Pretty Liar

Pretty Liar

TELEVISION, LANGUAGE, AND GENDER IN WARTIME LEBANON

Natalie Khazaal

S|U

Syracuse University Press

First Edition 2018

18 19 20 21 22 23 6 5 4 3 2 1

∞ The paper used in this publication meets the minimum requirements of the American National Standard for Information Sciences—Permanence of Paper for Printed Library Materials, ANSI Z39.48-1992.

For a listing of books published and distributed by Syracuse University Press, visit www.SyracuseUniversityPress.syr.edu.

ISBN: 978-0-8156-3595-6 (hardcover)
978-0-8156-3599-4 (paperback)
978-0-8156-5451-3 (e-book)

Library of Congress Cataloging-in-Publication Data

Names: Khazaal, Natalie, author.
Title: Pretty liar : television, language, and gender in wartime Lebanon / Natalie Khazaal.
Description: First edition. | Syracuse, New York : Syracuse University Press, 2018. |
Includes bibliographical references and index.
Identifiers: LCCN 2018040341 (print) | LCCN 2018046048 (ebook) |
ISBN 9780815654513 (E-book) | ISBN 9780815635956 |
ISBN 9780815635956 (hardcover : alk. paper) |
ISBN 9780815635994 (pbk. : alk. paper)
Subjects: LCSH: Television broadcasting—Lebanon. | Television and politics—
Lebanon. | Mass media and language—Lebanon. | Sex role on television. |
Lebanon—History—Civil War, 1975–1990—Television and the war. | Télé Liban. |
Lebanese Broadcasting Corporation International.
Classification: LCC PN1992.3.L43 (ebook) | LCC PN1992.3.L43 K48 2018 (print) |
DDC 791.45095692—dc23
LC record available at https://lccn.loc.gov/2018040341

Manufactured in the United States of America

In memory of my mother Marchella.
To my father Mikhail, my brother Ivan,
and my sister Alex.

Contents

Illustrations

Table

Acknowledgments

This book would not have been possible without the support of many individuals and institutions. I would like to extend special gratitude to television writers Camille Salame and Marwan Najjar, who were phenomenally gracious with their time and answered hundreds of questions about their work and achievements. They were also instrumental in connecting me to other interviewees and valuable resources, including providing copies of their works and their critical reception.

I am also grateful to those who contributed by sharing contact information, by reading drafts of chapters, by sitting for interviews, and in other important ways: Osama Abi-Mershed, Joseph Abu Nassar, George al-Asmar, Sepouh Alvanthian, Kelly Balenske, Michael Battey, Federica Ciccollela, Michael Cooperson, Dima Dabbous, George Diab, Joan Dunayer, Jean Feghali, Jerry Friedman, Melis Hafez, Melany Hawthorne, Amjad Iskandar, Charbel Khalil, Joe Khalil, Ahmad Khazaal, Zaven Kouyoumdjian, Marwan Kraidy, Tony Mhanna, Imad Moussa, Sylvia Onder, Maya Sadeq, Ralph Schoolcraft, Robert Shandley, Hassan Shaqqur, Alison Maura Shay, Zahi Wehbi, Gabriel Yammine, and Hana Zabarah, as well as Imad, Georgette, Sabah, and Vassia. This book was sponsored by a research grant from the Department of International Studies at Texas A&M University and a sabbatical leave for writing the final draft. Earlier stages of research were also sponsored by a Chancellor's fellowship at the University of California, Los Angeles. Last, thanks to the reviewers of the book for their invaluable advice.

Note on Transliteration

Common spelling has been used for well-known non-English names or terms (such as Abel Nasser). Other non-English names or terms have been transliterated using simplified phonetic rules. I have also kept the use of "al" in front of names in the first instance, omitting it in later instances (e.g., *al-Masira* followed by *Masira*).

Pretty Liar

Introduction

A New Look at Old TV

> Like old art, old media remain meaningful.
>
> —Lisa Gitelman, *Always Already New*

Entertainment or Treason?

On June 13, 1982, one week after Israel invaded a traumatized Lebanon, Télé Liban (Lebanon's national television network) began live coverage of the FIFA World Cup in Spain (June 13–July 11).[1] In the meantime, 20,000 to 30,000 Israeli Army troops, along with 200 tanks, aircraft, and naval ships, stormed Lebanon's borders and coastline, intending to oust the Palestine Liberation Organization (PLO), which had been attacking Israel sporadically from South Lebanon.[2] On June 13, the Israeli forces were on the outskirts of Beirut. The ten-week siege of the city began the next day and lasted until August 21. Heavy bombardment and psychological warfare, including agents planting car bombs, had driven most Beirutis to barricade themselves in their homes or shelters. Hundreds of buildings were destroyed; in fact the estimated material damage from the invasion exceeded USD$2 billion.[3] During the August 10 carpet-bombing alone, 300 civilians were reported dead in Beirut, adding to the total number of about 50,000 killed and wounded Lebanese and Palestinians.[4] Lebanon's president-elect, Bachir Gemeyel, had promised Israel peace after the PLO ouster. That promise disintegrated when he was assassinated in September, and subsequently his goons perpetrated the genocidal Sabra and Shatila massacres of mostly civilian Palestinians and poverty-stricken Lebanese Shi'ites.

Télé Liban had decided to hype its upcoming FIFA coverage with a soccer-themed game show during this unfolding national trauma. The show was hosted by one of television's doyens, Jean-Claude Boulos, and his tyro sports-anchor daughter, Josiane. Extraordinary athleticism engraved the 1982 FIFA in the world's memory. In a twenty-four-team elimination stampede, Italy won its third cup after almost half a century since its second win, defeating the favored Brazil in one of sports history's most sensational matches, while legendary forward Paolo Rossi scored six goals combined, topping Zico, Falcao, and Maradona. He also won the coveted Golden Boot and became one of only three players to have ever won all three awards in a World Cup: top goal-scorer, player of the tournament, and title winner. Lebanese audiences were mesmerized. Israel had cut off supplies of food, water, and electricity to Beirut, but fans took to the streets, connected their television sets to their car batteries, and seated themselves in front of the small screen. Some gathered to watch in shops or in bomb shelters. They plopped cross-legged on the floor when no seats were available. In the mid-1960s, Lebanese television had played an important role in the development of sports as a national leisure pastime and competitive sports as an entertainment sector,[5] which assured Télé Liban a committed audience.

Images of Lebanese men watching the Cup while the single ghastliest event of the Lebanese Civil War (1975–91) was unfolding stunned the world and caused a heated debate at home about the role of national television during wartime. On one side, there was the gravest trauma in Lebanese history; on the other, the most spectacular World Cup. Since the eruption of the war in 1975, television had been accused of occluding, minimizing, and sanitizing the conflict or sometimes sensationalizing the carnage (see chapter 2, this volume). With its ratings bottoming out, Télé Liban gasped for air. The FIFA World Cup couldn't have provided a better oxygen tank. Massive numbers of Lebanese followed the Cup, but Télé Liban's choice had split the country. Some believed it was a sign of Lebanese resilience against the invasion and an easygoing, fun-loving spirit (*damm khafif*) of which the Lebanese boast. During times of fear and suffering, the World Cup was a welcome distraction, a reminder that the ongoing siege was not normal, and a reason to hope for better days.

Yousef Barjawi, director of the sports section at Lebanon's second-largest daily, *al-Safir,* which was famous for resisting the invasion, described how audiences saw the tournament as "magic" and "a thrill" in his 2016 recollections of the events.[6] Others, however, saw the situation in much darker tones, accusing Télé Liban of treason. They quipped that the duty of national television was to reflect the nation's fate, not distract it.[7] In the years that followed, many have reframed Télé Liban's choice in much kinder terms. As Lebanese top political talk show host and author Zaven Kouyoumdjian writes, "If it was treason, at least it was worth it."[8]

State-owned Télé Liban grabbed the headlines again in 2014 during the twentieth FIFA World Cup in Brazil. BeIN Sports sued the outlet over broadcasting rights but a Beirut court threw the complaint out for lack of jurisdiction. Télé Liban had aired the tournament without authorization. According to the outlet, it was standing up for the rights of the Lebanese since BeIN Sports' exclusive package would have cost each Lebanese family an extra USD$100 to watch the games. After public outcry over the pricey package, the Telecommunications Ministry intervened and allowed cable providers to air it more cheaply. This solution, however, excluded the free broadcast Télé Liban and hurt viewers who could not afford the subscription. The outlet risked the consequences and aired the whole tournament for free, prompting a Twitter trend of hashtags like "#WeAreWithYouTeleLiban" and "#InSupportOfTeleLiban."[9] While some mused that Télé Liban broke the law, others saw the outlet as a protector of the poor.

Télé Liban's two controversial choices encapsulate how broadcast (terrestrial) television perceived its relationship with the audiences, which I explore in this book during the civil war period. These choices demonstrate the combustible mixture of spectacle, consumerism, compliance, defiance, public service, and patriotism that defines broadcast television in Lebanon as a modern medium and feeds its relationship with the audiences. The examples raise fascinating questions about media effects, media ethics, the ownership-censorship nexus, and audience reception, among others. But most importantly, they query the nature of the relationship between modern television and modern audiences and the means of negotiating such relationship—the two issues I explore here. Should television care more about patriotism and national unity or about leisure and entertainment? Which of these priorities defines the audiences' interests better? Should television defend poor viewers and provide public service or follow a law that doesn't?

Based on empirical data and grounded in theory by Arab and global researchers, *Pretty Liar* offers textual analyses of five Lebanese fictional series (over 150 episodes), four major and several additional periodicals, and nine literary works (a graphic novel, a short story collection, a memoir, a collection of prose poems, and five novels). Television cannot be separated from the content it produces.[10] Therefore, textual analyses of television content can provide valuable insights into the tropes and vocabulary for talking about modern television, modern audiences, and their relationship. On the other hand, the press and literary sources allowed me to understand how the Lebanese audiences themselves reflected on television content and the television-audience relationship. I chose to study entertainment formats because they made Lebanese broadcast television not only culturally important but also politically relevant. Since the Lebanese government censored primarily news and information programs, entertainment and even education formats enjoyed greater freedom and therefore were able to better connect to and communicate with the audiences. I weigh the analysis of entertainment formats with close attention to news and educational themes, all undergirded by a cultural studies perspective. "A cultural studies perspective can go a long way towards rejuvenating the study of Arab media," according to Mohamed Zayani.[11] In addition, I conducted unscripted interviews with twenty-five television administrators, anchors, actors, freelance contributors, print journalists, and audience members, which provided further context for the main themes and the analysis of the political economy of a media outlet. The political economy of media has dominated Arab media studies, leaving the areas of content analysis and audience reception wanting. My employment of textual analysis supplemented by a study of the political economy of one outlet answers Annabelle Sreberny's call to connect media and cultural studies to studies of political communication and political economy.[12]

Why Broadcast Television?

Questions such as those posed above are likely to lead to important insights. Yet academic accounts often dismiss Lebanese (and Arab) broadcast television as a mouthpiece of the government,[13] an inverse Habermasian public sphere, a "stagnant," "monolithic," and "paternalistic" medium "apathetic to audience views."[14] The industry and the users often also think of it as "static," "stifled by satellite," having a "reduced" audience, and inadequate given current "penetration rates."[15] "Alive" is probably the most negative qualifier as it shows surprise that broadcast television still manages to operate. Researchers have mined it mostly for government rhetoric (e.g., rhetorical analysis of political speeches, most notably those of Egypt's late president Abdel Nasser). Such choices are often justified with arguments that government censorship neither allowed for much institutional and programming complexity nor permitted journalistic resistance. As a result, broadcast television is a deliberately neglected area of research. Most research before the 1990s focused on the Arab press. Since the late 1990s scholars have heavily explored satellite television, and since 2005 they also have begun exploring social networks and the internet. A few studies of other media have also been conducted, including cassette tapes and the human body, which might inspire a broader following.[16] However, broadcast television continues to be invisible despite an increased interest in a more diversified agenda in the study of Arab media. For example, Helga Tawil-Souri thoughtfully stresses the importance of understanding the transition periods from one dominant Arab medium to another. Yet, she omits broadcast television when discussing the transition "from 'traditional' media such as newspapers and radio to 'new' satellite TV," although the transition from broadcast to satellite dominance has been enormously consequential.[17]

In many respects, qualifications about censorship and restrictions on broadcast television reflect the state of newscasts and political shows in presatellite Lebanon. Civil war newscasts often fed the audiences an absurdity posing as reality. Boring reports of pro forma government official meetings rubbed shoulders with nationalist clichés and chronic anti-Israel diatribes peddled by Lebanese and other Arab leaders. Worse, the clichés and diatribes often displaced meaningful engagement with the struggles of diverse Lebanese audiences. Censored news programs, frequently organized around the interests of the government rather than the public, conditioned the audiences to be lukewarm and uninspired. The government pretended to take care of the nation on the stage of this media theater while the nation pretended to listen to the government, cementing the protocol of disengaged media and passive audiences.

Censorship notwithstanding, the first of my main theses is that we should still study broadcast television for at least two reasons. First, studying it will recover some of the complexity that we have missed, giving us a more nuanced picture. A perception of Lebanese broadcast television as monolithic, stagnant, or static is misleading. News anchors, for instance, could circumvent restrictions in certain venues. Domestic news was regulated; however, television staff had a greater degree of editorial input in foreign news, which provided an opportunity to be more creative and develop audiences' global awareness. Another venue was breaking news, which anchors did not always have to run by censors and employed to outdo each other in developing an image of trusted professionals. On November 22, 1963, anchor Elie Salibi, who worked at Lebanon's second-oldest station, Télé Orient (Compagnie de Télévision du Liban et du Proche, 1962–77), broke the false news that Beshara al-Khoury—independent Lebanon's first president—had died. The report was based on a phone call the anchor had received from a trusted source. Within hours, he had to apologize to viewers for his mistake. When later the same day US President John F. Kennedy was assassinated, Salibi did not report it in fear of killing two presidents on the same day.[18] Camille Menassa, news anchor at the competing outlet, Lebanon's oldest station CLT (Compagnie Libanaise de Télévision, 1959–77), was awakened from sleep when the news hit Beirut, and he grabbed this golden opportunity to beat Salibi. Menassa rushed to the station and interrupted a live music program (shoulder-brushing and snubbing singer Samira Tawfiq) to tell the audience of the assassination.[19] When Beshara al-Khoury died two months later, Menassa scored another victory over Salibi, reminding the audiences that Salibi had "scooped" the story first.

Even the very format and content of news and political talk shows occasionally turned into venues allowing more liberty. A few years before the war, political talk show anchors had ditched presidential news for a more engaging opening consisting of headlines. While the war was raging in 1984, they added a "news introduction" segment to news bulletins—a type of subjective frame that colored viewers' perception of the story.[20] And a year later, they introduced live on-site reports for the first time, which subverted the government's and the outlet's ability to completely control the news feed. Journalists shaped the product they created rather than being mere servants of the government.

If descriptions of the "monolithic" or "static" nature of broadcast television do not do justice to information genres, they hardly reflect entertainment genres, which were often considered too silly or insignificant for serious political censorship and therefore enjoyed greater freedom. These genres made an important impact on Lebanese audiences and shaped the country's culture in the 1960s, 1970s, and 1980s. For instance, televised beauty pageants stimulated tourism, while the famous legal drama *Hakamat al-Mahkama* (*The Court Has Ruled*) catapulted the justice system into popular culture and inspired many law school applicants, according to lead actor Wahid Jalal.[21] The amateur video that captured the heart failure of Feryal Karim—one of Lebanon's drama and comedy stars—connected television to audiences in an unprecedented way, which we can fully grasp only today. The 1988 video was shot by a guest at the event where Karim was performing when she collapsed on stage, causing the country shock and grief.[22] Television stations aired the footage the next evening as a eulogy to their colleague, which raises questions about voyeurism, spectacle, and citizen journalism.

It is noteworthy that the anchors and entertainers whom the government punished for breaking the rules and de facto banned from television tended to be women. Leila Rustum's talk show was canceled after her guest, Alia al-Solh—the daughter of independent Lebanon's first prime minister—criticized the current government, whereas singer Maha Abd al-Wahhab was banned upon performing a song with allegedly provocative lyrics.[23] At the same time, when an opening act of strippers introduced CLT's Christmas special of carols, only some angry calls and the occasional joke in the press questioned television's choice: "Hello, Television? Sorry, I thought it was the brothel."[24] Instances like these reveal the amazing richness of broadcast television both as a historical phenomenon and as a gendered subject of investigation.[25]

It is also rewarding to examine the audiences. For example, why did they react differently when different fake news reports were exposed? Audiences remained calm after Beshara al-Khoury's death turned out to be false; they threw stones at television and government buildings in Beirut after learning that the Egyptians did not defeat the Israelis in the Six-Day War of 1967 as official broadcasting had claimed; and a few placed angry phone calls in 1971 when they discovered that Bariaa Meknas's marriage to her cohost,[26] a man forty years her senior who was also from a different religion, was an April fool prank.[27]

The above cases raise many serious questions that could support a healthy scholarly agenda focused on the development of broadcast television: How did journalists navigate among demands from the state, institutions, and audiences, and what kind of professional norms of conduct did they explicitly and implicitly follow in different periods of the history of broadcast television? How did television affect the development of the modern state and shape modern audiences? How did audiences shape television? What did early polling look like amid crowds stoning television buildings and descending on them to express their glee with particular programs? How was gender implicated in early television?

Broadcast television outlets were the main source of entertainment and news for four decades until the arrival of satellite television in the mid-1990s. This continues to be the case for some viewers. According to a report by Noura Abdulhadi, an Arab Advisors senior research analyst, 94 percent of all Lebanese have access to broadcast television, and 90 percent said they watched it.[28] Here lies the second reason to study broadcast television—given its continuing popularity, we need to understand its development. Analyzing its diversity is one starting point. Sometimes, people equate broadcast television with state-owned television, often labeled "national television." However, not only is broadcast television diverse in terms of ownership—state, regional (Kurdish in Iraq), private, or partisan (Lebanon), but it is also politically, religiously, culturally, and ethnolinguistically diverse. It is also in constant flux, given the region's turmoil (e.g., in Syria, Libya, Yemen, etc.). Broadcast television makes an excellent object for the study of class, especially from the perspective of audience reception, institutional production, and media policy. The perception of class differences among audiences who can afford satellite packages, paid television, or cable subscriptions and those who can only opt for the free broadcast outlets was clearly at play in Télé Liban's 2014 legal disobedience. Class can be explored on a regional level too. Compare poorer countries like Egypt, where broadcast television is very popular with 41 percent of Egyptians watching it in 2011, to wealthy Arab nations like Saudi Arabia, where only one percent watch broadcast television.[29]

More importantly, we need to understand how and why broadcast television has changed over time. The number of broadcast channels in Lebanon varied from two (1962) to one (1977) to fifty-four (early 1990s) to eight (2017).[30] What was the impact of this broadcast accordion? The 1994 Audio-Visual Law, which cut the number of broadcast outlets in Lebanon from fifty-four to six, has been addressed in multiple studies. However, scholars have not studied the cultural, economic, political, and social impact this first-of-its-kind law in the Arab world had on the publics these outlets served; research has mostly analyzed it as an act of institutional management and sectarian governmentality. Competition is another historical variable of great promise. The case of Lebanon is the poster child for exploring competition historically, as it has been the driving force behind its development since the institution's inception in the country in 1959. Even between 1977 and 1985, when Télé Liban was the only station, its two branches were often driven by competition or outright media war. The chapters of this book follow the competition between Télé Liban and the privately owned pirate channel Lebanese Broadcasting Corporation (LBC), which was launched in 1985. Each chapter contributes to the study of how competition created a unique Lebanese public space as a *cultural enterprise*, not simply as a commercial one.[31]

Understanding the development of broadcast television over time can finally help us understand the development of Lebanese journalism as a profession. There has been some interest in that area especially in terms of satellite television employees.[32] Yet, unless we study their presatellite counterparts seriously, how are we to understand what effect the shift in the dominant medium had on journalism? For example, why were many Lebanese journalists before the recent push for professionalization in fact people of literary skills—from the most prominent, such as award-winning Lebanese writers Huda Barakat and Elias Khoury (in print publications) or teachers like Sharif al-Akhawi (in radio), to individuals hired for having a decent command of Arabic grammar rather than for having received a degree in journalism? If television anchors were nothing more than hired guns who read the government's words off of the eight o'clock news scripts, then how did anchors like Camille Menassa earn the undying veneration of generations of Lebanese journalists as successful role models? How can we compare these models to those that scholars have attempted to articulate for the satellite era?[33] What are the changing bases of journalistic authority and television credibility? And what is the changing nature of the relationship between journalists and audiences or between the cultural institution of television and its users?

A new object of study not only broadens a field but also challenges it, according to Sreberny.[34] In sum, the discussion of broadcast television is crucial if we are to understand some of the evolution of Arab media over the last 150 years, including how the Arab satellite industry emerged within the rich context of presatellite media. What sets *Pretty Liar* apart from other accounts of media is its argument for wartime Lebanon as a harbinger of a new appreciation of national broadcast media that transcends the Lebanese context. Broadcast television is unlikely to disappear in the next decade, despite a decrease in households that watch it, because it is considered of national importance for mass alerts, disaster planning, and national emergencies.[35] It remains solvent due to government or partisan financial support, as well as to its specialization in local drama series that are "the major magnet for advertising revenue."[36]

The War Triangle

Television is shaped by social norms and values and cannot be examined separately from them or from the historical and political contexts in which it originates. A marginal, "thin discipline" before the late 1990s, Arab media studies is now a burgeoning field with an increasing amount of outstanding research.[37] Yet, it remains underhistoricized, which has triggered some scholars to call for its radical rehistoricizing.[38] The technological determinism inherent in misunderstanding broadcast television as satellite's "Other," or as a minority voice too insignificant to explore,[39] masks the political and economic regulation of the industry as well as the continuing suppression of dissent. Such masking is based on a normative assumption that the state is an obstacle to media development (and democratization) while the market is the solution.[40] Whereas such an assumption might hold some truth,[41] a nuanced historical narration of the wartime dynamics between state and market in relation to Lebanese television development exposes the assumption's overall essentialist nature.

Pretty Liar is the first lengthy study dedicated to war and television in Lebanon.[42] I chose the war period because I discovered that an important shift had occurred in the way television and audiences related to each other. During the conflict's first ten years (1975–85), television's disengaged relationship with the audience dipped to an all-time low because its occlusion of the war alienated them. Cashing in on the audience's disapproval with its competitor, the newly launched private LBC (1985) intervened and an intricate triangle formed, consisting of Télé Liban, LBC, and the audiences. The triangle played an essential role in negotiating a novel, increasingly engaged relationship between the industry and audiences, a relationship that boasted an effort, perhaps even a commitment, on the part of television to convey a new engagement with the audiences' tastes and concerns.

Two caveats are in order. First, it has been acknowledged that war has an important, often primary, role in the development of new media practices or infrastructure,[43] quite noticeably in the Arab world. For example, the US-led Gulf War (1990–91) is largely credited for CNN's rise to global stardom,[44] the regional adoption of Arab satellite television,[45] and the change in Arab journalistic practices.[46] Second, a shift from less active to more active audiences has been broadly attributed to the expansion in television choices in the 1980s globally,[47] as well as in the Arab world in the 1990s.[48] War's general stimulus and the shift in audience agency provide the backdrop for the events in Lebanon, yet both theories are too broad to be applied wholesale. Here I attempt a more radical historicizing of the development of Lebanese television, paying special attention to the local context of the civil war. I attribute the renegotiation of the television-audience relationship to (a) the positioning of each outlet in response to its own set of war pressures; and (b) the role the war played toward changing the audiences' expectations of television, rather than simply to ownership (state versus market) or global trends in agency. The war pressures in particular explain television's contradictory and ambivalent role during this period: from a nearly failing medium, which had lost legitimacy with audiences in the first war decade, to an enormously popular, legitimate, modern medium by the war's end.

The war broke out in 1975 and pummeled Lebanon for sixteen years, leaving 144,000 killed (one in twenty) and 184,000 injured.[49] Officially, an April 13, 1975, "bus incident" between Maronites (a Catholic sect concentrated in Lebanon) and Palestinians sparked the conflict; however, its beginning is rooted in a number of economic and political clashes over the preceding years.[50] These include internal sectarian contestations and class struggles, as well as a parade of opportunists from Syria, Palestine, Israel, Iran, and the United States. Even Lebanese arts arguably contributed to charging the prewar atmosphere. The war was not a single, prolonged battle but myriad shorter clashes followed by failed peace initiatives roughly split in three phases: 1975–77; 1978–82; 1982–91. It might have lasted only two years if Syria had not intervened on behalf of the Maronites; it would have also ended sooner if militias had not found war profitable. The civil war remains a defining moment for Lebanon not only in terms of damage but also in terms of the wellspring of culture it galvanized.

Lebanon had only two television stations when the conflict broke out, CLT and Télé Orient.[51] They had been struggling financially since launching in 1959 and 1962 respectively. Never especially attentive to the needs of their audiences, they were driven to the verge of collapse when the war destroyed part of their infrastructure and daily blackouts further reduced their viewership. In 1977, the government bailed them out by investing in 50 percent ownership of a new station that resulted from the two stations' merger, now called Télé Liban. Throughout the conflict, the outlets underreported, sanitized, and outright occluded the violence, having adopted the government's dystopian fears that television could further shake up the precarious balance of power among the seventeen Lebanese sects.

The broadcast mediascape changed in 1985 when the right-wing Christian militia, the Lebanese Forces (LF), launched its pirate television station, LBC. While Télé Liban was bound as a national outlet by pressures to keep the nation together even at the cost of occluding the violence, and the audiences rethought their expectations of television, LBC's militia owners had been in dire need of improving their negative image. This war triangle made the relationship between television and audiences significantly more engaged.

LBC marketed its brand as a game changer, solving the legitimacy crisis of Lebanese television with sleek technology, interesting content, and hip anchors and show hosts.[52] The "content of any medium blinds us to the character of the medium," wrote Marshall McLuhan.[53] Yet a medium's character, or its very meaning, remains important as it is created or negotiated both socially and perceptually.[54] That is why explanations that privilege technology or institutional business models alone, with no acknowledgment of social and cultural models, run the risk of essentializing the development of Lebanese television by granting it agency and power separate from people. Furthermore, the "self-evident" superiority of LBC's technology and content, and its anchors' "hipness," were as much superior to Télé Liban's as they were a continuation, intervention, and renegotiation of television's self-narrative. Instances like LBC's launch are never completely revolutionary, or points of epistemic rupture, because they engage with an ongoing negotiation of meaning. As Lisa Gitelman puts it, the media are not simply technologies but also include protocols—"a vast clutter of normative rules and default conditions, which gather and adhere like a nebulous array around a technological nucleus. Protocols express a huge variety of social, economic, and material relationships."[55] LBC may have rationalized its high-tech role as revolutionary, yet its protocols were in direct dialogue with Télé Liban's. For example, the quotidian greeting LBC's anchors used or the informal language they spoke during newscasts were not just new to Lebanese television but also direct comments and objections to Télé Liban's practices of disengagement from the country's fate and the audiences' trauma. Such protocols were of utmost importance for both the medium and audiences in understanding the positioning of the new outlet and its contribution to public culture and the meaning of television.

As James Zappen has observed, objections to older media constitute less a conflict over the merits of older media versus new media than a controversy about the cultural authority, values, and beliefs presumed to be embedded within older media.[56] The crisis of legitimacy of Lebanese wartime television then can be understood within the larger context of a crisis of confidence in traditional authority, which historian Ussama Makdisi sees as the underlying cause for the revolt against the hierarchical and unrepresentative social order that triggered the civil conflict.[57] Audiences saw Télé Liban as an authoritative, fixed, linear medium. The shows I discuss in later chapters that Télé Liban produced enhanced such views. By contrast, LBC attempted to dislodge the audiences' negative view of television and portrayed itself as dynamic, innovative, multidimensional, responsive, and espousing a multiplicity of languages and voices. The shows it produced that I discuss in later chapters reflected and enhanced such positioning. In place of Télé Liban's often authoritative and monolingual world, audiences found in LBC one that was more pluralist, challenging of authority, and dialogic. LBC also challenged the cultural hierarchy that Télé Liban represented: from government at the top, to national television, and then to audiences. Yet LBC's contribution was not a precondition for changing public space but an outcome of the negotiations for change already under way, of which Télé Liban was an essential party. Ultimately, the war triangle uncovers the historical context of television's struggle for hegemony over the national cultural space and how this struggle intersected with discourses on language, to which I now turn.

Language as an Analytical Paradigm

Mainstream linguistics postulates that language has two functions—instrumental (communicative) and symbolic (expressive). Language communicates information, emotions, ideas, and so on through its instrumental function, whereas as a symbolic tool, it expresses an individual's or a group's identity. Separating the two functions leads to problems, according to Peter Ives. Setting them in opposition to each other, or adding them up in different amounts "as if they were ingredients in a recipe," downplays the paradoxical nature of language, to use J. E. Joseph's expression,[58] and obfuscates the most important issue undergirding language—its political role.[59] Based on Antonio Gramsci's linguistic writing, Ives postulates that an understanding of the coterminous nature of these two functions unmasks the power struggles that take place among speakers.[60] Although Gramsci's ideas about language do not constitute a systematic theory of language,[61] they are relevant to my critical study of the social and cultural aspects of language on television because they are linked to his notion of cultural hegemony. In Gramsci's articulation, "Every time the question of language surfaces, in one way or another, it means that a series of other problems are coming to the fore . . . to reorganize the cultural hegemony."[62]

Scholars such as political sociolinguist Yasir Suleiman and linguistic anthropologist Niloofar Haeri began theorizing the political role of Arabic more than a decade ago. In fact, Suleiman sees language as a barometer for political, social, and cultural cleavages in Arab societies.[63] I'd like to extend their contribution that links language, culture, and politics by incorporating Gramsci's idea that language—in its coterminous nature—plays a crucial role in the reorganization of cultural hegemony. Whereas Gramsci sees language's role as a tool, I also see it as a trope. Hegemonic power struggles are not simply enacted through language when two parties are engaged in a direct exchange. They are also codified in affective terms associated with ideological readings of language varieties, nonphonetic language, or extralinguistic forms of communication. I argue that within this framework, language can be used as a core analytic category in the study of Arab media, and in the rest of this volume I suggest one template of how this could be done using the case of Lebanese wartime television. Inspired by Abdullah al-Ghathami's notion of "cultural criticism," the template includes exploring diglossia, heteroglossia, and nonverbal language (body, landscape, font), with specific attention to parody and the carnivalesque. Ghathami posits an approach to unveiling hegemony through the "cultural criticism" of texts.[64] Cultural criticism functions as a qualitative shift away from literary analyses of the aesthetic; it is "a theory of the critique of cultural consumption (rather than criticizing culture at large and exposing its defects)."[65] It works through uncovering contradictions between explicit and implicit cultural norms embedded in texts. Cultural criticism also notes resistance to the dominant "cultural norm industry," in voices that narrate the imagined, the marginal, the ugly, and the banal, in "neglected discourse . . . like jokes, songs, and rumors."[66]

My thesis is that during the war the discourse on language was implicated in reorganizing the hegemonic television-audience relationship; that is, in the dual process of contesting one hegemonic order and establishing a new one. The old hegemony encoded television legitimacy in privileging pure, formal language that befitted the making of citizens, whereas the new one strove to encode it in heteroglot, mixed language that fit better with the making of consumer-citizens. The Lebanese often boast of the country's linguistic heterogeneity and cultural and political pluralism, but that only obscures the hegemonic nature of the formal, standard Arabic (*Fusha*). Lebanese viewers overwhelmingly preferred local fictional and variety shows, which became the vehicle for the spread of Lebanese identity, culture, and spoken Lebanese language. Yet wartime television saw viewers more as passive receivers than active agents, despite instances of heartfelt feedback they volunteered. Television privileged a hierarchy of languages with *Fusha* at the top and a hierarchy of genres with news (presented in *Fusha*) above all else. The hegemonic relationship between television and audiences was shaken in the wake of the "crisis of legitimacy" because television occluded the war in its news and information genres and markedly stepped up the production of fictional series in standard Arabic. Such policy ran counter to a cultural trend noticeable throughout the country that I call "language pessoptimism." On the one hand, language pessoptimism privileged the spoken vernacular over standard Arabic, while on the other expressed deep cynicism in language itself as an unreliable medium. The launch of pirate television established a new hegemonic order under which television gained legitimacy once again. It was based partially on the actual acknowledgment of viewers' grievances with language and content, and the state of the television-audience relationship, and partially on conveying the impression of such acknowledgment by commodifying their tastes as active consumer-citizens. The new order was more palatable because it put the audiences at the center of representation.

I'd like to make several points regarding the scope of the language discourse with which I am concerned and the methodology I employ in explaining my thesis of language as a core analytical category in exploring television. I understand the changing relationship between television and audiences as a historically situated and socially dialogical process revealed (within my scope) through language. I am concerned here with three levels, or aspects, of language.

First, I am concerned with language as a tool of communication and identity construction. I treat language at this level as conventionalized as well as informal, constructed, socially shared, and dynamic systems of sounds, material signs, abstract symbols, and gestures. Language here includes verbal elements, such as written or spoken words and groups of words, as well as nonverbal elements, such as script, font, gestures, body posture, eye twitches, skin tone, music, silence, pauses, and geographic landscape. The nonverbal elements are understood in relation to the verbal elements. Hence, I analyze and also question the primacy of words (phonetic language) as the site for representation (signification) and construction of identity under particular conditions, adding other sites when appropriate, such as bodies, for instance. Second, I am concerned with language ideology; that is, the "cultural system of ideas about social and linguistic relationships, together with their loading of moral and political interests," as Judith Irvine has defined it.[67] Suleiman has persuasively argued that "amalgam" is a better term than "system" because language ideology may or may not be coherent or conscious.[68] He has found that language choice, font choice, and metaphors can all be elements of language ideology, initially constructed but later internalized and often communicated and consumed in unconscious ways. Language ideology permeates all spheres, including the media, especially when used to "comment or reflect upon language itself, producing a kind of ideologically impregnated meta-language."[69] Finally, I am concerned with ideology specifically related to language teaching/learning. Language, language ideology, and the ideology of language teaching/learning collectively constitute the language discourse of wartime Lebanon that shaped television and was shaped by it.

Popular language ideology (what Gramsci might term "spontaneous philosophy" and Suleiman has labeled "folk linguistics") inscribes local meaning.[70] Situating Arab media within local conceptual frameworks has been an aspiration for Arab media studies because most theory comes from Western academia and is hence often criticized for reflecting the conditions of Western liberal democracies. Its uncritical application to Arab culture has led to some misleading and inaccurate claims.[71] The internationalization or de-Westernization of media theory, though aspiring to create indigenous frameworks, has also been criticized for attributing media exceptionalism to the Arab region based on the exclusive application of Islamic frameworks, which reifies Arab cultures. The way I look at language ideology is consistent with the so-called double critique,[72] or de-de-Westernizing of Arab media studies, which is suspicious of a quintessentially Arab critical theory in the context of centuries-old traditions of intellectual exchange of knowledge among the globe's different regions.[73] A nuanced understanding of local contexts is paramount. I propose language as a culturally sensitive analytical category that reflects a dialogue between Western and indigenous theory to address the cultural underpinnings of Lebanese television. This category advances Arab critical theory because it critiques current understandings that ignore the role of language as a primary element of Arab culture in television.

Like other Arabs, the Lebanese are bound not only by a common Arabic language but also by their shared attitudes about it.[74] Native speakers describe their language situation as diglossia, or the coexistence of two varieties of the same language—a high variety (formal, standard Arabic, or *Fusha*) and a low variety (informal, vernacular Lebanese Arabic, or *'ammiyya*). This language dualism does not describe actual speech practice, which is dynamic and falls on a continuum. However, it reflects native speakers' ideas about the value and meaning of Arabic. Even though it might appear that the Lebanese speakers' attitude toward each variety is straightforward, it is better to see it as conflicted loyalties, especially during the war. (I discuss the political subtext of diglossia in more detail in the next section.) Given the importance of people's attitudes toward their languages for our understanding of the relationship between language and politics, Suleiman warns linguists against disparaging "nativist folk linguistics."[75] As Deborah Cameron argues in more general terms, studying native speakers' perspectives is crucial because language "generates social and political conflicts" as "practices and movements grow up around it both for and against the status quo."[76] Distinct from Haeri and Suleiman, I explore how language ideologies and ideologies of language teaching/learning inform creative choices of media employees and the fictional worlds of television series in addition to how language ideologies color overt discussions of the value of diglossia.

Language ideologies can be read through voices inherent in the fictional worlds created on television. Lebanese television, as a producer of texts, and the audiences, as their consumer, negotiated their relationship through a multiplicity of voices. My argument here extends Mikhail Bakhtin's notion of heteroglossia, a phenomenon that reflects how readers negotiate their relationship with texts. Bakhtin has a great potential for media studies as his ideas show how strongly culture and communication are linked. Within his constructivist and poststructuralist theories, the notion of heteroglossia designates the coexistence of multiple socio-ideological voices engaged in a dialogue and contestation within the same national language/culture.[77] Most importantly, heteroglossia is a dialogue among multiple meanings as each voice is laced with a different world view and value system.

> Every utterance must be regarded as primarily a response to preceding utterances of the given sphere (we understand the word "response" here in the broadest sense). Each utterance refutes, affirms, supplements, and relies upon the others, presupposes them to be known, and somehow takes them into account. . . . Therefore, each kind of utterance is filled with various kinds of responsive reactions to other utterances of the given sphere of speech communication.[78]

Every utterance is socially and politically marked because it comes with history that bears traces of previous uses. In its struggle for dominance, every utterance has to locate itself in relation to other utterances, not solely in relation to the context. Most importantly, the history of this dialogic struggle is linked to the history of society and changes in social relations. Although Bakhtin focuses on phonetic language, the extralinguistic features of perspective, evaluation, and ideological positioning that he examines in order to identify heteroglossia may in many cases also be extended to nonverbal language.

Dialogic relationships within heteroglossia are often performed through the carnivalesque. Bakhtin's notion of carnival is relevant, not in its historically situated expression (stemming from early modern Europe), but as a more general notion of parody, humor, and satire as means of expression of one's voice in relation to the social order and hierarchy of social relations. Bakhtin believed that humor and carnival were anti-authoritarian and liberating. However, well-documented evidence from early Europe shows that both were used by subordinated groups to challenge the hierarchical social order and by dominant groups to suppress their opponents, sometimes with the additional help of violence.[79] As Simon Dentith has suggested, the liberating power of humor may be a more utopian or populist view given that it was a mixed blessing for subordinated groups. It may have given them space for an emotional liberation during the act of its performance but it also reinforced the social order.[80]

A key problematic that stymies the broader interpretation of Arab culture is that many Arab scholars and intellectuals focus on the "official, homogenizing mediations of Arab cultures," according to Tarik Sabry.[81] They also disregard or disparage "the extraordinary range of contemporary and resistant heterogeneous forms of artistic and carnivalesque expressions" because they fail to recognize popular culture as "a site for the production of political meaning."[82] Sabry argues that the carnivalesque constitutes a serious subject of study that can free Arab cultures from the ideology of authenticity.[83] Used as a topos that reflects the degrading of dominant ways of perceiving the world, carnival can be a "useful key to understanding the transition to modernity."[84] The notion of the carnivalesque, then, and especially parody, is a useful tool to understand how the transition from one hegemonic regime to a new one—the transition in the nature of television legitimacy and authority during the Lebanese Civil War—was linked to competing visions of modernity.

Rival Visions of Lebanese Modernity

The trope of "a crisis of modernity" framed the Lebanese mental image of the civil war—a conflict powered by an allegedly backward sectarian tradition destroying an allegedly peaceful coexistence in modernity.[85] As the epicenter of the hostilities, a divided Beirut stood metonymically for Lebanon. "Cosmopolitan Beirut" featured glamorous high-tech hotels; steady circulation of a global economic, media, and political elite; prosperity; modernism; and hospitality. "Backward Beirut" surrounded the cosmopolitan enclave with a hostile periurban and semirural belt of poverty and slums with "static" sectarian loyalties, refugees, rural immigrants, and internally displaced individuals.[86] Over and over, Lebanese fiction, as literary critic Samira Aghacy found, narrated the inability of Lebanese society to achieve modernity.[87] One way or another, everyone was preoccupied with modernity, even those who blamed the war on modernity rather than on backwardness.[88] The two imagined versions of Beirut did not reflect an actual clash between modernity and backwardness—the clash is itself an ideological position created by modernity. According to Sara Fregonese, they represented a paradox of modernity, a kind of modern nation-state governmentality based on colonial and postcolonial sectarianism—a new way to experience reality.[89] While Muslim communities toyed with Arabism and Nasserism, and the Maronite Christian bourgeoisie painted Lebanon's "cosmopolitan vocation" as the mediator between Arabs and Europeans, decades of laissez-faire inequality, private initiative–driven policies, and the absence of public infrastructure impoverished hundreds of thousands of people.[90]

The felt "crisis of modernity" prompted a renewed attention to questions about Lebanese identity: Are the Lebanese modern? Inherently violent? Arab? Which is the right language to match a modern Lebanese identity? Modernity and language have been linked frequently. A tradition of nationalism scholarship links the modern social formation of the nation-state to vernacularization and the abandonment of sacred languages as a governing principle of community life. "Acting as a proxy for extralinguistic issues, the SA [Standard Arabic] versus dialects debate is used to signal metonymically the concern with identity, modernization, tradition, change, and globalization," Suleiman states.[91] Linking specific language varieties with modernity and contemporaneity began in the Nahda period (nineteenth through early twentieth centuries). At the time, the sacred language of the Qur'an—Classical Arabic—was modernized rather than abandoned for vernaculars (both Classical Arabic and its modernized version are known as *Fusha* [eloquent] in Arabic).[92] Since the 1960s, Western academia has popularized the term "Modern Standard Arabic" for the modified variety, leading Haeri to conclude that Western academia takes for granted this variety's link to modernity.[93]

Dominant Arab colonial and postcolonial thought tasked language with endorsing an authentic Arab modernity built around resistance, healing, and indigenous culture. Dominant ideology, especially in the heyday of pan-Arab nationalism, circumscribed *Fusha* as a trope for Arab unity and resistance against colonialism, an authentic and morally superior variety. Groups who experienced *Fusha* as a colonial language itself, however—a language of oppression rather than a language of resistance—challenged this trope.[94] On the other hand, dominant ideologies coded vernaculars as impure and morally inferior varieties, which were limited in vocabulary and aesthetic power as well as divisive. Vernaculars were perceived as a reminder of membership in a former colony,[95] thereby increasing the difficulty faced by Arabs from different countries in understanding each other.[96]

Dominant ideology notwithstanding, linguistic hierarchies leave Arabs ambivalent about modern forms of identity, according to Haeri, a conclusion she drew from a case study of Egypt.[97] She argues that Egypt formed a fraught relationship with its contemporaneity because Classical Arabic failed to create an indigenous Arab modernity, because the status of the modernized variety is ambiguous, and because the vernacular is degraded and excluded from official contexts.[98]

Whether it accomplishes an ideological mission or fails from a pragmatic point of view, what makes a language itself modern? For Haeri, it is the separation of form and content and the ability to translate that content into a different form (language).[99] As the language of revelation, Classical Arabic has lived in the shadow of the Qur'an and its untranslatability that has severely impeded Classical Arabic's ability to negotiate modernity. For

Moustapha Safouan, what makes a language modern is its speakers' ability to express their thoughts, feelings, and affects freely without restrictions in their everyday lives.[100] Hence, he comes to the conclusion that *Fusha*—the complex, written language learned only at school—is the cause of Arabs' oppressive political environment (a hypothesis that has been strongly disputed). He suggests that a major reform legalizing vernaculars as the official languages in Arab countries is a burning need.

In addition to defining a language's state of modernness from the perspective of its communicative function, a longstanding Lebanese tradition also defines it from the perspective of its expressive function as a site for constructing identity. Historically situated political interests have played a crucial role in constructing Lebanese identity through language. Christian minority sects (most prominently many Maronites) have constructed a version of Lebanese identity by "distancing" from the Arab-Islamic heritage—an Arab "Other"—and "identifying" with a mythological Phoenician past through the use of the Lebanese vernacular.[101] In fact, Phoenician mythology was key to the Lebanese nationalism that developed at the end of the nineteenth century. It was a direct response to Arabism and Syrianism, which Maronites saw as a threat.[102] The Maronite intellectual Jacques Tabet is one of the best examples of a whole generation of Lebanese who embraced the Jesuit legacy of Henri Lammens—father of the myth of the non-Arab, Phoenician origin of the Lebanese—by playing down the value of standard Arabic:

> In reality the Arabic language remains the universal language in the country. [But] it will soon find itself face to face with a new language: French. This new language, with its richness, beauty and organization, is certainly more powerful than the Turkish language. . . . [T]he Syrians had, at first, spoken all the languages: Phoenician, Egyptian, Chaldean, Hebrew and Greek; modern Arabic is very different from the pre-Islamic Arabic. . . . These continual transformations had singularly reduced . . . the national value of languages concerning the character of people.[103]

In addition, Lebanese nationalist intellectuals "began to draw on historical narratives describing the resistance of Mt. Lebanon's inhabitants against Arab and Turkish occupation" and created a Mardaite ancestry with the intent of claiming a Maronite resistance to alleged "Arab-Muslim invaders" (i.e., Muslim communities) of seventeenth-century Lebanon.[104] This put *Fusha* in an ambiguous position as the language of the "invaders." Michel Chiha—the cowriter of the Lebanese constitution who was of Chaldean-Melkite roots—later modified the Maronite mythology into a more acceptable one of Lebanese exceptionalism, linguistic diversity, and historical continuity.[105] In the act of "differentiation" between standard Arabic and the Lebanese vernacular, the former appeared downgraded. Further, Antoun Saade—a Lebanese intellectual from the Christian Orthodox community and founder of the Syrian Socialist Nationalist Party, who opposed pan-Arab and Lebanese nationalism and instead advocated a geographical (territorial) national identity—denied that language had a primary role as a basis for national identity.[106]

By contrast, identification with an Arab-Islamic heritage has prompted Lebanese Muslims to employ the ideological link between standard Arabic and an Arab identity as a marker of the Lebanese nation. They saw the elevation of the Lebanese vernacular to the status of a national language as an attack on the Arab-Islamic heritage and as a collaboration with the colonial powers. In response to the establishment of Greater Lebanon in 1920, Muslim communities initially denounced the new state as a French creation that served Maronite interests.[107]

Such traditional identifications raise the question of how steady is the link among language, modernity, and group identity. My study problematizes stable associations among the three, as multiple reasons beyond presumed subnational loyalties lead to language choice and the modification of language ideology. The complex visions of the two television outlets and their shows on modernity make it impossible to judge them either as failures of modernity or as a simple clash of "modern versus backward" outlets. Instead, I understand them as rival visions of Lebanese modernity proposed to the audiences regarding the right language for a Lebanese modernity and the right relationship between a modern television and a modern audience.

Rival visions of modernity are also often negotiated through gender and gender relations such as the practice of *ikhtilat*, or gender mixing, as Marwan Kraidy has perceptively theorized for reality television.[108] In addition, Lila Abu-Lughod has shown how television drama sparked negotiations of different versions of modernity and consumerist desire among Egyptian women.[109] Walter Armbrust, too, argues that television (and other media) are sites of experimentation when it comes to the treatment of women—the most contentious issue of Arab modernity and the latter's relation to the West.[110] *Pretty Liar* is distinct from other work on modernity and television because it zooms in on how language and gender interconnect in giving meaning to television's perception and organization of its own modernity.

Codifications of women and gender relations are key to the hegemonic positionality of modernity, and they are intimately connected to language as a symbolic system of meaning. According to historian Joan Scott, the analysis of gender and gender relations should include three components besides subjective identity.[111] The first is the nature and context of multiple, often contradictory representations of *symbols*. The second component involves *norms* that define how symbols are interpreted and how their meaning is limited by those norms typically through binaries of masculinity versus femininity. Last is the politics of *institutions*, such as in the labor market or education, that participate in the construction of gender norms and symbols. Gender is also a primary field to articulate and legitimize relationships of power.[112] Ideologies of teaching/learning language on different Lebanese fictional series interfaced with representations of gender and gender relations through a set of symbols and norms in order to communicate a unique relationship to the audiences. These representations did not exist a priori to politics but were instead embedded in local contexts and power differentials.

What does the link between language, gender, and modernity tell us about how institutions like television, the "vital creator[s] of modernity,"[113] negotiate modernity? I will show throughout this book, first, that such institutions have a dynamic relationship with discourses on modernity and multiple experiences of modernity, and second, that conveying a relationship with audiences itself became a sign of modernity during the Lebanese Civil War. Ultimately, television's rival versions of Lebanese modernity show us how we can dislocate hegemonic readings of broadcast television in Arab culture and incorporate new voices that reveal its richness and worthiness as an object of study without sanitizing its ambiguity.

About This Book

This book's central topic of media politics, language politics, and gender politics in the context of war raises questions, such as: What did it mean to become legitimate modern television for a modern audience? How was the new standard of legitimacy related to language and gender? How did it effect changes in the relationship between television and audiences? How was cultural hegemony renegotiated? My training in cultural studies and in language allows me to link the study of language, literature, gender, and culture with that of media, politics, and history, thereby translating the humanities to social scientists and contributing a unique perspective on the study of war and media. Therefore, I examine these problematics through different sets of cultural texts and the complex stories they tell.

To answer these questions, after a brief historical review of Lebanese television and the television-audience relationship (chapter 1), *Pretty Liar* tells the story of the civil war, which is also the story of how Lebanese television survived civil unrest and changed its philosophy from one of disengagement from audiences to one of greater engagement with audiences (part I). This story is not a linear march to an improved, more responsible media but rather a tough battle between the two major television stations that competed during the latter half of the war. Their responses to the audience were different because the war subjected them to different kinds of pressures. Télé Liban adhered to what I call "the television peace bubble"—a tacit ban on or lag in reporting the ongoing conflict. The bubble appeared because of Télé Liban's precarious position as Lebanon's national station, controlled by the government and by decade-long policies of avoiding the discussion or acknowledgment of hot-button issues (chapter 2). The audience perceived such an attitude as a moral failure of broadcasting to represent and engage with the audience's concerns and to address the audience in a language that represented and engaged it. On the street, at home, and in the popular press, the audience voiced its suspicion of the euphemistic language of the media and described its relationship with the media as dysfunctional, dreaming of a better one (chapter 3). Although romanticized, this vision reflects the beginning of a conversation about a new type of television legitimacy. Due to the unique war circumstances of its creator—the Lebanese Forces (LF)—the other television station, LBC, heard the voice of the disgruntled public. Wartime drug trafficking, piracy, extortion, illegal taxation, and arms deals had swelled the militia's coffers by hundreds of millions of US dollars, yet the increased power and visibility that came with this criminal revenue made it more difficult to garner the support of the constituency. Under pressure to switch to legal sources of revenue while dealing with popular outrage at the massacres of civilians it had committed and the ensuing internal power struggle, LF hoped for a new legitimacy with the launch of print and broadcast media like the journal *Masira* and LBC (chapter 4). LF's struggle to improve its image inadvertently provided the audience with greater leverage over the interpretation of what counted as public concerns and how media legitimacy was to be defined.

The two stations made the case of their modernity to the public through battles over language and gender politics (part II). While Télé Liban was committed to a more traditional division between formal and vernacular language (chapter 5), LBC mirrored the popular suspicion of language (chapter 6). These choices brought LBC and the stations that later emulated it greater legitimacy as a modern medium of communication. The war triggered a crisis of patriarchy and dislodged prewar employment patterns, which paved the way for a fundamentally new way of engaging and narrating gender on television and the language politics related to gendered space (chapter 7).

The history of television in Lebanon is not merely the history of technology or business. It is the history of a people and their continuing quest for responsive television even during times of civil unrest. *Pretty Liar* explores the rise of language and gender politics on Lebanese television to tell the untold story of the coevolution of Lebanese television and its audiences.

1

History of Lebanese Television and the Television-Audience Relationship

> Télé Liban was like a corpse
> shaking so intensely under the storm
> that we're erroneously compelled to believe it's alive.
> —Marwan Najjar

"I wanna bite you!" yelled a driver in the early 1960s at a twentysomething Jean-Claude Boulos, the future host of the 1982 World Cup game show.[1] At the time of the yell, Boulos, who was among the first employees hired in Lebanese television, already enjoyed celebrity status despite his young age and inexperience. From his first television job as an assistant engineer, he quickly moved to host a variety show and later doubled as a director of programming, a type of multitasking common for television's pioneers.[2] The driver's remark frightened him because the country had just emerged from the traumatic, albeit brief, 1958 civil war. Boulos gathered enough courage to ask what he had done to inspire such peculiar desire, only to learn that the driver was a huge fan. This anecdote illustrates how television symbolically transformed Boulos from a potential target as a member of a minority to a beloved hero endowed with the unifying power of entertainment. Lebanese television first emerged out of the 1958 civil conflict, riding on a wave of aspirations for national unity. Television was also a product of the 1950s, which brought financial and economic prosperity to many sectors in society,[3] including an increasing modernization and mechanization of domestic space. For its pioneers, its enthusiasts, and the country's administration, television symbolized Lebanon's transition to a modern nation marked by the marriage of national unity and technological advancement. Over the following decades, the Lebanese nation entertained competing notions of the role, meaning, and uses of television, although television's duty to serve the nation always drove the conversation.

Early Relationship (1959–1968)

Technological Novelty

The idea to launch television first came from Boulos Bros. Electronics, electronics stores owned by three brothers who pledged to import and distribute at least 5,000 television sets at a fixed lower rate.[4] Their idea did not come to fruition,[5] although they tested it in an experimental broadcast. The first official transmission came soon afterward, on May 28, 1959, at the hands of the twentysomething entrepreneurs Wissam Izz al-Din and Joe Arida, who obtained a nonexclusive license to operate a commercial television company called CLT.[6] The founders contemplated broadcasting one program on two channels, but they settled for separate transmissions in French on channel 9 and in Arabic on channel 7 given the cultural makeup of the audience whose native language was Arabic.[7] Entertainment and education programs of at least twenty hours per week were the main focus of the new enterprise under CLT's agreement with the government. Advertising time was limited to 25 percent and controlled by the separately established management company Advision, while news and political information programs were under government supervision.[8] A month before CLT's launch, a second group of Lebanese businessmen applied for a license to operate a commercial television station, Télé Orient, which began transmission on May 6, 1962. Early television programs were based on entertainment, which took up three-quarters of the schedule.[9] Some programs were local shows, but a sizable portion featured French variety, music, and talk shows; American thrillers; British comedy; and Egyptian drama. Most of the documentaries and educational programs came from France; even when subtitled they were apparently not that popular. There were also two daily news bulletins—in Arabic and French—both prepared by the National News Agency (NNA, est. 1961) and further censored at the stations by embedded censors from the Ministry of Information and General Security.

The beginning of television as a commercial product placed it squarely in the center of representation. The novel technology needed to be explained to the viewers as a sense of viewer necessity for it needed to be created. The local press reflected this familiarize-and-sell take on television. For example, in the early 1960s the famous weekly cultural magazine *al-Shabaka* (*Achabaka*, The Net) illustrated the columns and articles it dedicated to television with a series of revealing cartoons by staff artist Muhammad al-Qaisi.[10] In one cartoon, Qaisi tried to capture the magic of television technology by drawing a stilted television box with ladders on both sides. Lines of cameramen, actors, and studio audiences were going up each ladder to disappear inside the magic box. The year after, he drew a television control room with different types of equipment and the specialists needed to run it (stage manager, camera operator, floor manager, technical director, director, and video engineer/mixer). He also drew a series of cartoons with cameramen in their work environment, featuring heavy cameras, tripods, massive lenses, thick cables, and light projectors. Qaisi's work registers people's intrigue with the new commodity and its hidden world without overtly "pushing the sale." It reflects the central position of technology in this early period of the medium's history.

Modernizing Domestic Space

Although its inaugural transmission was received by fewer than ten sets, CLT's launch became a symbol of Lebanon's modernity, reflected in domestic space and its rituals. The family rearranged its whole living room interior to incorporate the television set, which could not be simply chucked in a corner and forgotten. These physical changes affected social dynamics too. Shows were viewed communally by the whole family, often in the company of relatives and neighbors who did not own a television and with whom the family regularly exchanged visits.[11] Modern domestic dynamics, then, no longer involved only private family members and the extended community of friends, neighbors, and relatives; the social visit now prominently included audiovisual technology as a symbolic guest of honor and a member of the family. Members now bonded by discussing what was on television and by sharing their impressions of entertainment hosts and news anchors. These intimate settings helped audience members form an emotional bond with the faces from the small screen. Incidents of overt admiration like the one Boulos relates show how the young country of barely 2 million citizens turned its local television pioneers into celebrities. They reveal how the audience understood its relationship with television as an emotional bond with these celebrities.[12]

Local shows also reflected the importance of the social visit to the new medium. For instance, the most iconic series of that period, the eponymous *Abu Melhem*,[13] which started in 1959 and ran for many years, opens every episode with a social visit: Abu Melhem and his wife are sipping coffee on their patio when a neighbor comes in with concerning news; the couple's efforts to find a solution and unite the good village people become the focus of the episode. Light comedy of the *Abu Melhem* type created a welcoming atmosphere for evening home gatherings with family, relatives, and neighbors in front of the television.

Series cost more to produce, though, and the pioneers always looked out for new talent that could be presented to the nation in cheaper genres. Variety shows, talent competitions, game shows, and in particular music performances came to dominate the period. Their cheaper production price was particularly attractive as the new technology had not yet penetrated the market and television executives needed more people to buy new sets before they invested large amounts in programming.[14] The popular variety shows mixed musical performances, sketch comedy, hosts' monologues, and talk show segments, but they often seemed vulgar to the cultural elite. For example, *Beirut fi-l-Layl* (*Beirut at Night*)—the Friday-night three-hour-long live program, which began in 1963 and ran for several years—hosted by Hassan Meligy, was a frequent target of such elite criticism although it was quite popular in its heyday. Whereas Boulos was the most famous game show host, audiences also loved Izz al-Din Subh, Gaston Shikhani, and prankster Najib Hankash.

Lengthy musical performances were often the central attraction of the evening either as part of a variety program or on their own. Musical performances on Sunday nights, for instance, were eagerly awaited, and *Shabaka* often documented them on its television page in the early 1960s—from the performances of the top television singer Samira Tawfiq to those of expats like Elia Baida.[15] The magazine offered more positive reviews than critical remarks. However, even the negative coverage, which almost always included suggestions for improvement, is evidence of the wide interest in this early genre and its resonance with viewers. As much illustration of the magazine's rubric as they were commentary on social mores and Lebanese modernity, Qaisi's cartoons reflected the popularity of the music and variety genres too. One cartoon in particular seemed to have a complex mission. It reflected the national craze over local musical performances and explained to the reader how they were an integral part of the television industry: in the center is a guitar-stroking musician under a heavy set of ceiling projectors, on the right a film crew of camera and sound operators handling bulky equipment, and on the left a producer clutching onto his papers.[16] The drawing is interesting because it presents a scene from which audiences are absent. Instead of focusing on them, the cartoon offers a glimpse into the secret chamber of television production "attached" to their home box that the lens never allowed them to see on their own set.

Musical performances also reenvisioned Lebanon as a folklore nation, as part of a process that had started a few years earlier on radio and live theater and that paralleled a global folklorization wave. When Lebanese folklore diva Fayrouz appeared in Télé Orient's inaugural broadcast as a lead in the Rahbani Brothers' musical play, *Hikayat al-Iswara* (The Bracelet's Tale), the program drew in 100 percent of the Lebanese audiences, even the diehard Francophones, according to Victor Khoury, pioneer at Associated Business Consultants, a Lebanese advertising and market research company.[17] (One should view such data with caution because the market research companies at the time did not rise to the professional standards of independent institutions.) Fayrouz, who had been a legendary theater and radio star never seen by a mass audience before, was deliberately unveiled to Lebanese viewers at Télé Orient's launch, which shows the strong bond between audiences and television entertainers.

If variety, musical, and game show genres were very popular with audiences, the press had a complicated view of television. It often celebrated it but just as often was harshly critical. At issue was the effect television

1. Television teaches hooliganism. *Shabaka*, issue 335, June 25, 1962.

had on viewers, and especially on children. *Shabaka*, for instance, ran a panic piece on children who had nearly died from ingesting tropical fruits while watching television.[18] Villainizing the new medium and, unwittingly, healthful snacks, the article opines that television is neither an educational tool nor a cultural awakening but "a joke" forced on audiences by advertisers' commercial interests. The accompanying Qaisi cartoon, said to be both the creator's visualization and a true reflection of the audiences' "disturbed attitude" toward television, features the television set as a long-legged mechanical troll (*qazam*). The gadget has arrived from an unknown world to stomp over the innocent, entranced audiences, and plunge its sharp fangs into their brains. A cartoon from a different issue carries a similar trope of entranced parents and damaged children (see Illustration 1). Puffing on a cigarette, the older brother bullies and shakes his fist at his younger sibling behind the backs of their inattentive, television-watching parents. The kids' school uniforms suggest that they should be learning morals from schoolbooks; instead, television finds a way to teach them hooliganism.

Several other cartoons reflect the trope of television as a pleasure trap that underlies the parents' behavior in the above example. In one a middle-aged man has crawled in front of the set to kiss the pretty young presenter (see Illustration 2). In the other, a heavyset housewife succumbs in an armchair in front of the set after hanging laundry on the indoor antenna instead of the clothesline away from the television (see Illustration 3). In the artist's view, the pleasure trap infantilizes and humiliates men by spiking

2. The man's pleasure trap. *Shabaka*, issue 333, June 11, 1962.

3. The woman's pleasure trap. *Shabaka*, issue 348, September 24, 1962.

their libido; men then "cheat" romantically on their wives, turning the family home into a brothel. On the other hand, the pleasure trap subdues women's sense of duty; women then "cheat" on the labor they provide to their husbands and family, turning domestic patriarchal order into a mess.

Qaisi reflects a more disenchanted vision of the modernization of domestic space ushered in by television. Threatening to break up family dynamics, this modern space panics each gender with a worst-case scenario about their partner's relationship with the magic box. His art also captures the intelligentsia's complaints that the new technology is arrogant and controlling. In one case, a revealing cartoon depicts a show host stretching out of the set and thumbing his nose at the shocked viewers (see Illustration

4. Television as an arrogant medium. *Shabaka,* issue 366, January 28, 1963.

5. Television's control of audience behavior. *Shabaka*, issue 337, July 9, 1962.

4). The image is the pictorial cousin of the magazine's plea to television to raise the intellectual and cultural level of its shows. Often *Shabaka* called for the abandonment of some popular genres, which it deemed vulgar, in favor of more sophisticated "prestige" ones, even if television lost money on them. But probably the most iconic cartoon was the one the magazine chose to accompany its television pages for several years. It is rather simple: a pretty presenter has stretched her arm outside the box to turn the knob on or to her channel or to prevent it from being turned off or to another channel (see Illustration 5). It is a gesture of television's ultimate control of audience behavior and the invasion of domestic space by modern technology.

It also references the desire modern technology promotes—the presenter's breasts are hanging outside the box, presumably turning the immaterial image into a material body part that could be grabbed.

Clearly, the series of cartoons captures the prevailing complex attitudes of viewers toward early television—from their curiosity to understand the materiality of the medium and how it affects domestic life, to how it creates national celebrity culture. They also capture the cultural elite's fears of the vulgarization of traditional Lebanese culture and the manipulation of mass audiences by arousing desire and promising to satiate it within the confines of domestic space.

Modernizing Public Space

Lebanon was the first Arab country with regular, uninterrupted television service, albeit not the first to attempt television transmission. Therefore, Lebanon's advancement over late television adopters—Arab, Israeli, and European—filled television employees, audiences, and the Lebanese press with national pride as pioneers.[19] According to Boulos, Télé Orient's launch made Lebanese viewers proud of having a choice of three channels (including CLT's French-language channel) well before French or a number of other European viewers could watch multiple channels.[20] In 1967 Lebanon became the third country in the world to broadcast in color on Secam, although color sets became the norm in the country more than a decade later.[21] Besides, the Lebanese public proudly saw Lebanon as a disseminator of technological progress to the rest of the Arab world. For example, Télé Orient began distributing foreign shows to other Arab countries after subtitling them, as well as selling its own local productions, which ensured it the coveted status of a regional leader.

The early adoption inspired the popular trope that Lebanese television was the "first television" in the Middle East, which would later prove to be a sticky talking point in accusations of decline. Another popular trope was that of a "foreigner" (researcher, traveler, etc.) assessing the quality of Lebanon's modernity by the state of its television development. The trope is an extension and inversion of the "first television" trope, usually used to point to perceived problems in the medium. In a 1962 article, *Shabaka* criticized the show *Abu al-Fahm*, created by the comedic duo Abu Salim–Abu Melhem, as vulgar (*mubtadhil*) and aimless by invoking this trope: "What kind of an idea would a researcher form about Lebanese culture if he saw a show like *Abu al-Fahm*?"[22] The following year, a similar story claimed that a foreign tourist would consider all shows on Lebanese television, except one or two, to be "the biggest embarrassment."[23] At issue was how such shows "represented Lebanon"—a question addressing the symbolic role of television as a measurement of the country's international status.

In addition to affording Lebanon prestige within a modernizing international public space, television also modernized public space in its capacity as a national institution. Those born in 1943, the year Lebanon gained its independence, came of age when the two television stations were launched (1959–62). In their imaginary, the new nation became synonymous with the modernized public space created by television. One dimension of this space was material-geographic. Since the young CLT founders 'Izz al-Din and Arida did not have the enormous resources needed to establish such an expensive enterprise, Lebanese television was partly financed by American companies and the French government. The US corporation Time-Life was briefly a partner in CLT's administration and advertising, while the French government financed CLT for years through its Ministry of External Affairs.[24] It repeatedly saved the station from going bankrupt, which forced CLT to pander to its foreign investor and choose the French-promoted SECAM instead of the more popular PAL system, for instance. The American Broadcasting Company (ABC) also partially financed the second Lebanese television station, Télé Orient.

Both television outlets depended on advertising, although the post-1958 situation was unconducive to it. Early television advertising was also quite primitive. For example, business owners used to bring their bulky products like fridges, furniture, and television sets to the studio to be shown live while the presenter would rattle off their qualities from a piece of paper.[25] As a result, television's small advertising revenues went to the investors instead of circling back for television development.[26] This left the outlets in a dismal financial situation despite brief periods of respite.[27] CLT was in so much trouble that it could not afford proper replacements for its recording equipment for a number of years.[28] According to Boulos, in 1963, CLT could not even afford to pay director Wassim Tabbara the "extremely modest" amount of 200 LL, so he left to found one of the most successful theaters in Lebanon.[29]

The importance of television technology for the creation of a modern public space overrode the conservative management of television finances. According to Lucien Dahdah, CEO of Télé Orient, the two stations made the grave mistake of overinvesting. A meager budget of an antenna and a telecine machine could have done the same job as the unnecessary fancy equipment and all the specialists needed to operate it, in his opinion.[30] Of course, such conservative policy made no sense within the perceived technological modernism on which the industry's legitimacy rested. Dahdah also faults the two competitors for building huge studios much larger than the current technology demanded, which ate up big budgets too. The stations bought or built multistory property, partly thinking ahead to a time when more studio space would be needed. The infrastructure not only housed grounds for technical equipment but also served as a landmark of modern enterprise to be reckoned with. For example, CLT's antenna was mounted on top of the building, visible from afar, projecting the station's might and legitimacy to the whole nation as well as the competition. In the end, technology had become part of the nation's geography, which symbolized its modernity and advancement among the other Arab nations. It wasn't only an implement that produced a product for consumption—the running time. It was also a spatial entity as much part of the institutional makeup of the nation as the courthouse, the national museum, or the parliament building, even though it was a private enterprise.

Another dimension of the modernization of public space came from the fact that television mediated between the independent nation and its people. The press regularly engaged with daily political, economic, and sometimes cultural events, but the literacy requirement restricted its customer base. Radio was more accessible to a mass audience, yet it was television that was able to constitute a true mass audience by combining sound and moving images. Moving images were available to the Lebanese audience before television in a number of movie theaters. But television boasted the ability to show the pulse of the nation in a sequence of frequently live, unrecorded, fleeting images and in synchronicity with the voices of its anchors and entertainers. As media historian Lynn Spigel has observed about the introduction of television in 1950s America, "Television's capacity for transmitting sight as well as sound would give its programs a sense of credibility that radio lacked, while its intimate privatized address would create a more compelling simulation of reality than film ever could."[31]

The faces and personalities of the entertainment show hosts, news anchors, and schedule presenters embodied television's intermediary role. Before anything, they were ordinary people with no journalistic or other professional training related to television. Boulos, for example, was an engineer; Lebanon's first announcer Najwa Qazoun was a simple young woman from the Beqaa Valley; and Salah Tizani, the creator of the top-rated eponymous comedy show *Abu Salim*, was a traveling amateur comedian from the north. This made them appear more accessible and less intimidating. And yet, their prominence turned them into celebrities far above any ordinary citizen who were able to translate Lebanese modernity to their brethren.

News anchors allowed the public to get a closer look at the machine of national politics. They were the symbols of a modernized public space that provided greater access to information. They also purposefully tried to create an image of trustworthiness and impartiality to reflect their status as the first heroes of television. Despite the censorship of news broadcasts, for instance, the most celebrated anchor of Lebanese television—Camille Menassa—managed to build a popular base. The demands of his job put him in close contact with the movers and shakers of the day—politicians, military figures, and entertainment stars. He even got a nickname, "harbinger of doom," when the public noticed that the famous and powerful died or suffered a coup right after he interviewed them.[32] His dry humor also seemed to have helped elevate his fame, as when he gave credit to his competitor for having announced President Khoury's death in error two months earlier. His fame continues even today. On December 6, 2012, Professor Menassa was a guest on Pierre Rabbat's talk show *Min al-Ekhir* (*Per Se*), which aired on Murr TV (MTV) as a "success story" of journalism and communications.[33] To the warm applause of the audience, Menassa was greeted by six other guests, some of whom were journalists. The guests expressed enormous appreciation for his role as an icon of Lebanese television and gratitude for being a role model for Lebanese journalism.

At the same time, an all-female cast of schedule presenters, as well as television's female anchors and hosts, were tasked to make the space of television feel intimate, welcoming, and attractive. Their beauty was the most and sometimes only important aspect of their performance because it symbolized a lot more than mere comeliness. It also represented innocence and domesticity that squared well with the image of television as a modernizer of domestic space. *Shabaka* policed this criterion relentlessly. Take, for example, Najwa Qazoun. In one article, the magazine held her as the model announcer in order to criticize those who failed to meet her profession's standards. The viewers, the article explained, think she is the best on television; her appearance is that of "a respectable girl" (*bint bayt*) and her "smiles are innocent."[34] The staff columnist juxtaposed her "calm beauty" with the less attractive faces of other female presenters that internal politics forced on viewers, as he claimed: "If you have to force them into television, why not give them some job in administration; why not have them hit on the type writer instead of hitting people's eyes? . . . Television has always been and continues to be about looks." The idea of the respectable girl may appear extreme; however, the language of an antiquated 1931 law on entertainment linked female performers with prostitution well into the 1990s.[35] Qazoun was so beloved that when she had a cold one time, the magazine lamented that "the beauty queen of television" was away from the screen for a whole twenty-four hours.[36] In a later article, though, the columnist dared go after the "queen" herself. He admitted that the magazine thought of her as "a piece of chocolate" but there was one thing that had bothered him—the "two black lines on top of her upper lip which look a lot like the budding mustache of a 14-year-old boy. . . . It's unnatural . . . I'm asking Najwa," he continued, "to find a way to get rid of her mustache. What's this way? I know not. All I know is that there is 'cream,' 'powder,' 'makeup.'"[37] Next to the text was a picture of Qazoun with no visible facial hair and a caption, "That's how we want her."

The earliest heroes of television—Boulos, Menassa, Qazoun, and others like them—played specific intermediary roles that projected a sense of modernity. Boulos and other entertainers showcased national talent and created an atmosphere of prosperity, merriment, and desire. Menassa and other anchors reflected and helped build the image of a serious nation whose daily political bustle was newsworthy. Qazoun and other female presenters showed the audiences that television was an intimate setting worthy of modern domestic space. These new domestic visitors became members of the Lebanese family who projected the unifying power of entertainment and a modern public culture created by television.

Amateurism and the Democratization of Public Taste

The early period was a formative period in the history of Lebanese television. It introduced many of the long-term trends and issues and the ways to talk about them that would manifest in the next several decades. One issue was the lack of professionalization in the industry, which the early celebrity culture may have obfuscated to some degree. Six out of ten television employees interviewed about their awareness of television flaws and commitment to combat them named lack of professionalization and amateurism as their greatest concerns.[38] "Popular shows? No, they're a joke!" protested *Shabaka*, accusing social show hosts of lacking any credentials be it in sociology, national education, or theater arts.[39] Technical crews, administrators, and hosts had no successful models or best practices from which to learn and had to create their own standards, often by trial and error. Early technology presented a particular challenge and the pioneers sometimes had to go to extraordinary lengths to put out a show. For instance, the technology CLT had gotten from the French did not allow the outlet to broadcast American shows with Arabic subtitles, and they had to hire interpreters for each showing. Eventually, the technical staff had to concoct a mechanism with a series of negative photographic images, wooden rolls, and an old typewriter to overlay the subtitles on the screen, effectively inventing the first mechanical captioning machine.[40] Despite a lengthy promotional campaign for color television, CLT discovered that the SECAM equipment shipped from France allowed them to broadcast either the television announcer or the shows that France had sent along but no other imported or local productions.[41] This put CLT in a tight spot as it wanted to keep its campaign promises of diverse, hundred-percent-color programs. Eventually, the technical staff fixed the problem with a series of off-the-cuff conversions through makeshift mirrors; however, 20 percent of the quality was lost along the way. In other instances, immaturity got the better of professionalism. News anchor Jean Khoury complained that some of the staff at his news department distracted their anchor colleagues during the bulletin delivery with jokes.[42]

Neither did television recognize the need for the professionalization of writing. As a result, television did not work with established, successful writers and often the show host or lead actors wrote the script. This led to repetitive, superficial, and unimaginative products. Undervaluing writers and their potential kept them hidden from the public and the early critics. The press, however, would not miss a swing to drive the point that its competitor was nothing but a bunch of amateurs. In one article, *Shabaka* "outed" actor Auni al-Masri for hiding behind the pseudonym Abu Tawfiq as the writer of *Qissati Qissa* (*My Story Is Complicated*), starring Elias Rizq, and followed with a slew of criticism for his amateurish script.[43]

The issue of language choice also triggered debates about the industry's professionalization. On one hand, the lack of professionalization led to a kind of democratization of language. Early television embraced all the accents of its pioneers—from Abu Melhem's village dialect, and Abu Salim's northern speech, to Muhammad Shammel's Beiruti accent. These accents entered the family living room and opened up the public's horizons as viewers became viscerally aware of the wealth of local language varieties and the social groups and regional communities that used them. When viewers first encountered Abu Salim and his troupe's northern speech, they admitted their surprise at the existence of Lebanese accents they had never heard before. However, the linguistic democratization had its set of challenges too. Some viewers found Abu Salim's accents too thick to understand, so mere audience interest became insufficient to justify using them, and in time the troupe softened its language considerably.

The variety of accents and local dialects within a given show were also issues when it came to exporting Lebanese television to the Arab world, a problem painfully familiar to Lebanese cinema. Professionals complained that the language bouquet prevented them from establishing Lebanese television regionally and edging out Egyptian productions whose language was already understood throughout the Arab world. Directors like

Muhammad Salman baited audiences by inserting an Egyptian character into the Lebanese story, while cultural icons like singer and actress Sabah were convinced that singing or acting in her native Lebanese had never been a problem for the broad Arab consumer.[44] *Shabaka* proposed a more permanent two-pronged solution: since local viewers were avid consumers of local shows, there was no need to change much of the languages and accents used currently. For the regional market, though, the magazine suggested creating a couple of television shows specifically geared toward broader Arab audiences that used a professionalized Lebanese language. This "proper Lebanese vernacular" was to be a single unified variety based on the speech of high-society Beiruti ladies who frequented literary salons and avoided obscure accents and vocabulary.[45] Professionalizing television language would continue to be a hot-button issue throughout the war and would only find a workable solution in the satellite era.

In addition to democratizing language, early television also reshaped public culture by interfering with the hierarchy of cultural taste. Earlier mass media and communal practices that organized public space were infiltrated by cultural notions of class. While theater tended to entertain the elite, night clubs were considered vulgar and lower-class. Traditional communal practices that needed no cultural authorization of taste helped community members form close bonds, but these practices remained parochial as each community created its own localized, unique set of cultural norms. The arrival of television challenged traditional hierarchies of taste and communal practices. For example, television destroyed a local practice known as "widow literature," in which elderly women gathered local communities in homes and cafes to entertain them with collective stories.[46] The new medium also hired and legitimized the mediocre performers radio had rejected, making them look "cool," which affected radio's legitimacy and cultural authority.[47] In the pretelevision era, B-rated singers were destined to wither away in cabarets and nightclubs where they performed for small crowds. Television turned them into stars featured in its top-rated genre—the variety show. Plucked out of oblivion, they were now bigger than radio, albeit occasionally accused of being tacky. For instance, the famous *Beirut at Night* was called a "vulgar cabaret" on account of the nature of its content and the caliber of its singers and dancers.

Television employees, to be sure, defended the variety of tastes, languages, and identities that the medium made visible. In an interview, news anchor Jeanne d'Arc Abu Zeid Fayyad explained that television flaws were just differences in taste. CLT's CEO, retired General Naufel, also firmly asserted that in case of any negative effect of television shows on children, "the father and mother only need to ban their kids from watching" rather than insist on banning television shows.[48] In sum, in the early period, television defined its role as a modern institution through introducing, reshaping, and popularizing what was considered vulgar, tasteless, or dangerous and turning it into mass culture. Only a few years later, that culture would be seen as the golden age of Lebanon.

Golden Years (1968–1975)

For thirty-five years in the business, Izz al-Din dreamed of creating a national television (*televizion watani*).[49] Television's "golden years"—the brief period between 1968 and 1975—perhaps came closer to his dream than any other period in the history of Lebanese television. The government's neoliberal policies during this Arab-Israeli interwar period boosted the rich classes' wealth while television opened a new chapter marked by policy changes, financial stability, a boom in the production of local entertainment, and the first wave of the industry's professionalization. An idyllic Lebanon emerged on television as a nation of prosperity, harmony, and modern vision. This trope masked the nation's classist and sectarian foundation and the deepening class cleavages that in great part led to the civil war. The trope of idyllic Lebanon also laid the foundation for the wartime peace bubble (see chapter 2) and the national postwar "amnesia" of all things war.

The maturing nation and the neoliberal economy produced the alluring notion of peaceful cosmopolitanism. This notion reflected an accelerating change from traditional rural values toward the modernism of a bustling urban culture. In the meantime, the television industry was maturing as well. Television was no longer a new product that needed to be explained to the consumer. It had established itself, and 75 percent of Lebanese households owned a set by 1974. From being a luxury item, it had become a necessity. The industry also resolved the two issues that restricted its independence and prosperity—foreign aid and relentless competition. CLT's commitment to French money, although proving a lifeline for the new Lebanese station, brought a set of problems that affected programming and impeded CLT's ability to attract audiences. The French connection also disrupted CLT's business relations with the Americans. In one case, the newly appointed director of Advision, the Frenchman Pierre Rocher, whom the Lebanese described as inexperienced and technologically illiterate, gave orders to start sending all official communication with foreign companies in French. [50] Boulos, who was director of programming, unsuccessfully opposed the orders. He complained to General Naufel that CLT had been corresponding with the Americans in English for years and that the Americans would find it time-consuming to look for a French translator. When his complaint fell on deaf ears and he became irritated by other disruptive practices, he decided to quit in 1970. By the mid- to late 1960s, the Lebanese were ready to take over from the French, who, too, wanted out of the perpetual money pit of Lebanese television. In 1974, this process was completed as Paul Tannous assumed the post of Advision's director after Rocher left.[51]

In the first television decade, CLT's and Télé Orient's rivalry for technological supremacy had drained most of the resources the companies had for other development like human capital, training, and the creation of original programs. The rivalry largely contributed to the dismal financial situation of Lebanese television. The dirty antics they played on each other were a matter of amusement in the press and for the audiences—from hacking and broadcasting the competitor's feed to poaching cadres, copying programming, and spearheading bluffing advertising campaigns. Eventually, competition strained the two stations so much that they decided to coordinate their efforts, which led to the golden age in Lebanese television. Out in the open there was fierce competition, but behind closed doors there had been negotiations about merging and coordinating their advertising budgets. In 1968, the two stations reached an agreement, and things started to get better. They chose a sole advertising representative—a company called "Telemanagement" owned equally by Télé Orient and CLT's Advision—and coordinated their sales of advertising time.[52] To save money, they also began coordinating their scheduling. In addition, news bulletins and political programs were to be produced and broadcast only out of Télé Orient's Hazmieh headquarters in order not to compete.

The newfound independence and peace in Lebanese television provided fertile ground for financial stability and a spike in production. Each station veered toward a specialization: CLT made local drama and comedy, while Télé Orient produced series for the Arab market, becoming the second-largest exporter of Arab television to the region. In 1974, the outlet was earning 12 percent of its revenue from these exports (while CLT's revenues from sales abroad were 5 percent).[53] The demand for Arab television production in the region was high in the presatellite era, while the supply was low, so Lebanese television was able to compete successfully and market its series and shows to twenty Arab countries.[54]

The new age of peace also inspired the professionalization of the industry. The earlier-produced, cheaper genres no longer satisfied the audiences' growing sophistication as consumers of television. Now, the industry had a decade of experience under its belt to guide it toward new, higher standards of production, professional behavior, and genre maturity. A new generation of television creators who understood the power of generic specialization developed the new genre of drama that came to dominate the period. They popularized thirteen-episode drama series, comedy, romantic series, satirical drama, and detective-crime series. Not only were plenty of drama series produced, but they also began choosing a subgeneric specialization, in contrast to the earlier period when genres were often eclectically combined in the same variety program. Some of their greatest hits have become an iconic part of the classic golden age archive: the 1972 drama *al-Mishwar al-Tawil* (*The Long Journey*, the first time a television series was filmed using cinematographic techniques),[55] the 1972 comedy *Masrah Shoushou* (*Shoushou's Theater*), the 1973 satirical drama *Akhwat Shanay* (*The Fool of Shanay*), the 1974 romantic series *Hawla Ghurfati* (*Around My Room*), and the 1974 romantic drama *Nisa' 'Ashiqat* (*Women in Love*, extended from three to eighteen episodes with rave critical reviews for director Samir Nasri's style), along with many others. The first wave of professionalization also witnessed the creation of Lebanon's private production companies. Sport and talent shows were very popular as well. This period birthed Lebanon's extraordinarily famous singing competition show *Studio al-Fann* (*Art Studio*). The show, which began in 1973, became a primary agent in the continuing shift of power from radio (where singing legitimized radio's cultural authority) to television.[56]

News anchors and political talk show hosts became facilitators in addition to their role as intermediaries. The year 1968 brought in a new style of interviewing with Marie-Therese Arbid's popular weekly show *Majallat Lubnan* (*Lebanon's Journal*) on CLT. Instead of the customary question and answer conversation between host and guest, Arbid sat behind the camera and let the guest speak directly to the audience in a confiding, revelatory atmosphere.[57] After President Frangieh came to power in 1970, he abolished the Second Bureau and other security apparatuses, doing away with some of the heavy censorship of the Shehab period. This thawing period allowed running and brand-new information shows to tackle censored topics and invite blacklisted guests. One was Adel Malek's popular political talk show *Sijill Maftouh* (*Open Record*). Other examples included the daring Leila Rustum's shows *Hadith al-Nas* (*Talk of the People*) on current affairs and the iconic *Sahra maʿ al-Madi* (*An Evening with the Past*), which introduced viewers to local politicians and to the previously "unspoken politics" they now shared openly on-air.[58] The hosts facilitated the direct communication of the nation's leaders to a diverse public much larger than the leaders' narrow constituencies.

Ultimately, the most profound of all golden age developments was that television won the media war over cultural hierarchy. Television remained at the center of its own representation, not simply as a miracle technology but also as an effective tool for cultural enrichment, multiculturalism, and peaceful cosmopolitanism.

Wartime Depression (1975–1991)

Things were going great for Lebanese television at the end of 1974. Total television advertising income was USD$4–5 million, which was a 20 percent increase from the year before.[59] Commercial success was accelerating at such a rate, in fact, that in December the government demanded 6.5 percent of CLT's advertising revenue when it renewed the outlet's license for nine more years.[60] Prewar television was apparently taking the country toward wealth and plenty, not just in images and boosted cultural output but also materially by financing the government.

Four months later, on the Sunday morning of April 13, 1975, the war erupted and derailed the television "car." The state institutions collapsed, advertising revenues quickly dwindled, local production dove from its prewar peak to only a few drama series here and there, and broadcast equipment was destroyed. Whole areas in the North, the Beqaa Valley, and the South lost television service for years, while the neighborhoods within a mile radius from the Tallet al-Khayyat (CLT) headquarters had either poor or no reception at all.[61] In 1977, the two television outlets headed for bankruptcy. In December, the newly elected president Elias Sarkis was forced to establish a new outlet, Télé Liban, with 50 percent government participation and the remaining capabilities of the extant private outlets to avoid the industry's total collapse as well as the label "the president who killed television."[62] The new outlet was managed by twelve board members, six of whom were from the government, and its chair was approved by the Minister of Information and the Minister of Finance.[63] The main contribution of the government in the new enterprise was to provide liquidity for the physical repairs to the damaged infrastructure and to restore service in the North and the Beqaa Valley.[64]

The war had other tangible consequences on television. On one hand, the industry became so politically volatile that it was uncontrollable by management, employees, or the Lebanese government. On the other hand, it was so deliberately oblivious to the ongoing violence that it became unresponsive to the audiences' needs. As a result, the relationship between television and audiences suffered a great deal.

Throughout several extended periods during the war, television outlets or branches were taken over by opposing factions and their news bulletins used in rhetorical battles. After the devastating 1975–76 sectarian takeover of Télé Orient and CLT, there was a general sense that television needed a makeover so the split would not recur. An international observer even recommended that instead of using the geographic names of the former Télé Orient and CLT branches—Hazmieh and Tallet al-Khayyat respectively, now marked by sectarian identities—Télé Liban should call them TL1 and TL2.[65] He also recommended it stop the monthly news bulletin rotation between them. To be sure, the branches split again in the mid-1980s.

The government not only failed to control the branches of its national outlet but also was impotent to guarantee Télé Liban's monopoly. President Sarkis and Télé Liban's CEO Charles Rizq tried to stop the militias from launching their own television service but they seemed to be working against an inevitable outcome. By the 1980s, equipment had become cheap and pirate service was easy to set up if one paid no taxes or aired bootlegged shows. The question for many was not whether the government would be able to guarantee Télé Liban's monopoly but which of the militias would be the first to break it with a regular service of its own.[66]

Besides, the government's quick-fix formula to repair damaged infrastructure in exchange for censoring programming and shelving all other concerns failed to gain popular support. Frequent voices began blaming the government for the lack of adequate funding to pay employee salaries on time, update equipment, and finance new production.[67] For instance, as late as 1986 the outlet had a single camera for outdoor shoots.[68] It was often hard to appreciate the difference between the outlet's newscast and a radio bulletin because the former aired little footage of local, regional, and international developments with sound and picture.[69] Télé Liban's financial neglect of its employees was another serious issue. Financial problems were mediated through a series of strikes, which usually ended with government promises for more funding that somehow never materialized. The strike of 1987 was different. The government had announced that it would allocate one billion Lebanese pounds to Télé Liban but the money was not forthcoming. After a week of unrest in national radio and television, the government resorted to its usual strategy of promises, but the employees stuck to their guns and picketed in front of both television branches, demanding back pay and improvement in working conditions. The higher levels of management were between a rock and a hard place. While the current chair of the board of directors, Raymond Jabbara, pledged support for employee rights and for the billion-pound increase in the outlet's capital (a decision within Parliament's purview), he also reprimanded "irresponsible actions" that might jeopardize these goals. The chair of the Parliamentary Committee for Media, Mahmoud Ammar, scolded the station for deserting its guiding and unifying nationalist role, which Parliament now felt forced to save; he even seemed to threaten the strikers that the legislators might reverse their decision.[70] But promises were no longer deemed acceptable. Strikers kept picketing, "Don't be silent. Don't back down. Your demands are right, and he who is right is king."[71] As tangible concessions were the only way out of the crisis, the government began distributing back pay, yet soaring inflation affected employees' benefits. Suspicion also remained whether working conditions would improve in other ways to clear the way for better television productions.

Télé Liban's neglect of its actors and contributors was deemed just as abhorrent. The hostilities and the decline in production pushed many actors abroad. Those who stayed faced television's unwillingness to pay. Seasoned actors of the magnitude of Layla Karam—"the Dame of Lebanese television"—were sidelined for cheaper, B-list alternatives.[72] Mahmoud Mabsout, who played the famous comedy character Fahman in the series *Abu Salim*, opened a juice bar in an effort to survive; other cast members of *Abu Salim* joined his new business.[73] Whereas Fahman of the golden age had earned a monthly income in acting of 1,000 LL (with 50 to 150 LL per episode), the juice income of Fahman in 1977 quadrupled to 4,000 LL. The press wistfully wondered if he would ever return to art given the income difference. Télé Liban seemed to care equally little about its deceased stars, although it still stayed in business in great part thanks to them—it continuously reran their early and golden age hits, plus they no longer required payment of wages. Yet, the station often only aired a last-minute, improvised commemoration of the stars' death or completely forgot about it.[74]

The most iconic thing about wartime Télé Liban was how the public viewed it. Télé Liban was "just around the corner" from turning a corner, the press mused, yet never seemed to get there. It cycled through a series of CEOs, some of whom did not stay for their full three-year term. None succeeded in solving the outlet's basket of problems, so employees, audiences, and critics moved from a peak of hope with every new appointment to subsequent disappointment and pessimism. In addition, the outlet's unresponsiveness to the public's needs and its occlusion of the war put constant public pressure on it, reflected in the popular press.

LBC's launch on August 23, 1985, changed the dysfunctional television-audience dynamic. The station's first competitor was Télé Liban's Channel 5 (Hazmieh), which covered the Christian areas where LBC could install its antennae.[75] Within six months, LBC had penetrated the whole Lebanese market; by 1987, it had launched its own French Channel C33 to compete head-to-head with Télé Liban's French Channel 9.

Initially, LBC attracted the curious viewer by illegally broadcasting the latest US and French shows, and especially by airing risqué movies like *9½ Weeks* uncensored. However, the outlet was able to rapidly increase and sustain wide viewership by two different strategies. The first was changing the public perception of its owners, the Lebanese Forces (LF), and LF's relationship with its Christian constituency. For the first time, hosts and anchors wore crosses around their necks. They did not change their Christian names to more Muslim or neutral-sounding names for marketing purposes and smoothly mixed Arabic, English, and French without framing it as mockery. All the above were done in an effort to construct a proud Christian identity.[76] The second strategy was developing innovative local programming that appealed to a national audience beyond the Christian enclave. LBC's cutting-edge news bulletins, gaming and talk shows, and later local fictional production made the pirate outlet the talk of the town. Not least, it offered special Muslim programming during Ramadan. The "hard to please" Lebanese viewers were completely enamored by LBC after just half a year,[77] because the outlet seemed to be of "a different caliber," especially in the way it connected to the audience.[78] Gone was Télé Liban's version of television based on neglecting the audience. Instead, viewers felt LBC's attention and interest in them: "We notice the effort," explained *Shabaka*, even if not all shows succeed.[79] The newcomer quickly attracted seasoned technical staff and actors who had been feeling mistreated at the national outlet or were looking for fresh creative opportunities. Since big actors were the major attraction for the audiences, booking them helped LBC strengthen its connection to the viewer. The outlet also started talking to Lebanon's most famous writers and early on made deals with private production companies (e.g., that of the al-Ashi brothers).[80]

LBC's success and the nature of its relationship with audiences invited harrowing comparisons to Télé Liban. The "new faces" of the "rising," "young" LBC looked filled with "vigor" and an "appetite for renewal" next to the "declining" old station and its "tired," "superficial" production. LBC's series on local social life appeared "twice as good" as Télé Liban's with their creative take on urban and rural communities.[81] In one of its articles, *Shabaka* fumed:

> Almost everyone you meet talks about the new shows on LBC, about their success, and how they attract a huge, enormous number of viewers. . . . Almost everyone you meet asks, "Did you see *Saturday Guests*?" Did you see this show? And did you see that show? When you open the television schedule, you realize that all these shows air on LBC. And where is Télé Liban headed? No one knows where it is going with this horrific pile of tired, worthless, dead shows and series that were produced right out of flat texts with no semblance of harmony, artistic value, or pleasure factor. And this, of course, strengthens people's interest in LBC's shows, satisfies their desires, and gives them what entertains and benefits them. . . . Doesn't Télé Liban know that the world is going forward? . . . Where are you going Télé Liban? Where to, when all your output is drowning in emptiness and dust?[82]

The connotation that LBC was headed forward to the future and Télé Liban backward to the past reveals the public's perspective on each outlet's relationship to modernity.

In 1989, leftist MP Zaher al-Khatib and breakaway LF member Elie Hobeika launched a second pirate outlet called Mashreq TV, which addressed middle- and lower-class socioeconomic groups to counter the right-wing leanings of LF's LBC.[83] The outlet came on-air in the midst of a fatal coincidence. President-elect René Moawad and twenty-three other people were assassinated a few blocks from the outlet's headquarters during the inauguration broadcast on Independence Day, November 22, 1989, just seventeen days after his election. Mashreq TV's trial period, however, was far from dramatic, causing some concern in the press. Its roster featured mostly Egyptian series and other foreign movies to distinguish its programming from Télé Liban's and LBC's fare. Later, it also covered the 1990s national cause cèlébre—the South Lebanon resistance. Some of the shows Mashreq TV broadcast were reportedly available for rent in local video stores, and viewers could watch them any time they wanted. This triggered a stern warning from the press to develop a rich local fare and ditch the Egyptian trial schedule if it ever wanted to "rise" (*Mashreq* means "the land of sunrise") and develop a good relationship with its audience. When *Shabaka* heard rumors that the outlet was interviewing anchors in preparation for launching its news bulletin, it warned the outlet again to compete against LBC, not copy Télé Liban's inferior newscast.[84]

The negative Télé Liban comparisons to LBC followed a decade of similar unfavorable analogies to private radio. The pendulum had swung the other way. Television's earlier victory in the culture war against radio had expired as commercial radio became the leading medium in the first war decade. One study from the late 1970s to the early 1980s shows an average Lebanese radio audience of 78 percent compared to a television viewership of only 53 percent, which is less by a third.[85] Nonetheless, television continued to assert its dominance over other media and cultural practices. After security concerns forced cinemas to close one by one and music concerts went into hiatus for a while, cinema- and concertgoers, who also doubled as television viewers, converted into exclusive television audiences. On top of that, viewers easily recognized amateur singers or new talent from television competition shows like *Art Studio* but had a harder time identifying concert musicians and singers with decades of live tours.[86] Television celebrity trumped traditional face-to-face art.

LBC took television celebrity to a whole new level by placing the audiences at the center of representation. On one hand, ordinary people, often from the lower class, were regularly interviewed in on-site news reports. Their raw emotions and everyday vernacular language provided the nucleus around which the report built its message to the broader audience. Regular people were also invited in new, bold social and political talk shows to share their opinions on controversial issues. On the other hand, LBC reimagined the cheaper game show genre that had reigned in television's early age and received a remarkable audience reception. The famous *Art Studio* singing competition, for instance, got a new set and sleek design. Originally launched on CLT, it was later produced on Télé Liban before moving to LBC in 1988. Its roots go back to the early, amateur days of Lebanese television and to the popular talent show *al-Fann Hiwayati* (*Art Is My Hobby*) hosted by Rashad al-Bibi, which was itself a successor of the show *Rukn al-Huwat* (*Amateur Corner*) hosted by Halim Bijani. The 1988 season was particularly difficult for *Art Studio*. As regular people could not move freely around Lebanon or among neighborhoods in Beirut, fear of crossing internal "borders" raised suspicions that LBC would only invite Christian contestants who could travel to its headquarters inside the Christian enclave. Everyone was watching if director Simon Asmar—often thought of as the genius of LBC—would provide transportation for the contestants and guarantee their safety.[87] The show ended up representing multiple Lebanese communities and turned into a resounding success. Nonetheless, its exceptional, carefully selected voices, despite being marketed as amateurs, represented an older model of competition and game shows. The new model, which LBC ushered in, made television heroes out of complete amateurs in shows like the top-billing game show *Laylat Hazz* (*Night of Luck*), directed by Simon Asmar and hosted by one of Lebanon's most beloved television personalities, Ziad Noujeim, an agnostic and unabashed critic of television, bureaucracy, and patriarchy. Dr. Noujeim, a Paris- and Harvard-trained oral surgeon and a university lecturer, started his television career in 1986 as an amateur. A decade later, he continued to describe himself as "a professional amateur."[88] In 2003 he became the lead anchor of Al Hurra, the US government–owned Arabic-language outlet, where he interviewed US Vice President Joe Biden among other notable guests. In addition to their focus on amateurs, shows like *Night of Luck* put the audiences in the participant position and commercialized their relation with television. *Shabaka* thought it was strange to gain so much success and advertising revenues watching amateurs, but it pointed out that they registered "the rhythm of life,"[89] perhaps more closely than the contestants on *Art Studio*.

Finally, the war spurred a revolution in television writing, which constituted a second wave of television professionalization. In the earlier periods, writers were often unknown to the audience, who instead saw actors, hosts, and presenters as the true stars of television and their points of connection to the medium. During the war, writers became among the most recognized names from television (e.g., Wajih Radwan, Marwan Najjar, Muhammad Shammel, Gulbahar Mumtaz, Genevieve Atallah, Anwar Tamer, Ahmad al-Ashi, Marwan al-Abd, Antoine Afram, Antoine Ghandour, Ibrahim Mirashli, and Dr. Najat Rifaat al-Khatib). Sometimes they were among the most recognized faces too, as in the case of Marwan Najjar. *Shabaka* followed their careers, conducted series of interviews with them, and regularly analyzed their roles in Lebanese culture.

During most of the civil war, Lebanese television failed as a medium of communication, which led to its crisis of legitimacy with the audiences. But by the war's end, it became hugely popular after going through a rebirth in great part due to a shift in the standards and practices of what made it a legitimate medium of communication. This shift from disengagement to engagement with the audiences involved paying attention to the audiences' cultural tastes, acknowledging their concerns, listening to them, and especially placing them at the center of representation.

Postwar Boom (1991–Present)

It is impossible to do justice to the incredibly rich and diverse television production in the postwar period in this short section, especially since it has lasted as long as all three earlier periods combined. Therefore, I will only briefly extend the themes I outlined in the previous sections. In the postwar period, television witnessed a further, much larger shift in ownership from government to the private sector; in attitude toward the audiences from disengagement to engagement; and in the object of representation from television to audiences.

The Challenges of Ownership

Following the example of LBC, a number of factions launched their own television stations. By 1991, their number was reported as thirty-nine,[90] and two years later it had jumped to fifty-four.[91] Most of the larger outlets became commercial, while the smaller outlets were primarily partisan-supported. In the early 1990s, the majority filled their rosters with Egyptian movies and series since local production had gone down considerably. There were good reasons to focus on Egyptian shows: they were cheap, had many fans, and brought in advertisers. But as in the case of Mashreq TV, people could simply rent many of the shows from a video store, which prompted *Shabaka* to call the new television outlets "video stores with antennae."[92] Some of them saved even more on costs by airing the same show multiple times, occasionally up to ten.

Local series could not ensure audience engagement until the mid-1990s when production increased drastically and local shows became a major attraction. The unlicensed outlets were understandably weary of investing large sums of money into infrastructure, equipment, and salaries for professionals because none of them owned studios or the technology to shoot programs for local production like LBC and Télé Liban. They could not compete with LBC, which produced 150 hours of local fictional series for 1992 (roughly three hours of airtime per week), for example, or even with Télé Liban's much more modest local production. The Ministry of Information did not impose any minimum quotas on local production because the government did not want to recognize the pirate outlets as legitimate enterprises. Even if it did offer such recognition, Lebanese television was regulated by the 1962 Press Law, which was inadequate for that purpose. The press and professionals from the television industry warned about the costs of meager local series production. Distinguished television director Antoine Rimi at one point reportedly stated that the new outlets wouldn't survive if they did not dedicate a large part of their efforts and budget to local shows.[93]

The early pirate outlets offset costs by creating engaging news and information programs. News coverage was completely unregulated and therefore could express the point of view of the primary constituency of the sect or faction that owned the outlet, or more correctly that of the sect's leader, as some have argued convincingly. The government did not censor their newscasts, again as a way of avoiding recognizing them as legitimate enterprises.

This political parallelism, or political influence over media, led to a rupture that embedded sectarian divisions in television's institutional memory. The media anarchy also endangered air traffic. As a result of these costs, and also based on political considerations, in 1992 the government announced that it would regulate the media and compel television outlets to stay out of news. This caused an enormous backlash. The public saw the proposed law as a tactic to silence political opposition and further promote the financial interests of the wealthy and powerful. Parliament nonetheless passed the bill in 1994 as Audio-Visual Law 382. The law revoked Télé Liban's monopoly and laid out a path for licensing a handful of private outlets, making Lebanon the first Arab country with a regulatory system for private television.[94]

The new legal system had at least two important consequences. The first was formalizing television's sectarian character.[95] Outlets associated with the larger minorities or main politicians received licenses; all other outlets were banned. These measures led not only to voluntary closures but also to forced ones as well as legal battles.[96] Some outlets were forcefully shut down despite having fulfilled all requirements for a license (e.g., New TV was shut down but reopened in 2000 after winning a legal battle). Others continue to operate without a license (e.g., the Catholic-run outlet Télé Lumièr).

The second consequence was sabotaging Télé Liban. During the tough war years, successive governments had failed to adequately finance the outlet and ensure its prosperity due to their slashed budgets. But Rafiq Hariri's reconstruction government prevented it from bouncing back even though the war was over. At first, Hariri bought 50 percent of the outlet's shares from the private sector (CLT's and Télé Orient's shares) before he became prime minister in 1992. (Later, the government bought them out and converted the station into a 100 percent government-owned enterprise.) Then, he launched his own station, al-Mustaqbal (Future TV). Like him, the other major private television owners were also government officials or very close to them; their interests trumped Télé Liban's. This left Télé Liban in disrepair for most of the following quarter-century. One 2009 plan to improve it, submitted to the Council of Ministers, was scrapped, for instance, because private outlets feared such improvement would come at their expense.[97] At one point, the outlet even closed down for six months, and when it reopened it operated at 25 percent of its previous capacity. Media scholar Sarah El Richani has warned of the dangers of "sidelining the public broadcaster, arguably a space where conflicting views may have been reconciled, and the presence of different political projects on the broadcasting landscape may therefore be contributing to what [Chantal Mouffe] calls the 'vibrant "agonistic" public space.'"[98]

Lebanese television continued to be regulated by the 1994 Audio-Visual Law for over twenty years, despite many challenges brought in by the new digital age. In December 2016, a new bill was finalized after five years of discussion to replace the pre–digital era law. The bill does not address, however, the serious financial problems from which all outlets suffer (their total annual advertising budget dropped from USD$100 million in 2010 to $60 million in 2015, according to Qassem Sweid, chair of NBN's board of directors).[99]

Engagement and Representation

Lebanese television experienced a second golden age in the 1990s with booming local production. Memories of the first golden age and Lebanese television's regional market power resurfaced together with the old trope of "the first television." To date, the Tallet al-Khayyat branch of Télé Liban is the oldest continuously operating television station in the Arab world, and it had its fifty-year anniversary in 2009. Its archives, which Caretaker Information Minister Walid Daouk called "our culture and our roots,"[100] are the most valuable resource the outlet and the Lebanese television industry have as a whole. Consequently, in the new era, the public expected Télé Liban to engage with its audiences as a key national institution, like it had in the golden age, and regain its regional influence.

Its 1991 makeover at first raised high hopes. Thirty-year-old equipment was slated for retirement, cables in walls were ripped out and new French brands installed, while ancient cameras were trashed. "Dead" shows and expired ideas got the boot for newer programs that were more responsive to the needs of the educated modern viewer. The biggest news perhaps came from the news department—the "retirement home," as *Shabaka* had called it on account of its sluggishness and incapacity.[101] "Loose hands and unprofessional behavior" reportedly stopped. Lone anchors were no longer solely responsible for the production of news based on official NNA briefings, and a committee was tasked to write the daily bulletin collaboratively, then hand it to three approved anchors to read on-air.[102] The broadly supported changes of this so-called white coup inspired premature pronouncements that Télé Liban had "come back."

The white coup eventually turned out to be another disappointment. According to the press, Télé Liban needed to produce local Lebanese stories and hire back the actors, writers, and directors who had left to work at new, unlicensed television stations, thus handing their considerable training and experience over to the competition. In addition, the outlet still lacked a strategic leader who could shape the makeover going forward rather than keep looking back to the golden archive.[103] No serious programming was produced to counter the brutal competition from the unlicensed channels. Instead, the outlet satisfied itself with a mere rebranding over several 1993 ad campaigns and finally changed the names of its channels to TL1 and TL2. The ads reflected the trend of audience-focused programming—"Whatever you like," "With you in every home," and "Television for all Lebanon"—but they were overly broad and related very little to actual programming. *Shabaka* bluntly accused Télé Liban of trying to manipulate the viewers with slogans and names "as if the problem is in the names."[104]

The outlet had a few successful years in the mid-1990s around the time when Jean-Claude Boulos was appointed CEO. It celebrated its thirty-eighth anniversary and finally completed production of the historic series *al-Raghif* (*The Loaf*) that had first started fifteen years earlier. It also aired a number of important popular drama series like *al-Asifa Tahubb Marratayn* (*The Storm Hits Twice*, 1994–96) with Roula Hamadeh and Fadi Ibrahim and its 1997 sequel, *Nisa fi al-Asifa* (*Women in the Storm*), as well as political and social talk shows like *Khamsa ʿala Sabʿa* (5/7) with Zaven Kouyoumdjian and *Kalam w-Nas* (*Words and People*). *Shabaka* criticized *The Storm Hits Twice* for oversexualization, but the 120-episode series had a number of progressive elements. For example, writer Shukri

Anis Fakhoury admitted that he often solicited audience feedback on the development of subsequent episodes, which *Shabaka* praised in a headline about its finale, "The Finale That Is Written by the Public."[105] In addition, the series was considered revolutionary in its treatment of women. It caused a stir because it depicted the right of women to divorce their husbands—something inconceivable for many Lebanese women. Télé Liban's boldness in its portrayals of male philandering and disrespectful attitudes toward women challenged the outlet's earlier portrayals of women who tolerated and silently suffered their cheating husbands for the sake of the marriage and public opinion. The series was a uniquely local achievement since its content was deemed inappropriate for marketing in the Gulf (like the station's earlier *Fusha* productions).[106] The prime time show 5/7 was also innovative in its discussions of unexplored topics and uncomfortable subjects. Using simple language that engaged the audiences, the show featured live call-ins from the audience and, according to the host, served as a site of connection between the political establishment and civil society. Climbing to ratings of 52 percent—the largest for a show of its kind—it brought in substantial revenue from advertisements. Considered among Télé Liban's most important shows, it is also iconic for the image of its Armenian-Lebanese host interviewing his guests from behind his laptop. After 1997, the station mostly stopped producing series, and its competitiveness decreased due to government policies that responded to pressures from the privately owned stations.[107] It is notable that shows like *The Storm Hits Twice* and 5/7 were exceptionally well funded by Télé Liban; both became landmark achievements for the outlet and for Lebanese culture in general. Therefore, Shabaka's claim that links government ownership with failure is misleading; "It [Télé Liban] was first in the East, then it became last in the world. Why? Because it's owned by the government."[108]

Despite these achievements, multiple administrators have failed to fix the outlet's endemic financial and programming problems, which Boulos captured in his book titled *Television: A Journey to Hell*.[109] When Talal Makdessi was appointed CEO in 2013, he pledged to build the outlet as a credible source of news and preserve the valuable archives, large parts of which have been lost.[110] The same year, Télé Liban attempted to strike a deal with France24, the BBC, and the Chinese state broadcaster (CCTV) to revive itself after years of debt, limited working staff, bureaucratic knots, and falling ratings. Eventually the Chinese helped with increasing information storage. The outlet's decrepit headquarters in Tallet al-Khayyat got a major facelift, fiber optics, digital cameras, a million-dollar van for live broadcasting, a new logo, and a lineup of new programming in 2014 (a quarter century after the last makeover).[111] "We will have a new sports program, a new kitchen for Chef Antoine, which has been around for 13 years next week, and entertainment programs and educational programs, so there can be more interaction between Lebanese citizens and Télé Liban," said Makdessi in an interview.[112] Yet, the Hazmieh branch has remained closed since 2000 despite multiple attempts to reopen it. According to Hassan Shaqqur, director of programming at Télé Liban, finances are available, yet the problem resides in the sectarian affiliation of the Hazmieh neighborhood, which makes the government reluctant to reopen it in that location.[113] After the makeover, the station's most important current concern consists of attracting an outstanding cadre, given its mission to create social, educational, and entertainment programming that is balanced, highlights the government's achievements, and does not irritate the family and the political structure.[114] All these issues might ultimately stem from the government's de facto promotion of the interests of the privately owned stations against the interests of its own station.

LBC had none of these troubles, although it has had its own share of political challenges. It remains Lebanon's top broadcast channel and the oldest continuously operating, privately owned Arab television outlet. Its eventful history since the 1990s is unlike that of any other media outlet. This history runs the gamut—from prestigious international awards to international battles over controlling shares, and from retaliation and twenty-four-hour evacuation orders to government-orchestrated transmission blackouts. Its anchors have been bombed and mutilated because of their anti-Syrian resistance during the hostile environment between 1990 and 2005 when Syria had control over Lebanese politics. Some of its owners have been outlawed and imprisoned.

In 2007, LF filed a lawsuit against CEO Pierre Daher for ownership over LBC.[115] A warrant for his arrest and that of LBC board member Raif Said al-Bustani was issued in 2010 over "misuse of trust, fraud, and embezzlement."[116] Daher immediately appealed, claiming LF "forgot" they sold him the station in 1992 for USD$5 million when LF's relationship with the state had gone sour and it could not obtain a license to operate a television outlet. (The outlet renamed itself LBC International, LBCI, at the time.) When the court dismissed the case against Daher for exceeding the statute of limitations, LF launched its web-based television: LFTV.

LBC started a number of new trends in the 1990s that continued to build on the closer relationship with the audiences it had begun forging since its launch. For example, shows like *Al-Awwal 'al LBC* (*First on LBC*) placed the audience at the center. The creators and host featured the most unique Lebanese people they found during their travels around Lebanon—the longest-mustache owner, the tallest Lebanese, and so on. The program was shot with seven cameras simultaneously, creating the impression that home viewers were present at the scene and able to connect to their many unknown compatriots. Another hit that placed the audience at the center was *Al-Shatir Yahki* (*The Expert Speaks*), hosted by LBC veteran Ziad Noujeim and created and written by Jinan Mallat. The show invited experts to challenge common perceptions on various controversial topics such as Freemasons, homosexuality, and more. It also featured discussions with people from these communities. Viewers expected Noujeim to do most of the talking, given the show's title. However, he let the guests speak, in an attempt to model "a democratic experience in a nondemocratic state."[117] Later, the show was hosted by Marcel Ghanem, who continued to discuss bold topics like drugs, sectarianism, domestic abuse, incest, racism, and others. Despite government objections and angry calls from Gulf viewers,[118] the show continued to air with high ratings.

Gaming shows continued to be popular too. News anchor Tony Khalife was particularly successful with *Btikhsar Iza Ma Btil'ab* (*You Lose If You Don't Play*), which started on a trial basis as special Ramadan fare. The temporary gig became so popular (audience ratings rose from 5 to 35 percent) that he eventually left the news department to dedicate his entire time to the game show. The popular quiz show *Wa'if ta-Illak* (*Hold on, Let Me Tell You*) was getting even higher ratings of 70 percent for quizzing regular people on the streets until someone answered correctly for a hefty prize. Simon Asmar continued to direct *Art Studio* and other successful shows like the dating shows *Qalbi Dalili* (*My Heart Is My Compass*) and karaoke variety game show *Ya Layl, Ya Ayn* (*Oh Night, Oh Eyes*),[119] which redefined cultural and social taboos as well as gender and class roles.[120]

Ultimately, LBC and Future TV, rather than Télé Liban, would achieve the revived dream of regional cultural power. LBC became a regional standard for entertainment and a precursor to the competitive pan-Arab television system, as it successfully partnered with the Saudis to conquer the lucrative Gulf market. As early as 1996, LBC opened *Art Studio* for non-Lebanese Arabs, foreshadowing the enormous success of reality television in the new millennium in singing competition formats like *Star Academy*, which enjoys vast regional appeal.

Part One

The War Triangle

From Disengagement
to Engagement on the News

2

Télé Liban

The Peace Bubble and the Crisis of Legitimacy

One thing was for sure. War was a television failure.

—Zaven Kouyoumdjian, *Lebanon on Screen*

Former Lebanese president Charles Helou (1964–70), a lawyer, journalist, and editor, complained that television had aborted its mission during the civil war.[1] Whereas its programs should have broadcast only "wisely chosen and calming depictions," they "led to deeper fissures and increased the alienation among the Lebanese."[2] It is curious that Helou should scorn television for its divisive impact, a kind of impact that is somewhat hard to prove, especially since he signed the Cairo agreement in 1969. The agreement allowed Palestinian guerillas to bear arms and attack Israeli military positions from South Lebanon. This transformed the Palestinian guerillas into a formidable force that clashed with the Maronites in 1975 to ignite the civil conflict. Helou is only one among many Lebanese who blamed television for fanning the fires of war. Politicians and television employees, like him, expected television to serve as a national forum of unity.[3] According to television's longtime executive director Wissam Izz al-Din, there was a dire need, even a mandate, to have a national service that unified all Lebanese during the war. Over the span of several decades, Izz al-Din fought to make television a symbol for all Lebanese, regardless of their affiliation. In the wake of his perceived failure, and in Helou's eyes, the medium loomed with monstrous warmongering power and unharnessed nationalist potential.

War Pressures on the First Side of the Triangle

The Television Peace Bubble

Actual television practices were more complex than the simplistic "divisive–unificationist dichotomy" as employees strove or were forced to keep viewers oblivious of the ongoing war to the extent they could. This resulted in what can be termed "a television peace bubble"; that is, the occlusion of the war on national broadcasting, which instead portrayed Lebanon as a peaceful, harmonious country.

The bubble did not appear suddenly in 1975. Its blueprint was drafted with the establishment of television broadcasting as a popular industry during the 1960s. As a country with a unique media experience unlike most other Arab states, independent Lebanon fostered its television industry within the private rather than the public sector. Private ownership gave the industry a large degree of executive freedom.[4] Despite such latitude, Lebanon shared with other Arab countries an experience in sanitizing news and other television programs.[5] Sanitizing emerged out of the independent Lebanese governments' fears over disrupting the country's precarious sectarian balance, which led to covering up domestic political, economic, and social problems in various degrees. Many critics thought that broadcasters were as comfortable with this deal as the government because it freed their hands to delve into entertainment without having to take a political stand that may have angered censors.

There were, of course, multiple avenues for exercising greater freedom even in the information genres. For three years after the Leila Rustum debacle, news anchors and hosts of information programs kept a low profile to avoid provoking the government again. But in 1974, Télé Orient's anchor Adel Malek got permission to host the first televised political debate in the entire Arab world.[6] It featured a live discussion between current Interior Minister Bahij Takieddine and former Interior Minister Raymond Eddé, then an MP from the opposition, that could not be censored. Televised politics had recently taken an entertainment turn, and this three-hour-long "televised court hearing," as the right-of-center daily *al-Nahar* called it, did not disappoint. Language became a thorny issue as Takieddine spoke eloquent standard Arabic, which worried the cynical francophone Eddé whose Arabic was flawed. Being on the defense for more than an hour, Eddé "pulled a theatrical stunt": he knocked on the table and demanded "a pause in the name of the Arabic language," then corrected his opponent for making a grammar mistake.[7] This was possibly the only grammatical rule Eddé knew, as Malek surmised, but it won him the debate. It is likely that this debate would have started a trend toward greater independence in political and information programs were it not for the outbreak of the war.

After the hostilities began, the demand for news increased greatly. The supply increased too. Télé Liban aired five daily news bulletins—three in Arabic at 2:30, 7:30, and 11:00 p.m.; one in English; and one in French. Its news department (including the technical staff) grew to 70 of the outlet's 500 employees.[8] The main bulletin was the 7:30 p.m. news, which was typically thirty minutes long. According to a study conducted by communications scholar Nabil Dajani at the end of the 1970s and in the early 1980s, 43 percent of all Télé Liban programming was news-related.[9]

The increase in news supply did not disturb the bubble. The media continued to support it in a climate of fear, leniency on disinformation, and self-muzzling, even though the government's power substantially weakened. In fact, the earlier cover-up was nothing in comparison to what transpired during the war. People were dying in the streets but television was afraid to discuss it. For instance, there were no images of the massacres in Karantina or Damour in 1976, nor of the bloody hotel war that destroyed Beirut's cosmopolitan downtown in 1975–76.[10] Malek describes his concern and confusion regarding the 1975–76 news blackout in his book *Harb al-Sanatayn wa-Ba'd (The Two-Year War and More)*, which the publisher called "a diary of an eye witness."[11] An unexpected call from a friend alerted him to gunfire and multiple victims in a "bus incident" on the day the war broke out, yet no news was forthcoming from official sources:

> I waited to receive any information from an official source about what happened—from the National News Agency or other—but to no avail.
>
> I remember that President Suleiman Frangieh was recovering from surgery at the hospital of the American University of Beirut when

> rumors started spreading about "the Ain al-Rummaneh incident." However, no information or news had been released from any official body that would explain or reveal what had happened in Ain al-Rummaneh. I tried everything to learn the truth, but a state of silence prevailed in the capital Beirut, the suburbs, and all other areas of Lebanon.
>
> The hour of the newscast was approaching, and all I had was a few items of ordinary local news and a lot of international news about the ongoing Vietnam War. I felt embarrassed as a professional: how can I appear on the small screen and deliver the news bulletin without any mention of what happened. I remember that while I was on my way to the studio, I received a call from the NNA and was told very briefly that "there had been some incidents in the area of Ain al-Rummaneh, and that the responsible authorities had initiated an investigation to find out what had happened!"

Malek's recollections provide a befitting description of how the broadcast media had to sanitize the war and talk in single lines about the ongoing hostilities, usually in the rubric of miscellaneous news on security. He describes news anchors as victims of the government news agency rather than as active agents of sanitizing the war, which dovetails with the hagiographic function of self-life narratives. Similarly, Boulos admits in his 1995 account of Télé Liban's history that until that day he was unaware of any convincing reason not to cover the incident. The blackout, he continues, "angered many citizens."[12] But according to Télé Liban's director of programming Hassan Shaqqur, NNA's agents feared going to their offices around the country because of the hostilities and as a result they were rendered incapable of covering the news.[13] That was certainly a contributing factor; however, there are other reasons for the news blackouts as well. The result was the same as far as the public was concerned.

The next morning, television's occlusion of the war was exposed. The dailies were filled with gory details about the "bus incident" and the violent events that unfolded for weeks afterward, commenting on the two main parties—the Palestinians led by Yasser Arafat and the Phalange headed by Pierre Gemayel. On April 14, an enormous headline took over *Nahar*'s front page:

> The Ain al-Rummaneh Incident: 30 Killed and a Number of Injured. **Arafat Pleads for Help from Arab Kings and Heads of State and Gemayel Blames Israel for Inciting the Incident.** Jumblatt and the Left Parties Demand "Disbanding the Phalange and Expelling Its Ministers." Sadat Gets Involved and Calls for an End to the Bloodshed and Nipping the Civil Strife in the Bud. During the Night: Explosions, Gunfire, Destruction of Stores, Cut-off Roads.[14]

All the lead stories were on the violent events, accompanied by four big photos: the bus, the aftermath on the scene, and the closed roads in the area. Most of the other pages dealt with the bloodshed as well, while the news of the president's surgery was bumped back to page four. The following day the headline was just as blood-chilling:

> The Massacre Continues: 33 Killed and Tens Injured. . . . Efforts to Hand Over the Wanted Men Continue. No Results! The Incidents and Disturbances Reach Tripoli, Sidon, Tyre, and Baalbek. **The Cabinet: No Emergency, No Army!**

And April 16's headline read:

> Day Three: 37 Killed, The War of Explosions and Missiles Continues. The Phalange Handed Over Two Wanted Men and 13 Kidnapped and Received Back Two Kidnapped. . . . **Explosion.** 1:30 A.M.: Solh Announces a Solution and Calls for Calm.

Meanwhile, the rest of the paper was filled with articles and photos of killed victims of stray gunfire, barricades, tanks, the burned bus, and scenes of explosions.

Safir similarly documented the tragedy from a more left-leaning, pro-Palestinian position on April 14, 15, and 16:

> **Lebanon Condemns the Phalange and Demands Its Disbandment.** 27 Killed in the Slaughter of Ain al-Rummaneh. The Government Is Storming the Area at Dawn If the Phalange Doesn't Give Up the Seven Responsible. (April 14)

The Number of the Victims Jumps to 55 Killed. Frangieh Confirms That the Palestinians Are in Danger and Summons Jumblatt to a "Historic Role." The Phalange Knot Worsens the Crisis: Khalid Jumblatt Resigns. The Resistance Informs Riyadh and the Arab Ambassadors: The Problem Is in the Phalange, Not in the Government. (April 15)

After 70 Killed, More Than 100 Injured, and 60 Hours of Horror, **the Phalange Hands Over Two of the Wanted Men**. The Resistance: Handing Over the Responsible for the Slaughter Helps Pacify the Situation. (April 16)

In 1977, President Elias Sarkis blamed the press coverage for exacerbating the war situation and introduced the most draconian censorship amendment to the 1962 press law. The press vehemently opposed it and was able to freeze its effect for a while, but the amendment nevertheless "altered [journalism's] nature" including television news, which was governed by that law.[15] According to the Lebanese daily *L'Orient Le Jour*, the Ministry of Information instructed television officials to make sure that "the Lebanese . . . [do] not sense [experience] the war."[16] When media scholar Douglas Boyd visited Lebanon in the mid-1970s, he was astounded how difficult it was to guess that the "country was in the midst of a devastating war" from radio and television programs.[17] Boyd's impression that the peace bubble was impenetrable is somewhat exaggerated. To be fair, the broadcast media did transmit information about ongoing battles, as we saw in the Malek example, but the information usually came after the battle and was sketchy, meager, and vague. Yet the peace bubble was not a hallucination, even if it was not impregnable.

Adapting to censorship led to the emergence of soft news.[18] This new genre was composed not so much of human-interest stories but of less factual, more general news unconcerned with the war. Soft news did not dampen the public's interest in the conflict's coverage; it simply reflected the unreliable access to facts and the unwillingness to report on the divisive strife. The majority of local news broadcasts continued to report on pro forma meetings among government officials and various political leaders in block A, occasionally spending a third of the bulletin on government lunches and the menus served at them.[19] In addition, journalists covered international affairs extensively, shifting the focus away from the conflict. Language also adapted to the necessities of war. Like in the rest of the Arab world, the official news medium was the formal *Fusha*, which is an appropriate vehicle to honor the solemn tone, formal trappings, and aspirations for national unity of the official sphere. *Fusha* also routinely introduced biases toward global and regional "big" issues, restricting access to public debate and hurting rapport with the public. Anchors bolstered the restrictive qualities of this formal tool by framing the meager information about the war with euphemisms, misleading understatements, a desensitizing passive voice, and other rhetorical techniques.

Furthermore, the hostilities made operating a television station much harder, in effect imposing unofficial censorship on events. During the December 6, 1975, "Black Saturday" massacre, CLT's Christian employees, who made up more than half of the staff, were forced to leave work under army protection.[20] The station was located in a predominantly Muslim area and it did not want to gamble the lives of its Christian employees. In 1975–76, the war was so intense that employees started commuting to work together, forming caravans of cars after programming director Paul Tannous fended off an abduction attempt.[21] In 1980, there was another abduction. Télé Liban's CEO Charles Rizq was thrown in the trunk of a white Volvo by unknown gunmen, likely connected to the LF militia—the future owners of LBC.[22] Apparently shaken from the abduction, Rizq resigned after his release. The resignation may have been an attempt to gain support in the "court" of public opinion as Rizq was tasked by the government to prevent militias from launching their own pirate television outlets.[23] In response, Télé Liban's employees turned television into a book when, during the evening bulletin, viewers discovered a frozen black screen with white text instead of a live newsfeed. The screen announced an employee strike until Rizq rescinded his resignation. Yet even this announcement was typically evasive. Rizq's abduction was called an "incident" (*haditha*) and his release a "return" (*'awda*).[24]

Production studios stopped operating even before their technical equipment and transmitters were damaged by the war. Soon a freeze on outdoor filming was enacted out of fear that a sniper or an armed militant would crash the shoot.[25] And, as it turned out, on the occasions the administration wanted to resuscitate production, it lacked the funds. This left television with a blank schedule. Dajani reports that "television officials went around collecting any film they could find locally."[26] For example, a Télé Liban official borrowed all the movies available in the library of a United Nations agency in Beirut to ensure program continuity at the station. The official was not interested in finding out what he was borrowing but instead focused on how each movie's running time fit the schedule. This demonstrates the administration's additional intent to do whatever was necessary to stay on the air rather than focus on actions to deliberately obscure the conditions of war. The effect, however, was the same.

In the end, the station was forced to fill its schedule with old shows from the archives.[27] Harking back to the golden era of the old shows induced nostalgia for an imagined bygone past when life was allegedly simpler and folks happier. The older production technology that the black-and-white shows from the archives had used amplified the nostalgia because that technology, too, was out of sync with the present. Despite the profound sense in which the war was absent in mediated images, sound, and meaningful commentary, the undercoverage did not leave a vacuum. Instead, the war was displaced by hopeful rhetoric for a peaceful future continually rekindled in numerous calls for national unity, tolerance, and coexistence.[28] The images of a former rural and conflict-free Lebanon, and the focus on peace talks and political leaders rather than on the public, fleshed out the narrative logic of the peace bubble.

Télé Liban (and before it the formerly independent branches CLT and Télé Orient)—the first side of the war triangle—experienced very particular war pressures to continue the government's nationalist and unificationist agenda. More a hope than a successful policy, the agenda stemmed from the government's dystopian fears that television would aggravate the conflict. This positioning tied the outlet's hands and demonstrated the neutered response of national television to civil wars.[29] During war, television is caught in a dilemma over its commitment to truth versus its patriotic loyalty to the government's nationalist rhetoric.[30] Even though the media theorizes a duty to witness the war, economic and political forces limit the act of witnessing and warp journalists' perceptions of reality. It is harder for the media to resolve this ethical dilemma, and ultimately journalists embrace self-censorship in a climate of fear. Since the Vietnam War, international mainstream media has shifted to superficially covering military tactics instead of covering war substantively.[31] Although television is now the main source of war coverage, it covers little of the actual "fighting, carnage, [and] loss of life."[32] The media also often choose to avoid rather than pose ethical questions. Ironically, sometimes the aesthetics of war images condition audiences not to ask ethical questions despite the images' great potential for underscoring violence as an ethical concern.[33] Journalists too fail to disperse the "fog of war" by using vague language in order to conform to government policies.[34]

This dilemma stems not only from the media's subservience to the government but also from their own protective policies. For example, to attract audiences, corporate media often deliver partisan reports of war. The tone changes in support of war alongside an increased tolerance for disinformation. Such reactive and proactive self-muzzling constitutes a failure to represent and mediate collective consciousness, which is why Andrew Hoskins speaks of electronic media that instead produces a "manufactured" public consciousness reduced to what is covered on television.[35]

When national media bear witness to a country's involvement in an international war, they are faced with the dilemma of balancing the ideally neutral act of witnessing with polemic patriotism. National suffering receives prime time, while that of the enemy is often callously suppressed. Assigning the labels of "defender" and "enemy" in a civil war, on the other hand, is much harder because the enemy is national. Group suffering should receive prime-time coverage. However, national media often restrict such coverage to avoid taking sides. This resembles closely the situation in Lebanon when the civil war divided the nation, the state collapsed, and television attempted to hold the nation together by underreporting, sanitizing, and occluding the war, thus creating a television peace bubble. Ultimately, the deliberate and unconscious politics of occluding the ongoing conflict consisted of soft news, self-censorship, toothless reruns, and endless mentions of peace initiatives.

Anchors, Protocols, and the Space of Journalism

A set of protocols that guided appropriate wartime news journalism outside of television content also helped maintain the invisibility of the Lebanese conflict and minimized unexpected surges of visibility. These protocols concerned anchors' appearance, emotional repertoire, body language, behavior, and audience address, as well as the mental representation of the space of journalism and its professionals.

Appearance, emotions, and body language betray specific attitudes toward the environment. Therefore, wartime protocols regarding appearance placed high demands for fashion and style on anchors of both genders and similarly onerous demands for hair and makeup on female anchors and presenters. Anchors' preoccupation with beauty and fashion, much discussed in the press, implied that their inner world was peaceful and that audiences should similarly be unencumbered by wartime anxieties. Protocols regarding visible emotions and body language on air were also intended to put audiences at ease and prevent mass panic. Calmness and positive attitudes became benchmarks for a successful broadcast, not how closely the news bulletin reflected the reality outside the studio. Anchors had to tightly control their facial expressions to suppress unsanctioned emotions, such as desperation or excitement, which could cause panic or betray sectarian loyalties. As Boulos observed, despite the fact that Beirut was showered with fire, "the smile never departed from Jean Khoury's lips, who seldom mentioned the military operations in his reports."[36] Anchors became fascinating figures striving for objectivity and neutrality yet, in the end, achieving the opposite as the war surged beyond the horizon of their coverage. (I discuss how the popular press negotiated the protocols regarding broadcasters' appearance, body language, and emotional repertoire in detail in chapter 3.)

Appearance and body language were not enough to seal the leaks in the bubble from which audiences sized up the threat. Anchors' behavior also had to comply with certain standards, especially with regards to anchors' reactions to unexpected developments during the bulletin. The bubble burst wide open on the evening of March 11, 1976, when Brigadier General Abd al-Aziz al-Ahdab, commander of the Beirut garrison of the Lebanese army, stormed CLT's studio. Interrupting the news bulletin, he commandeered the camera to demand the resignation of the president and the prime minister and declare himself Lebanon's new governor. After Ahdab left, news anchor Khoury apologized for the inconvenience and resumed the bulletin calmly as usual, as if nothing had happened.[37] There is no footage of the event, which was aired live. Ahdab's pistol does not appears on the few extant stills. Yet, some people vividly remember that the pistol was shown on camera, lying on the table in front of the general. Whether there was a pistol or not may be beside the point. What is striking is that in public memory (at least in some people's memory), even the fact that the pistol was threateningly visible did not diminish Khoury's compliance with behavioral protocol that demanded composure and neutrality. His reaction may have been brave, but it was also a demonstration of the efforts to diminish the visibility of the war even when viewers were live witnesses.

Khoury treated Ahdab's televised intrusion as a technical problem. But just what kind of a space for journalism did turning an attempted coup into a nonstory suggest? Overtly, this space was intended to be "calm and dignified" in order to resurrect a sense of hope among the Lebanese, according to a statement by CEO Rizq upon Télé Liban's launch.[38] Yet television protocols suggested that the anchors' address to the audience (e.g., Khoury's apology) was built upon both subtle and patent sanitizing of the war narrative.

Radio is outside the scope of this book, but Sharif al-Akhawi's traffic report on Radio Lebanon deserves special mention because it was often brought up in the press and public discussions as a counterpoint to television's address to audiences. Radio was the most available medium for most of the war. The cost of a transistor at the beginning of the war was six dollars and 90 percent of adults owned a set (29 percent owned two or more).[39] After the war broke out, the state-owned Radio Lebanon replaced a number of information and discussion programs with music blocks due to similar government and business continuity pressures. During the first eight months, between April and December 1, 1975, a record number of seventy-five new Lebanese songs was produced, compared to only around twenty new songs annually in previous years (an increase of almost sixfold).[40] *Nahar* complained that Radio Lebanon played music 80 percent of the time even though studies showed that the audience demanded talk shows.[41] *Shabaka* also harshly criticized the national station for playing songs of "love, rejection, and separation" that had nothing to do with the situation.[42] For example, the romantic Fayrouz-Rahbani song "al-Mahabba" ("Love"), based on Khalil Gibran's lyrics, aired more than twenty times in a short period of time, according to one *Shabaka* report. The author of the report complained that Gibran and his "love" were not present in front of the sniper, checkpoint, and gun, nor behind the barricade, while his bird chirping and spring gurgling were inaudible amid the sounds of bombing and gunfire.[43] The Egyptian diva Umm Kulthum was another favorite with her virtuosic performance of repetitive lyrical songs, many of which lasted 30 to 120 minutes.[44]

In contrast to these sanitizing and occlusionary radio protocols, Akhawi's legendary program *Salke wa Amne* ([*The Streets Are*] *Clear and Safe*, 1975–76) gave listeners detailed hourly information about ongoing battles, abductions, and closed roads.[45] The government sometimes maliciously misinformed Akhawi that a particular section of the city was safe; yet callers would inform him of ongoing battles there. He addressed the audiences as cocreators of the news and as citizens who deserved attention and honesty. Nonetheless, his traffic reports that merely acknowledged the war sparked tremendous backlash from militants. In addition to the regular threats he and his family received, he survived two botched assassination attempts before he stopped broadcasting in 1976 when militias invaded the radio station.[46] No comparable program replaced his.[47]

Clear and Safe had a profound effect on the Lebanese and a vast following across sectarian and class lines. Akhawi earned local and international fame as the voice of citizens and as a reliable source on the state of the war, as evidenced from the reactions of the local and international press. The local press reported on him for years. *Shabaka* alone published numerous positive full-length articles about him and countless shorter reports or mentions in other pieces. In fact, its extolling coverage of him was unmatched by its coverage of any other Lebanese broadcaster. His celebrity also spurred a number of documentaries and a nomination by the *Jerusalem Post* for the Nobel Peace Prize. Akhawi achieved such importance because he never addressed audiences as though they needed to be protected from the harsh reality. Instead he represented the space of journalism as one of honesty and collaboration between professional and citizen journalists.

Legitimacy and the Hegemonic Order

The Crisis of Legitimacy

How did these protocols affect television legitimacy? My answer is that the peace bubble caused a shift in the relationship between television and audiences.

Before the war, Lebanese media did not adhere to the public model of heroic journalism, made iconic in Hollywood movies of diehard journalists who fight for truth and transparency to prove their legitimacy. But even in Lebanon, journalists enjoyed a level of trust and authoritative control over the production of news and information programs. However, once the war broke out, the peace bubble led to a crisis of journalistic authority. Hyperfocus on foreign military and diplomatic news and underpoliticization of local issues of physical, economic, and cultural survival jeopardized the public's trust that television was concerned with the nation's safety. Specifically, the threat to people's physical survival that was brought on or exacerbated by the information blackout took a toll on the legitimacy of news television. Examples are numerous, but one is particularly salient. On April 13, 1975, neither the daily news nor the evening bulletins reported the bloody events in the Ain al-Rummaneh "bus incident" (as described earlier in this chapter). Because of the news curtain, the next day an engineering major named Samir Badaro was killed on his way to college while passing by an area with shootings. Boulos calls him the "first victim of the media deception."[48] Badaro is just one of countless victims over the years from snipers, militia battles, bombings, and massacres. It would be wrong to claim that the media blackout was to blame for all these deaths, but it is safe to presume responsibility for some of them. Journalists were free to depict the human cost of foreign conflicts such as the Vietnam War.[49] The government's silence on the human cost of its own civil war was eerie in comparison.

Also, the necessity to consume the sanitized news protocols critically forced the audiences to learn a new set of behaviors, further eroding their trust in the medium. To help "read" television broadcasts, whose words had lost their direct meaning, the audiences had to read between the lines of bulletins or simply assume the bulletins were rife with euphemisms. Viewers also had to learn that anchors' silences were laden with different kinds of meaning—panic, sorrow, or reserved glee. As voice and sound lost primacy as signifiers of meaning, their very absence acquired meaning. Body language can be deceptive and hard to decipher. Yet, the audiences had to learn to read anchors' faces and facial expressions. In a perversion of the technology of reading, the carrier of meaning was no longer words or sound alone but sometimes skin and muscle as well. Focusing on the anchor's lips, for instance, enabled the viewer to decipher the unspoken meaning hidden in its calm edges and polite, silent grins. Shades of cheek color, whether pallid, flushed pink, or sallow olive, were the currency of exchange in messages, while subtle twitches and muscle movements were the spikes and crashes in a frenzied marketplace of wartime communication.

In addition, television anchors conceived of their colleagues as enemies rather than as professionals for extended periods of time, which removed all doubts about the presence of journalistic bias. After Ahdab's coup, CLT and Télé Orient were taken over by warring factions. The Hazmieh branch adopted a frame friendly to President Frangieh.[50] In retaliation, leftist Muslim and Palestinian supporters imposed a frame friendly to Prime Minister Salim Hoss and the pan-Arabist, leftist National Movement at Tallet al-Khayyat. The stations began exchanging criticisms and, on occasion, insults. For example, Jacques Wakim, a Frangieh-appointed news reporter, called General Ahdab (*ahdab* means hunchback) the "Hunchback of Beirut." To retaliate, Ghassan Matar, an anchor at the other station, called the Christians of East Beirut "refugees to Larnaca and Limassol," suggesting they were leaving for nearby Cyprus because they were not very patriotic.[51] When the Beirut airport shut down during heavy fighting, Cyprus became a temporary shelter for Christian and Muslim families, who would be shipped to safety from the ports of Beirut, Jounieh, or Tripoli.[52] Because the LF-run port of Jounieh was the most active, temporary refuge in Cyprus acquired a Christian connotation. Whereas anchor Suad Qarut al-Ashi covered Ahdab's coup enthusiastically, Khoury tried to stay neutral, reporting, "For ammunition, they are using contradictory news flashes and endless rounds of threats, insults, 'we shall overcome speeches,' patriotic songs, and military marches."[53] The news split did not put substantive discussions of the war experience on television's grid. It showed the selectiveness in ignoring the war. If nothing else, for a while the vitriol displaced even the euphemistic coverage of the bloody events.

The on-air hijinks calmed down after the Arab peacekeeping forces arrived with the ascension of Elias Sarkis to the presidency on September 23, 1976.[54] The two branches, however, lost some of the seriousness and dignity that came with the news genre and the lofty language of standard Arabic it used, even though they finally united on May 16, 1977. That evening, the bulletin was preceded by a still screen with a white rose. A smiling Jean Khoury teased the viewers that he had a "surprise" for them. As the camera zoomed out, the audiences saw six anchors from both branches behind three small anchor desks. The two female anchors and the small-statured Jacques Wakim were seated at the edges of the tables in what appeared to be a gendered seat assignment. The other three male anchors authoritatively sat at the center of each desk. The next day rival newspapers were bickering about which of the two women—each working at an opposing branch—was more beautiful. Instances like these deflated the seriousness of news journalism, degrading the genre to a daytime soap opera, although the public still hoped that the reunification of the news was a sign of upcoming peace. But the two teams' unity pledge sounded like chest-beating against the backdrop of the melodrama: "A united media for a united Lebanon. A fresh start we hope will inspire Lebanese hearts and spirits to rally behind their love for Lebanon. One and only one news bulletin on all channels starting tonight: a segment that aims to cover current affairs from a proper nationalist perspective."[55]

The unstable protocols, which became visible in Ahdab's failed coup, abductions and attempts on the lives of television employees, and the ease with which militias commandeered the two television facilities, demonstrated the vulnerability in the space of journalism. The production of news and information was not an impenetrable stronghold of impartial journalistic authority but a revolving door defenseless against bias. Anchors could no longer persuasively position themselves as nonpartisan professionals, violating a fundamental principle of news journalism.

But when anchors themselves publicly called into question their own trust in the medium, television's legitimacy was in serious trouble. One evening during the intense two-year war (1975–76), Adel Malek lifted the cover off wartime protocols. Tired of not getting enough information from the authorities about what was happening, he asked the viewers to look out their windows to "see" and "hear" the news. "The situation is as you can see and hear," he said, looking defeated.[56] That was nothing short of an admission that the space of journalism where news was received, assessed, edited, and announced to viewers had failed. A new space seemed to have greater legitimacy—Beirut's geography. Its language was the raw sights and sounds of the outdoor space of the city: streets, debris, cars, buildings, people, trees, bombings, shelling, silence, shouting, laughter, sniper fire, breaking glass, wails, and cries. Geography, however, posed its own dangers as it had become a deeply sectarian space. The two branches of Télé Liban were now exclusively identified by their geographical locations—Hazmieh and Tallet al-Khayyat—on opposing sides of the Green Line rather than by their suggested neutral industry names TL1 and TL2. Malek's statement was an admission, too, that journalists' relevance as modern professionals was in trouble, as the audiences often served several functions. They were simultaneously their own news reporters that gathered news from the field ("see and hear"), anchors that made sense of the raw material and sieved the newsworthy items, and viewers that digested the news. The inadequacy and even absence of news journalism on the radio triggered a similar redefinition of audience functions and the instrumentalization of geography. Note how Jean-Said Makdisi links them in her memoir:

> Suddenly, the quiet catches my ear. With that sixth sense that Beirutis have developed, I go inside and turn on the ubiquitous radio. Martial music blares out at me, and my heart sinks. Another crisis. Where? Who is fighting whom this time? I go out to the other balcony, the one facing

> the city, where, as I expected, the white stars fade in the light of the red tracer bullets; the quiet of the evening is broken by the too-familiar sound of guns. . . . As I wait for the news bulletin, I take nervous mental stock of things.[57]

Professional anchors looked painfully aware of the increasing irrelevance of the current mode of news journalism as well as of their own impossible mission to serve their profession when the government was failing them.

Dajani's late 1970s–early 1980s study of viewer attitudes toward journalism corroborates these impressions.[58] All viewers from the elite and 83 percent of workers in the study owned a television set. In the elite category, the study found that 70 percent watched television daily or almost daily and 74 percent followed the news. However, viewership does not mean approval. Only 7 percent on average found local and national television news useful for understanding local and national issues, and a meager 5 percent found television a credible source of information. Most described it as "incomplete" and "biased." Similarly, only 7 percent trusted the NNA. When asked what medium they turned to for information in times of crisis, all respondents said it was their family. In comparison, 98 percent read the daily press regularly or frequently, 45 percent found it useful, and 41 percent found the local and national press to be credible. In the workers' category, on the other hand, 81 percent watched television daily or almost daily, and the same number followed the news. Out of them, only 19 percent thought the information they got on television was useful to understanding local and national issues, and an average of 16 percent found television a credible source of local and national information. By comparison, 37 percent found the daily press useful and 34 thought it was credible.

In the end, pre-1985 news television had failed as an oral communication medium, and the oral had been displaced by nonoral signs and signals both subtle and difficult to interpret. "Language journalism," where the news was based on understanding the anchors' verbal statements, had given way to "embodied journalism," where anchors' body language and on-air behavior carried significant information that supported or contradicted the text and its frame. Journalism of this kind changed the viewers' understanding of the nature of labor involved in journalism as anchors could not help but produce knowledge with their bodies, which viewers tracked with their eyes.[59] Lebanese viewers' experience was distinct from that of viewers in neighboring states who also tried to read truth from a deceptive government media because of the life-and-death stakes.

The growing loss of trust in news and information genres, mobilized by the peace bubble's rationale to shield the audience from inconvenient truths and the open display of bias and vulnerability, "unsettled traditional relations of journalistic expertise and authority," to use Dominic Boyer's expression.[60] Ultimately, evolving local historical contexts like the Lebanese Civil War matter because the pressures they exert on television affect television's perception of its mission. In its dereliction of duty to bear witness to the war, television's provision of news and information seemed only marginally relevant to a divided modern nation. Next, I show how the perception of news television's irrelevance provoked a wave of public cynicism about broadcasting.

3

Audiences

Sarcasm, the New Hero of Television, and the Components of Modern Legitimacy

Dedicating an excerpt from Abdel Halim Hafez's song "Helou w-Kazzeb" ["Pretty Liar"] to the listeners.

—Huda Barakat, *Hajar al-Dahak* (*The Stone of Laughter*)

Responses of the Second Side of the War Triangle to the Legitimacy Crisis

The second side of the war triangle—the audiences—responded to the crisis of confidence in journalistic authority and the unraveling of television legitimacy, which was at the core of the old hegemonic order, with a slurry of carnivalesque language.[1] They contested the dominant cultural norm of the television industry with sarcasm, parody, and narratives of the "imagined, ugly, banal . . . jokes, songs, rumors."

Street Politics

In 1990, at the tail end of the civil war, Jean Said Makdisi (Edward Said's sister) published a memoir about living through the conflict with her family. She is an important representative of a class of women writers who made an outstanding contribution to Lebanese culture during the war, especially by expressing ethical concerns about how the country was processing war trauma.[2] Her memoir, *Beirut Fragments*, can give us insights into the battle ordinary Lebanese citizens waged for more responsive broadcasting. When Makdisi describes life during civil conflict, she divides Lebanese society into two groups—insiders who had shared the experience of war and outsiders who had not.

> We are unforgiving judges of those who have not shared our experiences. We are like a secret society. We have our own language; we recognize signs that no one else does; we joke about our most intense pain, bewildering outsiders; we walk a tightrope pitched over an abyss of panic that a novice does not even perceive, let alone understand.[3]

Indeed, the Lebanese people formed overlapping publics that consisted simultaneously of distant, anonymous members ("a secret society") and of one's closest connections—relatives, friends, acquaintances, and neighbors. These publics—distant and close, from cultural elites to ordinary noncombatants from all walks of life—created and shared their own language to divulge the war trauma and pass moral judgment on the disengaged media. Joking about their pain, often in dark, cynical ways, was among the critical strategies to indict broadcasting.

The audience could not tolerate the "sanitizing" of television news during the conflict, because having accurate information about war developments was key to basic survival, according to communications scholar Marwan Kraidy.[4] The most dangerous moments of the civil war became the factory for the most intense political commentary. Often, Lebanese civilians faced a life of forced displacement or willful emigration. They lived on rationed water, power, and phone lines in an urban geography where sniper fire, bombings, and explosive street warfare often prevented them from going to work or school, leaving them without food or medication. Fights across the sectarian divide mutated into fights among those of the same sectarian colors. Abductions, summary killings, and genocide followed the theft of resources, infrastructure, and financial assets that made militias filthy rich and allowed them to carry on with the war for the sake of greed.

Punning the New Geography. When broadcasting was silent during such times of extreme need for information about conflict sites and danger zones, the people developed their own warning system based on language.

It involved using the vernacular in new contexts that allowed people to exchange life-saving information. For instance, everyday expressions like *Shu fee?* (What's going on?) and *Fee shee?* (Is there anything?) changed connotations to address a potential threat as in, "Are we in danger?" Another expression, *Ma fee shee* (There's nothing), now conveyed that one could safely continue going where one was headed.[5] A whole new vocabulary was created to reflect specifically how common daily tasks were upset by restrictions on movement, utilities, and healthcare. Examples include *hajiz* (the ubiquitous and sometimes lethal checkpoint), *maktab* (office; i.e., a militia's headquarters, which each neighborhood now boasted and feared), *salke wa amne* (clear and safe, which Akhawi's program on road conditions popularized), *ijit il-may* (the water came), *ijit il-kahraba* (the power is on), or *haram, biykhaf ktir* (poor thing, he's so afraid; i.e., of the shelling and bombing). When people walked "a tightrope pitched over an abyss of panic," as Makdisi put it, they created a much-needed vocabulary "that a novice does not even perceive, let alone understand."

A big part of this vocabulary dealt with urban geography and the dangers that lay hidden within it. Lesser-known areas, streets, or buildings in Beirut acquired vast significance during the war as part of a new sociocultural geography. Take for instance the Sodeco area, which was far from famous before the war. Its one important feature—the railroad passing through—had ceased operation in 1958. When the war erupted, Sodeco became a landmark of wartime culture. The Sodeco boulevard was the only road to connect adjacent warring neighborhoods, while the Barakat historic building (the House of Beirut) was taken up by snipers because it strategically overlooked a crossroads where hellish battles often erupted.[6] Although the area suffered a high population drain due to the severe threat level, those who stayed would clear the rubble as soon as a battle was over. As a symbol of wartime life, Sodeco was constantly on the news and in people's conversations; popular culture memorialized it in expressions like "*Sodeco boom-boom.*" The expression was popularized in theater plays, like those by Philip Aqiqi and others, and it was also used in the opening of *Arba' Majanin w-Bas* (*Just Four Idiots*), the only Télé Liban series that mentioned the war.[7] Other crossroads became equally infamous: al-Mathaf (the museum, a crossing in the middle of the Green

Line), al-Marfa' (the port), Galerie Semaan (a furniture store that became a landmark of the southern part of the front line), and Mar Mikhail (the roofless St. Michael church, which served as a checkpoint and a frequent heavy battle front on the south side of the Green Line).

Ruined symbols of Beirut's former glamour were also part of a new sociocultural geography, such as the twenty-six-floor Holiday Inn in Beirut's famous hotel district. The newly constructed hotel was open only for a year before bloody militia battles destroyed the area and scavengers later gutted it to the studs. Throughout the conflict, this ugly tower was both a geographic landmark and a symbol of the horrific toll of the war, as an interviewee of mine illustrated with the following story: In the summer of 1982, while Beirut was in the middle of the Israeli siege yet watching the FIFA World Cup, he was traveling in a truck from his residence in Qantari to a family home in the village of Aynata on the southern border. Qantari is a poor Beirut neighborhood adjacent to the hotel district with many immigrants from the south, and the Holiday Inn is just a short block away from his residence. On the road, in the midst of heavy traffic of people seeking temporary refuge, an army officer yelled at the truck, "Where are you coming from?" Umm Jihad, a relative who was traveling in the truck as well, bellowed quickly, "*Min el-'in*" (from the inn). Of course she meant the Holiday Inn, but everyone in the truck laughed as the vernacular pronunciation of "chicken coop" was also "'in," a poignant metaphor for rundown, poor Qantari.

These former hallmarks of Beirut's culture (the museum, St. Michael church), leisure (Holiday Inn), industry (Sodeco, the port), and trade (Galerie Semaan) lost their place as symbols of a thriving cosmopolitan nation. Now checkpoints, they became the knots of a net that trapped the city and homogenized its diverse cultural-economic geography. Yet, people used them to laugh at their misfortune and pun the grave or bland contexts in which they were cast in news broadcasting.

Dark Sarcasm as Political Commentary. In addition to developing a warning system and punning the new geography, the public also used the language of parody and sarcasm to demand empathy from the media. In this sense, Makdisi's assertion that the secret society speaks the language of tragicomedy is remarkable. It has been noted that during the war Lebanese writing became heavily experimental, as writers lost trust in the communicative quality of language, sometimes cynically berating it. The parallel with the public's disillusionment with the media's language is uncanny. Using cynicism, sarcasm, and parody as political commentary, people passed a guilty verdict on broadcasting, creating a vocabulary in which meaning was often perverted. For instance, *Ma fee shee* (There's nothing) was often used sarcastically for a bloody battle or heavy shelling to convey people's bitterness with the media's denial of the conflict. Another twisted expression was *La, hayda beb* (No, this is just a door). It was used as reassurance that the sound one hears is not an explosion but some other nonthreatening sound, like a closing door. It just as often cynically highlighted how television minimized what was indeed an explosion or other serious threat by calling it a "slamming door." The sarcastic expression *'Am biytsallu* (They're having fun, entertaining themselves) attributed militia battles to boredom, contemptuously denying them empathy and reason. While not overtly sarcastic, the understatement *al-ahdath* (the events) is a widely used euphemism for the civil war. Several of my interviewees referred to *al-ahdath* when they described the war's impact on their lives. Minimizing the impact of the war by diminishing its stature from war to "events" may have established their resilience to live, but it also brought out their bitterness about the occlusion of the war in the media and society.

Perverted Media Tropes. Not only did people develop their own informal spoken vocabulary to perform media critique and demand empathy, they also reclaimed favorite tropes that the media used euphemistically to occlude the war. These were words from the formal language register; however, when reiterated by ordinary citizens, the media vocabulary gained cynical, sarcastic, or understated connotations. For example, expressions like *ijtima'at mukaththafa* (intense meetings), *tawattur* (tension), *masdar mawthuq bih* (a credible source), *waqf itlaq al-nar* (cease-fire), or *hudu' nisbi* (relative calm) became favorite targets of parody. The expression *ijtima'at mukaththafa* was a cynical commentary on the media's pretense that this was not a time of war but one of peace, in which issues were resolved in meetings and discussions, not with guns. *Tawattur* usually masked a crisis or a violent flare-up. Because *tawattur* collocates with verbs of degree such as increase and decrease, even in combination its mild flavor does not express imminent danger. In ordinary citizen parlance, however, *tawattur* became a deliberate understatement signifying a full-blown crisis, a sudden outburst of violence, or prolonged battles with high casualties.

Television's favorite expression was *masdar mawthuq bih*, with which news anchors described just about any source—most notoriously ungrounded statements that the situation was rapidly improving, which no one believed but most hoped would somehow magically come true. Tropes such as "credible source" which seemed to herald intense meetings leading to ceasefire and peace, were the perfect vehicle for that. Wartime audiences fiercely contested television's Machiavellian production of public consciousness. For them, "credible source" meant nothing more than rumors or government subterfuge that loose tongues spread around. Calling any ludicrous story a "credible source," people critiqued the media for undermining the meaning of this expression and, by extension, for making it harder to engage in a mediated public discourse about the conflict.

While the media used *hudu' nisbi* as a hedging device to imply that the number of casualties from an incident was low, ordinary citizens used the expression to parody television's insensitivity. Calling the grizzly violence *hudu' nisbi* was a way to disempower television and showcase how it minimized the public's feelings and concerns. The term was so overused that it quickly became one of the most iconic symbols of wartime popular culture. Not coincidentally, it was memorialized by the poster child of wartime popular culture, Ziad Rahbani, in the instrumental "Relative Calm" from his 1984 album *Bala Wala Shi* (Without Anything). In an interview for the program *Shahid* on the Egyptian channel MBC, he shares, with a subdued laugh, how the militias entertained themselves by waging battles because they could not rely on the intermittent television broadcasts for entertainment.[8] Ordinary people were eagerly waiting for occasional ceasefires to go shopping for bread, water, and gas before the theater started again. Ziad conceived this piece during such "calm," which is ironic because when he could finally hear himself think, he created a piece with no words. The instrumental then betrays his suspicion that media language only packaged empty content, impotent to communicate his meaning or to resist occluding the war.[9]

People also contested television's methods of sharing information. Unofficial methods for sharing play an important role in Arab countries where mistrust in government-censored media abounds. Unofficial, oral methods, such as exchanges in the marketplace or coffee shop, are often more trusted than written documents, unlike in the West.[10] In Lebanon, ordinary citizens adopted oral methods to evade the entrapment that the government and news broadcasters had laid through linguistic channels that depend on formal, written Arabic. Oral strategies also actively competed with media discourses. The linguistic environment and shared symbols are the most important accompaniments of systems of trust.[11] Language and shared symbols are also incredibly useful vehicles to establish and popularize competitive moral discourses. When ordinary Lebanese citizens created a shared system of oral language symbols, they criticized the competitive system of media symbols and its moral bluster.

Literary Publics

In addition to contesting television's thick fog of war through public and private expressions of the carnivalesque (humor, ridicule, and sarcasm), the audiences also envisioned a new kind of engaged media and powerful audiences in a separate, overlapping space of literature.

Literature provides the broader context of the link between trust and language register. The problem stemmed from *Fusha*'s divorce (*ibti'ad*) from reality, according to Zahi Wehbi, the longtime cultural show host of *Khallik bi-l-Bayt* (*Stay at Home*).[12] Some blamed it on the failure of language in general, but most questioned *Fusha*'s truthfulness. Therefore, they challenged common cultural assumptions about *Fusha*'s supremacy over *'ammiyya*,[13] as novelist Elias Khoury bitterly summarized with the words, "the spoken is truth, the written is lies."[14] The quest for a new relevant medium that better reflected the environment led to the invention of a new Lebanese language Wehbi calls *lugha mumayyaze* (distinctive language).[15] It rejected former idealized models.[16] On the one hand, it infused *Fusha* with *'ammiyya*.[17] The wartime literary movement captured this development at numerous poetry nights and literary salons, which soon became a wartime phenomenon, and at the regular coffee shop gatherings of various Lebanese intellectuals and artists.[18] Even those from the leftist factions, which were more prone to support *Fusha* as part of a pan-Arab identity, embraced this cruder, colorful, vernacular-infused language as a special Lebanese tongue rather than think of it as a rejection of Arabhood. On the other hand, the "distinctive language" celebrated Lebanese vernaculars across the sectarian, political, and even ethnic spectrum, especially in performance art and popular music. Such emphasis on the vernacular as an important formal element of identity gave all Lebanese "a language that is unquestionably theirs and theirs alone,"[19] which cultural critic Elise Salem calls a "strikingly Lebanese" language.[20] Together, the distrust in the standard written language, the *'ammiyya*-infused *Fusha*, and the celebration of the different variants of the vernacular reflected the language pessoptimism characteristic of the wartime period.

A group of female and some male wartime writers has been credited for deflating heroic portrayals of the war and putting the genres of the novel and the life narrative on the map of the Lebanese literary world.[21] What has not been recognized, though, is that their writing was at the forefront of a literary culture that indicted the wartime media for its dereliction of duty. Half of a sample of eight literary works from the war, which I selected based on their popularity,[22] addressed the issue of the broken broadcast media. Some deal with television broadcasting and others with radio in very similar terms, which reflects the media's parallel survival pressures within the peace bubble. Broadcasting is usually not their main topic, but they dedicate from one to over ten pages on it and a number of other shorter references. Nonetheless, these works were a pulpit for a sophisticated language critique and political commentary on the nature of journalism. They painted a scathing portrait of the existing fraught relationship between broadcasting and audiences as well as an enchanted daydream for a new one.

The Fraught Relationship. Makdisi offers a stunning example of the fraught relationship. Her autobiographical voice, with pain and a dose of cynicism, projects her disappointment with the routine failures of the government-run Radio Lebanon to report on the war.

> Finally—in order to get a better grasp on things, a little in desperation to make sense out of the conflicting accounts offered by the partisan broadcasts—I turn to the official radio station. I say, "*Once more*," because I have tried dozens of times before, always to give up with impatience. Today is no exception.
>
> The state radio is much given to euphemism. Unlike the others, it attempts neutrality and achieves only confusion: "The sound of guns can be heard," instead of "So-and-so is fighting so-and-so." Almost invariably it speaks in the passive voice, giving syntax to the reality of its own impotence. The state is as powerless as the individual and goes through the same foolish, perfunctory motions of existence. I remember the moment in the early days of the war when the station, like the state for which it spoke, tried to pretend nothing was happening that it could not control. It was a fearful night. *We were huddled, as usual, by the radio.* Station after station around the world told the bitter news. The BBC, Voice of America, Moscow, Monte Carlo—the whole world was headlining Beirut and the deadly battles going on. When we turned to Beirut Radio, "La Comparasita" [*sic*] wafted out at our disbelieving ears. In the midst of our anxiety, we danced an impromptu tango, celebrating our own and our world's madness.[23]

It may be confusing that the Makdisis huddled by the radio, given her portrayal of the official media as part of the problem of war. But of course, as in any theater of the absurd, a plea for reason is a dead end. The contradictory webs of deception that the partisan broadcasts were spinning, along with the deliberate disinformation reported by the state radio, couched in euphemisms and understatements, sowed deep confusion among the public.

This scene lends itself to two contradictory impulses. One arises from a desperate hope to piece together confusing fragments of information, to make sense of life during a violent conflict. The other is a response to an incomprehensible world. The sounds and voices of news bulletins and militia babble allow limited, though distorted, knowledge of the war. However, the music wafting out in the Makdisis' living room, "La cumparsita," one of the world's most popular tangoes, is akin to garbled speech to the Arab ear or to silence. After all, unless the music stops, the station can broadcast nothing else. Of course, the radio could communicate meaning with its choice of music. But "La cumparsita," sometimes called "Tango Sensual," is a fusion of the sensual rhythms of tango and carnival march music. It is usually played as a grand finale of a musical or dance evening, expressing ceremonious sadness about the inevitable end of an unforgettable evening. In either case—as garbled speech or inappropriate mood-setter—"La cumparsita" reflects an absence of meaning, a parallel reality in which the country of Lebanon and its people do not exist. This explains Makdisi's feeling that her family and the world are in a state of madness.

Most striking in this account is the extent to which broadcasting organizes the public's experience. When "La cumparsita" frames war within formal dance music, the audiences respond with formal dance, an impromptu tango. Words and language give way to rhythm and body movement. No doubt, Makdisi is critical of the radio's cue that triggers the public's response, which she promptly labels madness. References to the civil war as "madness" are common in women's literature of this period; madness is a response to hopelessness. But I think what's at stake here is the health of the relationship between the media and the public. Notice the audacity with which the audience comments on the relationship and judges the media's performance. Whereas at the beginning of Lebanese television, General Naufel, CLT's longtime CEO, infamously dared the audiences to discontinue their relationship (turn off their television sets) if they were unhappy with the programming, Makdisi provokes them to engage in media critique. No longer powerless, the audience is now empowered to speak back to the media.

Mahmoud Darwish, too, evoked a painful memory of the media's perceived deliberate forgetfulness of the war trauma in his famous 1986 *Dhakira li-l-Nisyan: Sirat Yawm, al-Zaman—Ab, al-Makan—Bayrut* (*Memory for Forgetfulness: August, Beirut, 1982*). On a hot August day, heavy, "hysterical" Israeli airstrikes deafen Beirut's residents.[24] Yet, when he turns on the radio to hear the news, the sound box belches out upbeat commercials, nonsensical vocabulary chains, and songs reminiscent of a peaceful, romantic pan-Arab past.

> I turn on the radio and I'm forced to listen to happy commercials: "Citizen watches to keep correct time." "Merit cigarettes—more flavor, less

> nicotine." "Come to Marlboro, come to where the pleasure is." "Health bottled water, health from the mountain top." But where's the water? The dalliance of the female announcers at Radio Monte Carlo is escalating like they're just stepping out of the bath or some bedroom full of arousal. "Heavy shelling over Beirut." Heavy shelling over Beirut. Heavy shelling over Beirut? Is this called news, as if it's a normal day of a normal war, with normal news bulletins? I turn the dial to listen to BBC-London. Same deadly coldness in the anchors' voices who are smoking pipes so loudly that the listeners can hear them, voices broadcast on short waves transferred to medium waves that make them sound offensive and caricaturish: "Our correspondent says that from what it looks like to the cautious observers as far as it appears from what became clear from the spokesman, given some factual distortions, the whole thing points to surmising that both fighting sides are really trying to avoid mentioning the lack of clarity and not let on about some aircrafts flown by unknown pilots and if we want to be precise it might even be possible to confirm that some people look dressed nicely." Such grammatically correct Arabic! It all ends with a Muhammad 'Abd al-Wahhab song written in an Arabic which sticks to correct emotions: "Come to me, or tell me to come to you, or tell me to leave you alone."[25]

Disappointed but unsurprised, he switches from station to station in a desperate attempt to stir up broadcasters' war memory. Alas, neither local nor international Arabic-language newscasts say anything of consequence. The language of the newscasts is properly evasive and noncommittal, while that of the song selections reflects the similarly proper emotions—a romantic blend of passion, spurned love, and nostalgia for the golden age of Arabic music, which 'Abd al-Wahhab personifies.

Other jabs at broadcasting targeted the allure of the peace bubble. Despite their exasperation with the peace bubble, people spent extraordinary amounts of time huddled by their television or radio sets, tinkering with the dials. They watched or listened when cooking and cleaning; some even listened at work if they could. When battles, sniper fire, and abductions made roads dangerous, people would miss work and suffer depression and insomnia. If their days were television- and radio-centric, at night many escaped to the abundant radio programs that occluded the war. Listeners using pseudonyms called in to share their thoughts on nonwar subjects; some frequent callers even became minor celebrities. Their calls were like an unscripted radio serial that reassured listeners of a regular progression of life that couldn't be disrupted by the unpredictability of war. The frequent callers' pseudonyms became empty vessels into which listeners could slip easily, creating a feeling of closeness and belonging. The use of pseudonyms became a central part of the success of a radio genre that fed on the creation of a parallel reality where the war was reassuringly invisible. Huda Barakat's 1988 award-winning novel *Hajar al-Dahak* (*The Stone of Laughter*) poignantly describes and critiques this allure. The protagonist Khalil is not used to hearing talking on the radio—a dig at the occlusion of the war in meaningful news and commentary; one day while cleaning his portable radio he accidentally moves the dial to FM:

> There was never any news on the sentimental FM stations nor any mention of anything particular to the city's daytime existence . . . the host laughed a lot . . . [he] worked on the phone with individuals . . . using false names. . . . They speak in evasive, metaphoric language. . . .
>
> Ronnie [a caller] requests to get in touch with Gloria who was sad yesterday when she talked on the subject of "do you believe in luck," addressing Dani . . . only the priest [i.e., radio host] knows Gloria's phone number because she gave it to him to give to Dani. . . . Gloria or Fatima know Dani or Mahmoud but thousands of other listeners don't know each other and they know neither Gloria nor Dani . . . but Gloria and Dani become their heroes. . . . [Gloria] requests a song to thank Roni for his concern and assure him that it's just a passing cloud and that at any time of day or night—some things will make you happy while others will make you sad—and she asks if he's done fixing his car, which was on his mind, she asks him to take care of his health because health is the most precious thing in life. . . .
>
> They're people but they aren't real. Only their voices are real . . . real voices, empty and deceptive, these were the real voices of a city like this . . . the real city, people like me exist, then, they're real and they talk on FM.[26]

Dreaming a New Relationship. Literary accounts didn't stop at critiquing the fraught relationship between broadcasting and audiences. They also described the public's expectations of a new one, adding a different aspect to the carnivalesque I analyzed in the previous section. Two accounts best illustrate this. The first is a daydream scene from *The Stone of Laughter.* The war transforms the mostly homebound Khalil from a mild-mannered homosexual to a violent, rapist militiaman. Before this happens, he spends his time in menial domestic tasks like picking lentils for soup, mending old sweaters, wiping his portable radio with cotton swabs, or compulsively cleaning his tiny apartment. For hours he yearns to talk on a nighttime radio station and obsesses over how the talk show host will get in touch with him. When the host fails to call, Khalil daydreams their conversation: "The host asked Khalil what he wanted to say . . . the host began asking him questions and Khalil found himself answering them . . . expressing his opinion about honesty, then dedicating an excerpt from Abdel Halim Hafez's song 'Helou w-Kazzeb' ('Pretty Liar') to the listeners."[27] Talk radio broaches honesty at the exact point when Khalil daydreams himself into the scene. He explodes in glee, flashing a smile immediately after he dedicates the song. While the lyrics are not part of the scene, this is a popular, simple song, and most readers are likely to remember the opening, "Pretty liar, why did I trust you . . . why did you lie from the first time we met?" As the broadcast media stands for the pretty liar, Khalil derives uncanny satisfaction from exposing the bubble—the cover-up of the media.

A reflection of Lebanese audiences, the fictional Khalil harbors an irresistible desire for an honest relationship with the broadcast media. For one, the scene reflects this relationship's deeply personal nature—the host is even expected to know Khalil's phone number: "the host is a site of connection that becomes like a priest entrusted with the great secret, that is, the [caller's] phone number."[28] The host is "entrusted" with hearing and publicizing the "great secret" of the public's experience. This confessional yet public processing of the war trauma transforms private experience into public memory, thus giving meaning to the war. As a "site of connection," the host is an intermediary who helps create a sense of public by virtue of addressing the public. He validates the existence of the media through its users' perspectives.[29] Also, Khalil is happy because what follows next is an imagined sexual encounter with Rafat, one of the show's male callers. As a most intimate encounter, the sexual bond between Khalil and Rafat, though a dream, reveals how deeply Khalil desires to be connected with others and how much that depends on the media.

Two stories from Rachid al-Daif's 1983 surrealist collection *Unsi Yalhu Maʿ Ritta* (*Unsi Plays with Ritta*) capture a similar desire to be connected to the broadcast media, this time imagined as a visceral relationship with television.[30] In the story "The Elephant," the boy Unsi offers the banana he's eating to a television elephant, who takes it from across the screen.[31] In "Unsi and the Television," Unsi jumps inside the television set to save a drowning girl, then gets trapped when his mother turns off the set thinking no one is using it.[32] To return, Unsi writes her a letter and she replies to him with a letter of her own. In both stories, Unsi (the audience) is a keen observer—a judge—of television's troubles, a competent communicator with the medium, and its savior. Unsi detects that the elephant and the girl (i.e., television) need help and then proceeds to interact effortlessly with the medium. The two worlds are able, indeed ready and willing, to interact, to understand each other, and to react appropriately. The elephant picks up the food, while the girl thanks Unsi profusely, then invites him to meet her parents. Unsi speaks a language that television understands while his intentions, words, and actions are meaningful for television. Even though food for the elephant and a lifeguard for the girl are what television (rather than the audience) needs in the stories, providing food and saving one's life were the two most common needs of the Lebanese citizens (the audience) during the war. Therefore, Unsi's actions as a savior are equally directed to television characters and wartime concerns of the Lebanese public. In this sense, Unsi is television's moral savior who rescues the medium by reflecting the public's concerns.

Like Khalil, Unsi becomes the star of the show. Yet, Unsi is more than that. He is the means of television's existence and survival (at least for those characters who exist on television). Because he is a boy, without qualifications, a profession, or sufficient education, this savior is an everyman, an ordinary Lebanese. At the center of this relationship is Unsi's ethical compulsion to save television. Unlike Khalil, though, Unsi no longer dreams the relationship; it has become his reality. The audience becomes a protagonist in this reality—television's new hero. Television, then, constitutes the public, whereas without the public, television's meaning is at risk.

It is also a relationship that helps the public form a sense of its own existence and power and to imagine legitimizing television from the users' perspective. Previously, the broadcast media felt entitled to disregard the audiences, to leave them unheard, unseen, and unconsidered, because broadcasting had the power to dictate the scope of the relationship.[33] CLT's General Naufel notoriously advised viewers who were unhappy with programming to turn off their sets, as I discussed earlier. Whether the audiences stayed in the relationship or turned off their sets did not affect how television conducted its operations in the general's imaginary or in his public statements. Khalil though imagines that the power resides in him, which is why the show host is humbled to make the first move and call. Khalil is at the center of a relationship that revolves around his thoughts and feelings. This is also the case with Darwish's autobiographical protagonist who announces: "I want a radio host . . . who can put on a convincing show of sadness. Between tapes of *my* words, I want him to make short speeches."[34] Through Darwish's protagonist and through Khalil, the audiences imagine themselves as seen, heard, and sought after; they matter. Barakat's expressions "site of connection" and "family of listeners," as well as Khalil's dream of a sexual encounter with Rafat, beautifully showcase the intimate bonds among audience members that broadcasting allows. They also reveal the media's formative role in the emergence of the audience's sense of self and its power to validate the media's existence.

The importance of imagining a different social order before it could be transformed politically has been implicated in many cases. One is the fall of apartheid. In *Starring Cosby and Mandela: Media and the End(s) of Apartheid*, Ron Krabill suggests that *The Cosby Show* was critical in averting racial civil war in South Africa in the 1980s because watching it spoiled whites' taste for racial politics. According to him, the show substituted their unacceptable biological form of racism with a still globally tolerated cultural one by imagining what some see as a postracial society.[35] I believe similarly that imagining first a new, more equal relationship between the Lebanese audience and broadcasting was essential in the industry's eventual transformation. The literary examples analyzed here, then, corroborate Agnes Ku's suggestion that the imagined public (the audience) "is made possible and necessary through media publicity and cultural representations."[36] The examples suggest that the imagined general public could participate in the political discourse set forth by the media by altering such discourse through narrative ("between tapes of my words, I want him to make short speeches"), despite its unequal power.

The Press: A Self-Proclaimed Intermediary in the Television-Audience Relationship

In addition to ordinary citizens and writers, periodicals also followed, commented on, and tried to change the development of television and its relationship with the audience. Here I focus on the entire corpus of the weekly cultural magazine *Shabaka* between the war years of 1975 and 1991 because of the richness of information it holds on the topic. I also examined the top leading dailies *Nahar* and *Safir* to compare how discourses on television were treated in the political press, but discovered that titles primarily focused on politics were uninterested in television, and even the few important moments they reflected were quite brief. Against the background of such indifference, their criticism of television language is marked, as I show below.

Shabaka, a top seller in the Arab world, was founded in 1956 by the young publishing company Dar al-Sayyad, owned by the Freyha family.[37] Dar al-Sayyad also publishes the well-known daily paper *al-Anwar*, the leading weekly political magazine *al-Sayaad*, several leading monthly magazines (e.g., *al-Difa' al-Arabi* [*Arab Defense Journal*], the management and finance magazine *al-Idari*, the computer magazine ACCE, the fashion magazine *Fayrouz*, and the men's lifestyle magazine *al-Faris* [*Knight*]), and other publications. *Shabaka*'s readership is predominantly female (around 60 percent), skewing younger (around three-quarters of readers), and regional (only a third of the sales are in Lebanon). Sometimes it has to send censored editions to specific Arab countries to sustain its regional reach; for instance, toning down opinions on sensitive topics and removing revealing photos or replacing them with face shots. Although the magazine claims that its readers are middle or upper-middle class, research found that in the late 1970s the magazine was predominantly read by the working class, and none of the surveyed elites reported that they read it.[38] Much like today, during the war *Shabaka*'s main focus was Arab music and film. In addition, the magazine included a one- to two-page section on Lebanese television and also often had separate articles on Lebanese television actors, writers, directors, and administrators in other regular columns. Its penchant for the Arab music canon hardly left an issue into the 1990s without reporting on Muhammad Abd al-Wahhab or the Lebanese trio Fayrouz and the Rahbani brothers (it was practically obsessed with the relationship of the latter). The magazine also religiously documented the artistic career and sometimes private life of the Lebanese singer-actress Sabah, whose photogenic appearance and always joyful attitude made for catchy pictures.

Before the war, *Shabaka* dedicated extensive portions to the Lebanese cultural scene, including the booming television, film, and theater industries. It also reported extensively on the famous and sometimes infamous Beirut night life, local socialites, charity events, or leisure gatherings of local elites. When the war began, such cultural events took a hit. The magazine stopped covering local culture for months, cutting its pages from over a hundred to barely fifty that now covered mostly Egyptian actors and singers (with a separate page spread on Syrian television and film). *Shabaka* slowly regained its full size as the violence of the two-year war (1975–76) abated, but every now and then it lost coverage of Lebanese television depending on the ongoing circumstances. For instance, its coverage became weaker for over a month after national television's second split into two warring branches that occurred in February 1984. Between June 1989 and January 1996, *Shabaka* completely lost its section on Lebanese television, although occasional news on it appeared in other sections.

The magazine did not speak with one voice and sometimes reflected contradictory positions in its coverage of Lebanese wartime television. At the beginning of the war, Antoine Baroudi contributed to the television section. Then another writer, came on board, Abd al-Ghani Tlis—a poet in *Fusha* and the vernacular, journalist, composer, television writer, and later weekly talk show host of Télé Liban's *Masa al-Nur* as well as adjunct university professor.[39] Other contributors wrote in other columns about Lebanese television as well. Nonetheless, a number of common themes emerge, such as the poor state of the television-audience relationship, anchors' unique celebrity, the gendered discussions of anchors' professional qualifications, the female broadcaster–male viewer dynamic, and conceiving of television as a pretty liar.

The allure of television entertainment was driven by security, according to *Shabaka*; that is, such allure was imposed by the dangers of violence and death that lurked outside the home.[40] The magazine came up with the notion of a reluctant viewer to describe one party of the "contract" between audiences and television. Ideally, the viewer was to watch television more often, given that the war had restricted or destroyed other forms of leisure,[41] while television was to provide good entertainment in return. But television was scuppering the deal, in the estimation of the magazine. Thus, the most consistent theme in the magazine was, first, exposing television's failure by commenting on boring, superficial, or irrelevant programming; and, second, bringing attention to what it saw as viewers' justified anger and indignation with the "lemon deal."[42] This criticism culminated in denouncing the industry as a humiliating international pratfall from being the first television in the Middle East to becoming the last television in the world: "Who said Télé Liban doesn't 'develop'? It 'develops' by nosedive with an astonishing speed. As if it's racing the wind, even as if it's the wind itself."[43] In 1984, an article bluntly blamed national security for the poor quality of television,[44] which cost it over seven million LL lost advertising revenue. A few issues later the magazine pointed a finger at the inadequate government and private sector commitment to television upgrowth, desired to be between fifty and a hundred million.[45]

Shabaka saw itself playing four complementary roles in this context: an audience informer on all matters television, a commentator on television's performance and social influence, an intermediary between television and audiences (while often seeing itself as part of the latter), and finally an active agent arguing for television change. Its informative articles discussed new shows, interviewed actors and writers, and shared details about the latest administrative developments in television, especially the expectations of change with each new CEO appointment. As a commentator, *Shabaka* regularly published longer evaluative and analytical pieces and medium-length stand-alone critical rubrics such as "Missile Aimed at. . . ." Its shortest, paragraph-length comments were split between a positive section (named "Smile," "Nod," etc.) and a negative section (named "Frown," "Pinch," "Tack," and the like).

The magazine took its intermediary role seriously, given the broad perception of television's failure to live up to audiences' expectations. In 1979, it boasted of taking people's "whys" to Télé Liban.[46] Four years later it solicited for publication readers' suggestions for new cultural shows.[47] When unsolicited readers' letters were featured, columnists emphasized the readers' requests to reach television executives through the pages of the magazine to help improve programming. This was also, of course, a jab at how unresponsive television appeared to viewers' feedback. At one point *Shabaka* even called random phone numbers and interviewed the subscribers about their opinion of television. The resulting article painted a grim picture of the state of the medium and authenticated the negative feedback by printing the interviewees' actual names and phone numbers under their comments. That was necessary, the magazine explained, "because we want the Lebanese public to participate in building a superior television."[48]

From what I can tell, the magazine was able to affect directly only smaller matters related to individual persons, such as a writer who would modify an ongoing fiction series after reading specific criticisms of the initial episodes, or an anchor who would improve his or her grammar competency following a relentless grammar campaign on the magazine's pages. On the other hand, when LBC launched, it seemed to have taken to heart much of *Shabaka*'s feedback. Regardless of the magazine's actual impact, it is clear from its articles' structure that it had acute self-awareness of a greater social purpose. Many pieces began with a dedication "to so-and-so," and talked to their addressees directly (whether actors, administrators, anchors, directors, or writers), sometimes addressing them in the second person. Columnists admitted that their words were intended as suggestions, then followed with statements of hope that these suggestions would help the addressee in fixing the issue. Readers' letters were also occasionally sites for negotiations between readers and the magazine itself, as in cases where the television columnist shared readers' criticisms (and demands) of the magazine. On one occasion in 1987, a reader apparently requested the name of the anchor whom Tlis so often criticized for shaking her head, while in another a reader reprimanded the magazine for exposing by name news anchors who made grammar mistakes.[49]

As a self-proclaimed intermediary and active agent for negotiating a new television-audience relationship, *Shabaka* lambasted, chastised, and ridiculed television. It also praised, flattered, and cajoled the mass medium since the latter tended to see the press as an enemy. Although television had ups and downs throughout the war, the magazine remained consistent in bringing attention to two significant problems, summarized in a 1981 article addressed to Télé Liban's CEO Charles Rizq.[50] The greater of the problems was television's failure to answer people's needs in everyday life, culture, education, and so on; the lesser problem was the low production quality.

The magazine was widely read by nonelites.[51] Yet the columnists' keen interest in intellectual matters often dictated how they talked to television and monitored its response to the audiences' needs. Columnists often praised programs with an educated political leaning hosted by news anchors, such as Camille Menassa's show *Hadha al-Usbu'* (*This Week*) and Jean Khoury's show *Malaff* (*File*) in the 1977–78 season.[52] In the 1982 season, the magazine described Jean Khoury and Arafat Hijazi's cohosted program *Wara' al-Akhbar* (*Behind the News*) as "the strongest this and last season" for its focus on consensus and its goal to "develop people's ability for hope."[53] Despite praising these shows, the magazine continued to chastise Télé Liban for neglecting information programing. It wrote in 1986: "This long, never-ending wait is enough, Télé Liban. The audience is calling you to be at the forefront of Lebanese media. Enough with programs that don't respond to the sensibilities of the Lebanese viewers who are known to have the most sophisticated cultural taste."[54] A year earlier, *Shabaka* had lampooned the station for being "lost . . . on two hills" as its two warring branches were each "crouching" on a hill after the split.[55] What should the viewers do, *Shabaka* wanted to know: turn off their sets, keep switching back and forth between the two branches' news bulletins, or barricade themselves behind the partisan position of one of them? Later the magazine even suggested a solution that one of the news bulletins be pushed back an hour to the 9:30 p.m. slot so that viewers could watch both.[56]

At the same time, *Shabaka* relentlessly bashed television for promoting high culture and "stuck-up" programming. Television cartoons (seen as collections of good jokes) had become a prominent genre followed by adults since the two-year war.[57] Fictional series had large audiences too, while genres like theater plays, *zajal* (satirical poetry filled with invectives in the vernacular), and folk poetry thrived throughout the war. In 1982 and 1983 *Shabaka* ran several extensive articles criticizing how Télé Liban had massacred popular folk poetry in a show dedicated to the genre. The famous Salam al-Rasi had compiled several collections of folk sayings and stories from Lebanese villages and in 1982 Télé Liban created a show based on these collections that it called *Folk Literature*, directed by the young Ramzi al-Rasi. Ramzi filmed his improvised conversations with village locals. He would later discuss their sayings and tales in the studio with cohost Zainat Nassar al-Rayyes for fifteen minutes three times a week "in a simple understandable way, with no editing or making it sound urban," as *Shabaka* noted.[58] However, the January 31–February 7, 1983 issue of *Shabaka* was upset: "No, Marwan!" read the title of the piece dedicated to the show.[59] At issue was that Télé Liban had asked writer Marwan al-Abd to transform the folk tales and sayings into short television episodes played by actors. His attempt to rhyme every single line angered the magazine: "*Folk Literature*—our beloved and friend—lost one of its most important artistic and authentic features—its simplicity . . . as pompous, presumptuous pretension took over."[60] With "bitterness, regret, and sadness," *Shabaka* bemoaned a few weeks later, "why, every time Télé Liban touches gold, it turns into sand in its palms?"[61] Columnist Tlis promised to keep talking about this issue until Abd took a stand against his thick language. A few weeks later, Tlis reported partial success, as Abd had apparently decreased the number of rhymes.[62]

Encouraging Télé Liban to form a personal connection with the audience and to deepen it was a running theme in *Shabaka*'s coverage of television business. Shortly before an upcoming US-Lebanese diplomatic meeting, news anchor Suad al-Ashi had interjected in the middle of a report on a US space shuttle: "How we wish that the US initiatives on Earth would succeed like they did in space."[63] *Shabaka* was quick to reward Ashi with a "Nod" for acknowledging the audiences' deep-seated hopes and frustrations and building a personal connection with them. Also common were the magazine's requests that television focus on matters that personally concerned the public. It urged the medium to reach out to the public again in a 1983 comment on the show *Mashakil wa Hulul* (*Problems and Solutions*):

> Why doesn't this important and helpful show take its lens (this is its main goal) to the people on the street, at home, and in the office and ask them about their concerns and hardships? Why doesn't it go to the areas that complain from every day economic and social problems and document people's suffering on the ground, then take it back to the studio to discuss with the experts? I propose to my colleague George Abu Mashar [the show host] to head to Birj al-Barajneh, for instance, in the Southern [Shi'ite] outskirts of Beirut, because I am confident that he would be able to get a basketful of problems with no solution: roads full of potholes, suffocating traffic, no running water, power blackouts, a phone service that has become a memory, etc. Birj al-Barajneh, by the way, houses about a half million people, according to the latest statistics.[64]

Columnists deplored when hosts addressed their guests in the third person, or when news anchors corrected a mistake they made by saying "or" instead of apologizing to the audience.[65] Using the third person in situations where it is appropriate to use the second person is a distancing technique. It makes developing a strong television-audience bond harder because of the implications of distance, indirectness, formality, discomfort with intimacy, and even secrecy and duplicity. That Tlis picked on anchors' failure to apologize to the audience for the mistakes they made may be just an argument for common decency or a television format. But it may also suggest that the audiences saw television's failure as a lack of empathy or concern for them.

After LBC was launched, columnists doubled down on unfavorable opinions of Télé Liban, comparing its disengagement and anachronism to

LBC's engagement with the public and the latter's perception of modernity. This occurred even in instances when the columnist enjoyed Télé Liban's shows. For instance, when Camille Chamoun died on August 7, 1987, Télé Liban aired a rerun of a years-old Adel Malek interview with the former Lebanese president and major wartime political leader. In the next issue of *Shabaka*, Tlis praised at length the quality, depth, and sophistication of the interview and Malek's invaluable contribution to the outlet's archives. Yet, the columnist also skillfully jabbed at the missed opportunity to connect with the audiences. According to Tlis, the show had "served its function," while LBC's coverage was of a totally "different caliber." The new outlet had aired live from the late president's home, capturing how the mourning political elite paid its respects. However, the reason that Tlis gave LBC a "huge point" was its live coverage of the funeral procession and services, "which allowed all viewers to accompany the procession from their homes in sound, image, and commentary, and witness one of the faces of united Lebanon."[66]

The question of television's modernity and how it reflected that of the nation inevitably connected to the contemporaneity of television programs. In 1986, *Shabaka*'s editor-in-chief George Ibrahim al-Khoury argued that viewers saw only old faces on Télé Liban, yet television was supposed to be the medium of a modern voice and constantly renewing image.[67] "Sleeping on the past 'glories' of television series and airing reruns of anything one can grab from the locker is akin to falling into death," Tlis had written two years earlier.[68]

Shabaka's long-running commentary on the state of Lebanese television during the war years and its attempted mediation of the television-audience relationship provides ample evidence for the new cultural role that audiences had begun playing and the new demands this put on television. As Tlis reported in 1982, "television has had a problem since the cultural sense came to dominate the audiences; this sense that they would no longer lay back and receive, or accept what they are given; they have started participating in production, or in determining what they should be given."[69] Television needed to respond to that.

The "News" Is on the News, Again! Despite the hard line it took on behalf of the "reluctant viewer," *Shabaka* sometimes admitted that television was rather popular with the audiences. In one news item, the magazine related the story of an unsavory fight between a seventy-year-old man and a ten-year-old boy. The two got into a dispute about whether to watch a show on Lebanese *zajal* (the popular satirical poetry genre) or *Little House on the Prairie*. The dispute ended in the hospital after the man slammed a chair on the boy's head followed by the plate of *ful* (fava beans) he was eating.[70] Such admissions sometimes betrayed the magazine's bafflement. At other times they bore sarcastic overtones but never ceased to remind television that the press wanted it to play a national role because it had entered every home and become "more necessary than bread and water."[71]

Anchors were uniquely popular during the war. People's intense need for information focused their attention on individual presenters. The techniques viewers had to learn in order to decipher hidden messages from the anchors, or read their appearance, body language, and ripe silences personalized the experience of watching the news. Anchors were agents of the peace bubble yet also the closest viewers could get to witnessing the occasional challenge of the bubble. Anchors therefore became "friends of the Lebanese home," whom viewers loved and enjoyed, and "the only visitors" that viewers did not begrudge.[72] The magazine used the same metaphor of "the secret" that Barakat used in creating the scene of Khalil's conversation with the radio host: anchors were both gregarious informers and silent witnesses of each home's secrets. They could not disclose those secrets, the magazine wrote, but they could certainly keep them safe.[73]

Given anchors' unique celebrity, *Shabaka* dedicated many pages on them to quench readers' interest. The shorter items titled "Smiles," "Nods," "Tacks," and "Pinches" regularly addressed different anchors and hosts. Many longer stories humanized male anchors beyond the newsroom. There was a short story on George Qurdahi, who became schoolgirls' heartthrob (married, unfortunately, as the magazine noted).[74] Another focused on Pierre Ghanem—the young poet-anchor whose collection *Jasadiyat* (*Corporealities*) was "an escape from political news into the world of love and contemplation"[75]—and yet another on Jacque Wakim, describing him as "the closest anchor to people's hearts," especially the president's.[76] When Adel Malek became correspondent for Monte Carlo, columnist Baroudi called him "the companion of our evenings and one of our oldest mates."[77] There was even a piece on Maurice Nahhas—a Télé Liban employee who had been crossing the dangerous Green Line for thirteen years to get to work.[78] In 1980 *Shabaka* ran a three-page spread of profiles, featuring three female and four male news anchors together with seven female show hosts and schedule announcers.[79] The spread came in response to insistent requests from readers and included biological and career ages, marital status, job titles, and work slogans for each broadcaster. The two personal items in the profiles—age and marital status—reflected the readers' perception of the personal nature of the anchor-viewer relationship, similar to "Tacks" that were "Smiles" in disguise (e.g., "tacking" Jean Khoury for forcing viewers to miss him during his absence from the news bulletin).[80]

The stars of attention, though, were female broadcasters, who got several dedicated joint spreads and many solo articles, especially Suad al-Ashi and Gabby Latif. A joint spread called "Female Presenters: Happy or Miserable?" wrote, "We wait for them every night as if they've become one of us; they bring us a sweet smile, a kind word, and pleasant consolation," before it proceeded to interview the broadcasters about their job satisfaction.[81] The connection to female broadcasters seems to have been rather meaningful in one of the regular "Missile Aimed at . . ." columns, where the pseudonymous columnist Saroukh (Rocket) criticized CEO Rizq for deciding oddly to bar female anchors from appearing on screen and allow only their voices to be aired accompanied by stills of local historical monuments. Rocket cajoled Rizq into heeding the audiences' feelings: "This audience considers Télé Liban to be different only due to the presence of the seductive faces of the beloved female anchors. . . . As far as programs go, Télé Liban receives an absolute zero."[82] Articles of that nature confirm the transition from "language journalism" to "embodied journalism" and the viewers' keen interest in "reading" anchors (and the news) beyond the content of their contrived reports.

Considering the perception of the broadcasters' importance, their professional qualifications were widely discussed. The relative proportions of three main components—appearance, performance, and culture—underlay all discussions. According to a 1975 piece, some anchors

> absolutely fail to meet the standards for real, flawless anchors. One eats his words . . . and you can only get the gist if you rely on your intellect, eyesight, and cleverness in solving puzzles. Another is scared and shaking as he reads the news as if someone is holding a gun to his head from behind the curtain. A third one has a clear voice and confident tone but his tongue twists the sounds and turns the softer letter *ta'* into the emphatic *Ta'*, *sin* into the emphatic *Sad*, and the word *tansiq* for example into *TanSiq*. A fourth one has a handsome face, well-groomed hair, and poised eyes but he's weak in the language of *Dad* [i.e., Arabic], so you see how he struggles with his weakness, reading all words in their pausal form to avoid making a grammar mistake.[83]

This quote packs examples of failures in all three categories and shows the contradictory and multifaceted view of anchors as news celebrities and flawed professionals.

Appearance was a category singularly important for female broadcasters, especially schedule announcers, whose role was to announce the lineup and summarize the next program, sometimes killing the suspense. Many television employees insisted that the professional standard applied to female broadcasters did not require them to be beauty queens but to have faces that looked "acceptable" to the audience. Yet it was a public secret that most schedule announcers were hired for their good looks. Choosing beauty and elegant style over the "minimum degree" of other important qualities like culture and language proficiency prompted harsh criticism from May Menassa—a distinguished representative of Lebanon's first generation of broadcasters.[84] *Shabaka* regularly instructed anchors on appearance, on one occasion reporting an "expert's advice" on the single factor that sustains public attraction to women anchors: never go on camera wearing the same look twice in a row.[85] The magazine also frequently reassured female broadcasters that they were beautiful, as a prelude to chastising them for being superficial and vain in their focus on looks. Its reassurances nonetheless clearly conveyed that they were judged on appearance and being fastidious about their looks was expected of them.[86]

The contradictory expectations around female appearance manifested unambiguously in 1981 when *Shabaka* labeled its address to presenter Gabby Latif "Pinch or Nod."[87] The magazine acknowledged that Latif had a pioneer influence on the rest of the female broadcasters whom she introduced to new hairstyles and elegant clothing. Yet, it asked that she attend to her beauty and makeup less because her "disciples" spent more than three-quarters of their salaries on clothing and coiffures. The same year, the magazine also recorded the increasing requirements around the appearance of male broadcasters, apparently imposed by the mass popularity of color television.[88]

While appearance was easy to dismiss, praise, or critique, broadcasters' performance was a lot more complicated. It involved voice, tone, and bodily features like smile and gaze from which viewers determined the emotional state of the broadcaster. More importantly, it helped viewers determine the legitimacy of the information broadcasters presented, their qualifications as professionals, and even the ability of the medium to connect to the audience by telling or censoring truth. Voice and tone were even more gendered categories than appearance. When the news merged in 1977 after the insults on the air during the two-year war, for the first time there were five female news anchors—Jeanne d'Arc Abu Zeid Fayyad, Charlotte Wazen al-Khoury, Siham Asbar, Suad Qarut al-Ashi, and Maya Tabet (English news). Even though columnist Baroudi praised these "beauties" for giving the news a "'human' touch" and a dedicated fandom, he also unsubtly criticized the sexualized consumption of the female anchors by male viewers: "Having these beautiful women on has added a human touch to the bulletin as well as a male audience and fans. This guy is listening to the news to watch Siham, another one to enjoy Charlotte, a third one to see Jeanne d'Arc up close, a fourth one to check out Suad's glowing skin, a fifth one to track the English words that come out of Maya's mouth like the English girls. You ask them, what did you get from the bulletin? They pucker their lips [in confusion]—a human touch."[89]

The same issue also published the first part of a five-part series of articles by author and poet George Jordaq, titled "With the Voices of Female Broadcasters," under the premise that the human voice reflects one's personality and inner world better than the eyes or the face.[90] Jordaq was convinced that the human face was a good liar and could sell convincingly the party line of the broadcasting outlet, while the voice always told the truth of the anchor's actual emotions hidden behind the mask of her face. He argued that to know the truth one should listen intensely not just to the anchor's voice and tone, but also to her silences. Jordaq's premise was confusing, however, because he was writing about the female body rather than the female voice in an almost pornographically misogynistic account. The first part featured statements unrelated to voice: "I repeat: the smartest thing in a woman are her legs, lips, and eyes and the feminine charm that goes hand in hand. Everything else comes from male leaders, lion-hearted warriors, and women's rights organizations." In the second part, he tried to employ his poetic skills to describe his intense projections onto the voices of female anchors:

> Women's voices, specifically, can be heard, seen, touched, smelled, and tasted at the same time, if you are from those with taste. . . . This woman's voice is like a silk garment that covers her body yet hides none of its parts. That woman is calling and cajoling you; her words are saying: "Oh, baby!" but her tone is telling you "I'm a liar! . . . The female anchors' voices lead you into the bedroom without the slightest embarrassment from the watching eyes. . . . One voice undresses its owner in preparation for delivering the latest news to you. You think that this other voice is reading the news to you but its owner's head is down, her legs are up, and her dress is new. . . . That one is reading the news with passion and emotion but her voice isn't actually reading news; it intimates that the anchor is complaining to the listeners with her husband or fiancé for having run away with an uglier and less exciting friend of hers. That anchor is new; she's telling you about her exceptional interest in charitable work and about her regular engagement in social work, but during this talking charade her voice persuades you that she is only saying: "I want a groom!"[91]

Not coincidentally, the series featured multiple drawings of naked women with open mouths, semiclosed eyes, and perky breasts either with visible areolas or barely covered by a bikini top. The drawings were printed next to photos of actual anchors looking away from the camera, which made them seem both inaccessible to the ordinary male reader and objects of voyeurism. In addition, some of the series' sections were titled "I'm a (woman) liar," "I want a groom," "The lips of the beautiful woman," "In which dress?," "The most delicate legs," and "The taste of wine." After the more abstract two-part interlude, in the next three parts Jordaq described Suad Qarut al-Ashi, who read the same news bulletin on television and on Radio Lebanon, and Maggie Farah, who was a news anchor on the Voice of Lebanon radio station.

That the earlier Baroudi article sarcastically chided male viewers for sexualizing female anchors and de facto gutting the bulletin just pages before Jordaq glorified that very sexualization is, of course, evidence that *Shabaka* did not speak with one voice. It is also an indicator that very early in the war femininity became a site for the negotiation of television's (and radio's) relationship with the audience. Both accounts may actually be making the same point—that broadcasting outlets used female beauty to entice the male gaze and imagination and to stall, cut down, or obliterate demands for substantive, noneuphemistic, truthful, timely, and complete coverage of the war. If Baroudi registered the ongoing phenomenon, Jordaq gave away all the "secret" ingredients of the recipe and the directions for how to stir them in for a "happy" news hour. It came down to lying. In the opening part, Jordaq unequivocally announced that the voice cannot lie, yet he spent the rest of his breath to expose this delusion, perhaps without realizing it. First, he admitted that at least in intent a voice could hide things "like a silk garment that covers her body." Then he exposed the silk garment/voice as a pretty lie: "[H]er words are saying: 'Oh, baby!' but her tone is telling you 'I'm a liar!'" Going into "the bedroom without the slightest embarrassment from the watching eyes" can also convincingly describe television's (perhaps at some level reflexive) use of female sexuality to distract from the occlusion of the war "without the slightest embarrassment" on television's part and despite "the watching eyes" of the Lebanese public. The distraction—"voice that undresses its owner in preparation for delivering the latest news to you"—is a pleasure-generating mechanism—"You think that this other voice is reading the news to you but its owner's head is down, her legs are up, and her dress is new." Damage and pleasure cannot be easily separated and the audience was often a willing participant.

Describing the "talking charade" is not simply misogynistic. If she talks about charity and social work, translation: she wants a man. It also contains an indictment of broadcasting for those who could see it, even if it was not intended as such by the author, as I believe.

Jordaq's description of Maggie Farah brings this point to a home run.

> She reads the news of the war but it's as if it's news of peace because this voice doesn't agree with stories of killing and battles, because its connection to life and the living can only be that of love. Love has no relation to reading news or to the false amazement hatched in announcements, especially news about war and fighting and announcements about lunch and dinner parties in which so-and-so met with such-and-such, "studied" the issues, ate, then informed us about amazing ventures and miraculous achievements.[92]

Jordaq built the case of the "happy" news hour as a gendered distraction from the war and effectively dismantled it with sarcastic twists like "'studied' the issues," putting "studied" in quotes of irony that readers should have had no problem interpreting. His sarcasm provided another level of pleasure, this time the bitter pleasure of mocking broadcasting and Lebanon's political echelon.

Voice was so valuable as a measure of appropriate broadcaster performance that anchors, especially women, were frequently compared to singers. This comparison was accompanied by a host of assumptions such as harmony, melodiousness, leisure, joy, emotion, passion, beauty, and peace. Anchors were called artists, *fannan/a*, and *Shabaka* even proposed creating a special school to teach them the fundamentals of television performance, apparently based on melodious voice, proficient Arabic, and cadence, like a singer but without music.[93] Discussions of performance commanded public negotiation since the beginning of the war. A 1975 piece prescribed that a successful anchor needs "to rise to the performance of a stage actor in order not to react to one news item or another" regardless of his or her personal leanings.[94] Stage actors are trained not to hide but to exhibit emotions with their face, voice, tone, and gestures, even exaggerate them so they are readable to the public seated at a distance.

It is curious that the comparison to theater actors was deemed appropriate when wartime anchors were expected to do the opposite. "Being in the news business is to look for trouble," read Jean Khoury's motto in the fourteen broadcasters' profile spread—a little cynical and out of place among the touchy-feely mottos of the rest of his colleagues.[95] But it was a good warning. The ideal performance of news bulletins and schedule announcements required broadcasters to stay out of trouble by suppressing certain emotions and displaying others.

Worry and fear were off limits. Both risked that the broadcaster's state of mind be read as an acknowledgment of the war. Anchors had to appear to be smiling to stay out of trouble, which triggered one of the key concepts of wartime television—"the smile never leaves his/her face" (*la tufariq al-ibtisama wajhahu/ha*). Failure to do so triggered a round of discussion. When Niamat Azuri got promoted from a schedule announcer to a news anchor in 1985, *Shabaka* asked her to justify to the public why she got rid of her smile. Her answer was dangerously sincere—she felt she was forcing a smile at her old job because the raging war had made it too difficult to naturally wear one.[96] Now she was under the impression that her new position could not strong-arm her to keep the charade. In other instances, *Shabaka* also discussed the undesirability of "forcing a smile," or gave a "Nod" to presenters for not imitating other's fake smiles.[97]

Suzanne Abu Rizq was "pinched" for reading too slowly, making the viewer "imagine that she was afraid of the camera. Suzanne is beautiful," the pinch continued, "her television appearance is calm and she brings comfort to people's minds. . . . Hurry up a bit, Suzanne."[98] Rules about fear differ in times of peace and times of war. This pinch reminds us that any kind of fear, even of the camera, was double-marked during war. If slow speed had to be trimmed out, so too did fast speed because it reminded people of machine guns, as in the case of Fuad al-Kharsa whom *Shabaka* accused of going off so fast like a machine gun that wouldn't calm down until the whole magazine was empty.[99] Even the doyen of Lebanese news, Camille Menassa, could not always stay out of trouble and provoked a *Shabaka* comment for his proneness to anger if anything went wrong with the news. "Last week," the magazine reported, "the power went out in the middle of the bulletin. When it came back we didn't find Camille, who had left the studio and gone home. Should we consider this kind of behavior appropriate?"[100] Variable speed in speech and even in leaving the studio could easily remove the "silk garment" from television and remind the viewers how little it was doing for them.

To sustain the "magic," broadcasters were expected to exude a narrow set of well-defined positive-to-neutral emotions. According to Maggie Farah, the female presenter "needed to forget everything when she was at the studio and always be joyful."[101] The positive emotion set also included peaceful eyes, a relaxed face, a calm tone, and of course a comforting smile. When Charlotte Wazen was promoted to Jean Khoury's coanchor after being a show host for years, *Shabaka* praised her stellar observance of the criteria: "While announcing the news, her face was relaxed because she was well trained."[102]

Culture—the third category against which broadcasters were measured—was mostly concerned with language. At issue was what kind of language best reflected the identity and needs of the Lebanese and strengthened television's connection with them. *Shabaka* occasionally published readers' protectionist reactions against what they saw as the onslaught of the Egyptian vernacular due to the regular showing of Egyptian television series and movies. In one instance this kind of reaction registered readers' indignation that a swindler character on an Egyptian television series spoke Lebanese.[103] At the same time, the magazine also criticized Lebanese shows for being too narrowly nationalist, like *Abu Melhem*, which had suggested in one episode that those Lebanese who mixed French and Arabic were arrogant and thus seemed to target a specific group (Christians).[104] However, the perennial wartime dilemma was *Fusha* versus the Lebanese vernacular. It concerned mostly fictional series but it was discussed even with regards to the news bulletin.

Shabaka was an active agent in policing the purity of *Fusha*, as I show below, but even it complained about the principle of using *Fusha* on the news: "Thousands of illiterate and inarticulate people listen to *Fusha* news every day feeling as if they were deaf or born with ears filled with all sorts of noise."[105] On the rare occasions when anchors strayed outside the prescribed language medium, they received positive feedback. Jean Khoury did it a few times, and *Shabaka* reported on some of these occasions with great enthusiasm. It pointed out that people rejoiced and "discussed [Khoury's] words the next day, extolling the vernacular, doubling down on their praise, and saying that it was their language and that the news was meant for them. They understand this language, it's the language in which they love, swear, rebel, and pray. . . . Everyone who heard Jean Khoury wishes that he would make such mistakes once every day."[106]

The attitudes associated with policing the purity of *Fusha* were radically different from the enthusiasm and tolerance toward the vernacular. In a rare exception, Jordaq forgave Maggie Farah the mistakes she made in *Fusha*, going so far as to acquit her of all wrongdoing or ignorance. He blamed her mistakes on her aversion to an abtruse, hard-to-pronounce word or a burdensome expression, or even on the writer of the news report "because beauty and taste don't make mistakes."[107] The more widespread attitude, however, was that bad *Fusha* caused confusion (*balbala*). Beauty was not seen as an excuse for bad *Fusha*; its mention usually aimed at mitigating the offense of pointing out the anchor's mistakes. A piece addressing a bad night Suad al-Ashi had during one of the bulletins started by pumping up her confidence and stroking her ego. It described her voice as that of an exceptional singer that reflected her status as the undisputed star of news anchors: "Your voice is pure, your tone clear, your language correct, your start good, and your finish comforting . . . there is the pretty face, the sleek hair style, and the recognizable elegance, as well as the self-confidence, the neutral tone, and the forceful presence."[108] The author then laid in a serious criticism that the previous Thursday she had made many mistakes, uttered nonsensical words, and twisted sentences trying to fix her mistakes, making matters worse. The final judgment was also an offense-mitigating device: a newbie's mistake of not prereading the text, unworthy of Ashi's experience and status.

Instead of forgiving anchors their language mistakes, *Shabaka* insisted they improve their pronunciation and correct their grammar. In 1983 the magazine dedicated a full-length column to that objective, titled "Jalla Man la Yukhti'" ("Extolled Be He Who Does Not Make Mistakes").[109] Its writer, the Lebanese poet Younis Younis, who used the pen name Younis or Younis al-Ibn, quickly took over the whole page dedicated to television. The column ran for over eight months in almost every single issue. The changes in numbering the column's installments suggest that the magazine initially did not expect that it would take off or could be sustained for long. The first installment was unnumbered. The next seven were numbered 2–8, which suggests that the magazine envisioned the column would be a finite series. Then they got rid of the numbers and turned it into a regular rubric for the rest of the year. The initial installment laid out the rationale behind the column—Younis promised to hold female anchors and presenters accountable for their language faux pas since they had become a revered part of the Lebanese family and their mistakes could affect it negatively. The objective seems to have included public shaming as Younis intimated having tapes of the broadcasters' airtime that would turn faces red, yellow, or green for making mistakes "that even elementary students don't make." The column was envisioned as a gendered space given Younis's focus on female broadcasters. Their "dutiful" male counterparts made more mistakes, as he opined, but he was hoping to teach them by proxy. In later installments Younis broke that promise and also critiqued male anchors. The column's topics varied from pronunciation (*hawali* instead of the correct *hawala* [around/about]), to word choice (*muhimma* [important] when the anchor meant *mahamma* [important mission]), morphemes (mistakenly treating the voiced definite article "al" as voiceless "aj" before a "j"), and semantics (*fatra* [pause, weakness] for a chunk of air time). The column was occasionally interactive, keeping with the magazine's tradition. Some of the more memorable readers' criticisms that Younis discussed were by one reader who reprimanded the magazine for making the mistakes Younis condemned in the very same issue,[110] and by another who prompted Younis to justify his decision to shame anchors and presenters by name.

Outside of Younis's column, Tlis and Baroudi similarly critiqued broadcasters' language throughout the war and "invited" the latter to fix their mistakes. Their concerted efforts made an impression on Télé Liban after all. In a press conference with the outlet's top brass held at the Hazmieh branch, Arafat Hijazi—editor-in-chief at the news bulletin—admitted that hiring a separate staffer to write the text of the news and correct all the language was on the outlet's wish list.[111] Baroudi's tenure as the television columnist, which started before the war and included the first four years of the war, coincided with a period of professionalization of broadcasters triggered by the golden age of Lebanese television. Jean-Claude Boulos might have been one of the most beloved figures of Lebanese television, but since the beginning of the war Baroudi relentlessly criticized him as one of the most egregious cases of bad language. These instances included using the wrong word patterns (the incorrect *lahdha haseema* instead of *lahdha haasima* [critical moment]) and calling Salim Taqla's photo "Philip Taqla."[112] Baroudi also accused Boulos of lacking "full mastery of Arabic" and launching a new language "intercontinental ballistic missile" in every episode he hosted. In the end, though, the columnist hoped that Boulos would fix his mistakes so iconic grammarian "Sibawayh doesn't rise from the grave to abduct him."[113] Boulos's picture was displayed next to this critique at two-thirds the size of the column, creating the impression he was pinned on a wall of shame.

Whereas Younis stayed within the boundaries of linguistics in his contributions, Tlis approached language matters from the angles of identity, authenticity, and the social role of television. He had a keen eye for negotiations of femininity and masculinity and the changing standards of the television-audience relationship. When he commented on presenters who left off short vowels at the end of words or sometimes in the middle, his commentary revealed less about breaking grammar rules with which he "charged" presenters and more about uprooting *Fusha* from its linguistic-cultural network. After ten years, anchor Fouad Kharsa, for example, still failed professional standards, according to Tlis, because his omission of end vowels turned Arabic into "a half-breed" language "with no roots."[114] I suspect that three years earlier *Shabaka* had Kharsa in mind when it bluntly urged an anonymous anchor to "spend some of [his] money on a language teacher to teach [him] the fundamentals of grammar" because he made a language mistake "in every sentence, no matter how basic, casual, or close to spoken it was."[115] At issue was what Tlis and most anchors saw as the connection between the anchor's good language skills and his or her "presence"—a nebulous term that loosely designated the authority the anchor commanded in the audience. The anchor's presence then was closely implicated in the television-audience relationship. Mispronouncing the name "*Qasim*" as "*Qasm*," or the letter "*qaf*" as "*kaf*," therefore, did not just appear parochial and regionally dialectical, thereby creating something that only resembled Arabic but was not Arabic, as Tlis argued.[116] Such language processes also challenged Télé Liban's cultural authority, which was based in great part on the perceived authenticity of the standardized formal language. That is, not so much in its exclusive or pure use—as it is quite obvious the outlet's record with *Fusha* was anything but stellar—as in the claim that television was a protector of Lebanon's cultural standards, traditions, and identity. Yet, the widespread conversations on language and television were as much attempts at protecting that cultural authority by adhering to a perception of an authentic Lebanon as they constituted constant attacks on that authority.

In addition to cultural periodicals like *Shabaka*, Lebanon's political dailies also commented on Télé Liban's language and other faux pas. This stands out since these dailies were usually uninterested in television news as wartime polarization played up political news at the expense of other news. Indeed, research has shown that the top three newspapers dedicated about 48 percent of their space to political, diplomatic, and military news compared to 3 to 5 percent to all forms of entertainment.[117] As 65 percent of their content involved sectarian and government leaders as main actors,[118] the dailies' narrative framework was reminiscent of a theater script with the leaders carrying out a lengthy heated dialogue. By comparison, the boring television news could hardly sell the issue and support the 20 percent of space reserved for advertisements. In addition, the papers presented news mixed in with opinions and tended to eschew analysis, which made interpreting broader television trends just as out of place. The papers, then, only reported on major television events or if a television development related to politics. For instance, both leading papers *Nahar* and *Safir* reported on Ahdab's television coup, the unification of the two television channels in 1977, Charles Rizq's abduction, and occasionally on the destruction of television infrastructure or missile attacks on the studios. In April 1975, both *Nahar* and *Safir* also covered the beginning of self-censorship. Occasionally, the dailies reported on series like *al-Dunya Hayk* (*That's Life*) or on actors like Hind Abi Lama, Abu Salim, and Abu Melhem. Against this backdrop, having two *Nahar* reports on television's language mistakes just in the span of one week is significant. The first story appeared on page seven in the December 1, 1977, Thursday issue. It quoted anchor Arafat Hijazi's mistake in the title "The [Letters] '*Wow*' and '*Nun*' are Decoration for the News, So 'The Russians Remain Angry.'" The news bulletin, which had reported on a number of historic Arab summits, "skidded into 'historic' grammar mistakes," according to the article.[119] Hijazi had used the wrong nominative case ending of "angry," "*ghadibun*" (written with the letters *wow* and *nun*), instead of the correct accusative "*ghadibin*," which prompted a short grammar lesson from the article's writer Ismat al-Ayyubi. Like *Shabaka*'s authors, Ayyubi also suggested hiring a linguist to proofread the news items before they were read on air, and he ended bluntly with "the news department needs to get a grammar book."

Seven days later another contributor, M. B., reproached a schedule announcer for mispronouncing the English title of the 1976 US series *Rich Man, Poor Man* and for talking about one of the male characters, Rudy, in the feminine.[120] The author apologized for the criticism as a way of pointing out that such disrespect for the viewers occurred daily. Then he ended on a sarcastic note urging the announcers to care about the cultural aspects of their work as much as they did about their hairstyles and fashion. Both transgressions described in the *Nahar* articles provoked criticism because they constituted examples of deception. In the first case, Hijazi faked having mastery of *Fusha* and the cultural standards it advances; in the second, the schedule announcer feigned knowledge of the television content she was promoting. The broadcasters employed the seduction of cultural values associated with language authenticity or feminine beauty, ultimately revealing that television was but a pretty liar. It was no wonder that two of Tlis's pet peeves were when female broadcasters shook their heads seductively, which he found to be fake and manipulative, and when schedule announcers described every show as exceptional.

Truth and Lies. In 1982, the Directorate of General Security retroactively banned Wassim Tabbara's theater play *Shi Mitl il-Kizeb* (*Something Like a Lie*), reportedly upon the Lebanese president's wish.[121] The decision took the creators and the public by surprise, because when it was issued and the official media scooped the news the play's successful half-a-year run had ended three months earlier. The title of the play fit so well with common perceptions of wartime Lebanon and its institutions, including television, that thousands of ordinary people, politicians, and officials came to see it and laughed wholeheartedly. Tabbara, who also acted in the play, had put a television set on stage for one of the sketches. The president's Independence Day annual address was parsed to create a fictional television show for the sketch called "Meeting with His Excellency, the President." Tabbara played an interviewer posing questions to the recorded, cut-up president's answers. "Without being defamatory," the play employed a new technique of stinging criticism to deflate lies, falsehoods, and half-truths disseminated by the state, politicians, and television.[122] The physical prop of the television set simulated the home environment and transformed the theater audience into a television audience. The sketch, therefore, reenacted the television-audience relationship, reframing it in an audience-centric, empowering way much like Unsi and Khalil did to expose television and politics as lies. Whereas the play's title parodied the wartime culture of euphemisms—"something like a lie" instead of simply "a lie"—the sketch allowed the audience to participate in the commission of an act of resistance through the act of parody.

Shabaka's two-page spread on the censorship of Tabbara's play seems carefully designed as a wall of shame in which television figures prominently. A close-up of president Sarkis chosen from his televised speech is placed next to the three-line-long, bold-typeface article title, "The State Bans the Play 'Something Like a Lie' Retroactively!" Notice the punctuation at the end meant to convey the magazine's bewilderment and opposition as well as to invoke similar reactions in the readers. The caption identifies Sarkis with the simple "ustadh" (Mr.)—"the President of the republic Mr. Elias Sarkis"—in contrast to the more typical expression "fakhama" (excellency) used on television, which Tabbara cleverly parodied in the title of the sketch. There are five more photos in the spread: two are snapshots from the play and one is a group picture of the cast. The last two are photos of the laughing audience—one depicting Lebanon's future president Amin Gemayel and the other Druze Emir Faysal Arslan. Sarkis's face looms much larger than all other faces in the accompanying photos. In contrast to these faces' smiles and broad grins, his side gaze under the thick brows and pursed lips gives him a mean, vindictive look. Interestingly, on the snapshot where Tabbara looks down over the television set with his forearms resting on top, he seems to be having a conversation with the television itself rather than with the president because the screen is blank with no manifest images. Even the caption reads "Wassim in a television conversation," rather than "Wassim in a conversation with the president."

What *Shabaka* called the president's personal attempt to silence artistic expression was ineffective as far as Tabbara's play was concerned and even regarding theater in general. However, symbolic acts of that nature did have a chilling effect on television and journalism at large. Back in the first week of the war, on April 17, 1975, the daily *Safir* published a long piece on self-censorship under the title "Lebanese Journalism Begins Implementing Self-Censorship Today."[123] When a rerun of a prewar *Abu Melhem* episode was read retroactively as an indictment of the Palestinians after the war began in 1975 (it talked about dangerous "strangers" invading the authentic Lebanese village), *Shabaka* reported how television was repeatedly attacked on vocabulary.[124] This led to a second round of censorship of previously cleared old shows. Words like "war, battle, abduction, weapon, checkpoint, barricade, enclosure, coordination, committee, army, troops, armed, combatant, religion, state, government, system, anarchy, records, institutions, damage, destruction, hotel, corpse, bullet, situation, security, peace, etc." found themselves on the chopping block. Their ban led to "silent scenes and truncated situations" and suffocating artistic freedom.[125] In 1980, the magazine reported on how Télé Liban suddenly and with no public justification took off the air its political talk show *Sada al-Sinin* (*The Echo of the Years*), hosted by Mariam Shuqair Abu Jawde, allegedly to help establish a national consensus.[126] In that case, *Shabaka* blasted, "we demand that all television programs be taken off air."

The issue of truth versus lies was often invoked on the pages of *Shabaka*. Sometimes, the magazine bluntly pointed to the act of lying: when the war erupted, the broadcast media "began lying to people following its stupid media policy . . . of reassurance" since "it doesn't like disturbing people and instead treats them with courtesy because it's polite and doesn't like informing them of the facts even if that may cause their death."[127] When lying and broadcasting were mentioned, Akhawi's name tended to pop up as an example of successful resistance. His saying, "Don't believe what the broadcast news tell you. It's fake," was quoted as a strategy that transformed lies into warnings,[128] and inverted the standards of information from lies, deception, and half-truths to honesty even at the risk of embarrassing the government. "The road of honesty and truthfulness," *Shabaka* quoted him, is the only clear and safe road ["salik wa amin"] to reach the real Lebanon again.[129] Maggie Farah's interview with the magazine promoted a similar line: "What's most important for you?" "I always worry about the truth. I feel that no one knows the truth."[130]

Not surprisingly, the magazine encouraged all television writers to speak up and be unafraid to tell the truth in its entirety.[131] It even pointed the finger at Akhawi one time. He had reported that the Jdeideh road was unsafe but minutes later encouraged employees working there to go collect their paychecks upon request from their employers. *Shabaka* reported that people corrected Akhawi's blunder, letting it be known that they did not want to get a salary only to cover their hospital bill or grave plot.[132]

But the magazine saved its most caustic criticism for television. "The gun bullet wears its ugly face and attacks you in honesty; the television bullet is dressed in lamb's wool and rips through you with the fangs of hyenas. You, beautiful enemy, you, television, have mercy on us."[133]

Legitimacy and the Hegemonic Order

The Three Components of Modern Television Legitimacy

Trust is the main issue with which the Arab world is struggling, especially as it concerns interactions among government, media, and public, according to Mamun Fandy.[134] Indeed, trust had played an important role in establishing television's legitimacy with the Lebanese audiences ever since the medium's inception. But one of the biggest effects of the Lebanese Civil War was that it broadened the audiences' expectations beyond trustworthy information. Two new components of legitimacy emerged. To be perceived as a legitimate modern medium, television needed to become a site for the public processing of trauma and to form a strong, intimate connection with the audiences, placing them at the center of representation.

Site for the Public Processing of Trauma. As anthropologist Néstor García Canclini has argued about Latin America, when the government is unresponsive, the public needs someone else to pay attention to its concerns.[135] In most democratic states, an official failure is typically criticized and exposed by an attentive media. During conflict, the media in their capacity as institutions are one of the few public ways to organize and process trauma.[136] Although it is inaccurate to generalize about sixteen years of war during which Lebanese television had changing goals and functions, before 1985, when the workings of consociational democracy were put on hold, television was as inattentive as the government. Akhawi's traffic report responded to the needs of the public, but his one-man mission was doomed from the start.[137]

In that context, the wave of cynicism targeting broadcasting was a marker of people's anger with the industry's dereliction of duty to provide a public setting for the processing of the national tragedy. The variety of language strategies that people adopted—code words that identified different levels of safety, dark sarcasm, corrupting media tropes (especially those that feigned trustworthiness), and shaming television for its language and other flaws—expressed nihilistically their new expectation of broadcasting. A variety of distinct yet frequently overlapping publics raised significant concerns about media ethics and the broad cultural discourse on television. With their critique of broadcasting, these publics became part of what Asef Bayat would call a "social nonmovement." According to Bayat, the nature of power distribution in Arab states makes it extremely difficult to engage in open political resistance. Consequently, most citizens engage in what he calls "social nonmovements," or when individuals form a publicly visible, yet unscripted, unorganized social movement with no leaders or explicit programs. These individuals are changing the world by creating a new reality on the ground with their daily actions, not by directly challenging dominant authority.[138] This was the case that tied together government, media, and publics in wartime Lebanon. At the time, Lebanese civilians affected change through daily actions in the streets framed in language. They also resisted the war by sitting at home and expressing themselves, at least in part, through language, literature, and journalism since the streets were often unsafe. One of the most visible publics in that respect were novelists, memoirists, and print journalists. Charles Tripp has called acts of that nature "the art of resistance."[139] The Lebanese language nonmovement encompassed ordinary citizens like cab drivers, grocery peddlers, stay-at-home moms, literary writers, media freelancers, and columnists. Analyzing its "language politics" casts a rare glimpse of conversations about and responses to media policy that took place in people's homes, in the street, and on creative writers' desks, rather than in government offices or media headquarters. Its "language politics" reveals the audiences' (including writers and print journalists) increasing involvement in defining the nature of television journalism—what is usually seen as the sole purview of the medium.

The language nonmovement romanticized and inflated its role as a judge of the broadcasters' failure to reflect and witness the war. Yet, its members—largely lacking a metacognitive understanding of playing a role in a movement, albeit *Shabaka* was self-aware—engaged with some of the most significant questions that became emblematic of the 1980s and 1990s globally: What is the nature of television legitimacy and journalistic authority? How is the nature of information production and sharing changing? And what is the nature of the relationship between television and audiences? The nonmovement "unsettled traditional relations of journalistic expertise and authority" even if only in discourse.[140] Its importance also lies in providing a creative, artistic alternative to what we call today "wartime citizen journalism." Citizen journalists are active members of the audience who record and publicize stories or footage of suffering when it is ignored or suppressed in the mainstream media. Today, their visibility has triggered a paradigm shift in the power relations of news production.[141] The language nonmovement was never true citizen journalism because it did not document the conflict by collecting, disseminating, and analyzing actual news and information (except in the case of Akhawi, who regularly received oral information from citizens on which he based his reports). However, it raised issues similar to those today's discourse of citizen journalism addresses, albeit in creative, artistic ways. One issue is protecting civilians—a moral demand raised by writers in Lebanon.[142] Another is the dominance of state propaganda in televised war reporting, again targeted for disruption by writers and print journalists in Lebanon.[143]

In the end, audience voices are crucially important in articulating war concerns,[144] as 90 percent of the victims in modern conflicts are civilians, not combatants.[145]

Audiences at the Center of Representation. The multiple meanings produced by the public's contestation of television tropes coalesced around a second new expectation of television legitimacy that placed the audiences at the center of representation. The audiences portrayed themselves as the new heroes of Lebanese broadcasting. The old celebrities—the pioneer enthusiasts of early broadcasting, such as amateur show hosts, editors, programming directors, or stars of entertainment shows—never went out of fashion. However, ordinary people, like Khalil from *The Stone of Laughter*, saw themselves as new celebrities, a phenomenon that foreshadowed the sensational interest in Arab reality television and in ordinary Arabs on satellite television. Lebanese television's crisis of legitimacy, then, refracted the broader controversy on cultural authority and the dimensions of modern television and modern audiences embedded in television protocols. None of these harbingers of change appeared suddenly; they took years to develop, but the first signs that the old audiences had a new hunger were clearly visible. Perhaps this understanding of the active role of the public, in addition to its language politics, comes closest to the notion of "prosumers" (creators of media content and meaning). The notion gives the audience an "achieved citizenship," as Peter Dahlgren has suggested in a different context.[146]

By exposing the decreasing relevance of old television politics, the audiences questioned television's social role and helped shape a set of new social expectations for it, prominently reflected in *Shabaka*'s coverage. The user-inspired expectations of trustworthy, duty-abiding, and attentive television challenged in discourse the old disengaged protocols of supplying sanitized information to a passive public. Ultimately, the more people ridiculed the television-audience relationship, the more they made the case for its relevance as a marker of modernity.

Here I showed why the audiences were interested in the shift toward a new television-audience relationship. In the next chapter, I describe why LBC's owners—the third side of the war triangle—were too.

4

LBC

An Illegitimate Militia Seeks Legitimacy in Participating Audiences and Accommodating Media

> If, by some miracle,
> you could wipe out all the dope from Lebanon,
> the Christian camp, for example,
> would not last 15 days.
>
> —Beirut diplomat

War Pressures on the Third Side of the War Triangle

Lebanese Forces: The Brigand and the Legal

In 1989, in cooperation with the US Drug Enforcement Administration (DEA), the Lebanese Forces (LF) destroyed its hashish fields in Lebanon to stop the trafficking of drugs to Detroit.[1] Although LF dragged its feet as much as it could, it must have also understood the significance of showing a spirit of cooperation. The DEA's agents received support during their deployment there, and collaboration from the men of Samir Geagea (LF's leader since the mid-1980s) helped them improve their effectiveness during the mission.[2] In the end, LF might have outdone itself; the DEA telegraphed to congratulate it on its "efforts in cracking down on drug trafficking."[3]

Such cooperation was surprising given that, only three years earlier, LF was implicated in the infamous USD$60 million "Teflon Don" hashish bust in the United States. None other than major Phalange leaders like Geagea were linked to the notorious Canadian mobster Vito Rizzuto, known as the "Teflon Don," in this deal to import twenty-four metric tons of hashish.[4] A number of Phalange leaders had been dealing in hashish and heroin with the Rizzutos or their competitors, the Cotronis, for fifteen years, funding significant military strengthening of the Phalange camp. American journalist Collin Knox was convinced that "you can't have power in the anarchy of Lebanon if you're not involved in drugs."[5] As one Beirut diplomat divulged to French journalist Rémi Favret, without drugs, the Christian camp would have lasted two weeks. When the drug crops arrived in the Lebanese coastal towns of Byblos and Jounieh, the source continued, Geagea's men would hide heroin inside tires sealed with tape and then row them out to yachts at sea where smugglers handed over suitcases stuffed with money.[6]

Although LF continued its interest in the drug trade throughout the 1980s, these two events point to a shift in the militia's involvement—from criminal enterprises like the drug trade to legitimate businesses like LBC. To understand why LF willingly destroyed drug fields after being dependent on them for years, it is necessary to understand the changing relationship between the militia and its constituent population. This chapter therefore begins with the story of the two LFs and how each related to its constituency. The first is the brigand LF from the early 1980s, which was heavily invested in profitable criminality, yet still enormously popular with its constituency. The second is the LF from the mid- and late 1980s, whose criminality cost it popular support and had to be relinquished in an attempt at an image makeover.

This game of survival led LF to replace its criminal enterprises with legitimate ones, including in the media business, which enabled it to sway public opinion. The militia created three signature media during the war: Radio Free Lebanon (est. 1978), the biweekly journal *al-Masira* (The Course, est. 1983),[7] and the television station LBC (est. 1985). Being launched before 1982—a watershed year for LF's attitude shift—Radio Free Lebanon was a child of a different era and therefore will not be the object of analysis here. In contrast, *Masira* and LBC exhibit commonalities in that they struggled with similar needs to attract audiences in the post-1982 environment.

Fictional and biographical genres made a unique contribution to articulating the relationship between LF's media and the public. The focus of this chapter—a fictional graphic novel titled "The Story of a Hero Called Charbel" (hereafter, "Charbel"), published by *Masira*, was no exception. It documented LF's new understanding of the role of journalism and its ethical struggle to accept the new relationship of an engaged media and a demanding audience that public commentary had vocalized for years (see chapter 3, this volume). I therefore delve into the graphic novel to demonstrate the shift in LF's cultural imaginary, the crucial role of language in reorganizing cultural hegemony, and the resistance to the dominant LF cultural norm industry from the earlier era. The last section examines the outcome of these changes reflected in LBC's news bulletin. But before we learn how the print medium depicted its relationship with the public, we need to understand the reasons behind LF's makeover.[8]

The Cash Is Rolling. Bachir Gemayel (1947–1982)—a son of Pierre Gemayel (1905–1984), longtime leader of the Maronite Christian Phalange Party—founded LF, the organization's militia wing, in August 1976.[9] After the war began in 1975, a new generation of Phalangists, including Bachir, had begun to accuse the older echelon of focusing on political solutions at the expense of military investment. Although LF had begun to gather broad support on that issue in the Christian camp, it had problems. It was an insurgent player not elected by the then-nonfunctional Lebanese democratic system. Unlike the elected government, which enjoyed legitimacy despite its weakness, sectarian militias like LF, also relatively weak, suffered from their illegitimacy.[10]

LF overcame these problems by turning to crime in its first six years. A variety of dirty deals—extortion, racketeering, abduction for ransom, piracy, and illegal taxation—generated nontaxed revenue and made LF solvent. Redistributing its largess enabled LF to gain popular support and address its problems of illegitimacy and relative weakness. The militia set up what political scientist Marie-Joëlle Zahar calls a "revolutionary" taxation system. The system involved extortion of wealthy businesses (about 20 percent of their income in the biggest cases, bringing in more than USD$500 million), protection rackets that preyed on individual households, and the creation of a finance-ministry type of structure called the

"National Treasury."[11] R. T. Naylor calls this system "likely the world's most complex and thorough system of parallel taxation."[12] By 1982 reports, LF's estimated annual income was between USD$75 million and USD$300 million.[13]

The most profitable arm in LF's parallel economy was drug trafficking.[14] Sharing the drug economy among militias inspired intergroup cooperation.[15] Drugs proved to be the fastest and cheapest means to buy weapons and cover the militias' bloated payrolls.[16] They cultivated hashish (known as "the petroleum of Lebanon"), cannabis, and poppies, either exporting them immediately or processing them into heroin and opium in local labs.[17] Since drug cultivation requires at least six months, stability was necessary to guarantee profits. All warring factions (even the Armenians), prominent politicians (including the Gemayel and Geagea clans), police chiefs, judges, and bankers, as well as large sectors of the local population, colluded in creating temporary stability. They cooperated in the production, processing, and transportation of drugs out of the country to US and Canadian markets, with Syria and Israel tacitly condoning the trade in exchange for an added tax. The Beqaa Valley, mostly run by Shi'ite families and the impoverished farmers working for them, was the central production hub.[18] After being moved across the country, the drugs were usually shipped out of ports on the Lebanese coast. According to Jonathan Marshall, most sects opened their own ports through which they conducted illegal business. The Fifth Basin—Lebanon's busiest and most profitable dock (in the port in Jounieh, north of Beirut)—was run by LF, which seized the port early in the war in 1976.[19] By Favret's report, LF was getting most of its revenue from drugs, "whether operating clandestine ports, getting paid off by some big traffickers, or just using drug money to build hotels or leaving it sitting in banks."[20] The drugs were exchanged for weapons like "American M16 rifles and ammunition stolen from an armory in Boston, as well as heavy machine guns, grenades, and C-4 plastic explosives,"[21] which reportedly brought in close to USD$4 billion between 1978 and 1986.[22] LF's involvement in the drug trade was so bold that, in 1980, even the Gemayel family was openly implicated. Bachir's cousin, Jean Michel Gemayel, was arrested in Italy for attempting to transport two pounds of heroin. Turning a deaf ear both to his protests that he was just an LF arms dealer and to the Lebanese embassy's plea for leniency, the Italians sentenced him to nine years in prison.[23]

Despite the wealth of evidence, LF denied its involvement in crime. When US reporter Barbara Newman visited the militia in 1981, she was smitten with Bachir's charisma and perhaps the potential of a romantic relationship. Those close to Bachir believed that he was flirting with her to get good publicity and increase the militia's international legitimacy. Entire incidents may have been conveniently narrated so that Newman would get a favorable opinion about how intolerant LF and Bachir were of any involvement with drugs. She tells of an incident when Bachir's men caught four smugglers from the Beqaa Valley trying to sell six pounds of heroin.[24] Newman was impressed with Bachir's determination to punish the guilty, even going against his father, who apparently insisted that one of the men, a supporter of his, be released.

The massive cash influx, especially in combination with LF's vehement denial of its illegal source, also helped the militia to increase its legitimacy by establishing "a front of respectability."[25] For example, LF gave generously to the civilians under its control, thus treating them "responsibly" by setting up subsidized services such as public transport, education (including summer camps for children), housing, medical care, social security for militia members and their families, and even garbage collection.[26] To ensure order, LF also created a police force, a judiciary, representative offices abroad, and its own banking system, which it called Prosperity Bank.[27]

The quasi-state that LF created secured the loyalty of a segment of the population, even as Bachir was eliminating the leaders of other Christian groups who rejected his authority. When Bachir ran for president in 1982, he marketed himself as Lebanon's solution to the civil war, starting a widespread "Bachir-mania." His support base included a great number of Christians as well as the nation of Israel, with whom LF had forged a friendly relationship. Even Ronald Reagan's administration backed him with funding and weapons. Bachir's supporters were enamored by his larger-than-life figure, often calling him endearingly by his first name or the abbreviated "Bash" ("chief"). At a young age he became for Lebanese

Christians (at least those unaligned with leftist groups) what Ronald Reagan would become for American conservatives by the late 1980s. The degree of legitimacy LF enjoyed in that initial period culminated in Bachir's election to the presidency on August 23, 1982.

Crime becomes Inconvenient. The economic success of LF was a mixed blessing, as Zahar has convincingly argued. It did not simply enrich the militia and help finance some of its constituency's needs; it also made the former vulnerable. The illegitimate source of LF's strength became a liability after 1982 because it exposed the militia to harsh judgment nationally and internationally.[28] With time, the unethical rationale behind the drug economy, for instance, became difficult to overlook. Pressures from LF's new international allies led to demands for greater accountability. The United States in particular was committed to new Reagan-era antidrug policies, which primarily targeted leftist regimes. Lebanon also ended up on that list.[29]

Internal Lebanese pressures were even greater. General Michel Aoun, who served as disputed acting prime minister of Lebanon between 1988 and 1990, was the most influential voice portraying LF as a gang of drug traffickers who were building a "heroin republic."[30] At a cost of more than 440 lives, 1,700 wounded, and 75,000 refugees, Aoun's drug war on LF in the end seriously damaged the militia's economic base.[31] Sixteen uninterrupted months of fighting paralyzed drug smuggling and brought hashish and opium farmers to bankruptcy.[32]

Back in 1982, Bachir's older brother Amine had assumed the presidency after Bachir's assassination. In 1984 Amine tried but failed to seize LF assets (particularly the customs at Barbara, the Fifth Basin) to fund the government under the slogan of "national unity." Four years later, though, Aoun started a mass blockade of the illegal ports, calling them "dens of terrorism and drug trafficking."[33] Calling LF a "mafia" may have contributed to exposing its illegal activities, but for many that was the frosting on the cake—LF had done little to seriously hide its crimes from the Lebanese population. As a result, many Christians immediately supported Aoun's effort to end crime, and his strategy worked. By 1990 LF was on the verge of collapse.

The civilian Christian population was also disillusioned with LF because of the militia's 1982 genocidal massacre of several thousand Palestinian civilians and Lebanese Shi'ites in the Sabra neighborhood and Shatila refugee camp. Facilitated (or endorsed) by the Israeli Defense Forces, the attack was a retaliation for Bachir's assassination, which had been wrongfully attributed to the Palestinians. The civilian population was appalled at its brutality, and LF's efforts to blame the incident on rogue members, such as Elie Hobeika's Young Men gang, accomplished little.

In addition, LF's financial success was in stark contrast to the worsening economic circumstances of ordinary Christians. The militia made little effort to hide its ill-gotten gains, and Christian resentment increased. The aspirations of the Lebanese middle class for a consumerist lifestyle also caused withdrawal of support.

A pro-Syrian Maronite assassinated Bachir just twenty-one days after he became president-elect, causing disillusionment among the majority of the Christian camp. While alive, Bachir was seen there as a ray of hope for building a safe and stable Lebanon. These hopes crumbled. Although the cult of Bachir grew steadily after his death, many realized that he was a one-man show. The structures he left behind could not carry the same load that he had.

The intramilitary struggle for power that started with his death added to the disillusionment. Bachir's named successor, his cousin Fadi Frem, took office a day before the assassination, but LF leaders immediately began to compete for his post. The result was four years of internal conflicts, changes in leadership, and open military fighting. In 1986 Geagea emerged as the victor, and the militia has been under his leadership since.[34]

In sum, LF's criminal activities provided it with gains in initial potency and legitimacy that led to increased scrutiny. This scrutiny cost LF its relationship with its constituency. The latter's anger resulted from LF's criminal activities, including the illegal taxes it levied on the constituency, and LF's massacre of civilians. The previous patrimonial ties with the population were over. Regarded as the representatives of the Christian contingent while the charismatic Bachir was still alive, LF was now seen as a group of warlords.[35] As a result, LF's recruitment efforts suffered a great deal.

LF Solutions. The militia's attempt to regain legitimacy came with wavering dedication to make amends and meticulously hide the activities it was unwilling to give up. Soon LF's commitment was put to the test. The road ahead involved supporting the war on drugs and volunteering to fight piracy, both of which were prior occupations.[36] Driven by popular resentment, in 1985 the militia stopped direct taxes of households and businesses.[37] In 1990 the Lebanese army took control of the enormously profitable maritime taxation, including the Fifth Basin, and a year later the army destroyed the last of LF's financial institutions.[38]

Other solutions, such as establishing legal enterprises, reflected the era's changing ethos. The decision to enter the legal economy led to LF's most successful domestic undertaking—LBC—with a USD$5 million annual advertising budget.[39] The launch of LBC was indeed initiated to bolster LF's image, although the idea behind an LF-owned television station had appeared while Bachir was still alive. He discarded plans for an LF station after a reportedly productive meeting with Télé Liban's employees and administration, apparently intending to work with that station after he took office.[40] Nevertheless, when LBC was launched in 1985, the conditions that affected it clearly stemmed from LF's blessing-and-curse predicament.

In 1982 LF was less than a decade old, but it was about to start feeling the burden of its dependence on crime. By 1989–90 it felt cornered if not defeated. The pressure of its black-market deals pushed it to embrace the 1989 peace agreement in Ta'if to end the civil war. According to Zahar, "although the provisions of the agreement were more detrimental to LF than the terms of earlier peace settlements which LF rejected on ideological grounds, this time the negative consequences of LF involvement in black-market activities were instrumental in the militia's decision to compromise."[41] After the war, with its military and financial infrastructure destroyed, LF reinvented itself as a legal political party.

Over those eight years, the militia made the hard decisions necessary to change its image from brigand to law-abiding player in the body politic. Part of its new image remained mere rhetoric, but its need to recover its dwindling support forced it toward legitimacy.

Masira: A Response to the Audiences' Response

While in the public imaginary militias controlled public debate and imposed their visions on a disempowered population, each militia in fact operated within its own volatile space and depended on a specific constituency. This dependence compelled LF to strive to convince its constituency that it was a protector, not a brigand. LF needed to demonstrate, or at least pretend convincingly, that it was closer and more responsive to the changing public and more accepting of its demand for greater influence.

That meant finding common ground with the public, which rested primarily on understanding its sense of citizenship. According to Canclini, global changes in urban coexistence and a new economic ability to enjoy life's pleasures have led to new modes of consumption and consequently to new forms of citizenship.[42] Today the public exercises citizenship in great part through its role as consumers; hence, identity, and therefore politics, are structured "less by the logic of the state than by that of markets."[43] Mass media is key in that process because it stimulates consumerism with promises of pleasure and a political truth to be interpreted as cultural truth.

In addition, one of the effects of globalization and neoliberal politics is the multiplying of unmet needs in many groups.[44] The Lebanese Civil War is a painful reminder of how profoundly the government can fail to meet those needs. The mass media are key in this too. They are not more responsive to the public than the government, but they "fascinate because they listen," which is why they have been crucial in the creation of a public sphere organized around audio and audiovisual communication technologies rather than exclusively around a physical, political public sphere grounded in rational deliberation.[45] In some cases, manifestations of uncivil society such as LF significantly benefit from the inability of a weak state to hold monopoly over the mass media and from a severed or strained connection between the state and the public. As Canclini comments, "hegemonic forces manage to position themselves in the strategic settings of the economy and politics, and in communications, precisely the medium in which societies are transformed in this second half of the twentieth century."[46]

LF positioned itself strategically within mass-mediated communication by launching the journal *Masira,* with the potential to affect specific sectors of Lebanese society in uncivil ways. But *Masira*'s subsequent development, as I will show, was also proof that LF unconsciously glanced beyond the limitations of a partisan player. It understood how it could meet, or appear to meet, the broader evolving public and its new demand for power harnessed in mass-mediated entertainment.

The Masira Makeover and the Search for a Closer Relationship. LF's desire to appear closer to the public and its parallel anxieties over its own survival are wonderfully captured in *Masira*'s publication history.[47] *Masira* was cofounded by a group of young LF members—Amjad Iskandar, Imad Moussa, Jean Feghali, and Elie Khayyat (nicknamed "Tareq")—eager to prove their value to the militia and its cause. Two of them had professional training. Iskandar had studied marketing and journalism, and twenty-one-year-old Moussa started his journalism career in-house. They launched the publication in 1983 to preserve the LF that Bachir had created eight years earlier and that was now facing disintegration. In the months following the Israeli siege of Beirut in June 1982, LF had become stronger than ever. In return for Israeli support for his presidency campaign, military help, and training, Bachir was expected to sign a peace treaty with Israel. After his assassination in September 1982, though, depression among the militia members became a serious problem. This was greatly aggravated by the fact that one of its branches had already committed the gruesome Sabra and Shatila massacre. Thus LF was faced with a fallout among members and nonmembers alike. To counter this, the journal tried to reinvigorate members' loyalty, enable them to reimagine the group without its fallen leader, and provide talking points with which to justify their continuing relevance to the public.

Early issues of *Masira* were meant only for internal use because their goal was to rally the troops. Being a *nashra dakhiliyya* (internal bulletin), or an unofficial publication, under the regulations of Lebanon's Ministry of Information was sufficient in the beginning. Bankrolled by LF, the journal cost nothing to read, and it quickly became popular among LF's members. At this stage, the creators took pains to present an inspirational look at the individual militia member's life. To extol LF's military might, the journal's pages were filled with pictures of soldiers during drill training, soldiers killed in combat (referred to as "martyrs"), and drawings of weapons. To imagine life after the slain leader, *Masira* ironically and cleverly inundated its pages with his presence. Each issue featured a different full body picture of Bachir. Facing the contents page from the inside of the front cover, he looked at the readers as if to reassure them that he approved. Excerpts of his speeches and photographs of him standing among LF soldiers, or rallying his audiences, often made their way into articles.

The articles complemented the images by reporting military events and strategy and condemning violence against LF's Christian constituency. They communicated LF's objectives with interviews, commentaries, reports from the battlefield, the resistance against Syria, and historical accounts of Christianity. As a biweekly, the early *Masira* had to eschew events of the moment, which the dailies and the broadcast bulletins had already covered. Instead, the journal presented historical background on these events and issues of import to LF's constituency. The journal occasionally published hateful content about the Maronites' professed archenemy, Lebanon's Druze sect. One such item compares a Druze combatant to an LF soldier. The disheveled Druze is clothed in rural attire. Running barefoot and flailing his arms madly, he appears to be shouting angrily. By contrast, the LF soldier is dressed in modern camouflage fatigues. Kneeling in front of an altar, his palms touching in a gesture of prayer, he exudes serenity and loyalty to what is meant to be seen as a "rational" cause. The caption under the Druze's picture reads *al-qatil* (the killer) and under the LF soldier's picture, *al-muqatil* (the defender).[48]

LF's military logo (a delta triangle inside a circle) displayed on the front cover also buttressed the militia's sense of identity. In addition to symbolizing the holy trinity, the Greek letter delta stood for its predecessor—the Phoenician letter *dalet*. Because the rest of the cover had no images and little text, the logo suggested the Maronites' self-proclaimed specialness as descendants of the Phoenicians. This projected a fierce will to survive.

By early 1984, as more signs of LF's compromised position were visible, *Masira* had to reconsider its target readership. The Mountain War

(1983–84) ended with LF's defeat and its expulsion from traditionally Christian areas southeast of the capital. An internal struggle for power began, while LF's biggest supporter—the Lebanese Army—collapsed after the defection of Muslim units. The early *Masira*'s focus on rank-and-file LF members may have provided the proper framework for imagining a post-Bachir LF, but it had failed to attract a larger Christian readership. LF needed to recapture the minds and hearts of this crucial constituency, which was replacing its support with disillusionment.

Pressures against LF's illegal enterprises were mounting as well. Since LF's attempts to create a new image included generating legal revenue, *Masira* could no longer afford to funnel ill-gotten money from LF. It had to wean itself from LF's bankroll and become independently profitable from sales and advertisements. The journal began to target readers beyond LF members and their families, including those who might not be sympathizers. This required a serious makeover.[49]

Masira was LF's first journal, but it was not a first publication for the Maronite community. Its mother organization, the *Kata'ib* (Phalanges), had launched a newspaper, *al-'Amal*, in 1939. Although it experienced a successful run throughout the 1970s and 1980s, it could not compete against the revamped *Masira* among LF members and sympathizers. After 1985, when *Masira* broached the open market, it encountered a fiercely competitive arena dominated by established and well-financed periodicals, such as *al-Nahar al-'Arabi wa-al-Duali* (a sister publication of *Nahar*), whose high-quality production rivaled its broad distribution. *Masira*, then, needed more and better-trained people to staff its new social, political, sports, and culture departments. It also, for the first time, hired an editor-in-chief.[50] Despite the fact that readers now had to pay for it, the journal anticipated a wider readership and increased production. Now a weekly, it was available in bookstands and stores in many areas across the country.

Masira also changed its content and design to project a less partisan tone. Its content became more entertainment-centered. The military content shrank with each issue as its journalists changed their focus to cultural articles, movie reviews, international public figures, celebrities, crossword puzzles, and advertisements. Topics such as economics, Arab culture, and leisure mingled with international politics and American thrillers. The journal also began to interview people beyond its own political spectrum, such as members of Hezbollah and Palestinian fighters. Bachir's approving picture gave way to full-page ads of alcohol and jewelry. Back-cover ads of LF's new television station, LBC, replaced anti-Druze cartoons. In turn LBC began broadcasting commercials for *Masira*.[51] Collaboration between *Masira* and LBC occurred in other ways too, including sharing of staff. For example, in 1986 *Masira*'s cofounder Moussa began working simultaneously for LBC. Such collaboration assured similarities in outlook and audience engagement.

A bigger staff and a competitive spirit produced a better-designed journal. Before the makeover—between 1983 and 1985—its identically designed front covers were color-coded, which allowed an issue to be identified by its color, for example, *al-Masira al-Hamra* (the red *Masira*). That changed too after the makeover. The front cover was done in various engaging designs, while the earlier sepia-tinted pages were replaced with ones featuring vibrant colors printed on high-quality glossy paper, with proper attention given to fonts and layout.

LF's blessing-and-curse predicament and the need to develop a closer relationship with the public drove changes in the politics and character of media systems like *Masira*. Competing necessities challenged the journal's legitimacy and prompted a self-critical view of its role, resulting in a shift from political news organ to glossy lifestyle magazine. LF was learning to use legitimate ventures to ensure its survival.

"The Story of a Hero Called Charbel" and the Mutualistic Relationship It Embodies. Several months before the overhaul, the journal began featuring a graphic novel called "The Story of a Hero Called Charbel." The thirteen-part serial, which spanned seven months between April and November 1984, describes the life of an ordinary young man, Charbel, from the moment he decides to become an LF member through his service to the militia for several years. The story also weaves in the commemoration of LF's history and the slain leader Bachir.

This graphic novel is significant because of how it differs from the tone of the early *Masira* in a way that foreshadows the later publication and LBC. In parallel to the developments in novels and memoirs, "Charbel" depicts a media interested in public opinion in contrast to the national media's lack of interest. It also depicts a media-public relationship of a deeply personal nature. Such a portrayal mirrored popular expectations for a more responsive media, one whose legitimacy is based on more than providing information. Furthermore, "Charbel" reflects how audiences can inspire changes in media values within a new power differential. It is the clearest, and perhaps only, early example of how the journal and LF negotiated the changing relationship between media and public.

The character of Charbel illustrates much of this coevolution or mutualistic relationship. He embodies the changing media. Charbel is entrusted with recruiting new LF prospects and sympathizers and therefore with helping readers to digest LF's new image. He also embodies the changing audiences whose ability to use the media for political purposes was emerging. Readers identified with him. They felt a sense of power, genuine or not, over the narrative. Therefore, as an avatar, Charbel's character was a site where the media and the audiences met—a site of connection, or *mahattat ittisal*, as Barakat described the talk show host in *The Stone of Laughter.*

The cocreators of "Charbel" embody the mutualistic relationship. Amjad Iskandar, who wrote the text, was an insider—one of the cofounders and the de facto editor-in-chief. His friend C. N.,[52] the artist, was an outsider—a medical student and an amateur artist in his early twenties who in 1983 began frequenting the journal's headquarters and occasionally irritating the contributors with the sketches he made of them during his visits. Inspired by the popularity of Batman comics with Lebanese audiences, C. N. persuaded Iskandar to collaborate on a comic strip about an LF hero. That was C. N.'s first contribution as an advocate from outside the medium on behalf of the public.

Initially, no one expected this marriage of insider institutional power and outsider advocacy to amount to much. That's why Iskandar and C. N. decided on the content of the next installment spontaneously, rather than envisioning a series that would grow to thirteen segments. However, readers' reactions were overwhelmingly positive, far more so than toward coverage of military maneuvers or articles on the history of the church. To generate installments, Iskandar drew on his personal experience of visiting LF fighters on the front. He listened to their stories and asked questions, then with C. N. modified the answers and used them in "Charbel." In order to protect their authors' safety, *Masira* did not allow them to sign their work, so no one knew that Iskandar and C. N. were creating the "Charbel" narrative.[53] According to Iskandar, the issue that came out a few weeks after an impromptu visit to the front impressed LF members with how closely it reflected their life. We can think of these LF fighters as cocreators in a less technical sense. In fact, Iskandar seems to have used their input to gauge the novel's shape and tone. We can judge the mutual relationship more confidently because of this spontaneous nature of the novel's creation.

Merely by its launching, the early *Masira* appeared more responsive, albeit to a narrow Maronite public whose war trauma it passionately depicted. It was still true, though, that the journal didn't truly cater to this public's interests because it remained muzzled by LF's partisan agenda (even though the Lebanese press enjoyed greater freedom than the broadcast media to discuss war-related subjects). Accordingly, *Masira* minimized the suffering of the other communities, at times even vilifying some of them. It could afford to disregard the broader public's needs, partly because it did not depend economically on its readers. But when matters worsened, the overhauled *Masira* became more responsive to a broader public of readers who were driven much more by entertainment than ideology. In this context, "Charbel" is very valuable as it illustrates how Lebanese society's thinking about the media-audience relationship transformed and how the media began reflecting public tastes in its messages.

Three questions frame the discussion below to show how the graphic novel and therefore the journal as a whole were part of the transformation of the media-audience relationship: (1) How do generic and narrative conventions embody the changing relationship between LF and the Lebanese public (homologously, between *Masira* and its actual and prospective readers)? (2) How does "Charbel" reflect LF's anxieties and conflicted commitment to the transformation of the media-audience relationship? and (3) How does the novel attest to LF's eventual acceptance of the new "engaged media/demanding audience" dynamic? The answers to these questions will allow us to see how, slowly but steadily, LF was creating media that valued audiences in a new way and was choosing to fulfill some of their preferences and cater to their cultural tastes.

Generic Conventions. The sequential visual-verbal art form we call the graphic novel spans fictional and nonfictional genres. It is a global medium with roots in American satire and political cartoons, European comic albums, and Japanese manga.[54] Although initially geared toward young readers, graphic novels now appeal to diverse audiences. In the 1970s and 1980s the genre witnessed a period of fast growth and is now part of mainstream culture. In the Arab world comic strips are also widely popular and have a diverse readership. They began to flourish there in the 1970s, paralleling the increase in the genre's global popularity and aided by the enrichment of Arab economies from oil.[55] Arab comics are influenced not only by US and European strips but also by traditional Arabic forms such as the popular, humorous shadow plays (two-dimensional shadows of puppets moving behind a screen) as well as medieval illustrated ("imaged") narratives such as *Kalila wa Dimna* or *Maqamat*.[56] Arab comics are closer to European comics, which appeal to both mass and elite adult audiences and have refined aesthetic values, rather than aligning with US notions of high and low culture that regard comics as an inferior genre (at least before Art Spiegelman's *Maus*).[57] Their authors—among the most respected fiction writers, artists, or editorial cartoonists in the Arab world—consider these comics a serious political and cultural genre with themes ranging from secular to Islamist.[58]

Traditionally the comics genre has been a format for presenting the hero or heroine, the individual who has extraordinary skills to fight for justice, such as Superman, Wonder Woman, Tintin, Asterix, Ultraman, Astro Boy, and the Shojo superheroines. Over the years, the genre's heroes and heroines acquired a more literary tone in the United States and have begun dealing with socially meaningful, even heavy, topics such as drug addiction, racism, and inner-city youth. In addition to presenting fictional heroes, the genre has also become known for its use in presenting historical personalities as heroes, mostly through their life stories. Will Eisner, an innovator and a theoretician of the genre whose 1978 multiple-story *A Contract with God and Other Tenement Stories* is framed biographically,[59] wrote that the comic strip was very well suited for creating the intimate atmosphere of a personal story and the dreamlike mood of memory. In this, the genre closely resembles television and film.

Heroic characters of political leaders have been developed in biographical Arab comics too. The 1973 Egyptian graphic novel "Jamal Abd al-Nasir" tells the story of a close relationship between Egypt's famous president and his nation.[60] Another history-based narrative, the Iraqi graphic novel "Al-Ayyam al-Tawila" ("The Long Days"), about the young Saddam Hussein's failed attempt on Prime Minister Qasim's life, is an adventure narrative of a solitary hero whose legitimacy comes from personal character rather than popular support.[61]

Since an overwhelming majority of early American graphic novelists and comic strip creators were Jewish, often first-generation Americans, their work portrayed the history of the American Jewish community.[62] This format, then, has been widely used by authors for whom questions of communal identification are important. In Arabic comic strips, communal identity has been explored throughout the Arab region, making the genre perhaps "the most pan-Arab of all modern forms of cultural expression," although less appealing to minority cultures.[63] "Charbel" is one example to the contrary in that it portrays the history of Maronite Christians and the militia that considered itself their protectors.

By several reports, "Charbel" attracted many new readers. The reason, I believe, is the conventions of the comics genre that "Charbel" employed. Well adapted to readers' tastes for entertainment and play, these conventions spoke to an evolving public that demanded power through entertainment. The format of "Charbel" became a harbinger of the journal's upcoming entertainment-infused content and increasingly reader-oriented design. A bridge between the old and the new *Masira*, the graphic novel stood out against the somber tone and military pathos of the surrounding contents, foreshadowing the journal's new and broader cultural message.

To the chagrin of parents and teachers, the novel was irresistible to the teen and preteen siblings of LF members and their friends,[64] since it translated militia life into a captivating spy log and adventure story. Spanning over one-quarter of the novel, the spy adventure calls attention to its key role. The borderless first panel of each episode anchors Charbel as a

6. Opening panel, Charbel at the watch post. "The Story of a Hero Called Charbel," *Masira*, issue 36, July 31, 1984.

lookout who stares intently at the empty valley and mountain ridge on the other side, surveilling LF's Syrian enemy (see Illustration 6).

But most importantly, "Charbel" is a story within a story, and therefore it requires an internal audience. During a home visit from the front, Charbel gathers children around him when a raid forces his building's tenants into the bomb shelter. He dazzles them with stories of his war adventures, as his audience validates the perception that LF members lead attractive, adventurous lives. Full of gadgets, night incursions, a debauched enemy, and swift victory, Charbel's story fascinates even the girls, painting an Ali Baba–like kismet full of abundance and ordeals. A tale of male camaraderie, effortless bravery, and a taste of technology, the novel makes the children around Charbel impatient for the day when they too will be part of LF. More than a tool to validate LF's new image, though, the fictional audience dictates the story. Placing it within the adventure/spy comics genre reflects the contemporary "youthquake" (a culture shift influenced by young people). The fictional audience, then, is not passive but rather important to the conveyance of the meaning. This indicates that the novel has given readers power to change the journal's output.

LF and Sexualized Masculinity. If the adventure/spy comics genre is one way to attract broader readership, then sexualizing the male body is another. Most comic strips exhibit homoerotic themes and characters with

7. Street warfare, LF militiamen defend the neighborhood. "The Story of a Hero Called Charbel," *Masira*, issue 29, April 13, 1984.

a "highly eroticized physical presence."[65] Two examples from "Charbel" show the presence of such themes and the force with which this generic feature contributes to the negotiation of the media-audience relationship—the LF fighter's homoerotic body and his phallic gun.

"A handful of our defenders fought ferociously like heroes," the caption from the panel in Illustration 7 reads. It is payback time for terrorizing the quarter's dwellers and shelling their family shops. The defenders are silent, but their biceps, throbbing under tight, sexy T-shirts, promise to protect the neighborhood. Clenching their double-barreled shotguns, the men fire in sync. Blam-blam-blam! The slugs pierce both attackers, leaving puffy clouds in their trajectory. This panel from "Charbel"'s second installment creates a fantasy of sexualized masculinity. One defender fights from the threshold of a half-opened storefront, reassuring readers that LF will do anything to protect its constituency, but also seducing them with his tense posture, fitted jeans, and slender, athletic body. The panel's point of view is the gaze of another fighter over his gun, seemingly positioned around the groin area, firing in an orgasmic outburst to sully the enemy and establish the erotic frame of the panel. Similarly, a phallic gun is depicted in the opening, borderless panels of almost all installments (see Illustration 6). Controlled by the young Charbel and pointed at an invisible enemy, the gun spews a sense of physical threat and erotic fantasy over the whole series.

At the heart of youth popular culture, comics formulate new trends and reflect changing ideologies and popular tastes. Employing entertainment genres with homoerotic subtexts of male bodies and phallic weaponry enabled LF to play with its changing identity and to test its attractiveness and viability.

In addition to seductive visions of masculinity if not outright homoerotic voyeurism, "Charbel" also used heterosexual encounters to suggest what life as an LF member could be. Close encounters with women liberated from watchful parental eyes, and the possibility of such encounters resulting in sexual relations, as well as hints of military life as leisure, were common themes. LF's members often portrayed platonic real-life encounters with women as romantic interactions. The ambiguity of such gendered encounters recalls how traditional boundaries of propriety are transgressed within marked military spaces, including the front lines, headquarters, training camps, watch posts, and college campuses.

"Charbel"'s newly painted image of LF fighters as seductive heroes and its erotic iconography dislodged the earlier brigand image and captured the imaginations of youth and young adult readers. By speaking directly to their desires for leisure, romance, and adventure, these images translated the militaristic view into experiences enticing to nonmilitants. This allowed LF to formulate a new vision of its relationship with *Masira* readers, one in which the readers developed respect for the media and the media listened to the public.

Charbel as an Urban Qabaday. The generic conventions of spy/adventure stories allowed for play with sexuality. This combination attracted new readers and, in the process, gave them a sense of empowerment. Another way "Charbel" empowered readers was to pit LF's leader and protocols against the challenge of the lower-class Charbel. Thus, the honoring of public disapproval of LF's brigand behavior brought the media and the audience closer.

In the public eye, the civil war is blamed (at least domestically) either on sectarianism that rose to the level of violence or on the greed and brutality of the militias.[66] In either case, class contestation played an undeniable role. According to historian Ussama Makdisi, militia politics were as much about sectarian strife as they were an uprising against Lebanon's elite class.[67] Elites had placidly sliced Lebanon along sectarian lines to spoon off the richest parts. Militia elements violently contested this disenfranchisement of the common people by attacking elites, but more often they directed their fire against the militias of other sects.[68] In addition, between 1970 and 1975 the elite class used state forces to brutally crush strikes for higher wages, decreasing ten-hour workdays, and protection against monopolies, as well as demonstrations aimed at toppling the sectarian elites.[69]

These kinds of contests reverberate in "Charbel." In the fourth and sixth installments, he is called *qabaday*—a lower-class tough guy with street clout who both helps and opposes the elites.[70] According to sociologist Michael Johnson, the urban *qabaday* is a moral leader, "a man of the people, a helper of the weak and poor, a protector of the quarter or neighborhood, and a communal and confessional champion."[71] Ordinary people were ambivalent about the *qabaday.* They admired him for his code of honor, masculine values, and ties to the street, but they resented his bullying. Many considered him a thug.[72] Political leaders and clergy were also ambivalent about the *qabaday.* On the one hand, *qabadays* were valuable to traditional *za'ims* (political-sectarian leaders who provided important services to their constituencies in exchange for votes and loyalty). *Za'ims* used *qabadays* as "recruiters and enforcers of that part of the *za'im*'s organization composed of low-status, poor, and politically weak clients."[73] The *qabaday* was therefore "a mediator between clients and *za'im*, a settler of disputes, and a protector of people and property."[74] On the other hand, *za'ims* felt that *qabadays* threatened their leadership. *Za'ims* had no control over *qabadays* who had become popular militia leaders. For example, although the traditional *za'im* Saeb Salam—a carnation-wearing six-time prime minister—and the *qabaday* militia leader Ibrahim Qulaylat catered to the same Sunni constituency, Salam had no power over Qulaylat, who in 1958 had fought as a partisan of Salam. In fact, Qulaylat apparently opposed Salam's agenda in the fight against the Phalangists in downtown Beirut.[75] Qulaylat and other *qabadays* such as the popular Faruq al-Muqaddam from Tripoli presented a powerful challenge to professional politicians such as the *za'ims*.

As an urban *qabaday*, Charbel is a protector of the neighborhood and his community: he fights in the Mountain War, helps victims rebuild their villages after attacks, masterminds spy missions against the Syrians, and so on. He is also a recruiter for LF, unofficially as a teller of LF spy stories to children, and officially as a teacher to recruits about slain leader Bachir's life and mission. Yet when Charbel becomes more powerful than the *za'im*, he begins to challenge the authority of Bachir himself—the upper-class *za'im* of the Maronite community. Bachir himself had challenged the authority of traditional Maronite *za'ims*, including his father, but that challenge was contained within the boundaries of his privileged class. Charbel's challenge to Bachir's leadership and status, however, disregarded class boundaries.

Hero and Superhero. According to graphic design scholar Zeina Maasri, after 1982, when the militias felt secure, they toned down the rhetoric of their political posters. They moved from inflammatory prints that insulted opposing factions to portraits of their leaders (a still vibrant tradition in Lebanon). Charismatic leadership thus became a cornerstone of militia politics, rhetoric, culture, and practice, and the image of the *za'im* offered the needed charisma. This was most pronounced in the Christian sector, where the cult of Bachir was booming. LF started commemorating his birthday together with key events and battles. Similarly, in the graphic novel Bachir is depicted as an infallible, sacred, and untouchable superhero, whose life story is a fundamental part of LF's image. Many of the events in the novel include his actions and words, his inspirational floating bust, his mini-biography, and other characters' reminiscences about him. The novel takes great pains to protect Bachir's status as the eternal leader and an unchallenged site for constructing identity. For example, Fadi Frem, who took over LF's leadership after Bachir, is intentionally suppressed. Since Frem's face is meticulously drawn to achieve good likeness, it is inconceivable that he would not be recognized. This conflicts with the fact that he is never named. Nameless, he cannot be recalled unless one uses the term "leader."[76] Unfortunately for Frem, any reference to a leader is inevitably redirected to

Bachir, who in this way cannibalizes Frem, thus liquidating any threat to his own leadership position.

Given these efforts to neutralize potential threats to Bachir's reputation, the challenge that Charbel poses is astonishing. In this battle of heroes, neither Bachir nor Charbel gives in easily. Each intrudes on the other's space, tries to wrest control of the narrative, and seeks to win the audience. The superhero invades Charbel's space because some of the events in Charbel's story are clearly narrated to invoke Bachir's eternal presence. But Charbel's story interrupts Bachir's too. While at a 1979 political rally, Charbel and his friends interrupt Bachir's commemorative speech with character introductions. In a later panel, they challenge Bachir's authority again when they start a conversation about joining LF in the middle of his speech, perhaps equally signifying that it has inspired them and that it is not important to pay attention to it. Despite Bachir's random appearances throughout the novel, his personal story seems banished outside the main frame. Being added as an afterthought in the last fascicle makes it appear artificial and calls into question the ultimate superiority/control of the historical Bachir. Besides, Charbel is the one who relates Bachir's mini-biography, which is a final testament to the former's greater power and even subjugation of Bachir. As the *rawi* (reciter), Charbel controls the narrative and can tell Bachir's story as he wishes, change it, appropriate it, and decide where and how to use it. The title "The Story of a Hero Called Charbel" frames the novel as a narrative of the fictional LF rank-and-file member Charbel, with no mention of Bachir's story. Such omission captures the attention of a readership used to framing stories with a Bachir flavor. The word "called" implies that Charbel is just one of many such heroes, challenging Bachir's status as the only hero (clearly intended by most LF literature).

If Bachir's story reflects the cult of the *za'im*, which caters to a tradition-bound, elite-ruled public sphere, Charbel's story reflects the daily life of the normal person, the domestic spaces which that person occupies, and his or her interactions with other regular people. In other words, it reflects a new public that is less official and more diverse. The lower-class *qabaday*'s challenge to the elite *za'im* alters the power relations between the two. It also acknowledges or at least indexes readers' concerns about

LF's brigand image, in the process making it easier to overcome such concerns. The graphic novel, therefore, challenged traditions in sectarian politics. Its portrayal of the *qabaday* and his challenge to elitism and the status of the slain leader reflected a debate over unrepresentative politics.

Communal Narrative and Myth-Making. Such a challenge, however, was done quite carefully because Bachir is not just a historical character in the novel but also a site for constructing the collective identity of LF and the Maronite community. His story represents that community. Education scholar Nemer Frayha confirms that "a biographical approach has been used in recording Lebanese history." He observes that presenting historical events as illustrations of the leader's role and biography is a format used to teach history.[77]

In a sense, the tensions between Bachir and Charbel are also tensions between communal narrative and personal story.[78] In "Charbel" as well as in other graphic novels, a contradiction exists between portraying the group (here the political-religious minority) and creating the intimate atmosphere of the personal life story.[79] As I will show, whereas "Charbel"'s communal history misleads the public, its personal story more accurately displays the struggles and desires of the people to be free from the dictates of communal history's sanctioned interpretation. This implies that "Charbel" helped to increase the visibility of the public as well as to diminish the media's gatekeeping.

Consuming a Troubling Record. The main purpose of Bachir's communal narrative was to transform LF's troubling record into a positive story that the Maronite community would buy, peddling in this way a partisan ethics of historical remembrance. "Charbel" is a commemorative microhistory. Microhistory—the history of a group—is a relativist accounting of a group's historical symbols. "Charbel"'s first installment, which appeared on April 13, 1984, and was mistakenly labeled as second fascicle, commemorated the ninth anniversary of the beginning of the civil war—a cornerstone in Maronite microhistory. The tenth installment, which portrayed Bachir's last speech and the fallout of his assassination, appeared on September 14, 1984, to coincide with the assassination's second commemoration.[80] The last fascicle appeared on November 15, 1984, for Lebanon's Independence Day on November 22.[81] These events form a relativist account because some of them, such as Bachir's last speech, are meaningful only to the in-group. Microhistories also build group identity by educating new members about communal protocols. According to Lebanese intellectual Ahmad Beydoun, by the mid-1980s, the Lebanese focused on local or sectarian microhistories, most likely when all warring factions needed to replenish their ranks.[82] Under these circumstances, "Charbel" played an important role in recruiting new members and educating them about protocols.

Microhistories were not simply sites for preserving and consuming the history of the group but also a format for socializing the group into communal mythologies. For instance, in the Initiatives of Change brochure, "Breaking the Chain of Hate: Visit to the U.K. of Lebanese Former Militiamen, April 19–25," Chehab, the notary public of the Ras Beirut neighborhood, shares: "When we were teenagers, we Muslims were told that the Christians intended to slaughter us, throw us into the sea, and found a Christian state similar to Israel and allied with [it], to spearhead the war against the Arabs and Muslims. Those ideas mobilized us to fight against the Christians. But I discovered later that the Christian youth were told that the Muslims wanted to establish a Muslim state, oust all the Christians, and join the Arab countries in their fight against Israel. Hence, neither of the two versions of the 'conspiracy' were true."[83] Microhistory's mythologies made their way into the loosely regulated schools, especially in Lebanese history, with each school promoting the vision of history privileged by the sect that had established the school.[84] In 1980 Nakhle Wehbe and Adnan al-Amine found that history textbooks from public, Christian, and Muslim schools differed significantly in defining concepts like independence, hero, enemy, and so on.[85]

Microhistory's promotion of communal identity and loyalty allowed mythologies to be consumed more easily. In particular, "Charbel" peddled a vision of the militia as a heroic protector of a victimized Maronite community, which had given up its traditional pacifist thinking only after multiple attacks from outsiders. The graphic novel is based on a conventional triangle of stereotypes—heroes, victims, and villains. The sexualized masculinity panel from the novel described above depicts an urban battle of good versus evil with clear winners and losers. Its whole installment, which deals with the clash between LF militiamen and Palestinian commandos that ignited the sixteen-year-long war, is an obvious example. The panel places all three LF defenders in the foreground. Their everyday clothes (jeans, T-shirts, dress shoes) invite readers to identify with them. Closely cropped hair and clean-shaven faces show that they have nothing to hide. Their double-barreled shotguns suggest that they didn't expect the attack and grabbed the first guns lying around; they are occasional fighters, minutemen, not trained militants with automatic weapons. Despite their unwillingness to start wars, their steady stand, confident grip on the guns, and placid facial expressions speak of their commitment to finish those wars and protect the neighborhood. They kneel, take aim, and fire, prevailing over the enemy with their superior urban warfare strategies.

In contrast, the Palestinian commandos look threatening in their combat fatigues and heavy boots. Their automatic machine guns, grenades dangling from their waists, and vests of dynamite sticks display their aggressive intentions and identify them as willing militants who have had the time to dress and train for an all-out war. Their kufiyahs (checkered Palestinian headscarves worn by men) hide their faces, making the commandos indistinguishable from each other. In addition to these accoutrements, the Palestinians' movements and body postures label them as pathetic. They quiver, shake, bend, fall, and sprawl. In the end, they die, rightfully punished for the attack they have presumably initiated. Before falling over dead, one of the attackers drops his machine gun. His fingers go out, pushing against the concrete to protect his skull. The second attacker, shot and dying, loses his balance. His legs bend, and the grenades attached to his belt quiver below a vest of dynamite sticks. The muzzle of his AK-47 ogles the sky. The illustrator relegates the commandos to the middle of the street in the background, which offers them—the enemy—no protection.

The events in this panel and many others are mythologies of microhistory. They are carefully crafted to rationalize LF's participation in the war—an unjust and unexpected attack by an evil enemy that forces the community to exchange its peaceful disposition for a defensive stand. As one of the captions reads, the attack is "a new stage in thinking and logic and it is a fundamental [framework] for our future actions."[86] Here

"Charbel" lionizes LF members, although as I described earlier, the militia's actual record is genocidal, criminal, and selfish. The graphic novel used the spy/adventure and other generic conventions to convince its readers that they wielded increased influence over the journal's output. At the same time, the conventions of communal microhistory, along with the mythologies created by microhistory, managed to safely expunge LF's record even as they invoked it (of course, after multiple redactions).[87]

Transgression in the Personal Story. Simultaneously, however, "Charbel" challenged its own success at downplaying LF's wrongdoing. While LF's mythologies of microhistory rewrote the militia's troubling record, Charbel's personal story confronted this myth-making. Take for instance the most engaging and piquant part of the graphic novel—the fictional spy mission that Charbel narrates to his siblings and their friends in the bomb shelter. Up on the mountain, Charbel and seven other LF members sneak in and kill a small post of enemy troops. This mission challenges the "new stage in thinking and logic" because it is prompted by a combination of bravado and boredom. The fighters' desire to end their idleness and raise morale on the front moves them to action. Since multiple panels depict this attack as unprovoked—making clear that LF's actions are not retaliatory—Charbel's personal story unequivocally depicts LF as the aggressor and exposes the false message of LF's microhistory.[88]

The intimate settings in which this story is told to its bomb shelter audience is as significant as the plotline. Among family and neighbors, Charbel is not as much an LF member as one of the afflicted citizens. He runs from his family home to the shelter at a moment's notice together with everyone else. Impotent to protect anyone (contrast this with his phallic gun in most of the opening panels), he waits out the raid listening to the radio and his neighbors and telling stories. Here he witnesses the experiences of the Lebanese people. They resent the war but instead of looking for someone to blame, they search for someone to bear witness to their trauma. Charbel the aggressor has become Charbel the witness. As this witness struggles to free himself from the communal history and publicize the war trauma, he makes visible the public of which he is a part. Communal history (the narrative), LF (the group), and *Masira* (the medium) stand challenged by the personal story (the counternarrative),

Charbel (the individual), and Charbel (the public). No doubt the creators included Charbel's witnessing to elicit sympathy for LF's "mission" to protect its constituency. However, Charbel's role also suggests a budding interest in the welfare of the Lebanese public or at least an attempt to give the impression of such interest.

Including a marketplace of recruitment prospects (the children in the shelter) within the narrative of spy comics is likely to make the reading audience more willing to redefine LF's troubling record as a heroic mission. It demonstrates the lengths to which the media (*Masira* and print periodicals, backed by LF) are willing to go to attract that audience (adopt new entertainment genres, depict a strong challenger to LF's iconic slain leader, and transgress the communal protocols of microhistory). What does this willingness ultimately tell us together with "Charbel"'s sophisticated use of the generic and narrative conventions of heroes and superheroes, portrayals of sexualized masculinity, the clash between the traditional *za'im* and the urban *qabaday*, and the use of communal narratives in myth-making? I believe they all demonstrate the novel's vision of a modern medium and a modern public. And I believe it is the same vision we find in LBC just a few months later. This vision links LF's search for a closer relationship with its constituency and the broader public to the new budding roles of participating audiences and accommodating media. *Masira* is unique because it provides us with important evidence not simply about the shifting roles of the audiences and media in broad terms but also specifically about the new role of television.

Legitimacy and Hegemonic Order

Participating Audiences and Accommodating Media

The new functions of participating audiences were defined through three important roles within *Masira*'s vision. First, audiences were active agents who could transform their relationship with the media into a more intimate, personal bond; such a bond is the hallmark of television. They also demanded that modern media should be attentive and coddle the public. And third, audiences wielded the power to influence media politics through entertainment, again with entertainment as a feature through which television tends to exceed other media such as print. Inspiring the media to take entertainment within politics more seriously helped broaden the space for public discourse and increase the access of a previously invisible, unorganized public, or a social nonmovement, to the discussion of relevant issues. The audiences now more easily contested the production of public consciousness in the media in a sphere that was both attractive and comfortable to use.

Despite their impressive new agency, the audiences were limited in their ability to inspire a more socially conscious position. For example, they were unable to spark a truthful conversation about civilian victimization on the pages of *Masira* (outside an idealized Maronite plight), because LF, a perpetrator of this victimization, stood to lose face from it. Instead, *Masira* and "Charbel" emphasized the public's desires for change in the media-audience power differential (and, as I will show in the next two chapters, the meta-discourse on language and gender), rather than in matters of truth, balance, or clearing the fog of war.

The modern forms of media were defined through three main characteristics too. First, they needed to satisfy popular and mass cultural desire. That's why *Masira* explained its relevance as a champion of such desire (especially that of nonelites). Second, and most importantly for my thesis, mass cultural desire was satisfied above all through television and other forms of audiovisual media. That is why the graphic novel frequently portrays lecterns, podiums, and microphones in an effort to resuscitate the atmosphere and enthusiasm that Bachir's speeches inspired. The novel does not depict television cameras and crews. However, 40 percent of the panels that portray Bachir present him in mediated venues—audio or video recorded speeches; widely known shots of his pictures, often popularized through other mediated contexts such as posters, newspapers, and journals; or depicting actual angles from which he was filmed. One explanation for this is that the artist C. N. wanted to achieve naturalistic likenesses of his subject. The most widely known photos of Bachir would have been the most able to further this goal. The panels therefore adopt the viewpoints of the cameras. Since the novel's creators could have depicted him in imagined postures, the mimicry suggests that they saw audiovisual media as a primary means for driving audience interest. Therefore, the media's own understanding of its nature and role reflected the importance of audiovisual communications within the scope of consumer-citizenship. That is why *Masira* is so relevant to the exploration of television in this study, not just in terms of media in general.

Third, the modern media spoke a language closer to the people. "Charbel" uses *'ammiyya* almost exclusively. According to Allen Douglas and Fedwa Malti-Douglas, Arab comic strips, like most cartoons and animation, are traditionally written in *Fusha*.[89] Since the majority of Arab comics are created for children and intended for wider regional distribution, using *Fusha* serves a pedagogic function and a mass-marketing strategy.[90] Adopting the vernacular in "Charbel" is even more poignant, considering that the rest of *Masira* was published in *Fusha*,[91] and therefore cannot be simply explained by an assumed Maronite preference for the vernacular. In only a few instances does the journal employ phrases from the Lebanese vernacular (*lughat al-hayat*), mostly as a way of emphasizing the uniqueness of Lebanese identity and how it should be distinguished from other Arab (Muslim-majority) countries.[92] Rooting "Charbel" in the vernacular was a conscious choice that created significant implications.

The graphic novel reached out to the public not only with its choice of language but also with a calligraphic style. Its dense speech and thought bubbles, numerous context captions, and pre- and post-panel text use a handwritten calligraphic style to distinguish it from the typewritten *Naskh* style used in the rest of the magazine. The use of the handwritten style invokes everyday experience and the intimate atmosphere of writing a note to a family member, a letter to a friend, or an entry in a personal diary. This script then resembles *'ammiyya* as a marker of intimacy. Framing the novel with the medium of the Lebanese vernacular and the handwritten script ultimately suggests closeness to the spoken medium of Lebanese audiences and implies sharing their concerns. The graphic novel enjoyed instant credibility among its readers because it avoided official language and style in favor of the vernacular.

In the end, the journal's new vision of a modern audience and a modern media preceded, paralleled, and contextualized that of LBC's programs. The interconnected changes in tone of the print and broadcast media provide a measure of the Lebanese public's success in applying leverage to the television industry. Being a response to LF's conundrum, these changes also help understand how the newly established television outlet was similarly invested in the shift toward a media that branded itself as relevant.

LBC, News, and the New Relevance of Television

As chapters 2 and 3 argued, Télé Liban's news bulletin failed to establish an intimate, personal bond with audiences through content, format, or language. Its boring content was not based on catering to the masses' cultural desire. Instead of attending to and coddling the audiences, the outlet was loyal to the government's aspirations in preserving the television peace bubble. Even when anchors wanted to cover the news more substantively, government information blackouts, such as the National News Agency providing them no official information, led to an end result that put off the audience just as much. The television-audience relationship was further damaged because of constant technical difficulties such as power outages, poor reception, and damaged infrastructure. The bulletin's format commonly lacked audiovisuals, while its language was formal yet frequently flawed. The bulletin's only connection to the audiences was based on the anchors' habitual presence during the family's evening routine and the audiences' need for information and hopes for a change in the production and delivery of that information.

LBC's news showed a radical improvement in all the abovementioned aspects of news reporting, as if it was listening to the pileup of public criticisms. The outlet developed its brand as edgy and shocking,[93] bringing entertainment into politics. Its very launch broke the political taboo on challenging the government's monopoly in television news. LBC began broadcasting its bulletins at 8:00 p.m. to preempt its competitor's, which significantly damaged Télé Liban's ratings.[94] Sometimes subtly, at other times openly, LBC's news content contradicted its competitor's.[95] LBC's news desk, full of young professionals headed by the Télé Liban–trained veteran Elie Salibi, developed an aggressively fresh profile that appealed to a new, younger generation unafraid of strategic, substantive controversy on the airwaves. It did not hesitate to scandalize even its early core constituency. In November 1986, for instance, the outlet secured an interview with Yasser Arafat—LF's biggest enemy. After the PLO had left Lebanon in 1982, the animosity had calmed down. In the mid-1980s the two sides discovered that they had common enemies (like Syria's Hafez al-Assad) as well as common supporters (such as Iraq's Saddam Hussein). LBC's eagerness to show with this interview that it had no problem with Muslims and was independent of the LF agenda raised accusations of treason to Christian interests but also attracted a huge audience.[96] Newscasts usually ended with Pierre Sadeq's political cartoons, an innovative format choice that mirrored the general public attitude and its use of parody and the carnivalesque in degrading the television peace bubble.

According to *Shabaka*, LBC's newscast was "the real bulletin in Lebanon as far as the production of information is concerned."[97] Audiovisual footage always supported domestic and regional news items and even international stories, which had a steep price.[98] Its sophisticated montage allowed every sentence to be accompanied by its own separate set of moving pictures and sound. In addition, voluminous field reporting widened the scope of the reporter's job,[99] placing the audiences in the middle of the action and often interviewing them as well. The bulletin featured spot-on reports about everyday people's struggles and tackled important social concerns that had never been broached before, responding to public demands for more attentive television.

The 8:00 p.m. newscast was so successful that a second news bulletin called *Last Hour News*, featuring reporters Dolly Sabbagh (Ghanem) and May Tabet (Matta), launched at the end of 1986. It aired at 11:30 p.m. and was inspired by the emerging aggressive CNN signature formats. The *Last Hour News* was more liberal, modern, and dynamic than the 8 p.m. bulletin.[100] Getting anchors Sabbagh and Tabet out of the studio and chasing stories in the field aimed at producing more engaging news about everyday social and human interest stories. The bulletin also included live studio interviews with analysts and an international stock market brief with Emile Baroudy. According to Kouyoumdjian, the most innovative feature of the *Last Hour News* program was that it transcended the two earlier phases in Lebanese news production—the "hellogoodbye" news and the politically motivated announcement news.[101] Instead, it focused on more engaging analysis of the news items' relevance to viewers and the country. The 11:30 news also revolutionized the image of the anchorwoman, placing her on par with her male counterpart.[102] Despite some mixed reactions that disparaged women and a cancellation due to a spike in the war, the show developed a cult following and affected the 8:00 p.m. news as well as Télé Liban's bulletin.[103]

In addition to the radical changes in content and news production, the audience address and news delivery of the LBC news desk were particularly innovative or, as the press called them, "of a different caliber."[104] Anchors read the news on autocue, looking straight at the camera to forge an intimate bond with the viewer through uninterrupted eye contact, whereas at Télé Liban anchors looked down at their papers frequently, thus breaking eye contact. The LBC programs also adopted a new, closer-to-the-people language approach, which elevated the vernacular and simplified the standard language. The very first words uttered by the outlet were Lilian Andraus's address to audiences in the vernacular during the inaugural broadcast. LBC's news also replaced the earlier customary greeting *As'ad Allahu masa'akum* ("May God bless your evening") with the simple *Masa l-khayr* ("Good evening").[105]

Most importantly, the outlet did something unprecedented on Arab television news: it began airing its bulletin in the vernacular. Télé Liban and television news bulletins in other Arab countries, to my knowledge, have traditionally been conducted in *Fusha*. Of course, minor regional differences permeate *Fusha*. In general, one can tell an Egyptian from a Lebanese anchor based on the pronunciation of "j," or even a Lebanese from a Gulf anchor based on the pronunciation of "a" (the so-called *imala*), although the latter is much harder. Some regional vocabulary may give region or nationality away as well. Overall, however, news bulletins stuck to the written variety, rendering news a dignified, official sphere, inaccessible in various degrees to regular vernacular speakers. By contrast, LBC's in-studio anchors adopted standard Arabic with simplified terminology and a less formal style, so long as it sounded more familiar and closer to the audiences, and sometimes flavored it with generous helpings of the vernacular. On-site reporters and interviewees exclusively used the vernacular.[106] Despite the hybridization, the *Fusha* segments were radically superior to Télé Liban's bulletin, whose incorrect vocalization and broken grammar markers had been a thorn in the critics' side for years. LBC hired a language proofer to ensure that the anchors' grammar and pronunciation were impeccable. This strategy was so successful that *Shabaka* praised LBC in the form of a warning to the audience—if anyone was looking for mistakes on the LBC news, their basket would remain empty.[107]

Télé Liban responded aggressively to its competitor's challenge in an urgent fight to stay relevant, pointing out that it had been promised monopoly by the government until 2012. Its CEO at the time was a Maronite Christian by the name of Michel Sameha, who served his three-year term between 1983 and 1986. Sameha sided against his traditional Maronite allies at LBC and threatened the advertising companies and individual advertisers not to deal with LBC.[108] It took a while to convince the older outlet to ease up on the pressure, according to Boulos, who worked in advertising at the time. At first, Télé Liban chose to fight the grid rather than create programming or language geared toward viewers. It moved its news to 7:30 p.m. and slapped LBC with a lawsuit, which eventually failed.

It is tempting to read LBC's decision to embrace the vernacular as a simple reflection of Maronites' traditionally positive attitude toward it. As the military arm of the Christian community, LF of course shared this attitude. But linguistic attitudes are not set in stone; for example, some important nineteenth- and twentieth-century Christian intellectuals were staunch proponents of *Fusha*. I argue that LBC's choice was in fact a dynamic response to the general feelings around language in the country. As I explained earlier, in the new language climate, *'ammiyya*'s challenge to *Fusha*'s authority found widespread support (chapter 3). The hybridized language variety on LBC therefore answered the nation's call for a "special," "strikingly Lebanese" language. In addition, the hybrid was a publicly relevant response to the audiences' demand that a modern television reflect the language tastes and sphere of competency of the public. LBC "'uplifted' the vernacular to a formal status, which other mass media adopted in an unprecedented language coup," in the words of media scholar Nassim al-Khoury.[109] According to linguist Mahmoud al-Batal, the hybrid variety, still very successful, constitutes a new language register, which calls attention to a uniquely Lebanized linguistic-nationalist identity.[110]

LBC's news reached educated and uneducated social classes alike with its more accessible language and appeal to mass cultural desire.[111] In Khoury's view, the outlet's broadening of the televised public sphere and acknowledging the public's concerns was first and foremost a linguistic reformation.[112] This is why the language on LBC's news challenged Télé Liban's nationalist peace bubble even more than the stories its anchors reported.

Ultimately, language offers a meaningful avenue for examining negotiations over the modernity of television news and information in wartime Lebanon as well as the development of television in Lebanon (and more broadly in the Arab world). Part I of this volume demonstrated that we should not separate language in its capacity as a medium to communicate a message to an interlocutor (audience) from its symbolic value as a medium to share and define identity. From the analysis of Télé Liban's peace bubble, to the carnivalesque in the language nonmovement and *Shabaka*'s critique of Télé Liban, to "Charbel"'s reflection of the shifting media/television role and LBC's news reformation, Part I illustrated that the political role of language resides in its coterminous, instrumental-symbolic potential to index and challenge unequal power relations. On the one hand, it showed how informal linguistic systems (akin to Gramsci's "folk grammar") challenge the hegemony of formal ones (akin to Gramsci's "normative grammar") and the power relations in which they are based. On the other hand, it showed that thinking of informal linguistic systems as pure and untouched by power struggles is to misread them. This is clearly evidenced in the complexity of power struggles indexed in "Charbel"'s language, plot, and characterization or LF's motivations for launching LBC with its hybrid language and willingness to break down taboos.

Part Two

Language Politics and Gender Politics on Entertainment Television

5

Télé Liban in Defense of *Fusha*

This is our language.
If we do not know it, it is our fault, not the language's.
—*Mister Mandur*

"I wish this letter finds a way to your pages and therefore to the ears of those in charge in television," a reader wrote to *Shabaka* in 1982.[1] "All Lebanese series speak in *Fusha*," the letter complained. "This might be appropriate for a historical story, but it's confusing to our ears and taste when a contemporary story speaks the language of the ancients. What stirs our resentment the most is when a servant in a series speaks *Fusha*. Is it reasonable for a servant, a madman, or a plain everyday person to speak like Sibawayh and al-Akhfash?" The reader refers to Sibawayh, the most famous Arabic grammarian, who lived in the eighth century CE; al-Akhfash was his teacher, who also edited Sibawayh's signature work on the fundamentals of Arabic grammar. A year earlier, an article dedicated to the issue of the Lebanese vernacular summarized the general frustration about the lack of vernacular fictional shows:

> Vernacular, vernacular, vernacular. . . . Many times our attention is commanded by the constant calls to produce television works that speak in our everyday language instead of the language of Sibawayh whose grammar and pronunciation are full of jagged ridges and sharp needles. And many times these calls are persuasive since if answered, they would ensure the good artistic qualities whose loss we feel bitterly.[2]

In 1980, *Shabaka* had published a series of interviews with television writers George Ibrahim al-Khoury, Gulbahar Mumtaz, Marwan Najjar,

Genevieve Atallah, Ahmad al-Ashi, Wajih Radwan, Marwan al-Abd, and Muhammad Shammel. A question was posed to the writers: "Do you prefer to write in spoken Lebanese or *Fusha*?"[3] The magazine admitted that the responses reflected "one of the most dangerous television controversies."[4] The opinions were split. *Fusha* was found to be completely inappropriate for comedy and light social drama, given its formality and distance from everyday life, yet it befitted historical work and serious drama. The majority of those interviewed expressed confidence that the vernacular could bridge the gap between television and the audiences but that its multiple regional dialects presented some challenges. Wajih Radwan put it bluntly when he said that he preferred *Fusha* because language was a creative process first and for all, despite many people's love for the vernacular.[5]

By a popular conviction in the wartime industry, writing in *Fusha* was necessary to market Lebanese work on the Arab regional market, given the collapse of the local television advertisement industry and the difficulties this caused for showing Lebanese series on the local screen. Yet there was also a general sense that this could be overcome if writers developed creative, appealing, and "uplifting" work in the vernacular. That kind of work was to help with the acceptance and assimilation of the Lebanese vernacular in the region, turning it into "literary, creative language."[6] Several critically acclaimed examples, which were very popular with the audiences, supported such convictions. Faris Youakim's *The Long Trip*, Wajih Radwan's *Around My Room*, Antoine Ghandour's *Barbar Agha*, and Ibrahim Mirashli's *Aghani wa Maani (Songs and Thoughts)* all put the vernacular at the forefront of television, prompting the press to describe each as the best show in years. Columnist Abd al-Ghani Tlis even pled to Ghandour to leave everything aside and write a show at the level of *Barbar Agha* "that will add a great, great deal of confidence and respect to the relationship which Télé Liban wants to build with the audience."[7] "In sum," *Shabaka* had argued in 1981, "the vernacular on television needs authentic writers. Where are these authentic writers?"[8]

This chapter and the next discuss how fictional television series demonstrated that language was topical to the negotiation of modernity and how, as in news bulletins, language in television series also became a referendum on television's relevance to the times.

The 1980s: A Decade of Language on Lebanese Television

The debate over language had such political import that 1980s Lebanese television witnessed the emergence of a fictional mini-genre: sitcoms and drama-comedy shows about teaching and learning Arabic. Several classic television series exemplify how the mini-genre negotiated language politics: Télé Liban's *al-Mu'allima wa-l-Ustadh* (*Miss Teacher and Mister Professor*, 1984), al-*Ustadh Mandur* (*Mister Mandur*, 1985), al-*Ustadh Mamnu'* (*Professor No*, 1986, Hana'a Media Productions), and LBC's signature series *Bayt Khalti* (*My Aunt's Home*, 1988–90) and its sequel *Niyyal al-Bayt* (*What a Fortunate Home*).[9] The earliest of the series was the thirteen-episode comedy *Miss Teacher and Mister Professor*, broadcast on Télé Liban in 1984 and packed with a star-studded cast: Ibrahim Mirashli, Hind Abi Lama, Layla Karam, Alya Nemri, Amalia Abi Salih, Shafiq Hassan, and the prolific Michel Tabet. In 1985 Télé Liban broadcast another language series, the thirteen-episode drama-comedy *Mister Mandur*, which kicked off the career of a young George Diab and a decade-long working relationship with his costar Toni Mhanna and scriptwriter Marwan Najjar. A year later, the light comedy *Professor No* caused friction with *Mister Mandur* because it appeared to be an imitation. The series used standard Arabic instead of the vernacular and its lead, historical and drama actor Abd al-Majid Majzoub, reportedly found the role of a grammar zealot to be close to his own real-life personality.[10] His costar was famous Egyptian actress Sherine. Two years later, the rival and still pirate station LBC aired its wartime signature series *My Aunt's Home* starring Rada Khoury, Toni Mhanna, Antoinette Aqiqi, George al-Asmar, Asad Haddad, Julia Qassar, and Gabriel Yammine. After a three-season run in the 1980s, *My Aunt's Home* was revived in the 1990s under the title *What a Fortunate Home* because Rada Khoury, the actress who played the aunt, had developed Alzheimer's and stopped acting, and writer Claudia Marchalian joined the cast. Despite this hiatus, I discuss the whole series that reached ninety-six episodes to present a more comprehensive picture of its language politics. (This mini-genre includes other series such as Elie Maaluf's thirty-five-episode sitcom *Talamidh Akhir Zaman* [*Latter-Day Students*, 2001], but because they did not participate in the civil war debate on language politics, they are beyond the scope of this work. Three of *Miss Teacher*'s cast also played characters on *Latter-Day Students*: Layla Karam, Amalia Abi Salih, and Edward al-Hashim.)

Miss Teacher and *My Aunt's Home* are among the Lebanese sitcoms widely known to multiple generations of viewers in Lebanon and beyond. The mini-genre as a whole followed shared generic conventions about representing a language environment and the questions commonly raised in that environment. Although the series appeared only a few years apart and dealt with similar domestic and global circumstances, they promoted rival positions on language politics. The particular ideology about teaching Arabic championed by each series was at the heart of its premise, social dynamics, and language conflicts. Therefore, the mini-genre reveals important battles over television's relevance enacted through language ideology.

Language Comedy and Global Flows

Why did language education emerge as a mini-genre on 1980s Lebanese television? Why then? The short answer is that it occurred against the backdrop of international cultural exchange. Between 1977 and 1979 British ITV aired a sitcom on teaching English called *Mind Your Language*.[11] It became an instant hit when it appeared in Lebanon a few years later. The show focuses on a recent Oxford graduate hired to teach an evening ESL (English as a second language) class to new immigrants after they have driven the previous teacher mad. In a reversal, and even parody, of the plot of Bernard Shaw's 1913 play *Pygmalion* and the 1964 American musical adaptation *My Fair Lady*, the teacher fails to inspire his students to learn the language and, it is assumed, to climb the social ladder that goes hand in hand with the increase in language capital. The students are not his sole concern, though. His feminist boss frequently drops by to check up on him and criticize him, especially since she despises male teachers. Created a few years after Britain was admitted to the European Economic Community (EEC), the sitcom made fun of some of Britain's new EEC partners as well as its own largest immigrant minorities. The audience in the United Kingdom considered the series xenophobic and it was canceled after three seasons (twenty-nine episodes) because of the offensive stereotypes of foreigners. In 1986, it was revived, making it a four-season, forty-two-episode show. Following its worldwide DVD release in 2003–7, the Virgin Megastores in Lebanon stockpiled it in an attempt to cater to the nostalgia of the civil war's cultural milestones.

Despite its cancelation in the United Kingdom, *Mind Your Language* made an international run in many former British colonies, including Australia, India, Malaysia, Pakistan, Singapore, Sri Lanka, New Zealand, Ghana, Kenya, Nigeria, and South Africa. Its premise of teaching a language spurred a global format adapted in spinoffs such as the US syndicated sitcom *What a Country* (1986, starring Yakov Smirnoff), where a night course teacher prepares recent immigrants to pass a citizenship test; the Indian show *Talk with Care* (1993), where students from around India learn Hindi; *Second Chance* (Nigeria); *Raja Kaduwa* (Sri Lanka); *Classmates* (Kenya); and several others.[12] The Lebanese shows analyzed below were influenced by and adopted some of *Mind Your Language*'s settings, as some of the writers told me and as we can see from a number of plot choices. For example, the lead character Mandur in *Mister Mandur* is hired because the students have driven the previous teacher mad, and the supervisor in *Miss Teacher* frequently shows up in class to berate the teachers. *Miss Teacher* was also influenced by the iconic Egyptian comedy *Madrasat al-Mushaghibin* (*The Troublemakers' School*, 1973), which shot comedy superstar Adel Imam to fame. The international context, then, ceded the comedic framework of the Lebanese mini-genre.

Domestic War on Illiteracy

The long answer is that the global run of language teaching shows was a stimulus that happened at an opportune moment in the history of language debates in Lebanon. This was the time when a polemical war on illiteracy was raging and when the value of *Fusha* and *'ammiyya* was a flammable issue.

Public perceptions of the factors that affect illiteracy, that is, poor or no command of the written variety of *Fusha*, were sometimes delusional. In 2000, Niamat Kanaan, director general at Lebanon's Ministry of Social

Affairs, stated that the most important reason for increased illiteracy in Lebanon goes back to the civil war.[13] The Ministry estimated that it needed to spend USD$1.5 million over three years to combat illiteracy in a population of about three million. The figure was supposed to shock the Lebanese as much as assure them that they could blame the civil war, and especially the militias who ignited it, while relieving the noncombatant public from personal responsibility. During the war, discussions of the problems with the educational system had become a common placeholder for pessimism about the future of Lebanese education. Over the two-year war of 1975–76, *Nahar* had extensive regular coverage of the massive problems in education: schools' destruction, closures, temporary relocation, gradual repair and reopening; the launch of education television in November 1975 to prevent the school year from being canceled; teachers' strikes, and so on. Students were reported to have somehow become duller, unmotivated, distracted, and less prepared, while teachers were angrier about their meager salaries and insecure pensions. It is true that the unstable and traumatic circumstances of the war took a toll on students and teachers; eventually entire academic years were canceled and some teachers were gunned down by their students over grades.

But, by and large, the actual data are conspicuously at odds with opinions like Kanaan's. Between the start of the war and 1997, a few years after the war ended, illiteracy rates had dropped by 10 percent.[14] This decrease might not appear significant; however, it was a watershed considering that the rate had not changed for decades before the war. In the early 1970s, people praised the government's and educators' efforts to raze illiteracy. Yet, actual survey statistics showed that illiteracy rates were at 32 percent and had not declined for the previous thirty years.[15] Public opinion changed quickly after the war started. Over the next decade and a half, language education and illiteracy became vexing, highly political topics where polemical swords were drawn, opinions clashed, and passions exploded. Fearing the onslaught of illiteracy, people debated what had gone wrong with language education. Some blamed the perceived language crisis on the sectarian war, others found fault in teachers and the curriculum, while still others focused on *Fusha's* difficulty. A war on illiteracy was born.

According to sociolinguist Zeena Zakharia, who researched language attitudes during the 2006 Israel-Hezbollah war in Lebanon, in times of conflict two simultaneous phenomena take place in relation to language.[16] First, *Fusha*'s importance as a symbol of the Lebanese nation skyrockets, and many start publicly and privately asserting the value of learning and using it. Second, *Fusha*'s practical value plummets, and the Lebanese rush to learn foreign languages, which helps them emigrate or get better jobs at home. These tendencies were largely in play during the second half of the 1970s and the 1980s as well. For instance, the number of hours spent on teaching the Arabic language in school diminished once the 1975 war began (especially in private schools), while the country witnessed the promotion of a number of strategies on how to "fix" language and the country. Some poets sang in defense of language and its role for uniting the nation; some educators revised the curriculum; and a few private entrepreneurs opened centers for "wiping out illiteracy" (*mahu al-ummiyya*).[17] A number of these centers sprang up throughout the country, teaching illiterate adults to read and write at an adult level.[18]

Lebanese fictional television did not remain silent on these issues. Local series, which favored the vernacular in the early history of television, now steadily shifted to *Fusha*. Between the outbreak of the war in 1975 and the Israeli invasion in 1982, out of thirty-five notable fictional series,[19] thirty were in standard Arabic and only five in the vernacular. That means that only one out of seven series used the vernacular. Even topics as mundane as comedy, romance, and melodrama used the standard language, thereby emphasizing the unprecedented increase in the production of series using this language variety over the entire history of Lebanese television. While in the preceding period, 1968–75, the production in the standard language had increased because Télé Orient was selling it successfully on the regional Arab market, the production in the local vernacular thrived just as much and its numbers were greater. Out of thirty-eight notable series produced before the war, twenty-three were in the vernacular, fourteen were in *Fusha*, and one was in a Bedouin dialect since its plot was about Bedouins. Some of the production in *Fusha* can be explained with the collapse of the local advertising market during the hostilities and the need to earn revenue from the regional market, which preferred *Fusha* rather than the Lebanese vernacular. But this explanation is limited because, by 1979, the advertising market had bounced back and slots were hard to find.[20] Zakharia's explanation, therefore, seems to add an aspect that can help make fuller sense of the *Fusha* wave. Even though local series were popular—59 percent of the audience followed them and 58 percent found them important[21]—the outcome of Télé Liban's language choices alienated viewers (as testified by the reader's letter to *Shabaka* quoted at the opening of this chapter).

The *Fusha* wave wreaked havoc on some actors' careers. For instance, Layla Karam had established herself as one of Lebanon's preeminent actors before the war, despite being illiterate, because the vernacular was the dominant medium of early fictional television. When the *Fusha* wave began, her career dried up. This period was so difficult for her that she prefers not to remember it. In a 1983 interview, she was quite frank:

> Don't remind me! After I'd become famous during the early days of Lebanese television and played major roles, I was stunned when the production shifted to *Fusha*. I was out of work for a long time because I don't know *Fusha*. . . . Isn't it sad when an actor reaches an important stage in their career to find out they are getting back to zero . . . [to] oblivion because [they] don't know how to pronounce *Fusha*![22]

Eventually, Karam began studying correct enunciation but never learned the grammar of the standard language.

Another set of measures in the war on illiteracy was built around the 1980s United Nations (UN) global initiative on children's rights and welfare. The increased attention to the abuse of children through low access to education, child labor, and lack of healthcare spurred a global awareness of the need to keep children within the education system. This awareness, which inspired a search for more effective methods of education and teacher training, affected Lebanon. In 1990, the country signed and ratified the UN Convention on the Rights of the Child after a decade-long public debate on child education. A few years later, researchers registered the proliferation of NGOs dealing with children's issues in the country.[23]

Modern Media and the Power of *Fusha* to Save the Nation

Mister Mandur is a drama with comedic elements about a year in the life of a substitute teacher of Arabic language in a junior high school somewhere in Lebanon. The aging, still unmarried Mandur lives in an apartment with his single sister Assia, who is at once his cook, cleaning lady, tireless matchmaker, and chaperone. Disillusioned with human nature after a blackmail incident, Mandur suffers from what today would be called post-traumatic stress disorder. He has left his former position as a schoolteacher after the relative of a female student threatens to expose him publicly for acts of sexual harassment that Mandur has not committed. The relative extorts a large amount of cash from him at gunpoint. In the beginning of the series, years after the blackmail, Mandur reluctantly returns to school when an Arabic teacher quits in the middle of the year. The season covers how Mandur embarks on a heroic quest to fix the language, circumstances, and families of his students. His goal is to revive language nationalism by promoting *Fusha* as a nationalist symbol.

Télé Liban did not commission *Mister Mandur*, but it found the show's nationalist language platform highly agreeable. The vision of the series' creator—freelance writer Marwan Najjar—to uplift a society that he felt had fallen behind in nationalism, education, and literacy aligned with the vision of the station. Both understood the media's power as a tool of nationalism. *Mister Mandur* was an important stage in Najjar's writing career, which linked his passion for television (he was twelve when Lebanon launched its first station), his language degree, and his desire to create a nationalist public.[24] After graduating from the American University of Beirut with a degree in language, Najjar opted for a job in journalism and later became one of Lebanon's most prolific and successful television, theater, and movie writers. However, teaching Arabic was never far from his heart, and he worked briefly in a junior high school.

Some of Najjar's earliest work was influenced by local and international attention to children and education in the second half of the 1970s. In its December 25, 1978 issue, *Shabaka* praised him for being a notable representative of a new television trend.[25] When 1979 was designated the international year of the child, Lebanese television was motivated to take advantage of the distinction and create fictional series with children in lead roles. Najjar penned two series, *al-La'ba* (*Game*) and *Sami*, which inspired *Shabaka*'s praise and a passionate appeal to other writers to follow suit. In 1979, he pitched an educational show to CEO Rizq, who reportedly liked the idea; however, it did not come to fruition.[26] During a flare-up of hostilities the following year, Najjar created a televised teaching course called *Durus Musanida* (*Support Course*). The program was meant to help high school students prepare for the baccalaureate exit exam, which many had failed in past years because of the war. The televised lectures were expected to give students electronic access to instructors from Beirut's most expensive schools. The same year, Najjar also convinced Télé Liban to produce a game show with an educational flavor under the title *al-Mutafawwiqun* (*The Vanquishers*). The fifty-two-week quiz show, which aired during prime time on Saturday evenings, featured young people competing for the ultimate prize of 23,000 LL. The press's initial reaction was slightly negative, apparently pressuring the show for stronger contestants. After the show found four smart young men, the press was ecstatic. The contestants, Najjar (who was also one of the judges), and the show host Suad Qarut al-Ashi turned into stars and became subjects of heated discussions among the public.

Najjar had also been hosting the cultural show *Majalis al-Adab* (*Literary Assemblies*), which generated some positive press. However, since 1983 he had produced a series of works that were reviewed more negatively. The 1983 *Hayk Rabbuna* (*That's How They Raised Us*) did not adopt the "modern educational approach" he had applied in *Game*, *Sami*, and *The Vanquishers*. It started as a drama revolving around a forty-year-old mama's boy, Faris Ibn Imm Faris (Faris, Son of His Mother), who could not let go of his mother's skirt. When critics pointed out that the "unrealistic story" and "backward character" did not correspond to the social purpose and critical outlook to which the title alluded, Najjar reportedly wanted the public to see the series as a comedy, not as a drama.[27] That did not convince the press, who thought the whole thing came out of "pure fantasy, or perhaps out of a strange and perverse 'reality' that borders on fantasy."[28]

Shortly thereafter, Najjar went back to the theme of education with *Mister Mandur,* which featured a new kind of knowledge idol. It was intended to work around Muslim sensitivities toward Arabic, the language of the Qur'an, in order to inspire a national audience united by language. In an ironic twist of history, *Mister Mandur* was canceled after episode thirteen, when sectarian violence cut off all communication. A year after its run, in the battle lull following 1986, Najjar tried to revive the story. He adapted it for theater but, according to his recollection, security conditions prevented a successful run and it did not sell well. *That's How They Raised Us* and *Mister Mandur* bewildered the press as to why an intellectual like Najjar could not translate his culture into his works: "Marwan the intellectual (he created the show *The Vanquishers*) is superior to Marwan the artist. . . . What's in his mind is not on the screen. . . . Why is Najjar at peace with the language of 'books' and at war with the language of television?"[29] Apparently, in 1986 matters worsened and Najjar chose not to be listed in the credits of his show *Hanadi*—allegedly the first time in the history of Lebanese series when a show did not mention a writer.[30]

Embarking on more commercial stories such as *'Ariseyn Midri min Weyn* (*Two Grooms God Knows from Where*), which makes fun of racist attitudes, paid off. *Two Grooms* sold a whopping 230,000 tickets in 1986–88. Columnist Jean Shahin swore audiences cried with laughter from the very start—something they badly needed, he claimed, after twelve years of war.[31] More successful plays and television series followed, some of them adapted from European works. For instance, when Najjar visited London in the 1980s, he got a bargain deal from playwright Ray Cooney, who charged him only 25 percent for the rights to adapt all his work in Lebanon. Cooney's 1983 play *Run for Your Wife,* about a polygamist cab driver, turned out to be a huge success in its Lebanese adaptation *Jawz al-Jawz* (*The Couple's Husband*). In Najjar's words, "When I saw Cooney's play in London, the audience laughed for one reason—because it was funny. I laughed for two—because it was funny and because it was designed for Lebanon. It was my play, not Cooney's. I came back rich. *The Couple's Husband* ran for sixteen consecutive months."[32]

After a decade away from television to produce theater plays, Najjar returned to the theme of education in the 1990s with two long LBC series—the social comedy with a happy ending *Talibin al-Qurb* (*The Matchseekers*, 136 episodes) and the drama *Min Ahla Buyut Ras Beirut* (*Best Homes of the Ras Beirut Neighborhood*, 45 episodes). He considers a 1998 episode of *The Matchseekers* to be his ultimate victory as a champion of children and their right to education by showing Lebanese legislators the importance of banning child labor and keeping students in school. Najjar cast Mona Hrawi (Lebanon's first lady at the time) as the ban's parliamentary proponent. A law similar to the fictional ban was passed a few months after the episode aired; according to Najjar, it passed as a result of Hrawi's involvement, although it is unlikely.[33] Two years later, LBC broadcast Najjar's series *Best Homes*, which depicted how broken and abusive homes harmed Lebanese youth and how supportive environments helped them reach their educational and personal potential. Both series frame education as a primary right and obligation for a united Lebanese youth, although the series do not specifically address language learning.

Quixotic Quest for Reviving Linguistic Nationalism

Throughout his career, Najjar has insisted that his work is relevant because it caters to popular sensibilities. By his admission, when television came to Lebanon in 1959, intellectuals and the wealthy considered the new medium too populist. He shared this attitude as a college student, but later he insisted that his television shows, plays, and movies were dedicated to the masses. This sentiment is perhaps at odds with his rebuke of the public, manifested in some of his creative choices and in his stated goal to "initiate the masses to build up new sets of ideas and attitudes."[34] Supporting the linguistic elitism that lies at the heart of *Mister Mandur*, actor and *Nahar* journalist Joseph Abu Nassar praised the series for uplifting Lebanese comedy from the down-market vibe of *Miss Teacher* to a tasteful, elevated standard.[35] Abu Nassar brought up matters of tastefulness and propriety not because the series avoided exploiting "handicaps or gays for cheap laughs," as he claimed.[36] In fact, a minor but recurring character—the despised snack vendor Anwar—has a lisp, not coincidentally paired with the role. I believe that Abu Nassar ignored such examples of off-color taste and talked about propriety in part because the series defended the borders of an elite national culture (*Fusha*'s symbolic value) by rebuking those who did not protect language nationalism.

The Israeli invasion, the Mountain War, and the battle of East of Saida in the four years preceding the series (1982–85) were particularly damaging to Lebanese nationalism. The cultural elites were searching for common causes to deliver the nation from its fratricidal violence. In response, Najjar rooted *Mister Mandur* in nostalgia for a lost, idyllic nationalist Lebanon. Episode 2, for instance, depicts the character Salim and his friend Najib strolling along a beautiful forested hilltop and dreaming of nationhood with passion, idealism, and their favorite *amus* (vocabulary): *watan, hawiyeh, intima* (nation, identity, belonging). The portrayal of their intellectual discussions rehashes cultural tropes of natural beauty and idealism that invoke Gibranian imagery and the Fayrouz folkloric tradition.[37] Likewise, Mandur's students respond to linguistic nationalism when they are inexplicably motivated by pastoralist descriptions of Lebanon's natural beauty, even though they come from urban backgrounds.

The series' reasons for the paradise lost are more curious than those Lebanese audiences typically encounter. Salim marries out of obligation but soon realizes that his wife is uneducated and superstitious. Seeing no path to marital happiness, he is driven to despair and violent alcoholism. As Salim's marriage suffers, the link between women and illiteracy threatens to destroy Salim's intellectual dreams from the beautiful hilltop. His only chance for recovery is Mandur and the teacher's enthusiastic aid for fallen linguistic nationalists like Salim. With passionate conversations, in which he idealizes language and nation, Mandur succeeds in pulling Salim out of the rut and setting him on a path to healing.

Despite Mandur's promises for revival, the audience was not enamored with the show. Reviews in the press were lukewarm or negative. Even the positive reviews expressed concerns with the show's simplistic understanding of language education. The audience and critics had difficulty disregarding Mandur's quixotic quest to educate the public and instead thought of his cause in the intended positive terms.

The Weak Teacher and the Mental Student

Mandur's language nationalism promised to reclaim the lost paradise by improving Arabic literacy. Sketching the debate on the appropriate educational procedure to achieve this is helpful for understanding the rationale behind the show. One of two schools of thought with rich and influential history blamed illiteracy on *Fusha* itself. In particular, it faulted Modern Standard Arabic (MSA) (the *Fusha* version used in the modern educational system) for preserving too many of the difficult structures of classical *Fusha*. The policy recommendation was to modernize MSA focusing on its functional capacities. The new MSA was to be "unencumbered" by "the dead rules of the past," the number of synonyms in it reduced, and flowery language forsaken for meaning.[38] The second, a pedagogical position, saw the problem in teaching methodology. In addition to envisioning new, simpler, and more student-friendly ways to explain grammar, it put demands on teachers to be inspiring and committed. The pedagogic view undoubtedly forms the backdrop of Mandur's efforts as well as the series' discussion of teacher conduct and the value of *Fusha*. As Mandur explains, "This is our language. If we do not know it, it is our fault, not the language's."[39]

The bell rings and Mandur's predecessor Fahme starts the Arabic language class. His students snub him and chase each other around, shouting at the top of their lungs. Fahme tries to control them in vain, his sense of powerlessness clearly visible. After they lock him up at recess, the exasperated teacher quits, leaving a vacancy for Mandur. Although the anarchy in the series' opening scene—a trope of Lebanese educational shows—seems exaggerated, it resembles many Lebanese classrooms.[40] Besides, blaming students' misconduct on the teacher's allegedly weak personality is the conventional wisdom in Lebanon. According to research, failure to manage student behavior is among the top reasons why teachers quit. Meanwhile, debates in the field of pedagogy regarding carrots and sticks rage on. During the war, most Lebanese classrooms relied on corporal punishment or public shaming to maintain discipline. Yet Fahme fails even at administering punishment. In fact, he himself receives it when the students lock him up. In the pilot episode, his first order of business is to tell the students of his family life, perhaps in an attempt to forge friendly relations. The students are irritated, though, as one of the class ringleaders, Ziad, bemoans in a song:

> Instead of the lessons we're to learn
> And for which we bear
> All that's unfair
> I get a teacher whose only concern
> Is to brag of his hobbies and his affairs
> Nobody cares
> Nobody knows what's going wrong
> How time is wasted by that lively tongue. . . .
> I run and toil, I'm angry and annoyed
> So I can get some knowledge, not that void.[41]

The series reframes the pedagogical issue as a character flaw—Fahme's weak personality—avoiding a discussion of the ineffective conventional methods of lecturing and rote memorization as well as low teacher training and compensation.[42] When the war broke out, the education budget began to shrink from its highest of 22 percent in 1974–75 down to 11 percent in 1990.[43] There was also a drop in the number of graduates from the few teachers' schools. In response, the government simply loosened admission requirements.[44] Ironically, given its ineffectiveness, teacher training in Lebanon was expensive. To lower the costs of the two-year programs, the government began summer courses and even hired high school graduates with no teaching experience. According to a UNESCO study, more than 50 percent of elementary and junior high Lebanese teachers were unqualified for their jobs.[45] Recruiting untrained teachers became popular because they were paid minimum wage, which forced many to find second jobs.[46] According to a 1981 study published in *al-Majalla al-Tarbawiyya* (*Journal of Education*), 49 percent of male teachers and 17 percent of female teachers worked overtime; 34 percent had a second job in another field (usually commerce or agriculture); and 20 percent of private secondary teachers had degrees in fields such as law and engineering.[47] Only 3 percent chose teaching because they liked it. During the particularly hard period of the 1980s, many schools had to focus on boosting profits to stay open, which greatly increased corruption. At an interview for a teaching position with a private school, Nemer Frayha was told by the owner that unless the school made 250,000 LL each year, he would turn the building into an apartment complex and collect a comfortable profit.[48] In light of teachers' images as uncredentialed, overworked, and underpaid, it is not surprising that a study found that parents blamed their children's poor performance on "teachers' disrespectful, nervous, and careless attitude toward their children."[49] Such tensions were fertile ground for shows like *Mister Mandur* as well as *Miss Teacher,* where weak teachers' soft personalities, laid-back attitudes, and ineffective pedagogy caused the students' boredom, disillusionment, and rebellion, dooming the students to fail.

Depictions of ineffective teachers lay the foundations of the mini-genre, on which the vaudeville *Miss Teacher* drew diligently. At first, its teacher duo of Hind and Ibrahim are too weak to take charge of their classes at the private school for adults focused on wiping out illiteracy. As a result, they regularly suffer insults and physical abuse from the students. Eventually, the squabbles caused by the teachers' budding love affair forces them to stop coming to class. The principal Zarife is equally unfit to be an administrator. Unable to inspire changes in teaching practices or institute appropriate curricular reforms, Zarife voyeuristically spies on the teachers through the secret cameras she has installed in their classrooms.

Miss Teacher drew on a second generic convention it borrowed from *The Troublemakers' School,* which depicted students as blowhard under-achiever hooligans. *Miss Teacher* was the most notable embodiment of that trope in my corpus. Over the span of three fictional years, the motley student crew of a butcher's apprentice, a senior citizen, a stay-at-home mom with a three-year-long pregnancy, a speechless young black woman, a forty-year-old man-child, an effeminate gay man, and a lady in a red hat have been stuck on the same lesson in their elementary Arabic textbook. The toddler rhymes, children's songs, and basic proverbs that fill their lessons imply infantile consciousness and arrested intellectual development. They get cheeky and know-it-all when the teachers push them to move forward, and they inflict corporal punishment on their educators after getting bad grades. The reviews in the press were rather harsh, wondering why writer Mirashli, who also played the main role of Ibrahim, created characters who looked like "runaways from a mental hospital."[50]

Mirashli had been a comedian since his tenure with Shoushou's theater in the 1960s, but he finally got his breakthrough as a writer and lead with the highly acclaimed 1983 sketch comedy series *Songs and Thoughts* against debuting costar Rolla Hamede. The press was bitterly disappointed: the writer who brought back a forgotten star from the golden age of Lebanese fiction television with each episode of *Songs and Thoughts* had sunk into hackneyed "juvenile punchlines" and canned laughter inserted after "word clichés resembling jokes told by taxi-drivers" with *Miss Teacher.*[51] Mirashli asked the press to be patient and eventually the high ratings of the show plus the multiple ads it attracted persuaded a few journalists to give the series a chance.[52] But most remained uncomfortable with the name-calling and ageist, sexist, anti-gay, and racist jokes, clearly inspired by *Mind Your Language.*

We can look at *Mister Mandur* as a criticism of *Miss Teacher*'s indecision to push generic conventions. I believe *Mister Mandur*'s critique addresses Mirashli's failure to find a solution for the students' linguistic incapacity and the series' dark sense of doom. The transition between *Miss Teacher*'s opening sequence and its first scene foreshadows a desperate situation. The camera shows a close shot of the school building's plate—"*madrasat mahu al-ummiyya*" ("school for wiping out illiteracy"), projecting confidence in the mission of education.[53] Yet the accompanying music—Charlie Chaplin's popular song "Titine" from *Modern Times*—implies that our trust in modern education is misplaced. In *Modern Times,* the little tramp is a waiter in a trattoria whose task is to entertain the customers with a song. The historical audiences had never heard the king of silent cinema speak before and they placed great importance on the words that would come out of his mouth for the first time. The tramp teases them with a long instrumental opening as the proper lyrics (written on his cuffs) fly away while he trots in from the kitchen. To save his job, he sings in gibberish. His ruse may have deceived his fictional boss and the restaurant's crowd, but hardly the viewers. Like Chaplin's language ruse, *Miss Teacher*'s depiction of language pedagogy is eerily counterfeit and doomed to fail.

The Benevolent Language Dictator

Frankly, idealization had never been Mirashli's forte, but that was exactly where *Mister Mandur* found a niche. If *Miss Teacher* portrayed a traumatic stage in the development of Lebanese education, *Mister Mandur* presented a fantastical solution to the trauma—a lone savior, a superteacher. The larger-than-life figure of a benevolent language dictator, woven into many nationalist traditions, indexes the molding of a shared national identity through unified language. In hopes of creating a shared Lebanese identity around standard Arabic, the series invented trickle-down linguistic nationalism. The fountainhead is superteacher Mandur who educates his students to use formal grammar correctly. Overflowing with newfound knowledge, this new generation of language activists correct their parents' speech and then lecture them on standard grammar, like Sami does with his father, the snack vendor Fadlu.[54]

In addition to policing proper speech from vernacular grammar and pronunciation, Mandur also polices it from French. If foreign languages threaten *Fusha*'s practical value during war, as Zakharia argues, then the biggest offenders are Mandur's sister Assia and her vain female friends, who snobbishly use Franbanais (a mixture of French and Lebanese vernacular) over a game of bridge. In Episode 1, he lashes out at his sister for using the French word "régime" in the sense of "diet" instead of the *Fusha* term *himiya.*[55] An invocation where the Arabic homophone *rajim* means "evil, damned" ("*A'udhu bi-Allah min al-shaytan al-rajim*" ["I take refuge in God from the damned Devil"]) fuels Mandur's efforts to assert patriarchy over Assia and in Episode 4 over her and her friends for vulgarizing Arabic and shame them for alleged national betrayal.[56] As language is one of the fundamentals of identity, Mandur's archnemesis could very well be Franbanais, which embodies both foreign and vernacular threats to *Fusha*.

What *Mister Mandur* offers to the viewers goes beyond the common tropes of nationalist traditions. Consider how the lyrics below, which come from the series' theme song, introduce Mandur as a hyperbolic avatar, a superhero, rather than simply a national hero.

We'll only learn Arabic
With the method of Mr. Mandur . . .

If on occasion my tongue slips
Over a tiny unguarded mistake
He will turn this world upside down
Demanding correct speech

No one's as smart and wise as him
Always alert to capture mistakes . . .

We think he wants to correct a word
A short vowel, a little "o," a short "a"
A blunder that has lost its way
He ends up correcting the whole family . . .

He wants to fix this world
And teach the planet how to spin
Mr. Mandur, Mandur, Mandur.[57]

After ten years of war, no pessimistic, dead-end education bashing such as on *Miss Teacher* has any appeal for Mandur. In fact, it appears to be dangerous if we accept Zakharia's framework. As the song clues us, exclusivity ("only learn . . . with the method of . . . Mandur"), unanimity ("the whole family"), and hyperbole ("fix this world . . . teach the planet how to spin") form a sui generis pedagogy that pushes the boundaries of the comedic mini-genre toward altering the status quo rather than reasserting it. Ironically, the whole series uses the vernacular, including the theme song, which praises Mandur as a staunch champion of standard grammar. *Fusha* only appears in some instances when Mandur or his students discuss grammar, in some of Mandur's statements, musings, or mutterings, as well as in the poetry recited on the series. I believe this strategic decision on Najjar's part resonates with his expressed opinion on the "dangerous" *Fusha/'ammiyya* issue: the former is easy on the writer, he claims, while the latter bridges the gap with the modern audience.[58] It also brilliantly illustrates the validity of Zakharia's notion of *Fusha*'s high symbolic and low practical value.

By contrast, the series *Professor No* uses *Fusha* exclusively, which takes *Mister Mandur*'s premise to its logical end—another reason to think of it as a creative imitation. *Professor No* featured Abd al-Majid Majzoub's first comedic role after playing a romantic hero for over a decade. The press had followed his career and that of his costar from the romantic blockbuster *Around My Room*, Hind Abi Lama, with an obsession due to Lebanon's legendary romantic TV couple. *Professor No* was Majzoub's child, proudly birthed after multiple delays that dragged over two years of war and an expensive trip to Athens, Greece, where the indoor scenes were shot. (The outdoor scenes were filmed in MP Pierre Helou's garden in Hazmieh, which had been featured in many other films and television series.) Its thirty half-hour episodes were scheduled to appear during Ramadan when fictional series about Islamic civilization typically fill the grid and *Fusha* features prominently in the month's high cultural atmosphere. But the show was a miss for Lebanon's idol. The press unapologetically remarked on his stiffness as a comedic lead, the shockingly low number of female roles, and the romantic couple's big age difference. When asked at an interview if he himself liked the show, the vexed Majzoub bluntly affirmed his commitment to the role.

The role itself is a step up in the social ladder from his counterparts in the other series of my corpus that portray teaching junior high students or illiterate adults. Fadil Zahrawi (Majzoub) is a university professor who wages a "war on mistakes" and also hosts a television show called *Minute before the Mistake*. Interestingly enough, his unflappable language fundamentalism and hypercritical attitude toward faulty grammar help him to attract an extremely favorable marriage prospect. The series' most notable feature is perhaps its disdain of audience sentiment. Consider the following scene: Fadil's servant Aziz, an uneducated *sha'abi* (folksy) character, leaves a feather duster on the coffee table. The annoyed Fadil summons him to receive punishment in the form of a grammar-literary task—Aziz must immediately memorize two poetry lines. Without further ado, Fadil recites two verses from the most famous Arabic poet Mutanabbi. They happen to be the strangest verses the medieval genius produced, entirely consisting of twenty-three irregular verbs conjugated in the imperative. This is quite a feat since some Arabic verbs have all sorts of defects and may lose one, even two, of their three root letters. Fadil recites:

> *Ish ibqa smu sud qud jud mur inha ri fi sri nal. . . .*
>
> Live, survive, distinguish yourself, lead, command, be lavish, rule, forbid, hurt your enemy, redeem your pledge, attack your enemy by night, submit him to your will.[59]

When Fadil stops, Aziz asks to be given instead a verse in Arabic on account of not speaking foreign languages. The implication is that these imperatives are not recognized as Arabic by Arab speakers. Fadil is furious: "You, ignoramus! The verse is by Mutanabbi and it is one of the most important verses. Get ready and listen again!"[60] If Aziz had retorted in the vernacular, it would have made for a legitimate comedic situation. But a servant who speaks *Fusha*, yet does not recognize it, is fundamentally implausible. In addition, it stirs the audience's "resentment," as the above reader's letter (written years before the series) pointed out—a bridge Najjar was smart not to cross.

The Patina of Age

George Diab (who played Mandur) admitted to *Dalil* that his childhood dream was to be a movie hero.[61] After dabbling with chemistry upon finishing high school, Diab eventually graduated from the Lebanese University Film School and his dream became reality when he landed the role of his career as Mandur. The actor fell in love with the strong character immediately. The comedic elements of the series were supposed to lighten the mood of heavier topics like child abuse, alcoholism, blackmail, failing educational standards, and corruption. The role of Mandur in particular was meant to bring out this fusion of serious talk and light mood.[62] Nonetheless, Diab confessed to having trouble warming up to *Fusha*.[63] The toughest part was giving the solemn variety the quality of intimacy.[64] That such a matter emerged at all exposes the hardship the formal language presented even to those who worked with it. I believe that Diab's struggle to relate to *Fusha* indicates how the series' quest for language was simultaneously endearing and outdated. Insisting on everyone learning *Fusha* and understanding Lebanese identity within *Fusha*'s boundaries, Mandur demands obedience to a restrictive ideal rather than encouraging looser boundaries in speaking and behaving.

Modern trends in set design and characters' wardrobes, hair, and makeup, which could have created the impression that the audience's modern tastes mattered to the media, were disregarded too. Instead, *Mister Mandur* boasted 1960s and 1970s sets and garments, decades out of sync with audiences' expectations, which gave the show a passé feel. Here, too, Mandur makes a strong impression. His shoddy, featureless suit jacket apparently fits any season; his dusty headwear resembles an Alpine fedora or Trilby hat; and his old leather bag—falling apart at the seams, its clasp rusty and squeaky—could have been wrested from a hoarder's home. When Assia trashes it to slip in a new one, Mandur throws a tantrum and demands his old bag back. Télé Liban's policy to remain neutral by choosing uncontroversial prewar settings was consistent with the time lag in its sets, wardrobes, hair, and makeup. The audiences also knew that the station struggled financially and thus demonstrated no interest in responding to their changing tastes in these matters. Nonetheless, *Mister Mandur* shows that Télé Liban's choices went beyond the financial constraints within which it had to operate. The show's creators could have made Mandur a younger character to match the actor's actual age. Yet, the young Diab, cast not long after college, had to feign the patina of age under the heavy makeup that aged him thirty years.

In news bulletins, the *glamour of fashion* distracted from the occlusion of the war. In fictional series like *Mister Mandur,* on the other hand, the *patina of age* authenticated a kind of modernity that looked back at the past and its treasures, wisdom, golden archive, and powers of hyperbole and idealization. Mandur uses the power of idealization to inspire his students to learn Arabic, especially those who, like Walid, have dropped out of school demoralized by the poor pedagogic system. Calling on the power of idealization to increase language capital contradicts some of the conventions of the global genre inspired by *Mind Your Language*. In fact,

Mister Mandur reverts to the very scenario of *Pygmalion* and *My Fair Lady* that *Mind Your Language* had parodied,[65] thus staying faithful to its own commitment to a modernity that lives through links to the past.

By moralizing on the shortcomings of viewers' everyday speech, Mandur and Fadil painted a modernity marked by trust in authority and hegemonic power relations organized within the domain of language (although Mandur also tries to empower children). The fictional warriors exhibited the "unconscious and contradictory effectivity of the hegemonic within the popular."[66] But that kind of modernity was no longer popular with the public, with only 5 percent preferring the formal *Fusha* as the language of broadcasting.[67] Instead, the public was eyeing the media for signs of change.

6

LBC and Language Pessoptimism

Arabians learn Arabian with the speed of summer lightning.
—*My Fair Lady*[1]

"Older than you is the owl, wiser than you is the kitten" is the most bizarre proverb ever uttered in Arabic.[2] It boggles Rayya, a fired phone operator at a radio station who has now become a television show host, in a scene from *What a Fortunate Home*, the sequel to *My Aunt's Home*. A distortion of one of the most famous Arabic proverbs, "He, who is older than you by a day, is wiser than you by a whole year," Rayya's bizarre utterance reflects her struggle to make sense of common proverbs after unintentionally perverting them.[3] Given her status as a minor celebrity, this scene reveals the irrelevance of linguistic capital in capturing a modern national audience—an idea that would have appalled Mandur in *Mister Mandur* (see chapter 5, this volume, for discussion of the show). But other ways in which LBC's fictional series imagined television's role as a modern medium would have equally appalled the superteacher Mandur. *My Aunt's Home* maintained neither Mandur's and Fadil's insistence on moralizing, idealizing, and the patina of age nor their claim to linguistic authority and *Fusha*'s hegemony. Instead, it conceived of a television modernity that hinged on ambiguity, parody, and the pastiche of place, as well as doubt and self-reflection.

Bonds of Intimacy and Moral Ambiguity

My Aunt's Home/What a Fortunate Home was so popular with the audiences that LBC produced ninety-six episodes spread over more than a decade. *My Aunt's Home* had three seasons of thirteen episodes each between 1988 and 1990; *What a Fortunate Home* made thirty episodes in 1998–99 and had another season of twenty-seven episodes after a year-long hiatus.[4] The sequel reflected the time jump but remained faithful to the original premise.[5] *My Aunt's Home* tells the story of a language teacher, Kamal, who struggles to impart the standard *Fusha* and the Lebanese dialect to his four students: Rayya, Farme, Dara, and Salah.[6] Unlike *Mister Mandur*, language education provides the glue that ties together the plotlines, but it is not the moral center of *My Aunt's Home*. If there were any moral center, it was in scenes such as Rayya's discharge from the radio that engaged the language politics of everyday people, as I show below.

In addition, the show connected to the audience by establishing an emotional bond with it—something that fictional television does best. Both the general public and the cultural elites received the show's language puns and upbeat atmosphere exceptionally well,[7] and they waited impatiently for their "rendezvous" with the weekly installments.[8] The press captured the prevailing sentiment in every article, some pieces openly proclaiming their love in the title, such as "We Loved *My Aunt's Home*."[9] The interviews I conducted with members of the audience confirmed journalists' impressions that the characters Saber, Dara, Farme, and Rayya had become "engraved" in people's memories.[10] No character was too insignificant to inspire attention. Even writer Camille Salame's eleven-year-old son Karl Salame, who joined the sequel's cast to play Kamal's son Samer, got his own newspaper special.[11] The sitcom and Karl's role were so popular that his middle-school teachers called him "Samer" in place of his "forgotten" real name.[12] Asad Haddad, too, became famous in the role of the plump, adorable Farme, a professional success that he could not achieve with his creative roles in three serious works of the Rahbanis—*Socrates' Final Days*, *The Will*, and *Summer 840*.[13] Salame and the series' actors I interviewed described the audiences' passion for the show with a common narrative trope—the streets became eerily dead at 8:30 p.m. when the prime-time show aired right after the news; only the voices of the show's characters broke the silence through the open windows.[14] Using far less descriptive words, a member of the audience I interviewed summarized the general feeling, saying that she tried not to miss it. Another, a foreigner, was very enthusiastic: "As a foreigner I could have watched French or English shows but I instead watched it [*My Aunt's Home*]. Their diction was good, I understood everything even though my Arabic was not ideal. I never watched another Lebanese sitcom."

A large number of commercials lined up to air during the show, and their steep costs corroborated the more subjective views of its success.[15] In fact, LBC aired so many commercials during the show's time slot that *Nahar*'s Jana Nasrallah warned that if it didn't pull back, the show might lose its comedic flavor.[16] Instead, LBC deployed one more heavy-handed tactic to squeeze the show for market shares. The outlet held back a number of episodes from *What a Fortunate Home* for over a year, moving the show from its original Friday slot to a Monday one, apparently hoping to compete against a popular program on another station and displeasing even the soft-spoken screenwriter Camille Salame.

There was a lot to like about the show—from its quality, focus on family lifestyles, and positive atmosphere to its lack of didactic, symbolic, or pretentious language. Considered a "successful experience in local production" amid the low-quality Lebanese scene, *My Aunt's Home* was compared to high-quality American sitcoms and praised as the first local series to ever use special effects.[17]

But *My Aunt's Home* connected with the audience because it reflected the strength of family bonds.[18] Even the sequel's title was said to anchor the sitcom within local family values—*What a Fortunate Home* was often compared to the Lebanese proverb, "A home [of family values] that gives birth to another is a fortunate one."[19] People watched how the sitcom's family, neighbors, and friends forged deep bonds because they reflected people's "need to connect to the other" and shield family members from the war.[20] The show's fictional family even welcomed strangers. According to *Nahar*, it was the only place for the Indian guest worker Dara (one of the four fictional students)—a stranger in a strange land.[21] Besides, the bonds of harmony and cooperative spirit that connected the actors were real in contrast to the fake harmony of the peace bubble.[22] The team was so tightly knit and congenial that *Nahar* called them "the gang" (*awba*), while *Afkar* described them as an "orchestra."[23] Reports about their good relationships emerged in the press. When fiction writer and actress Claudia

Marchalian joined the show, she felt instant closeness to the rest of the team, whom she described as "my friends" even though, just days before, some were characters she had followed for years.[24] *Shabaka* argued that *My Aunt's Home* was a good title for a show that became a platform for the presentation and promotion of new talent. The journalist called Rada Khoury—a seasoned actress with a long career in theater who played the aunt—"mother" of the creative team because the many young actors and junior director Faris al-Haj learned a lot under her guidance.[25] According to Salame, "working with Haj was one of the best kinds of cooperation," and after the director's premature death a journalist wrote that *My Aunt's Home* team was orphaned.[26]

These bonds made it easy to project empathy even for an outsider such as Dara, whose character had "fascinated the audience," as one of my interviewees put it. Empathy was also evident in the series' reflection of "the real conditions of the family home" as it was threatened with economic and social crises.[27] *Nahar* commented that the series didn't let the audience deny their "reality," adding, "We see our truth in about a half hour."[28] Describing the series' closeness to the public, *Shabaka* offered that "Camille Salame left his abstract aunt's home to enter the real one of the audiences."[29] Although Salame often denied that the show was about politics, and the audience members I interviewed in general supported that view, the show did treat social and political problems of public relevance, such as unemployment, poor communications, the peace bubble, or taxes.[30] In fact, it was described as the only truthful social comedy show in Lebanon, given its critical presentation of "the complex problems of Lebanese society and its serious faults."[31]

Unlike the shows featuring Mandur and Fadil, *My Aunt's Home* spoke to audiences that tolerated ambiguity without offering simplistic solutions. The press applauded it for eschewing symbolism,[32] academic mumbo-jumbo, and moralistic lessons. Instead, the show was said to venture opinions without pretense, mannerisms,[33] or "a shadow of conceit" toward the audience.[34] Its language and characterization were likewise highly praised because they eschewed didacticism and imposed no role models. *Nahar* wrote that the characters "don't present flawless persons, even Mr. Kamal with his desires, habits, and personal traits doesn't boast perfection (*kamal*) that would make him the show's spiritual guru, problem-solver, or authority that teaches the audience a moral lesson every episode."[35] Other characters often eclipsed Kamal, sharply contrasting with Mandur's status as a lead character on *Mister Mandur.* In place of Mandur, at one point *My Aunt's Home* had the blowhard wise-fool Saber, whom *Nahar* characterized as an illiterate, obnoxious, pretentious, and conceited person. The makeup team took special care to give Saber a disheveled hairstyle that would make him "unacceptable to society" to match his repugnant behavior.[36] Interestingly, the seasoned actor Gabriel Yammine who played the role had previously studied to become a priest, then a teacher of Arabic, only to reject both lines of work and throw himself into acting. Despite or because of his shenanigans, imperfect language, and awkward grammar, Saber was a widely beloved character, maybe even a center of gravity in the sense that Mandur was for his show.

Parody: Why Idealization Doesn't Work

Vanished Villains

Unlike Mandur's student Walid or *My Fair Lady*'s Eliza, the formal Arabic skills of Kamal's four students are not helped by effort, magical thinking, or a lapse of time. Farme and Rayya rarely speak *Fusha*, and when they do, they make hilarious mistakes. Dara remains illiterate, while Salah tries to fool the whole country that he knows *Fusha*. It's not Kamal's fault; it's the genre. The linguistic disability of his students speaks to an audience already cognizant of local generic conventions. Featuring an Arabic language teacher presupposes students with poor Arabic skills.

However, rather than becoming villains or antiheroes, the four students contest the conventions that created them. Take social status, for example. When a character like Eliza learns the skill of idealization, she climbs the social ladder from a common flower peddler to an upper-class socialite due to her language improvement. In *Mind Your Language* and *Miss Teacher*, both reversal shows of *My Fair Lady*, the students never learn the language and consequently never climb the social ladder. In contrast to all three, in *My Aunt's Home* social prestige is possible without good language skills. That's how Rayya and Salah become celebrities. Salah is Lebanon's "best actor in *Fusha*"; Rayya rises up from telephone operator to radio announcer to television game show host, while her linguistic skills worsen. The link between class status and language capital is reversed—better language does not elevate one to a better class; jumping to a better class might cause one to lose one's language skills. Linguistically poor yet socially rich, the four language outsiders are welcome at the national table as they are, contrary to the ways in which Télé Liban's shows dealt with the conventions, that is, demanding speakers to improve and atone.

Moreover, *Fusha* ceases to be the coveted end goal of linguistic enrichment. Whereas in the original show Rayya's misunderstanding of language stems mostly from her poor skills in *Fusha*, a decade later her profound uncertainty includes her mother tongue—the Lebanese vernacular. She misinterprets, mispronounces, and misuses it when she deciphers the Lebanese proverbs, welcomes her television audience, or interviews contestants and guests on her game show. Dara inexplicably attends a *Fusha* class to learn the Lebanese vernacular. The tragicomedy of this gas station attendant is paying part of his meager guest-worker salary to be in a class not designed pedagogically to provide the practical language skills he needs.

In the end, Kamal's four students are complicated characters that bring out the audience's compassion rather than the righteous indignation reserved for villains and antiheroes.

Fallen Heroes

If generic villains vanished from *My Aunt's Home*, then what happened to heroes? Within Télé Liban's negotiation of generic conventions, language nationalism and literacy dictated the heroes. *Mister Mandur* acknowledged the unsung feats of language nationalists like Mandur, a descendant of the great romantic-folklore tradition of Gibran and Fayrouz. Ironically, one of the diva's most popular songs during the war, "Bhebbak Ya Lubnan" (I Love You Lebanon), mourned (and tried to recoup) people's loss of faith in an idyllic, folkloric Lebanon as the basis of Lebanese identity. But people were disillusioned with heroes, unconvinced that villains were villains, and mistrustful of representation. As cultural critic Elise Salem observes, "'Techniques' of survival replace[d] larger issues . . . villains and heroes of some early war fiction . . . disappeared."[37] Thus, Fayrouz was no longer a hero. As Khalil from *The Stone of Laughter* lets on, the prewar music icon was at best a stranger who did not speak to his concerns: "he had nothing in common with this woman's songs . . . with empty words . . . a symbol that symbolizes nothing to him."[38]

In that environment, *My Aunt's Home* reflected the somber atmosphere in which fictional heroes all but disappeared. Kamal's title and profession speak to that effect. He is variously called "Master" and *Ustadh*, the Arabic word for teacher, professor, or Mister. His degree in Arabic language and literature puts him squarely in the intelligentsia, and as a teacher of Arabic, Kamal should be an intellectual role model to his students. However, the pilot episode reveals that his private class is just a tutoring side gig and his breadwinning occupation is waiting tables.[39] From one angle, this reflects the reality of the teaching profession during the war. Because of their depreciating salaries and the government's inability to find funds to cover back pay, retirement, or benefits, as well as the comparably low pay at private schools, teachers turned to extra sources of income like private tutoring. It is unlikely that teachers created a high demand for "discreet tutoring" at their homes by performing poorly in class, but many factors contributed: tough curricula, hard official exams, and pushy parents with cash on hand. Private teachers were assured additional income when their students did better at school or at qualifying exams, and they gave word-of-mouth recommendations to the families of other prospective students. Alas, Kamal achieves no improvement with his students; neither does he get more foot traffic at the tutoring business. From another angle, when a master becomes a servant,[40] his domain (*Fusha* and education) becomes perverted and inadequate. He is a fallen hero.

Ironically, his student Salah enjoys higher socioeconomic status despite doing so by a ruse. Actors in *Fusha* are supposed to mark their lines in the script in advance with the correct short vowels and grammatical endings. To avoid being caught unqualified for his job, Salah arrives late at the studio, so someone else marks the script for him. Therefore, Salah tries to pass as a member of a higher class, while Kamal is reduced to a lower class than he has earned. Yet, like Kamal, Salah is addressed as *Ustadh*, in his case a term of high respect. Perhaps Salah is represented as more authentically Lebanese than Kamal, as Salah is called "teacher" only in Arabic.[41]

With Kamal and Salah losing what distinguishes them from each other, education loses its significance as a means of sublimating reality. Kamal is no hero. Whereas he himself is not the object of ridicule, despite the better pay and greater respect that his uneducated student receives, the teacher's domain is a target. Salah is no hero either. His celebrity is depicted as a liability. Kamal and the other students make fun of him for covering his head with a scarf so no one recognizes him when he goes to Kamal's private lessons. The truth is, Salah fears that his reputation would be destroyed if the nature of his business with Kamal were discovered, for which he is even blackmailed. Learning *Fusha* becomes an embarrassing secret, as does consorting with a teacher of Arabic, albeit in the context of the ruse.

In the world of *My Aunt's Home*, then, linguistic capital is irrelevant and the likes of hyperbolic superteacher Mandur no longer possible.

Peace, Quiet, and Parody

The war is raging in the capital Beirut. News anchor Rayya enters a small radio studio, takes a seat behind the bare desk, and inhales deeply as she begins to speak into the microphone to announce the evening news. It is her first assignment. She is all nerves; her eyes flare wide, exaggerating their roundness. Her face, frozen into place, masks her fear and uncertainty. Behind the glass partition of the control room, the production director watches her carefully, wary of any slip she might make. As she begins reading the first item, a bulletin about the progression of the war, he watches and listens anxiously. To his relief, she has been well coached. All she utters is *hudu' tamm* (peace and quiet), before she switches to the international news.

This scene is a flashback Rayya shares with Kamal and the other students when they resume their private language class after the summer break (more on that lesson in the section below). The obvious reason (to the audience) that the production director fears what Rayya might say is that he is worried about her inadequate language skills. Twentysomething Rayya has worked on the phones and scheduling at the radio station for a few weeks in the hopes of becoming a regular announcer. When she is asked to fill in for the sick news anchor, she humorously mispronounces common media vocabulary in *Fusha* (e.g., "news briefs," "international," "Kuala Lumpur") in a way that a nonnative speaker would. At the end of this live experiment, she is shown the door. Rayya is too ashamed to admit what has happened when she relates the story to the class. Intending to say that she has resigned (*ista'alet*), through the same mishandling of Arabic that caused her to get fired (this time in the vernacular though), she actually says that she no longer works at the radio station because she got annoyed (*istas'alet*).

Superficially, the scene appears to entertain viewers with an unprepared anchor and her innocent mistakes, but beyond that it tells us how the language of news bulletins alienates the audiences, who feel like foreigners trying to navigate this language. As an interpretive community, the listeners realize when the station is insensitive to the language they understand and when it speaks down to them. If Rayya represents the ordinary person—the taxi driver, the stay-at-home mom, the doorman—is not the newscast alienating all of them? If the station severs its relationship with Rayya the first time she fails to properly use its language, then how should other Lebanese expect the newscast to treat them? True, the viewers of the sitcom are supposed to feel superior to Rayya and to laugh at her fumbles with language, but shouldn't they also feel disturbed by her unfair dismissal? After all, she was fired for trying to help out the station. No wonder Rayya says she's annoyed—her annoyance is at her rough treatment.

A closer look at Rayya's mistakes shows that she mispronounces the very words that the media uses to displace meaningful reporting on the war—the local news briefs that are too short to reveal the war trauma, and the international news reports that focus on conflicts like the Vietnam-Cambodia war, which occludes Lebanon even further. But most of all, it is the terse and bland commentary, *peace and quiet* (lit., "complete calm"), that renders the war officially invisible. Rayya's "news" is clearly a language parody, being a redoubling of the infamous expression "relative calm" (*hudu' nisbi*) and the equivalent of the dark sarcasm with which the language nonmovement challenged equally radio and television practices, in particular Télé Liban's (see discussion in chapter 3, this volume). Hardly an ignorant telephone operator, Rayya is a keen observer of the core issues that upset the public.

In sum, this scene illustrates the discourse on the ethics of broadcasting and its relationship to modernity through the lens of parody. Rayya's take (and by extension the series' and LBC's) is similar to that of the language nonmovement: dark sarcasm as the most viable strategy to expose the peace bubble and dismantle the linguistic idealization that perpetuates it.

The Pastiche of Place

If *Mister Mandur* privileged time, especially through a patina of age and looking back to the past, *My Aunt's Home* narrated the modern condition through a pastiche of place anchored in the present. In 1988, historian Kamal Salibi published his classic history of Lebanon, *House of Many Mansions*, in which he argued that Lebanon was a divided nation because its multiple communities had forged clashing identities rather than a united one.[42] Salibi exposed the oblivion in the idealized histories of each community as self-serving delusions that could not avoid contradicting each other. Like Salibi, *My Aunt's Home* saw the country as a house of many mansions, but each was a mansion with a different language.

A scene about Farme's visit to grandma's house is a good example. Farme, the happy-go-lucky teenager, gets up from his seat. Gathered around the dining-cum-conference table, Rayya, Dara, and Salah are eager to hear Farme's report of the summer break (their over-the-summer homework). Puckering his lips in a proud expression, Farme recites a *Fusha* poem about grandma's house. His eyes burn with exhilaration as he declaims the stanzas, all in full inflection. Finally, he's done. Suspecting a ruse, Kamal exclaims, "Does your grandmother's house truly resemble this description?"[43] Farme makes a lemon face, collapses on his chair, and breaks down into colloquial expression. It turns out that the real house is a disaster. Over the span of a few lines, Farme gets himself in trouble too familiar to many Arabic language students. Eager to please his teacher, he goes too far. Instead of showing Kamal that he's making the progress in *Fusha* he so badly needs for a passing high school grade, Farme plagiarizes a poem above the register of an average homework assignment:

> My grandmother's house has beauty
> Built as it is of red brick
> It is set in a wonderland garden
> Which holds noble towering trees
> From the soil spring colorful flowers
> About which the butterflies flutter
> While the bees suck their nectarine flavor
> For us sweet honey to bring.[44]

After the recitation, Kamal remembers that last year he had asked his students to memorize this lyrical piece—a fictional children's verse. The house in this *Fusha* poem comes from another person's verse. After Kamal urges him to tell the truth, Farme picks up in the Lebanese vernacular again: "My grandmother's house is an old one: it has two bedrooms, a sitting room, and a kitchen. The toilet is out in the field."[45] A heath (*bura*) surrounds the house instead of a garden.

The language and imagery of the idealized house from the *Fusha* poem contradict those used to describe Farme's grandma's real home in three significant ways: whereas the former is depicted in positive terms, the latter is negative; while the former is panegyric, the latter is derogatory and down-to-earth; and, finally, the two are opposites in linguistic register. From the beautiful, stalwart architecture to the anthropocentric image of nature, the setting of the *Fusha* poem is one of harmony between humans and the rest of nature, written entirely in positive terms. The real house is quite negative in comparison. It lacks in epithets, thus pathos, and its only adjective—"old"—distorts the idyll of the *Fusha* poem. Grandma's "old stone" bricks invoke ruin in contrast to the stability of the "red brick" of the *Fusha* house. And while a garden full of flowers is pleasant to see and smell, a *bura* full of weeds and thorns is torture to the eye as well as to Farme's legs when he goes to the outhouse.

The intended panegyric style of the *Fusha* poem alludes to a vast corpus of schoolbook texts depicting a pastoral, idealized Lebanon, in which natural beauty and serene internal states of awe define the nation, closely reminiscent of Ilyas Abu Shabaka's and Al-Akhtal al-Saghir's poetry. The extensively taught Abu Shabaka composed verse filled with romantic individualism whose pastoral scenes guaranteed that it would be politically unthreatening. Instead, the conflict in his work centered on how the denatured world of the city threatened the ideal pastoral life in the mountain.[46] As the poet Yusuf al-Khal wrote of authors with a similar oeuvre from that period, "We used to praise nature . . . her virtues and beauty . . . [with] primitive optimism."[47] According to literary critic Robin Ostle, that kind of romantic awe reflects a tendency to ethereal and spiritual amatory poetry.[48] In contrast, Farme's lack of "primitive optimism" makes the second account appear derogatory. There is nothing to replace the wonderland garden, the noble towering trees, or the industrious bees as symbols of beauty and harmony. In fact, the outhouse and the surrounding *bura* have conspicuously taken their place. These images are not only grotesque caricatures of the idealized house, but they also deflate its imagery and language. In this sense, Farme's colloquial words are down-to-earth and contradict their idealized double.

The third difference is the linguistic register: *Fusha* versus the Lebanese vernacular. Farme's idealized lyrical description is entirely in *Fusha* with the proper final vowels, as in poetry, but the real house is described fully in the Lebanese vernacular. The high, almost heavenly imagery of the *Fusha* poem is matched by the "high" style of its standard register, while the down-to-earth, rustic imagery in the description of the real house harmonizes with vernacular's "low" style. Farme's body language, his facial expressions, and the pitch and intonation of his voice during the two descriptions reinforce his view that the two languages have a hierarchical relationship. And so does Farme's reason for not describing grandma's actual house first: "The other one [the poem house] is better. It is in the grammatical [formal language]."[49] When he starts reciting the idealizing lyrical description, he stands up out of respect for *Fusha* or to show his pride in being able to recite in the language of solemnity. His face acquires a solemn expression, and he recites in a high-pitched, confident, and rhythmic chant. By contrast, when he starts describing the real house in the vernacular, he sits down, rocks in his chair, frowns, and knits his eyebrows. His voice becomes lower and coarser and loses its festive quality. The camera shows Farme's shaggy forearms. Even worse, his potbelly is in the way of the table as he is trying to adjust his chair.

Grandma's real house is a direct parody of the ideal house that reflects an idyllic Lebanon that commonly appears in textbooks as a prewar icon and is reproduced in series such as *Mister Mandur.* As a parody, the real house represents not only its own imagery, language, and style but also the characteristics of its double from which it derives its own meaning. In this sense, their relationship can be interpreted as what Mikhail Bakhtin has called a "dialogical relationship" and the space they occupy as "a zone of dialogical contact."[50]

Of course, grandma's house is fictional. Nonetheless, its description in the vernacular, at least within the scope of Farme's narrative, implies that it is more truthful to Farme's reality. That is, until Farme recounts his actual vacation in a mixed *Fusha*/vernacular register while a third house in silent moving images mocks his narrative. He recounts that he wakes up early when the roosters crow, yet the accompanying images show him getting up only after grandma beats him awake with a broomstick. He says that he shares meals with his grandparents, but the camera shows how he elbows the old couple away from the meal, leaving them a single piece of flatbread. The camera, therefore, exposes Farme's languages and shows what really happens in a series of images that do not have diegetic human voices. Yet the reality in Farme's village is by no means ridiculous. The subject of humor is Farme, not his grandparents. They retain a kind of dignity. In this sense, they do not possess the quality of parody in themselves, nor does the first lyrical description if taken alone. Rather, the humor surfaces retroactively when the ideal house is compared with the one Farme narrates and with the silent images, as Bakhtin has posited for heteroglossia. If grandma's house and its media of representation—vernacular and prose—expose as fraud the lyrical house and its media—*Fusha* and verse—then the silent house exposes all of them. This parody questions the ability of language to authentically represent Farme's experience. Even though moving images appear to be the most truthful representation, perhaps in a way that Ziad Rahbani's instrumental piece appeared to be more truthful than songs with lyrics, uncovering consecutive levels of self-delusion suggests that there might be more underneath.

Indeed, the house of many languages is also a commentary on the divorce of the idyllic Lebanon of school textbooks (the kinds Mandur teaches to his students) from the reality of the civil war. Farme's reference to a thicket of weeds and thorns in the *bura* parodies the beauty, timelessness, and anachronism of idealized textbook verse, reminding the audience of abeyant lands, abandoned and destroyed homes, and a dislocated population suffering from loss and ruin. A close up of Rayya silently reciting the lyrical verse alongside Farme hammers home the point. Perhaps Rayya repeats the verse because she enjoys it, but the camera mercilessly reveals that she knows the verse by heart, which makes Farme a fraud even before Kamal squeezes the truth out of him. Mocking the technology of idealization is remarkably similar to the famous challenge of idyllic poetry by the Poets of the South. When the cause of the South became prominent after the Israeli invasion of 1982, a newly emerged group of Shi'ite poets resisted the common impulse to idealize the southern village. Instead, they "repeatedly challenge[d] a romantic nationalism that sought to imagine Lebanon within a strictly beautiful, physical landscape."[51] Mocking romantic nationalism on *My Aunt's Home* is a declaration radically opposed to a "culture that eradicates truths," as Hassan Abdallah described those who tried to cover up social problems and instead wrote about beauty.[52] In *The Stone of Laughter*, too, Barakat describes the desire to sweep wartime problems under the rug because exploring these problems may lead to uncomfortable discoveries, "seeing it [the city] in its ugliness would make them [the Lebanese] see their own ugliness, its repugnance would make them see their own repugnance, that is why they prefer twisting the truth about it and staying their course."[53]

If *My Aunt's Home* suggested that circulating images of a beautiful sanitized Lebanon was a fraud that led to sweeping problems under the rug, the show also exposed how *Fusha* led to detachment from wartime reality. The show portrays *Fusha* as an obstacle to communication, not its means. *Fusha* and the Lebanese vernacular can be used in separate speech acts, as in the two descriptions of the house. They can be also combined through code-switching; that is, switching between languages (or linguistic registers) within a single sentence or a group of sentences. *My Aunt's Home* uses code-switching as a device to parody *Fusha*'s detachment from everyday life and conversations:

> "Is your grandmother's house as you described it? (*Wa-hal baytu jaddatika bi-hadha-l-wasf*)"
>
> "What? (*Kayf*)," asks Farme.
>
> "The description you just gave (*Alladhi qultahu-l'an*)," Kamal explains.
>
> "I do not know (*La a'rif*)," answers Farme.
>
> "How come? Did not you just give me a description of it? (*Kayf? A lam tasifhu li*)," Kamal has to explain again, still persisting on using *Fusha*.

After his three-word answer in *Fusha* (*kayf, la a'rif*), the chatty Farme finds it impossible to use it and switches to the Lebanese vernacular:

> "I memorized it [the poem] but I didn't know what I was saying (*Ana hafaztu w-ma fhimt shee min il iltu*)."
>
> "How does your grandmother's house look like? How? (*Bet sittak kifu, kifu*)," Kamal now switches to Lebanese vernacular as he wants Farme to understand him.
>
> "My grandmother's house exactly as it is? (*Bet sitti mazbut, mazbut*)," Farme double checks in the vernacular.

The parody here is directed against the difficulty of *Fusha* as a means of intelligible communication and transfer of meaning. That is why Kamal has to explain things twice, once as a teacher by using *Fusha* that his students don't understand well (or don't want to understand), and a second time as an everyday person using the Lebanese vernacular. In this short dialogue exchange, the Lebanese vernacular establishes itself as the appropriate means of communication, no longer just as *Fusha*'s double; the joke is on *Fusha*.

In sum, *My Aunt's Home* destroys the elitism behind the notion of language register with its pastiche of place. But it also creates ambiguity about the communicative value of language in general as well as skepticism that any language variety (*Fusha*, the vernacular) can properly reflect one's experience and communicate one's thoughts to others. It is here that *My Aunt's Home* comes closest to the skepticism about language as the medium of communication prominently reflected in 1980s Lebanese culture (see chapter 3, this volume). Salame questions the medium of his art like 1980s writers question the medium of their own trade. The show also makes the case for television as a superior medium of modern communication because it introduces multiple special-linguistic realities, allows them to challenge each other, and tolerates ambiguity through the pastiche of place. In this sense, it embraces the sensibility of language pessoptimism or the parallel suspicion of language and the development of a "distinct," "strikingly Lebanese" language so characteristic of wartime Lebanese culture.

Self-Reflection and the Death of Trust

In an environment where ambiguity was fair game and language was far from reliable, trust in authority ceased to be an operational principle of media legitimacy. *My Aunt's Home* took stock of television's own relevance by becoming increasingly self-reflexive and meta-critical of its standards. Such meta-discourse was influenced by the suspicion with which the audience and other technologies (novels for example) now looked at broadcast media and its purported legitimacy.

A clever illustration of the medium's introspection on trust in authority and meta-cognition is the ode (*qasida*) Saber composes in the episode titled "The Camel."[54] Saber is a former hospital nurse who wakes Kamal after surgery to give him sleeping medication. A savant who suffers from logorrhea, Saber tires the other characters with his constant commentary and unwanted presence, which prompts Kamal's wife Jina (Claudia Marchalian) to call him *makhluq* (entity, creature). He never joins Kamal's class, although he is similarly incompetent at communicating. Even his French, which he uses to show off his education, does not escape the other characters' mocking as it tends to be mispronounced and grammatically wrong. Sometimes, like any wise fool, he is accidentally insightful. Besotted by the impression that Indian fakirs sit on nails and eat glass to entertain vast audiences, Saber convinces Dara to disguise himself as a fakir to make money as a fortune-teller for a charity cause. To help Dara with the promotion of the fortune-telling gig, Saber brings Farme to a camel and a tent on top of a hill—traits reminiscent of Bedouin Arabs' lives rather than those of an Indian fakir. In preparation for the promotion, Saber tries to strike up a friendship with the camel and composes a short *qasida* for him.

The traditional Arabic *qasida* is a rhymed poem—the ultimate icon of Arab culture. Composing and reciting eloquent poetry was a revered, distinguishing characteristic of Bedouins. The best pre-Islamic poets idealized the nomadic life in the desert with their female camels—their cherished companions—and the campsites that the tribe abandoned seasonally. After the advent of Islam, the pre-Islamic *qasida* became one of two main sources (the other being the Qur'an) for Arabic grammar and vocabulary. It was also considered a kind of historical record of the Arab tribes, especially because it enlisted the names of campsites and geographical regions and often described tribal battles and other events. The high style and complex meters of the pre-Islamic *qasida* are difficult to imitate, while their obscure vocabulary is often hard to understand. Yet eloquence rooted in imitating pre-Islamic poetry has been a goal for generations of Arab poets and professional reciters of live poetic performances.

As I have shown above, poetry is so important to Arab and Lebanese culture that all the series analyzed here engage it. When used skillfully, poetry signals belonging to Arab culture and respect for its heritage. By contrast, a negative attitude toward poetry might mean losing one's right to belong. For instance, in Nizar Qabbani's play *Jumhuriyyat Jununistan: Lubnan Sabiqan* (*The Republic of Insanitolia: Formerly Lebanon*), sectarian militia members lose the right to belong to the Lebanese nation and Arab culture when they axe a long list of Arab poets and writers from the republic's literature textbooks.

Convinced of having remarkable literary skills, Saber begins composing a *qasida* about a camel, like the famous Bedouins, leading the audience to expect that he will follow the traditional *qasida* requirements. This is the *qasida* he produces ("Saber" is the Arabic for steadfast):

> O' Bub'a, O' Camel,—Ya steadfast (Saber) in the desert sand
> On Wednesd'y ya travel—Ya leave me aband'.[55]

Despite its many transgressions, Saber's *qasida* meets some of the requirements (subject, rhyme, vocabulary, live performance, linguistic code, and style), perhaps to establish the ground for the work of parody. Convinced that he has produced a masterpiece worthy of the pre-Islamic Bedouins, Saber points to the traditional subject of camel, desert, hardship ("steadfast"), departure, and abandonment. His *qasida* properly rhymes on each line's final syllable ("sand"—"*aband'*," in Arabic *sahari—la-hari*), as well as on the hemistich ("camel"—"travel," in Arabic *Bub'a—urb'a*). In fact, when Farme does not understand what aband' means, Saber explains that the word should have been "abandoned" (in Arabic "alone," *la-hali*) but he perverted it to save the rhyme. As a bonus, this word is a simulacrum of an obscure pre-Islamic lexicon. Some of the *qasida* is in *Fusha*, its style clearly ceremonial, which Saber intentionally underlines as he recites it in front of Farme.

In a Salame-style double parody, Saber's recital contradicts the expectations set up in the beginning. The subject is deviant. The tribe does not abandon the old campsite (as in old poetry); rather the camel abandons the hero. Additionally, instead of using place names to anchor the *qasida* (e.g., names of abandoned campsites), Saber marks his ode with time (a weekday's name), a highly unusual category for that type of poetry. Next, rhyme and register suffer too. The rhyme clips two words—*Wednesd'y* (*al-urb'a*) and *aband'* (*la-hari*)—mutilating the *qasida*'s style and meaning. Saber's *qasida* also mixes the linguistic codes of *Fusha* ("steadfast" and "the desert sand") and the Lebanese vernacular (*al-urb'a*, and the use of the predominantly vernacular active participle, having left me [*tarikni*]). Although the *qasida* boasts the obscure word *aband'* (*la-hari*), this word is a fabrication, not part of the idealized treasure chest of the Arabic language. This sets up the language in the *qasida* as deception. Style is compromised too. When Farme hears Saber's *qasida,* he recognizes the first words ("O' Bub'a, O' Camel") from the beginning of an old song, which is not a masterpiece, but an earworm with second-rate lyrics. It is so unremarkable that if Saber's copy-ode were the result of real poetic effort, it would be bottom-of-the-barrel tacky. Finally, despite the ceremonious live performance, as in old customs, Saber's audience (that is, Farme) is unable to understand high poetry. Besides, Farme openly discloses that he is perplexed with a compromise such as *aband'*, which is easy to decipher.

Saber follows the *qasida* rules only in semblance, while in fact shrewdly transgressing them. His poetic effort disappoints the audiences' expectations because his *qasida*'s subject is perverted, its rhyme based on deception, its vocabulary seemingly incomprehensible, its recital uninspiring, its registers mixed, its style weak, and its content juvenile, not least because Saber manages to sneak in a vain, but generically appropriate, reference to his name ("steadfast"). The most significant observation that the audience could make is Saber's spectacular failure of taste, on the one hand, and the parody of *Fusha*, poetry, and high culture, on the other.

The effort and detail with which this scene was created seem pointless, since shortly afterward the audience's beliefs about the characters turn into a delusion. Dressed in a long abaya, Farme recites a rhymed retort to Saber's ode imitating a Gulf accent. This scene mocks Bedouins, the *qasida*'s inventors (as Gulf Arabs are supposedly closer to Bedouins than the Lebanese are), as much as it does the fictional world of *My Aunt's Home,* in which Farme should be a literary ignoramus. The series mocks itself as a medium for creating meaning that audiences could trust.

Ultimately, allowing, even inviting, audiences to challenge the media's legitimacy and trustworthiness allows them to see television as a site for behaving politically and for assessing the media and their relationships with it. The carnivalesque played a crucial role in that process for defining the parameters of television and audience modernity on LBC.

7

War, Modernity, and the Crisis of Patriarchy

Aesthetic quality is the most potent medium for
the passing on and perpetuation of cultural tricks.
—Abdullah al-Ghathami, "Cultural Criticism"

A Televised Flop

During one of the episodes of the quiz game show *al-Mutafawwiqun* (*The Vanquishers*), audiences witnessed the spectacular downfall of the most famous contestant of the show, Dr. Jacque Kondakjian.[1] The young Kondakjian had been moving forward in the contest, answering increasingly more difficult questions for three months, "*armed* with knowledge, information, and a brilliant memory."[2] On the early evening broadcast of April 12, 1980, he could not answer a relatively easy question about the date of the Nazi siege of Leningrad, nor could he answer the rescue question asking him to identify the first military coup in the Arab world. He simply muttered "impossible" three times.[3] The audience gasped, while the show's creator Marwan Najjar looked shocked and buried his gaze in a piece of paper in front of him. Later he admitted he could not find an explanation for the mysterious fiasco. The press churned up whole articles reliving the Kondakjian scene in lengthy descriptions of the atmosphere, the dialogue between Kondakjian and host Suad al-Ashi, and the reactions of audiences and the creative team. Trying to make sense of his stunning fall from the 16,000 LL award level, *Shabaka* wrote, "An important bridge that connected the people to *The Vanquishers* and rallied them around the show collapsed with Jacque Kondakjian's downfall. We hope that Télé Liban's administration will take better care to encourage the vanquishers, instead of sticking a rod in their wheels and robbing them of their self-esteem with one hand after having handed it to them with the other."

The left-leaning pro-Palestinian daily *Safir* had already been circulating rumors and accusations that the show was marred by pro-Christian bias on account of the identity of its four famous contestants. But eventually the show regained its standing, especially after Charbel Taia, who had exited earlier at the 8,000 LL award level, returned, perhaps in an attempt to shift the focus away from the Kondakjian debacle. The accusations are interesting, though, given Najjar's own statements in the contemporary press (and years later in a personal interview with me) that his goal was to combat the militias' recruiting efforts among youth and promotion of the militiaman role model. According to Najjar, the show allowed "young talents from different confessional backgrounds to play the role model of national heroes whose only *weaponry* is books, and whose *battlefield* is knowledge. Kids aspired to look and act like those worthless fanatic warriors, and parents needed badly a substitute, like idols, to motivate their children to follow their steps. *The Vanquishers* created a whole generation of superheroes of knowledge."[4]

The word in the show's title, *mutafawwiqun* (sing. *mutafawwiq*), means "superior"; surpassing, outstanding; or victor. It is a relational adjective describing a person who has outperformed or prevailed over someone else or who stands at a higher level than someone or something else. The title thus reflects the game show's ambition to present an alternative model of masculinity that could defeat the dominant militarized masculinity of the 1980s militiamen. As evidenced in Najjar's statement, the assumptions each model undergirded—about the modernizing nature of knowledge and intellectuals versus the backward nature of violent, crazy, sectarian militarism—were central not just to the show's title but also to its expected outcome. The geeks were supposed to distinguish themselves from the bullies by winning the prize and the admiration of the young male audience. Kondakjian's downfall confounded such expectations as it suggested that the geeks might not be ready yet to vanquish the bullies, but it became truly devastating with the revelation that the geeks were the bullies. Allegedly, Kondakjian and his Christian militia friends had threatened one of the judges—Palestinian historian Dr. Nasri Zarubi—demanding that he give them the answers to the next round.[5] When the judge alerted the show's team, Najjar reportedly wrote a set of new questions at the last minute. The team tried to hush up the whole affair, but Najjar's attempt to popularize an alternative model of masculinity suffered a sharp blow.

The televised flop of the alternative model did not deter Najjar, and a few years later he reimagined it in Mandur's character in the show *Mister Mandur.* Since the war opened new spaces to challenge codes organizing gender and to remake masculinities and femininities, the other shows on teaching Arabic also offered their own take on alternative gender models. In previous chapters, I discussed the important role the carnivalesque played in these shows for defining the parameters of television and audience modernity. Here, I analyze how the carnivalesque and discourses on modernity intersected with gendered discourses in the same language shows.

The Crisis of Patriarchy

The immediate aftermath of World War I, famine, and the establishment of the French Mandate (1923–46) undermined male authority in Lebanon during the mandate. As a result, Lebanon experienced a period of "gender anxiety" characterized by a struggle among paternal privilege, republican fraternity, and universal democracy, according to historian Elizabeth Thompson.[6] Negotiations of gender relations ensued at home and in the civic order, and these changes spurred fierce conflict over women's rights. The struggle over gender decreased class and religious conflict among males and rounded off with a "gender bargain" that deprived women of many rights, preserving male privilege in a reasserted class and sectarian hierarchal order. Thompson defines the "gender anxiety" at the three levels of nation, community, and household as a "crisis of paternity"; however, it is more broadly a "crisis of patriarchy."[7]

The Lebanese Civil War was a similarly turbulent period of "gender anxiety" that could be called a "crisis of patriarchy" at the levels of nation, community, and household, albeit with different dimensions. Historian Suad Joseph has argued convincingly that Lebanon's dominant social system is a connective heteropatriarchy.[8] It occurs when people construct their identity as citizens on the basis of the relationships they forge with high-status male members (sectarian patrons) within the hierarchy of the consociational minority. Individual citizens seek such relationships because only the minority's political leaders, rather than the actual individual, can secure rights and benefits from the state.[9] The civil war posed serious challenges to the structures of patriarchal connectivity and personalized state-citizen relationships.[10] Public institutions collapsed or only vestiges survived, forfeiting the state's ability to collect revenue and consequently provide services for its citizens directly. For instance, lost customs revenues cut total budgetary revenue significantly: from comprising a third of the total budget in 1974 to 3 percent of a much smaller budget in 1987.[11] At the same time, the power of the traditional sectarian patron, the *za'im*, was assaulted by the militia leaders. The local population now had to appeal to the militia for services like sanitation, housing, police, protection, and others because it was the militia who ran them in each sectarian enclave.[12] Neither the government nor the army were in a position to protect civilians from the rampant intimidation and violence from militias. Civilians lived at the mercy of the militiamen, from the higher-ups to the lowest-ranking members. Therefore, the viability of the traditional male politician model decreased, and with it there was a decline in the hegemonic masculinity associated with the workings of the prewar heteropatriarchal nation-state.

At the level of the community, the militias' challenge to connective heteropatriarchy sparked a crisis of parental authority and paternal protection. Michael Johnson attributes militia mobilization to the changing family patterns of the urban poor after they moved from the country in the decade prior to the war. Extended families back home shared stable notions of gender roles and familial loyalties, which modernizing, cosmopolitan-looking Beirut challenged, pushing young men to look for a replacement of the repressive family order in new sectarian youth groups.[13] After the war erupted, over 100,000 young men (and a small number of women) left their families to join one of the thirty-plus militias and smaller gangs.[14] In their new militia family, young recruits enjoyed greater freedom and status and were socialized into specific codes of militarized masculine swagger as a rite of passage into adulthood.[15] Kinship relations, in the meantime, had become indispensable for survival in the absence of the state and the constant threat of militia violence. Families, therefore, competed with militias over the loyalties of their young male members.[16] When Joseph studied kinship relations in the immediate aftermath of the war, she discovered a widespread set of tropes that described the perceived tensions, pressure, and blame among family members over their loyalty, such as a "ruined generation" of "corrupted" children who failed in their filial duties and "nervous" mothers "burned out" from daily responsibilities.[17]

What I focus on, though, is the crisis at the household level, which pitted men versus women in terms of employment. The Lebanese economic system remained unchanged, despite the conflict, with a dominant private sector and a free foreign exchange market.[18] In fact, the national Bank of Lebanon, which dictated monetary policy, was the only stable government institution.[19] The system owed its survival to the formal private sector and the expanding informal economy.[20] Civil society contributed to the stability too because it continued to push back against total collapse. However, the economy incurred heavy costs such as inflation, budgetary deficits, reduced government services, and eroding purchasing power (per-capita gross domestic product [GDP] for 1990 was estimated at a third of what it was in 1974).[21] The third phase of the war (1982–90) experienced rapid economic and financial deterioration following the Israeli invasion.

The war had diverse and contradictory effects on professional opportunities for men and women. The number of male jobs decreased as many companies closed down or relocated abroad. The nonfinancial service and trade sectors declined as did manufacturing, but the construction sector grew.[22] Real wages dropped and the standard of living declined. This caused an accelerated emigration of skilled male labor that checked the level of unemployment to a degree (e.g., unemployment was 8 percent in 1970 and rose to an estimated 10 to 35 percent between 1987 and 1992).[23] Overall, the business and professional class that remained in the country was better off.[24] However, men in unskilled labor had to seek multiple jobs to survive the downturn. In addition, they had to compete with an inflow of non-Lebanese unskilled labor. Extreme pessimism about shrinking work opportunities and the bleak future was rampant, all the more since the heteropatriarchal state imagines a household with a male breadwinner and a mother-housewife.[25]

As male employment was under strain, the family's diminishing financial security pushed women to seek opportunities for employment outside the home. Many were forced to find work instead of their husbands and brothers because when women left home they were less likely to be harmed by the militias.[26] Therefore they could earn a living, bring back food and medications, ensure the survival of the family, and guarantee their men safety from abductions.[27] The need for every household member to contribute to survival "turn[s] men's economic protection of women into a myth," according to Deniz Kandiyoti.[28] As the Lebanese woman became a "full partner in family economics and often its sole provider," women's employment increased by 10 percent and their employment span shot up by twenty years.[29] Consequently, women faced new situations where they "suddenly found themselves heads of households, caring and attending to every aspect of their family's needs."[30]

The labor drain caused by the emigration of Lebanese men did not trigger a transformation of the workforce in favor of women. In many places, women's roles decreased after industrialists mechanized the process, let go their women employees, and hired unskilled foreign men in their place to run the new equipment.[31] By 1982, 64 percent of all male workers were foreigners, mostly from India, Sri Lanka, and Thailand. Because "employers gave in to their deep-seated biases and misconceptions about women's suitability for mechanized labor," hiring women in the textile and food processing industries, for example, decreased by about 75 percent.[32] By comparison, the powerful tobacco industry, which relied heavily on nonmechanized labor, preserved and increased the number of its female employees and the benefits for which they had fought so hard in the previous decades.[33] These developments, according to Malek Abisaab, were not inspired by frozen cultural attitudes that discouraged female labor in general. That women wanted to work is clearly visible from the fact that industrial companies received a large number of applications for work from women, who were nonetheless sidestepped in favor of hiring men. Poor working conditions and lack of benefits, rather than negative social attitudes, were another substantial reason that kept many women away. That is why improved labor conditions in the tobacco industry, for instance, attracted committed female workers, who formed 41 percent of all the industry's workforce in 1981 and 42 percent in 1987.[34] These uneven effects placed women in complex situations that required them to move strategically to maximize the possibility of their desired outcomes and minimize the pressures of the patriarchal system in which they operated.

Becoming breadwinners, however, did not free women from house and motherly duties. Instead, they became subject to new patriarchal pressures as they had to learn a whole new set of routines. They pulled an "accordion work day" that increased as needed to accommodate paid labor and housework.[35] An interviewee of researcher Maha Charani, who studied female attitudes during the war, shares: "It was men's war and women had to pay the price. I remember every day we used to spend two hours getting water and carrying it to the seventh floor for cooking, cleaning, and drinking. Our whole life's routine and rituals changed. How we cooked, how we cleaned, how we took showers."[36] Despite the double shift that many women now faced, men in general were not prepared to lessen women's burden and take on some of the household and child-rearing responsibilities.[37]

While lower-class women were less restricted to find jobs, middle- and upper-class women had to fight more explicitly for them. In the early 1970s, career choices for middle-class women had been limited mostly to working as teachers, bank tellers, and nurses.[38] During the war, when the number of employed eligible men shrank and single women could rely less frequently on marriage as a financial plan, greater numbers of women enrolled in secondary and higher education to ensure their own well-being. With this forming cadre of empowered women, careers became more important to Lebanese women and many became highly protective of them, such as hiding a pregnancy in fear that it would delay a promotion at work.[39]

Whereas women entered a variety of fields such as law, engineering, science, and business,[40] a considerable number chose to become writers, journalists, and activists. As jobs in media became one of the socially acceptable venues for women during the war, 75 to nearly 90 percent of all media majors were women. According to an unpublished study by Najah Abdallah, between 1982 and the end of the war in 1991, female students averaged 75 percent of all students enrolled as media and communication majors, peaking at 87 percent for the 1988–89 academic year.[41] These numbers are much higher than the general trend for other majors, where female enrollment increased from 25 percent in 1973 to 48 percent in 1993.[42]

Just as journalism careers rose in popularity with middle-class women, private engagement with writing also became popular. A cluster of women writers emerged to become one of Arab literature's modern phenomena (e.g., Ghada al-Samman, Hanan al-Shaykh, Emily Nasrallah, Etel Adnan, Huda Barakat, Jean Said Makdisi, etc.).[43] Writing allowed women—as a counterpublic—to resist the state and the official male-dominated public sphere. It also became frequently depicted in women's wartime novels as a women's profession. According to Joseph Zeidan, creating fictional female characters who were often journalists, writers, artists, or fighters appears to have been a semiautobiographical trend.[44] The compulsion to write among some women should be considered against the fact that many other women could not dedicate their time and energy to reading and writing. As another of Charani's interviewees shares, "The war set me back intellectually. I did not have the time or the luxury of reading."[45]

Prompted by migration, loss of male jobs, and the stresses of survival, shifting patterns of employment caused systemic change in familial control. Extended families broke apart and familial control over women loosened—males could no longer exercise it exclusively.[46] This lowered familial resistance to female paid work and ultimately allowed women greater leverage and bargaining power within patriarchal culture.[47]

Due at least in part to the decrease in familial and male control, women assumed public and volunteer roles. Activists commonly push the boundaries of acceptable policies and behaviors in society. Lebanese women activists were no different. They found ways to thrive even within the patriarchal contexts they were navigating. Women increased their participation in governmental and women's organizations whose mission was helping the displaced, orphaned, or injured in dangerous circumstances.[48]

After training as a volunteer with the Emergency Medical Service for only ten days, a woman's group was called to report for duty following an Israeli bombing. She remembers:

> It was one of the worst days of my life. Bodies everywhere, blood, pieces of skin and guts were hanging out everywhere. I was terrified. I felt my legs shaking; my heart was pounding very fast, and I thought it was going to stop. I was afraid of collapsing and fainting but I had to be strong and courageous. We started picking up the dead bodies and looking for survivors in the rubble. As we were pulling the dead, Israel hit again. . . . We started running toward the ambulance. . . . Most of us made it to the ambulance, but two of our colleagues were still far away. Some of the volunteers in the ambulance wanted to move and leave the two behind; the others did not want to leave them. Luckily they showed up before any decision was made. We saw them running toward us, we stretched our arms and held onto theirs while the ambulance was moving. . . . I looked at my friends and to my astonishment they were all laughing. I think I was too. We were trying to hide our fears from what we just experienced. After a few days I got used to it. I was not afraid to see blood or death anymore while I was working, but when I went home at night I could not sleep.[49]

Many women across national, religious, and class lines also entered the arena of political activism to resist oppression and to fight for peace. Some joined the resistance movement against Israeli occupation.[50] Ain Helweh, the largest Palestinian refugee camp located in South Lebanon, was destroyed by the Israeli military. The camp's women defied the Israelis and rebuilt the camp using female labor. Other women frequently contested what were considered matters of common concern by engaging in political activism through peace rallies, sit-ins, hunger strikes, and petitions, and at times they tried to dismantle militia checkpoints.[51] For instance, a spontaneous twenty-three-day sit-in at the American University of Beirut began on August 1, 1982, when about a hundred women protested the shortage of water, power, and medications caused by the Israeli siege. Sometime during the sit-in, the women engaged in a three-day hunger strike. Grassroots organizations like the Lebanese Council for Women also organized a series of conferences and peace demonstrations.[52] A famous photograph taken by Roger Moukarzel in 1978 Beirut shows an elderly woman giving a flower to a soldier.[53] This photograph conveys a widespread idea that women are more peace-loving, while men are more prone to fighting and violence. Not all Lebanese women protested the war, though. Some enrolled in militias in what can be seen as temporary military careers. There were three all-women fighting units, called *Nizamiyyat* (Regulars), which trained and fought alongside their male counterparts. Interestingly, one of the female units refused to raid a building with a sniper upon hearing the cries of a baby inside, as they believed they had to kill the baby to get to the sniper.[54]

As a result of women's activism and resistance of patriarchal codes, they scored a number of victories, including in 1983 when the ban against the sale and use of contraception was revoked, which afforded women more control over their life choices.[55] Under the contradictions of patriarchy augmented by the war, Lebanese women developed new attitudes toward their paid labor that challenged earlier social and gender codes (e.g., no longer regarding writing and journalism as male professions). With the changes in women's own attitudes, society began developing new attitudes too. No one cared about the gender or able-bodiedness of relief workers, as one activist states: "During a situation of war, no one thinks about the fact that you're a woman. They think about getting help: who can provide help."[56]

In sum, the three levels of gender anxiety—the national, the communal, and the household—involved conflict within and between the genders (see Table 1). On the national level, a dominant, militarized model of masculinity, which governed the militia mini-state system of citizenship, challenged a prewar model of cosmopolitan masculinity, which governed the patron-client system of citizenship. On the community level, the conflict was generational. A more attractive model of younger, militarized masculinity challenged a traditional model of older, patriarchal, parental authority. In the household, an increase in female employment and decision making rubbed against a decrease in male employment and control over women's behavior, placing the two genders in a bind. The older, patriarch-ruled order appeared to be under attack from younger males

Table 1
Challengers to Dominant Gender Models

Model	*A. Challenger*	*B. Challenged*
1	Militarized masculinity (militia mini-state)	Prewar, cosmopolitan masculinity (patron-client system)
2	Young, militarized masculinity (community of militia "families")	Older, patriarchal parental authority (community of traditional families)
3	Women (more egalitarian household)	Men (traditional patriarchal household)

and women at all three levels, and the hegemonic masculinity the older patriarch represented appeared to be in crisis.

Competing Models of Masculinity and Femininity

Bullies, Geeks, and Tyrants

The militiaman is an iconic wartime signifier with positive and negative connotations. We saw "Charbel" portray the militiaman positively as a protector of the community and a reluctant, self-sacrificing hero. Positive tropes were openly celebrated by the community in its own historiography, in public rituals, and in private settings even as the community suffered at the militias' hands. Najjar's statement about *The Vanquishers*, on the other hand, depicted the militiaman critically, and similar negative images circulated widely in multiple other cultural products from the war. For instance, Qabbani's *Republic of Insanitolia* portrays the militiaman as a villain, an uneducated savage, and the main agent of sectarian violence against civilians.

The militiaman often presupposed a monolithic form of militarized masculinity. In reality, as we saw in "Charbel" (and as is also the case in *The Republic of Insanitolia*, where the low-ranking militiaman pins the violence on the higher-ups), militia culture was brimming with internal contradictions and struggles among multiple forms of militarized masculinity. The rank-and-file militiamen tasted few of the rich spoils from rackets, drug money, and arms deals that the higher-ups enjoyed, and instead they were forced to serve in ways that offered little benefit.[57] By the mid-1980s, many of these militiamen became disillusioned and left the group,[58] as militarized masculinity experienced a downturn.

But when Najjar proposed the vanquisher model in 1980, militia culture was at its peak. Hegemonic prewar models of masculinity based on assumptions of cosmopolitan tolerance were under tremendous attack. I believe Najjar's proposed model acknowledged the failure of prewar cosmopolitan masculinity to prevent the encroachment of sectarian militia violence as it acknowledged the need to experiment with new models that would attract the modern young male. According to Walter Armbrust, the media are "significant sites for social experimentation because they are at once removed and engaged, observers of the public space that their activities also define."[59] Najjar's early experiment with the vanquishers suggests he tried to channel violence and aggression into nonviolent competitiveness and play, positioned alongside monetary markers of success (the prize levels) rather than the perpetration of brutalities. The vanquisher identity was unattainable for most young Lebanese men, who would not have performed well in the competition. In fact, even the four famous contestants had to cram for months, and some left because they got tired of the lifestyle. But it demonstrated to males displaced from the labor market a creative way to earn extra money that did not involve the militiaman's "breadwinning" of extortion, theft, drug trafficking, and illegal taxation. The competition was also potentially attractive to a thrill-seeking young man because the contestant could lose his "earnings" with one wrong answer and diminish his status vis-à-vis other competing males.

After the young geek revealed himself to be tarnished by the militia bully culture that he was supposed to vanquish, I believe Najjar reimagined alternative masculinity and came up with the Mandur model of linguistic nationalism. If the geek is secretly sectarian and therefore untrustworthy, he needs a lesson in nationalist loyalty. In addition to addressing the crisis of citizenship, the benevolent grammar dictator also tackles the generational crisis. As a strategic patriarch, Mandur berates older males for failing to take seriously the socialization of younger males (e.g., Jad's alcoholic father, Walid's absent father). Najjar then reclaims their power by reimagining the failed younger vanquisher as an older patriarch; hence the "patina of age" makeup and styling applied to young actor Diab. Last, Mandur is a problem-solver worth hiring who is also in control of his household. Ultimately, his alternative masculinity is the triumph of bourgeois nostalgia for the prewar cosmopolitan era when employed, educated professionals were representative of hegemonic masculinity, while the uneducated, unemployed, sectarian poor were its nemesis.[60] Mandur the intellectual modernizer is a response to the marginalization of the older hegemonic male and intellectual. But he also reminds us of a widespread denial that many cosmopolitan and modern elites benefited tremendously from the war by serving as business partners, bankers, and speculators for the militias.[61] Dr. Jacque Kondakjian may have attempted to do just that by teaming with his militia buddies.

Women on the Periphery

In addition to replacing the younger vanquisher with the older patriarch, *Mister Mandur* also displaced women. I believe the real purpose was to sweeten the male-by-male replacement deal. If the militarized male was to ultimately transmogrify into the prewar cosmopolitan male, the potential resistance and conflict between the two may be averted with a male coalition and male visibility at the expense of women. Further, if the militarized male were to give up his power, swagger, and freedom in order to return to an economy of strain, unemployment, and gender competition, a world that lowers male anxiety by displacing women may just be attractive enough to make the sale. This seemed equally reassuring to men outside the militias, whose "he-men" fantasies of superiority over women's interests may be enough to lower anxieties generated in the labor market where women appeared to be outcompeting some of the men.

Thus, women disappear as main characters, relegated to the periphery of *Mister Mandur*'s fictional world. When anything important happens on the series, it is done by men and as a result of interactions among men. As a central character around which the series is built, Mandur's interactions with the other characters—mostly male administrators and teachers—bring them into the spotlight and bestow significance on them. Most importantly, though, all the school kids whom Mandur tries to help, in fact to save, are boys—Jad who suffers physical abuse from an alcoholic father, Sami who is expelled when his father is kicked out of the school's snack kiosk, Walid who refuses to go to school because he sees no benefit in the teaching styles he experiences, Mazen who searches for his birth parents, and even the depressed tall boy Deeb.[62] When Mandur is not part of the scene, the plot revolves around other males, like the fight between the two snack vendors Fadlu and Anwar, or struggles over the principal's job with seen and unseen school trustees.

In their supporting roles, women are an extension of the male characters or their mission. Noticeable, though limited, stage time is allocated to Mandur's sister Assia and, toward the end of the series, to Hala—his sexualized student. Neither, however, challenges the main premise of center-stage males and peripheral women. For example, all of Assia's desires and concerns center around what is good or bad for Mandur. She looks for a bride for him, serves food and drinks to his colleagues, takes care of the school kids whom he shelters, or chaperones his private lessons. Assia seems to have no private life apart from Mandur, except for playing cards with two women friends whom Mandur resents and berates throughout the series.

Although the show's men and women are portrayed as incompetent parents some of the time, men are motivated to grow and with Mandur's help they shed their limitations. Women resist growing. Walid's mother, who is raising him on her own (as her husband works abroad), has lost control. Instead of finding a way to get to Walid, she yells at him in desperation. But when Mandur steps in to help and finally gets to Walid by breakdancing with him, the boy's mother gets upset and throws Mandur out, preventing herself from growing as a parent and her child from being heard and understood. Jad's mother is a particularly interesting example. Although Jad's father is an abusive alcoholic, with Mandur's help he discovers that the core of his rage lies in his wife's superstitious, uneducated personality. She makes amulets to ward off evil spirits, tries to predict the gender of her unborn child by different methods of divination, and is worlds apart from his intellectual concerns. When Mandur steps in to liberate the husband from this suffocating atmosphere, he advises the husband to accept his wife the way she is—superstitious, uneducated, and naïve because she can never develop a higher consciousness. The series portrays male growth as predicated on accepting a presumed female inferiority.

The comedic genre, or the carnivalesque, makes female displacement more palatable. But *Mister Mandur* is not nearly as extreme as *Professor No*. Writer Anwar Tamer included very few female characters in the *Fusha* series, the main one played by famous Egyptian actress Shirine. The small number became a topic of discussion in the press as well as the fact that Majzoub chose to hire an Egyptian actress for the role of the romantic interest instead of a Lebanese actress. Nor could *Mister Mandur* compete with the chauvinist flavor of *Miss Teacher.* Under a thin guise of gender equality in casting, *Miss Teacher* depicts the outright abuse of women. For example, the male protagonist hits a female African student when he gets frustrated with another character.

Career Women as Villains

Miss Teacher's plot does not suppress women's roles because it approaches the defense of male economic interests differently. The show resolves the paradoxical expectations of women in the changing economic environment—equal to men in the workplace on the one hand, dutiful wives and mothers on the other—with an instructive comparison between the supporting and the lead female role (Zarife versus Hind). Both develop career appetites and aspirations for starting a family. Yet the former is punished as a threat to male economic interests, while the latter is rewarded for playing to them.

While it is difficult to find full-bodied villains on the show, *Miss Teacher* nonetheless has an antihero—the school's incompetent *nazira* (principal) Zarife. Zarife is a marked character. Her name, which means "nice" or "companionable," is carefully crafted, evidenced by the series' use of the actors' real first names for almost all other characters (e.g., Ibrahim, Hind, Shafiq, Amalia, Aliya, Jean, Yousef, etc.). Using their own names allowed the other actors to bring into their roles a part of their own personality. The audiences too could read them as composite characters against the background of their many earlier roles. This was especially true for Ahmad Khalife who instead of his real name brought his character Abu al-Abed al-Beiruti that had made him famous since the 1960s. Abu Abed is a *qabaday* (street tough) from Lebanese folklore known for his bamboo switch, jellabiya, red fez, and handlebar mustache. By contrast, Zarife's character could be read as a marked character, one that audiences should pay special attention to. Such attention walls her off in a separate category as the antihero and puts her negative qualities into stark contrast. For one thing, Zarife is violent with the students. She orders them to stand perched against the wall with their arms up, whips their feet, and marches them to class at gunpoint as punishment for misbehavior. She also abuses teachers and students verbally, bemoaning their trickery, stupidity, and laziness. But despite these obvious flaws, I propose that Zarife's markedness is not based on her negative qualities. Rather, it is based on her ambition to own marital property and her drive to be a powerful career woman—the two very desires that patriarchy finds unforgivable. Patriarchy operates through the construction of gender-appropriate desire that divides "active males" from "passive females." According to Bourdieu, male desire is constructed as the desire for possession.[63] Zarife's multiple desires, including for different kinds of possession, constitute a punishable transgression against dominant patriarchal norms.

Zarife wants it all—career, success, power, romance, marriage, and property. However, she is a victim of sexist politics underneath the comedy of her villainy. Her downfall comes with her struggle to succeed as a school principal in a profession traditionally held by men. In the end, she stands accused of incompetence at running the school and of its eventual closure. Here, the show eliminates the middle tones to achieve a greater contrast between Zarife's failure as a career woman and her self-described, and delusional, mission as an "educator of the up-and-coming generations." The show abounds in examples of how Zarife fails at her job—from misusing her authority with subordinates and wasting her working hours for romance to incompetence at managing the school's property—allowing displaced individuals (*muhajjarin*) to occupy one of the classrooms. Yet the damages that Zarife allegedly causes the school in fact come from factors outside her control. For one, the students go on strike when the two teachers stop coming to school as they are busy bickering over matters of the heart. Further, in the real wartime Lebanon, a large portion of the population was turned into squatters in the forced war migration, and sometimes schools were taken by the squatters. The show depicts how, in a situation of constant threat to one's life, the students' interest in learning is understandably low, which inspires the teachers' sarcasm. But war, displacement, poverty, and rampant political opportunism melt away as Zarife takes the fall. Most of all, though, she fails to effect the school's mission—neither her administrative philosophy nor her subordinates' teaching methods educate the students. The students' failure to pass the same exam for three years could not have been more obvious to the audience since it is frequently discussed by multiple characters, and the series opens with a close-up of an entrance plate that says, "School for Eradicating Illiteracy." Eventually, Zarife is punished for her misdeeds—the owner fires her and sells the school.

Other desires that she has, such as being wanted and romanced, although punished verbally with ridicule, are forgiven as they do not transgress the boundaries of acceptable female status within patriarchy. Take for instance, the show's double standards in age and appearance. The Mirashli style of comedy was to saturate his shows with heavy-handed antics and burlesque wisecracks. Some of the offensive nicknames thrown at Zarife seem to have been modeled to fit the actress's age. Ibrahim calls her *mjanzara* (old, ancient; lit., covered in verdigris), which ridicules Zarife's desire for love and romance as well as her capacity for being an object of romantic desire. Layla Karam, who played the supporting role, brought to it a certain gravitas that comes with a well-oiled acting persona. Although her heyday was in the late 1960s and 1970s, she had been a fixture on Télé Liban and its premerger ancestor since the beginning of Lebanese television. As a veteran, Karam listed on her long resume series like Télé Liban's signature shows *al-Dunya Hayk* (where she played Warde; the series featured a few of *Miss Teacher*'s cast as well, like Shafiq Hasan, Yousef Fikhri, etc.) and *Abu Melhem* (where she played Abu Melhem's wife despite being twenty-five years younger than him).[64] In interviews, Karam openly complained about being cast as a mother and never as a romantic lead despite her illustrious talent and heaps of praise from critics and audiences. The press shared her disgruntlement. As early as 1963, *Shabaka* warned that it was a mistake to cast twenty-six-year-old Karam in the role of Nadya Hamdi's mother since the two were the same age.[65] When Abd al-Ghani Tlis interviewed her in 1982, he was astonished that she had never played the lead, only to hear in reply that the audiences wanted them looking young.[66] She costarred with Hind Abi Lama on *Around My Room* and was Mirashli's mother-in-law in *Songs and Thoughts*. In addition, Karam acted in several Fayrouz-Rahbani plays and films like *Safar Barlik*, *Mays al-Rim*, *Bint al-Haris*, and others. When Karam played Zarife, she was almost fifty and her own age enhanced the role's inverse alignment between age and romance. In contrast to Zarife, neither Hind's nor Ibrahim's fathers' age is considered a problem when they get involved romantically. Karam's broad-boned physique was also exploited when Zarife is called *biftek 'umri* (beefsteak of my life)—a Mirashli-style perversion of the expression *habibat 'umri* (love of my life). The butcher's apprentice Abu Abed, a student in the school, gives her this nickname when he admits to being in love with her, a complete non sequitur in the plot. The name offensively objectifies Zarife as a product and is a crude reference to Zarife's/Karam's failure to live up to dominant notions of femininity, beauty, and desire. The fact that only the butcher is in love with her presents a link with the sexual politics of meat.[67]

The show forgives Zarife for her age and physique after it sufficiently pokes fun at them. However, it does not forgive her desire for power and influence. She is portrayed as a gold-digger who has manipulated her new husband (Ibrahim's millionaire father) to sign all his property into her name after their marriage. Divorce for many Muslim Lebanese couples can easily be initiated by the husband (e.g., in the case of *talaq* [repudiation]). It is enough for the husband to repeat that he divorces his wife three times with no justification or court decision for the divorce to be considered legal. Consequently, women's desire for stability, especially financial stability that does not depend on the fickle desires of a philandering husband, led to cultural fears of powerful women who can dominate and control their husbands if the marital property was signed to the wife's name. The show plays on these kinds of fears when Zarife's move for financial control angers Ibrahim, who has become her stepson and is now disqualified from receiving his dad's fortune. Pretending to be an apparition, he frightens Zarife that her husband would divorce her unless she belly dances for him like a cabaret dancer. (Cabarets are a type of shady establishment, a cross between a nightclub and a brothel with strong connotations of prostitution.) Interestingly, Zarife heeds this ridiculous advice despite earlier assurances of her chastity and decency when she warns Ibrahim not to educate her on certain subjects, implying that she is ignorant of sex. Even more interesting, she chooses to dance in lingerie at an important meeting convened to decide the fate of the school, rather than in the privacy of her marital bedroom. In addition to revealing that she is naïve and superstitious, this decision proves to her husband that she is not the cultured, educated woman he thought he had married. Again, this portrays her as incompetent in her career as an educator. As a result, he promptly divorces her. Zarife goes insane and is sent to an asylum while Ibrahim restores his inheritance. The meeting at which she performs the belly dance is a school board meeting over which her husband presides after he buys the school. Zarife has admitted her desire to be the school's director, and since all the property should have been in her name (as the series alleges), it only makes sense that she preside over the meeting as the owner of the school. Clearly, women's power is symbolic, yet it is still so threatening that it requires Zarife's disposal in an asylum.

Women's Career as Silly Entertainment

While *Miss Teacher* allows female characters like Zarife to express serious aspirations in the work arena in order to punish them accordingly as villains, it simultaneously celebrates female characters with no serious career ambitions. The show infantilizes women's aspirations for a career, alleging that they enter the job market for any number of superficial reasons, such as boredom or looking for a husband—all nonthreatening to patriarchal men and thus appropriate for dutiful women.

In contrast to the negative though humorous portrayal of Zarife, Ibrahim's love interest Hind is depicted in positive terms that affirm gender stereotypes but ultimately question her viability as a career woman. As an unmarried woman from an affluent family who can afford several real estate properties, drivers, and personal servants, Hind has some independence that allows her to dabble in humanitarian service. Nonetheless, she has dedicated herself to eliminating illiteracy not out of social activism or financial need but out of a desire to entertain herself and to "build character." As serving society comes last on Hind's list, her self-proclaimed humanitarian mission is only skin-deep. She questions it and so does her mother, who suspects that Hind is in fact running away from an unwanted marriage prospect. Furthermore, Hind's father tries to prevent her from having a career, even one as acceptable for unmarried women as a language teacher, instead of trying to prevent her from having a romantic partner he disapproves of (a more typical parent concern).

A discussion of women's career is central to the series' response to "the crisis of patriarchy." While Hind and Ibrahim have identical job descriptions, the series' title *Miss Teacher and Mr. Professor* (*al-Mu'allima w-al-Ustadh*) introduces him with the more respectable title *al-ustadh* (professor, teacher) while she is just *al-mu'allima* (grade-teacher, also master of a trade). The titles of *Mister Mandur* and *Professor No* also use *ustadh* to describe the male educator—*Ustadh Mandur* and *Ustadh Mamnu'*—and only *My Aunt's Home* excludes the male teacher Kamal and instead builds its title around the female role. Curiously, the press occasionally misremembered *Miss Teacher*'s title and put the professor first, rendering the title as *Mr. Professor and Miss Teacher* (*al-Ustadh w-al-Mu'allima*), offering a read on the series' gender dynamics and perhaps subconsciously fixing a slip-up in patriarchal ordering. Hind is also called *mademoiselle*, while her student Pierrot (who is about her age) invalidates her credentials and status when he addresses her as *tante* (French for aunt), a term frequently used in Lebanon to address women from an older generation. Thus, the series introduces an alternative discourse of age that derails, even parodies, the discourse on women's career and status. Indeed, age hangs over Hind; since she's no longer a young girl, she is afraid that she might be waiting for Prince Charming until "[her] hair becomes white." This thought convinces her that she needs a man. Career, it seems, is just a distraction until that man appears, which again depicts her as a nonthreatening character.

The show also injects uncertainty in viewers about female skills at motherhood. Half the female characters are bad mothers in some sense—Zarife's reproductive clock is dead, yet she has failed to become a mother; the pregnant Amalia fails to birth her baby for three years; Ibrahim's mother abandons him by dying; Youssef's mother fails to raise her son, committing herself to extramarital affairs and playing cards instead; and Pierrot's mother, Aliya, hopes to learn the recipe for green peas from her son's textbook, forcing Hind—who is an odd choice for criticizing a mother—to berate her as a woman that should not be a mother if she does not know how to care for her children. The fact that Pierrot is forty enhances the joke, yet also makes for a more caustic bite. These and other examples involve female characters who do not have careers, implying that women should first become competent at motherhood before they have any aspirations for a career outside the home. The real-life parental choices of actress Amalia Abi Salih may also be relevant. Her adoptive daughter Jessica was abandoned as a toddler by her biological Jamaican mother and given to the mother's friend, Amalia. Amalia raised Jessica through two marriages and a period of single parenthood and would occasionally bring Jessica to act with her. Jessica is the young African woman whom Ibrahim hits in the series, physically punishing and perhaps symbolically devaluing the one real example of responsible, committed parenting.

In sum, there are at least two similarities in the ways the three shows on Télé Liban convey their concepts of modern masculinity and femininity to their audiences. First, a modern male is one who spends time and effort to restore male privilege or get to the socioeconomic top in some sense. Higher-status, older males (Mandur or Fadil; i.e., Professor No) engage in a master-disciple relationship with younger or lesser males (Mandur's pupils, Fadil's servant Aziz) to develop the latter's masculinity. This relationship indexes a primary dynamic on which prewar cosmopolitan masculinity is built, thus restoring its hegemony. Alternatively, males that fall between the older/dominant and younger/lesser types (Ibrahim) bluff, maneuver, or swindle their way to the top to assume the patriarchal position. Second, the modern female is an obstacle in some sense to the presumed centrality of negotiations of maleness to modernity. Masculinity only develops when femininity is neutralized, diminished, or removed altogether.

Competent, Powerful Career Women

The negotiation of modern masculinity and femininity on LBC's *My Aunt's Home* is radically different. Maleness is not central to the portrayal of modern society, nor is the male in any rush to the top. The majority of the male characters are in a state of confusion and ambiguity, especially in terms of employment. Kamal is a servant-teacher, Sabir and Kamal's brother Mazen are predominantly unemployed, Lamya's father-in-law is retired, Farme is a student (also unemployed), and Salah is an actor under threat of losing his job because technically he is unskilled for it. A minority are unskilled or low-skilled laborers like Dara, the immigrant gas station attendant. Only Lamya's husband is a young professional working as a television director, yet even his status is at the "lower" ranks because he directs food advertisement or assists the actual director. In other words, older males are retired, low-skilled, or in a state of ambiguity, no more established or secure than their confused, low-skilled, or free-floating younger counterparts. (By comparison, males on *Mister Mandur* tend to be professionals like teachers, administrators, and journalists; *Miss Teacher*'s males are teachers and wealthy business owners, while on both series the low-skilled males like butchers or snack vendors are the ones being educated, admonished, or disciplined.) Neither do *My Aunt's Home*'s males register great achievements in status or employment in the sequel. Most remain where they were in the original, while Kamal is hired as a grade teacher, a respectable job but nothing spectacular.

Modern maleness is decidedly not a return to the past nor to cosmopolitan heteropatriarchy. It is in step with the changing scripts for normative gender behavior. *My Aunt's Home* features strong, confident women who often exceed their male partners in power, skills, and success. Aunt Suad is an independent unmarried woman who manages to raise her niece and nephews, provide for them, and educate them so they seek intellectual careers. Suad's background is not explored either, which makes it even more interesting as she needs no explanation to justify being able to raise three children. In her house and outside she is a strong character whose value is never questioned—it is assumed as normal.

Other women on the series have successful careers outside the home. The niece Lamya for instance is a successful journalist, as is her friend Hind. In the original show Lamya is more successful in her career than both her brothers. While Kamal is struggling between giving private lessons and waiting tables and Mazen has no known employment, dedicating his time to funny schemes, Lamya is making money churning out articles for the paper where she works. The episode treats her career with respect that dwarfs concerns about marriage: Mazen approaches Aunt Suad to break the news that Lamya has found herself a marriage partner, hoping his aunt's deepest wish for her niece is to get married. But when Suad says matter-of-factly that her wish is for Lamya's successful career as a journalist, he is a little disappointed at being deprived of the chance to prove himself an excellent intermediary. Suad still matter-of-factly adds that she would be happy to see Lamya get married if that is what Lamya wishes. Contrary to Télé Liban's shows, women on *My Aunt's Home,* as Lamya's case demonstrates, are celebrated for being more concerned with their career than with being wives and mothers. She finds meaning in employment outside the home in a field that has long been dominated by men—the press—but which during the war opened up to many women. Lamya also finds her self-worth in writing (as Suad implies), as did many actual middle-class women during the war.

Employment obviously is not a matter of concern, but cultural traditions around motherhood might be. Take for instance the episodes on the birth of Kamal and Jina's daughter Hala. Sabir's friend and former coworker, nurse Tammam, has been fascinated with the nursing profession since childhood when she used to give the other girls shots instead of playing with dolls. She invites Sabir out for dessert and reveals that, when she was a child, parents used to scare girls with the imaginary monster Abu Dibe, who "eats girls but does not touch boys" (*biyekol el-binet, biykhalli ssabe*). Sabir has never heard of this sexist character and his rhyme. Tammam is not surprised at the surgical precision of gender discrimination and admits she is happy the newborn's gender no longer matters in this culture like it used to. However, when put to the test herself, she feels disappointed that Kamal has a baby girl rather than a boy. Similarly, Kamal's female supervisor chooses to deceive the school that Kamal has a newborn son in a plot to increase his prestige among his colleagues. Modernity, then, is a dynamic where women have to figure out how traditional scripts, such as those around motherhood and birth, can be negotiated. For Jina, it is simply to affirm Kamal's satisfaction with having a daughter. But the series might just be suggesting that the pleasure trap of patriarchy makes women equally likely to affirm their own oppression.

According to Ghathami, his "cultural criticism project seeks to unveil tricks used by culture to carry its discourse under different guises, with aesthetics being the trick that is the most outstanding when it is used to pass on the most dangerous and domineering norms."[68] Patriarchal norms are so deeply embedded in texts and discourse under the guise of aesthetics and desire that they are de facto invisible. Ghathami's cultural or norm criticism is useful to uncover the symbols, norms, and institutions that participate in the construction, representation, and communication of gender and gender relations theorized by Joan Scott. How does one then unsettle deeply embedded patriarchal norms or the habitus of patriarchy within which gendered consciousness is generated? According to Clare Chambers, the "most effective form of social change is the combination of an enforced, structural change together with active promotion of a new set of norms," for example, through "positive portrayals of working women."[69] As I showed with the above examples, such a lens is helpful in exploring how the different visions of a modern television-audience relationship put forth by Télé Liban and LBC were refracted through gendered discourse.

It might be tempting to conclude that Télé Liban promoted inherently misogynistic cultural norms while LBC embraced an enlightened course toward the dismantling of patriarchy. Lila Abu-Lughod warns us, however, that resistance against patriarchal norms and symbols should not be romanticized because it is never external to structures of power. The institution of Lebanese television operated within structures of power to construct competing visions of relevant gender identity and relations. Neither vision arose from an actual egalitarian television-audience relationship. Given the pressures of the war, both outlets' relationship with the audience was fundamentally based on enormous differences in power, not to mention the capitalist, patriarchal relations of production among the employees of the institution that were still in force, despite LBC's impressive female employment. What the different gender portrayals ultimately tell us is that each outlet employed them to convey a special vision for a new, modern relationship with its presumed audience.

This deep dive into the complex analysis of gendering on LBC and Télé Liban therefore serves as a helpful lens into how each station conceived of its own modernity. Within the confines of the mini-genre, Télé Liban conceived of its modernity as a protector of patriarchal, family values and male employment, while LBC conceived of its modernity as a trendsetter in women's empowerment and female employment. More broadly, the entwined histories of the two channels, of which the gender lens is part, reflect the broader issues raised during the war: the negotiation of a modern television-audience relationship; the connection of global trends in television production and consumption to local historical context; e.g., negotiating gender relations in response to changing local scripts for normative gender behavior, and interpreting political truth as cultural truth where language and gender became sites for behaving politically.

Ultimately, these broader issues raised by the gender analysis set us up to think about the importance of broadcast television in Lebanon and the region, or how working within structures of power, the field of patriarchy, and the institution of television led to the establishment of a new hegemonic order based in consumer culture rather than the breakdown of hegemony, which I discuss in the conclusion.

Conclusion

The Case for the Study of Lebanese Broadcast Television

So we bought the intellectual rights to the series' title to use in our restaurant.

—Jean-Claude Ghosn, restaurant owner

Pretty Liar offers three contributions.[1] The first is to make the case for the study of Lebanese broadcast television by suggesting that its historic exploration is relevant to understanding the present relationship between television and audiences, as may be seen in the following two examples.

In late 2008, Lebanese streets buzzed with a hit campaign, "Khidi Kasra w-Harriki al-Umur" ("Change in One Bold Stroke"), created by advertising magnate H&C Leo Burnett Beirut, which had launched the controversial Johnnie Walker bridge campaign during the 2006 Israel-Hezbollah war.[2] The edgy "Khidi Kasra" campaign was commissioned by the Hariri Foundation (an NGO established in 1979) as a step toward women's empowerment. The name of the campaign is a play on words: *kasra* means both a diacritic mark for feminine gender (a short vowel written with a slanted stroke) and a habit. Thus, the slogan meant "Get a *kasra* and vowel things" and "Get into the habit of making things happen."[3] The campaign's creative team teased this phrase by exhibiting big signs in the streets of Beirut that displayed the words "Your responsibility, your right, your will," unmarked by gender diacritics (see Illustration 8). All passersby who read the sign pronounced the words in the default masculine gender, leaving women invisible.

8. Slogan of the Khidi Kasra Campaign. Khidi Kasra Campaign, Hariri Foundation, conceived and developed by Leo Burnett, Beirut.

Then the main, interactive phase of the campaign demonstrated the engaged relationship between civil society and television. The campaign organizers invited people to attach a red *kasra* sticker under displays featuring the campaign slogan at university campuses, in supermarkets, and inside the pages of popular magazines (see Illustrations 12 and 13). Members of the public soon took to adding the *kasra* to the language of bus ads, traffic signs, graffiti, and social networks (see Illustrations 9 and 11). On March 8, 2009—International Women's Day—the campaign hit the media: hosts and anchors on all Lebanese channels wore the campaign's pin and opened up lively discussions of women's rights (see Illustration 10). The campaign also reached the broader region through the most famous Arab reality show, LBC's *Star Academy,* as well as through Arab channels outside Lebanon.

A few years later, nostalgia for golden age television hit the restaurant business. Restaurants and cafés named after iconic golden age Lebanese

9. Street art replicates the campaign message. Khidi Kasra Campaign, Hariri Foundation, conceived and developed by Leo Burnett, Beirut.

10. Discussing the campaign on satellite television. Khidi Kasra Campaign, Hariri Foundation, conceived and developed by Leo Burnett, Beirut.

11. Advertisements on city transportation replicate the campaign message. Khidi Kasra Campaign, Hariri Foundation, conceived and developed by Leo Burnett, Beirut.

12. Passersby write in the feminine gender marker under the campaign slogan. Khidi Kasra Campaign, Hariri Foundation, conceived and developed by Leo Burnett, Beirut.

13. Local celebrities add the feminine gender marker under the campaign slogan. Minister of education, Bahia Hariri. Khidi Kasra Campaign, Hariri Foundation, conceived and developed by Leo Burnett, Beirut.

series or characters began popping up in Beirut, such as "Shoushou Snacs," "Abu Melhem," "Abu Salim," "Such Is Life," and "Sitt Zmurrud: Lebanese Authentic Restaurant" (Sitt Zmurrud was Feryal Karim's character in *Such Is Life*). "Such Is Life" opened on Mar Mikhail Street in Ashrafieh after the former old residence of the Gharius family was renovated to become a nostalgia-themed restaurant. Old wooden doors, mosaics, an artesian well with a large copper pail tied with a thick rope, cushions, backgammon, and a *baladi* (authentic) menu conjured up the village atmosphere of the golden age. Those who had not seen the series could watch it in the restaurant or learn some of its characters' catchphrases from the placemats: "Leysh Heyk?" ("Why's that?"), a character asked the *mukhtar* (mayor) at the end of each episode; "Al-Dunya Hayk" ("Such is life"), answered the *mukhtar*. The restaurant advertised its relationship with golden age television at the entrance, which featured large images of two stylish Lebanese men—one sporting the *tarbush* (fez), the other dressed in 1970s attire.

The waiters also featured male fashion by dressing as *Alloush*—the series' character famous for his quaint clothing and numerous hats.

The television-themed restaurants appeared against the backdrop of a recent trend across the Middle East to style cafes and restaurants in what anthropologists Lara Deeb and Mona Harb call "heritage style."[4] The civil war had destroyed the country's vibrant leisure culture and the downtown cafes had closed.[5] There were a few restaurants and coffee shops in residential areas and along the beach, but most eateries became takeout food stands, juice bars, or food caterers.[6] People were apprehensive about sitting down to socialize in public, given the dangers of exposure to sniper fire or sudden outbursts of violence. After Hariri's assassination in 2005 and the 2006 war, coffee and restaurant culture expanded rapidly and developed an eclectic style of interior and exterior design to capture a growing diverse clientele with middle-class income and aspirations.[7] One among four categories of design (heritage, nature-garden, formal dining, and contemporary),[8] the heritage, or Eastern style, features themes of idealized Ottoman, Bedouin, and village life with clear nostalgic overtones. Its faux-stone or wood decors, traditional arches, corbels, balconies, canopies, low couches, checkerboard tabletops, and antique objects (e.g., copper pots, gramophones, or sepia photos of prewar Beirut) are intended to promote customers' learning "about their origins and their identity while they are being entertained," according to the architect of one of the cafés.[9] Even conservative neighborhoods like the Shi'a-majority Dahieh have witnessed a rapid expansion in café and restaurant leisure culture that caters to a mixed-gender clientele of different ages. Eating and coffee establishments offer multiple attractions, including playgrounds, internet rooms, unique Turkish baths, swimming pools, gyms, museums, souqs, and poetry rooms.[10] "What all these cafes have in common," according to Deeb and Harb, "is an emphasis on consumption as part of leisure or participation in commercial leisure—purchasing coffee, food, or argileh [hookah] in order to spend time in a place as opposed to spending time in a public park (though those are scarce in Beirut) or visiting people in their homes."[11] The "heritage" style of ethnic chic reflects trends of upwardly mobile tastes; a desire to distinguish oneself as urban, modern, and inclusive against the pastiche of the rural environment of the establishment.[12] The style also reflects nostalgia for a period presumed to be superior to a present that reflects deep sectarian divisions.

While the television-themed restaurants and cafes exhibit the abovementioned general characteristics, they also feature a unique trait related to television. Their choice of theme signals the continued importance of broadcast television in the modern Lebanese mediascape. They strategically offer customers an environment where the notion, experience, and memory of broadcast television helps them to distinguish themselves as inclusive modern consumers who can skillfully navigate between broadcast and satellite media.

"Khidi Kasra" and "Such Is Life" demonstrate the intersection of language, gender, and consumerism that lie at the heart of the new hegemonic relationship between television and audiences; I have discussed aspects of this transition in the previous chapters. "Khidi Kasra" is a descendant of *My Aunt's Home* and its challenge of cultural norms in the negotiation of modern femininity. Like the 1980s series, where Lamya and her colleague Hind established their independence through careers in print journalism (i.e., language), the nexus of gender and language in "Khidi Kasra" marks a modern go-getter woman who summons her power through language revisionism. The campaign was able to question the cultural norm industry by calling attention to the presumption of maleness in Lebanese (and Arab) culture and also by a subversive mixing of *Fusha* and the vernacular, reminiscent of *My Aunt's Home*. While the words in the slogan were written in *Fusha*, the interactive diacritic marks were placed and vocalized in the vernacular (e.g., *mas'uliyyatik* rather than *mas'uliyyatuki*). On the other hand, the television-themed restaurants are descendants of the nostalgia for the prewar heteropatriarchal male (Abu Melhem, the *mukhtar*, etc.) that lies at the heart of *Mister Mandur* and *Professor No*. This idealized male commands the power to solve problems with a catchphrase. Hence, these restaurants do not simply bring back Lebanon in its gender-neutral glory.

The apparent clash of the femininity model of "Khidi Kasra" and the masculinity model of "Such Is Life" should not obscure their ultimate support for the same hegemonic order. For example, "Such Is Life" offers a mixture of a selectively reinterpreted past and contemporaneity (customers park their twenty-first century vehicles in front before going in), packaged and sold for consumption. "We wanted to introduce a new concept in the restaurant world, which carries a spontaneous mix between Lebanon of the past and Lebanon of the present, so we bought the intellectual rights to the series' title to use in our restaurant," says Jean-Claude Ghosn, one of the restaurant's founding members.[13] "Khidi Kasra" in turn was birthed in one of Lebanon's most successful advertising agencies—the epitome of consumer society.

The engagement of "Khidi Kasra" and "Such Is Life" with television is not a free-floating signifier inspired by globalization, though; it has roots in historical Lebanese culture. *Pretty Liar*'s first intended contribution therefore aims to inspire a recognition that many of the current trends in Lebanese culture have deep roots in the war period and therefore this period should be investigated more thoroughly, especially its broadcast television. For instance, the roots of the state-sponsored amnesia of all things war made prominent by the Hariri reconstruction government lie in part in the wartime peace bubble and the game of avoiding the blame that both television and civil society played. Anchors blamed the NNA for the lack of news briefs, NNA agents blamed the militants for unsafe conditions, the audience blamed anchors and television administrators for occluding the war and ignoring public concerns, while, with few exceptions, all avoided their own responsibility.

Pretty Liar's second contribution lies in making the case for the study of Lebanese broadcast television by narrating its rich and dynamic negotiation of a modern television-audience relationship. The discussion covers the lengthy breakdown of the old hegemonic television-audience relationship (a disengaged relationship between an authoritative medium and more passive citizens) and the negotiation of a new hegemonic relationship (an engaged, yet commercialized relationship between an attentive medium and more active consumer-citizens). While a global paradigm shift toward more active audiences and television diversity occurred in the 1980s and 1990s, *Pretty Liar* has narrated the unique, local historical context of the Télé Liban/audiences/LBC triangle that brought about Lebanese television's greater engagement with audiences. War pressures put Télé Liban and its formerly independent branches, CLT and Télé Orient, in the tough position to downplay sectarian conflict in fear of adding fuel to the fire, thereby creating the phenomenon of a wartime peace bubble. The news bulletins therefore sanitized the news about the conflict with self-censored, belated, euphemistic, and meager coverage. The bulletins also occluded the war's meaningful discussion in favor of on-air hijinks during the television split and dedicated coverage to grandstanding around peace initiatives. Other war pressures led to the same effect, such as electricity blackouts, damaged technical equipment, unsafe working environments, and the lack of proper budgets due to the collapse of the advertising market and the hit on government revenue collection and budget allocation. The audiences began doubting Télé Liban's news relevance and lost confidence in its authority because of the station's intentional, unintentional, and at times unavoidable occlusion of the war. As a result, television suffered a crisis of legitimacy, while the audiences—a growing nonmovement of ordinary people, journalists, and writers—engaged with critical questions of television legitimacy, journalistic authority, and the nature of the television-audience relationship. The audiences expressed themselves with a flurry of carnivalesque language (sarcasm, parody, perverted media tropes) and contested broadcasting and the dominant cultural norm industry with public cynicism. They also imagined the ingredients of a new, more engaged television-audience relationship: trust, ethics (where television was a site for the public processing of trauma), and a deeply personal relationship placing the audiences at the center of representation. The future owners of LBC channeled the audiences' expectations of modern television and a modern audience out of sheer necessity to survive a blessing-and-curse conundrum. Redistributing a portion of their criminal gains had initially afforded them temporary public support but ultimately discredited them nationally and internationally. To get out of the conundrum, LF positioned itself strategically within mass-mediated communication and attracted audiences with attention, promises of pleasure, and a political truth interpreted as cultural truth. Ultimately, LBC had a role in reorganizing hegemony but not creating a television-audience relationship outside hegemony, thus commodifying audience taste and intimate experience with the medium.

Pretty Liar's third contribution has been in showing how language on wartime television and the way it intersected with gender became a site for behaving politically. I presented a flexible template for the study of television through the lens of language to which one can add more items—including diglossia; heteroglossia; nonverbal communication (body language, landscape as language); language ideology and the ideology of teaching language; and cultural norms embedded in language and the resistance of such norms. This template is innovative because it engages common themes across news, education, and entertainment genres and does not sever the natural ties among them. For instance, we see how all genres reflected the flammable language question (the war on illiteracy, *Fusha* versus vernacular, the increasing symbolic versus plummeting practical value of *Fusha*) because language became a referendum on television's relevance to the times. News on Télé Liban struggled to hold onto the elevated style and formal atmosphere of the government-centered, political public realm. The glamour of fashion and female beauty tended to distract predominantly male audiences from the occlusion of the war, while the anchors' grammar fumbles sidetracked male linguists who saw them as a failed expression of an authentic, rooted linguistic identity. In the end, while the content and format of its news was deemed boring and its language too formal and disconnected from the public's daily concerns, Télé Liban's audiences stayed tuned in for at least two reasons. First, audiences hoped for any information on the conflict. Second, they felt a connection to news anchors due to the latter's habitual presence during the family's evening routine. In a battle for institutional relevance in the eyes of the audience, Télé Liban's competitor LBC created an edgy vision of modern television. This vision was presented by a younger generation of bolder broadcasters who brought entertainment into politics, broke political taboos, and appealed to modern audiences unafraid of controversy. The station used parody and the carnivalesque in degrading the television peace bubble, and it embraced the vernacular to develop a hybridized, "strikingly Lebanese" language that better reflected the language tastes and sphere of competency of the public.

In entertainment shows that dealt with education—the comedy mini-genre about teaching and learning Arabic—as with news bulletins, language also became a referendum on television's relevance to the times. Local series on Télé Liban, which had favored the vernacular during television's early history, shifted to *Fusha* to sustain the station through regional sales but also in part to counter the perceived threat to standard Arabic and to create a shared Lebanese identity around it. *Miss Teacher* portrayed a traumatic stage in the presumed arrested development of Lebanese education, while *Mister Mandur* and *Professor No* presented a fantastical solution to the language identity crisis—a lone savior, a superteacher, a man with a mission. By moralizing on the shortcomings of viewers' everyday speech, Mandur and Fadil painted a portrait of modernity marked by trust in authority and hegemonic power relations organized within the domain of formal language. Unlike news bulletins, where the glamour of fashion distracted from the occlusion of the war, fictional series like *Mister Mandur* showed the patina of age and authenticated a kind of modernity that lived through links to the past. On the other hand, series on LBC like *My Aunt's Home* avoided moralizing, idealizing, and the patina of age or a claim to linguistic authority and *Fusha*'s hegemony. Instead, the series conceived of a television modernity that hinged on ambiguity, parody, and the pastiche of place as well as doubt and self-reflection. *My Aunt's Home* spoke to audiences that tolerated ambiguity without offering simplistic solutions or superheroes along the lines of Mandur. It embraced the sensibility of language pessoptimism—or the suspicion of language and the parallel development of a "distinct," "strikingly Lebanese" language—so characteristic of wartime Lebanese culture. Trust in authority ceased to be an operational principle of its media legitimacy. Instead, challenging television legitimacy and trustworthiness allowed audiences to see LBC as a site for behaving politically.

Intersecting with the language question, a second category important to the negotiation of modernity—gender—became central to news bulletins and entertainment shows. News on Télé Liban became a gendered site for reinforcing the peace bubble through the dynamic of female broadcaster–male viewer. While the roots of that dynamic may be traced back to early television, the war made it a central protocol in the television-audience relationship. The launch of LBC preserved the marketability of that model while adding a parallel go-getter female anchor model (e.g., Dolly

Ghanem from *Last Hour News*). On the other hand, the entertainment shows featuring Arabic teaching engaged with female employment and the search for viable masculinity models to oppose the militarized masculinity of the militias. The war-induced "crisis of patriarchy" (exemplified in the decreased viability of the traditional male politician model, competition between families and militias over the loyalties of young males, and gender conflict due to deteriorating economic conditions) produced more vigorously competing models of masculinity and femininity. Shows like *Miss Teacher, Mister Mandur,* and *Professor No* responded to the crisis with alternative models intended to cure the marginalization of the older hegemonic male. Indexing bourgeois nostalgia for that model, they tried to revive it by arguing for the centrality of masculinity to discussions of modernity versus the relative unimportance of femininity, evidenced by the latter's displacement, marginalization, or being rendered unthreatening. By contrast, LBC's *My Aunt's Home* did not position maleness as central to the portrayal of modern society, restore male privilege, or try to neutralize femininity. Modernity in *My Aunt's Home* was a place where men and women had to figure out how to negotiate traditional gender relations in response to the changing scripts for normative gender behavior. Ultimately, with the help of the norm criticism posited by Ghaddhami, *Pretty Liar* has uncovered deeply embedded gender norms within the changing scripts and analyzed how the visions of a modern television-audience relationship put forth by Télé Liban and LBC were refracted through gendered discourse.

Finally, *Pretty Liar* hopes to stimulate three areas of future research: research on broadcast television in Lebanon and the broader Arab region, research on language in Arab television as a key component in negotiations of multiple modernities, and exploration of the carnivalesque in popular culture and television. In addition, it adds to other researchers' voices that articulate the need to preserve and study television archives. The archival collections of television footage, especially that of Télé Liban, are disappearing fast due to lack of preservation efforts. They are also rarely accessible to outsiders. When Gladys Saade and her graduate students conducted research on Lebanese television archives in the early 2000s, they observed that most stations showed hostility to the researchers.[14] Another serious issue was entrusting the archives into the hands of unspecialized staff, and assigning them exclusively for internal consumption by resident journalists, although amateur search procedures often made even this functionality challenging.[15] Kept under lock and key as precious personal property prone to theft, archives were not envisioned as a source of interstation market income or as a matter of public interest, although they are part of a national heritage and a collective memory.[16] Yet, they are an indispensable resource for the study of early television.

The stress and trauma of Lebanon's civil war was a crucible that brought about rapid development in the relationship between its media and audiences. It should be expected that other rapid developments occurred outside the scope of this book that are valuable for media history and cultural studies. Observing how media and audiences shaped each other during times of trauma may also add to our understanding of the human condition.

NOTES

BIBLIOGRAPHY

INDEX

Notes

Introduction: A New Look at Old TV

1. The epigraph is from Lisa Gitelman, *Always Already New: Media, History, and the Data of Culture* (Cambridge, MA and London: MIT Press, 2006), 4.

2. Thomas Davis, *40 Km into Lebanon: Israel's 1982 Invasion* (Darby, PA: Diane Publishing, 1995); Ellen Laipson and Clyde Mark, *Conflict in Lebanon: From the Missile Crisis of April 1981 through the Israeli Invasion, August 1982* (Washington, DC: Congressional Research Service, Library of Congress, 1983), 32; Robert Fisk, *Pity the Nation: The Abduction of Lebanon* (New York: Nation Books, 2002), 200, 211.

3. Samir Makdisi, *Lessons from Lebanon: The Economics of War and Development* (London: I. B. Taurus, 2004), 33.

4. "The 1982 Israeli Invasion of Lebanon: The Casualties," *Race and Class* 24, no. 4 (April 1983): 340–43. The source reports the following statistics: 19,085 deaths and 30,302 wounded in the invasion (as reported by the Lebanese police); 49,387 plus 3,500 casualties in the following massacres of Sabra and Shatila (as reported by Israeli journalist Amnon Kapeliouk); and 52,887 total casualties on the Lebanese/Palestinian side.

5. Zaven Kouyoumdjian, *Lebanon on Screen: The Greatest Moments of Lebanese Television and Pop Culture* (Beirut: Hachette Antoine, 2017), 211.

6. *Bala Tul Sire*, Future TV, https://www.youtube.com/watch?v=2AxOWNB3qw8, published March 27, 2016.

7. Lebanon sent its first team to the World Cup qualifiers in 1994.

8. Kouyoumdjian, *Lebanon on Screen*, 135.

9. The outlet's CEO, Talal al-Maqdisi, stated in an interview he was prepared to air the cup "no matter the cost" even if that meant "his personal resignation," which inspired the press to muse about the dynamics between the government and the state-owned outlet. "Telefiziun Lubnan Yunaffidh Wa'dahu: Al-Mubarayat Mubasharatan li-Jami' al-Nas," *al-Akhbar*, http://www.al-akhbar.com/node/208650, "Court Throws out World Cup Lawsuit against Tele Liban," *The Daily Star* (Beirut), July 5, 2014.

10. Walter Armbrust has made this point for new media in Muslim societies. Armbrust, "Bourgeois Leisure and Egyptian Media Fantasies," in Dale Eickelman and Jon

Anderson, eds., *New Media in the Muslim World: The Emerging Public Sphere* (Bloomington: Indiana University Press, 2003): 102–28, 104.

11. Mohamed Zayani, "Arab Media Studies: Between the Legacy of a Thin Discipline and the Promise of New Cultural Pathways," in Tarik Sabry, ed., *Arab Cultural Studies: Mapping the Field* (London and New York: I. B. Taurus (2011), 55–78.

12. Annabelle Sreberny, "The Analytic Challenges in Studying the Middle East and Its Evolving Media Environment," *Middle East Journal of Culture and Communication* 1 (2008): 8–23.

13. Noha Mellor, "Media: An Overview of Recent Trends," in *Arab Media: Globalization and Emerging Media Industries,* ed. Noha Mellor et al. (Cambridge, MA: Polity, 2011), 12–28; Muhammad Ayish, "Political Communication on Arab World Television: Evolving Patterns," *Political Communication* 19, no. 2 (2002): 137–54.

14. Muhammad Ayish, "Arab State Broadcasting Systems in Transition: The Promise of the Public Service Broadcasting Model," *Middle East Journal of Culture and Communication* 3 (2010): 9–25; Muhammad Ayish, "Arab World Television in Transition: Current Trends and Future Prospects," *Orient* 41, no. 3 (2000): 415–34.

15. "121 Terrestrial TV Stations Broadcast in 18 Arab Countries," January 9, 2013, http://www.broadcastprome.com/news/121-terrestrial-tv-stations-broadcast-in-18-arab-countries/#.WQVWn1eFitA; "Terrestrial TV 'Stays Static in Arab World,'" *Trade Arabic Business News Information,* Amman, June 7, 2009, https://www.tradearabia.com/index.php?/news/MISC_162612.html.

16. Flagg Miller, *The Moral Resonance of Arab Media: Audiocassette Poetry and Culture in Yemen* (Cambridge, MA: Harvard University Press, 2007); Marwan Kraidy, *The Naked Blogger of Cairo: Creative Insurgency in the Arab World* (Cambridge, MA: Harvard University Press, 2016).

17. Helga Tawil-Souri, "Arab Television in Academic Scholarship," *Sociology Compass* 2, no. 5 (2008): 1400–1415, 1402.

18. Jean-Claude Boulos, *Al-Televizion: Tarikh wa Qisas* (Beirut: Sharikat al-Tab' wa-al-Nashr al-Lubnaniyya, 1995), 177; Kouyoumdjian, *Lebanon on Screen,* 75.

19. Boulos, *Al-Televizion,* 177.

20. Kouyoumdjian, *Lebanon on Screen,* 91, 149.

21. Ibid., 309.

22. Shafiq Ni'me, "Ferial Karim Tamut 'ala al-Masrah bi-l-Sakta al-Qalbiyya," *Shabaka* 1688, July 11, 1988, 14–17.

23. Kouyoumdjian, *Lebanon on Screen,* 101–2, 218.

24. Ibid., 199.

25. Male presenters were also sometimes banned, but that seems to have been temporary. For instance, in April 1975 Jean Khoury and Arafat Hijazi were banned for several weeks from appearing on the news over a dispute with the government censors. More research is needed to uncover the gender dynamics of censorship.

26. Bariaa Meknas is George Clooney's mother-in-law.

27. Kouyoumdjian, *Lebanon on Screen*, 235–37.

28. PARC press release June 5, 2009; see Mellor, "Media: An Overview," 17. In Egypt, broadcast television is very popular; 41 percent watched in 2011 and in Oman it was 48 percent (*Arab Media Outlook 2011–2015: Forecasts and Analysis of Traditional and Digital Media in the Arab World*, 4th ed., [N.p.: Dubai Press Club, 2012], 141, 198).

29. *Arab Media Outlook 2011–2015*, 141, 159. According to the World Bank, Egypt's gross domestic product (GDP) in 1980 was USD$22.9 billion, while Saudi Arabia's was USD$164.5 billion. In 2014, Egypt's was USD$305.5 billion, while Saudi Arabia's was USD$756.3 billion. For 1990, Lebanon's gross national income (GNI) per capita was USD$1,360, Egypt's was USD$740, and Saudi Arabia's was USD$7,340.

30. Sudan has 18 broadcast channels; Egypt has 17, Iraq between 16 and 21, and Palestine 25–30 (as of 2017). Tim Miller, Val Jervis, and Tim Hogg, *Terrestrial Broadcasting and Spectrum Use in the Arab States: A Report for the GSMA* (London: Plum Consulting, 2015).

31. Since the satellite era, broadcast outlets have developed dramatically in an atmosphere of severe competition from privately or semiprivately owned satellite channels. Conversely, the popularity of satellite television may be driven by competition from terrestrial broadcasters, especially in the production of local drama.

32. Noha Mellor, "Arab Journalists as Cultural Intermediaries," *Press/Politics* 13, no. 4 (2008): 465–83.

33. Lawrence Pintak and Jeremy Ginges, "The Mission of Arab Journalism: Creating Change in a Time of Turmoil," *Press/Politics* 13, no. 3 (2008): 193–227; Mellor, "Arab Journalists"; Lawrence Pintak, "Border Guards of the 'Imagined' *Watan*: Arab Journalists and the New Arab Consciousness," *Middle East Journal* 63, no. 2 (2009): 191–212; see also Jihad Khazen, "Freedom of the Press in the Arab World: Censorship and State Control in the Arab World," *Press/Politics* 4, no. 3 (1999): 87–92; Naomi Sakr, "Freedom of Expression, Accountability and Development in the Arab Region," *Journal of Human Development* 4, no. 1 (2003): 29–46.

34. Sreberny, "Analytic Challenges," 10.

35. This is so even if some have made the case that just one broadcast channel would be enough in case of emergency; see Miller, Jervis, and Hogg, "Terrestrial Broadcasting," 26.

36. Mellor, "Media: An Overview," 16.

37. Tawil-Souri, "Arab Television"; Zayani, "Arab Media Studies."

38. Lena Jayyusi, "Internationalizing Media Studies: A View from the Arab World," *Global Media and Communication* 3, no. 3 (2007): 251–55, 253.

39. Ayish has noticed that state broadcasters were seen as "minority voices" after the advent of satellite television and later the internet ("Arab State," 10).

40. Gholam Khiabany, "Iranian Media: The Paradox of Modernity," *Social Semiotics* 17, no. 4 (2007): 479–501, 487.

41. Kraidy and Khalil's nuanced argument that examines both private and state-owned satellite outlets is a welcome challenge to this assumption, and I believe its intention should be replicated. Marwan Kraidy and Joe Khalil, *Arab Television Industries* (London: Palgrave Macmillan, 2009).

42. Despite the vast global literature on war, on the one hand, and on Arab media, on the other, the growing need for a historical exploration of the Lebanese media during the important wartime period has barely been tackled. The subject of war and television politics is a sensitive matter in the Lebanese environment, like numerous other topics related to the war and sectarianism. The religious sects or political factions that own, or owned, broadcast outlets suppress the exploration of their businesses because such exploration may include investigating their politics and powerful patrons as well as the latter's alleged crimes. This sensitivity partially explains why the subject has not been researched in depth. With the exception of a few valuable but scattered chapters or articles, neither histories of LBC nor any lengthy academic studies of the role of Lebanese television in the process of cultural change have been published. Television veteran Jean-Claude Boulos's memoir, *Al-Televizion*, relates his personal experience as a founding employee of Lebanese television. Rich as his book is, it focuses on the technical, managerial, and financial battles of early television, glossing over critical questions of cultural politics, for example, or users' perspectives and their relation to the medium. Talk show host Zaven Kouyoumdjian's books *As'ad Allah Masa'kum: Mi'at Lahdha Sana't al-Televizion fi Lubnan* (*God Bless Your Evening: 100 Moments That Made Television in Lebanon*, 2015) and its expanded English version *Lebanon on Screen: The Greatest Moments of Lebanese Television and Pop Culture* (Beirut: Hachette Antoine, 2017) are important as fascinating yet brief accounts of 100 to 160 memorable moments chosen from the inaccessible Télé Liban archive, organized along news and entertainment formats (as a former employee, Kouyoumdjian was able to access the archive). The books' explanatory sections also deal with some of the outlet's cultural impact as a medium. Yet, this is a form of popular reading that should inform, not substitute for, theory-driven scholarly work. This situation is especially irksome: the recent increase in scholarly exploration of Arab cultural production from a number of theoretical frameworks could benefit significantly from studies of television, especially since the history of Lebanese television is one of the most tumultuous in the region.

43. Ronald Zboray and Mary Zboray, *Encyclopedia of War and American Society*, ed. Peter Karsten (Thousand Oaks, CA: Sage, 2006); Des Freedman and Daya Kishan Thussu, eds., *Media and Terrorism: Global Perspectives* (Thousand Oaks, CA: Sage, 2012).

44. Thomas Allen, F. Clifton Berry Jr., and Norman Polmar, *CNN: War in the Gulf: From the Invasion of Kuwait to the Day of Victory and Beyond* (Kansas City: Andrews Mcmeel, 1991); Barbie Zelizer, "CNN, the Gulf War, and Journalistic Practice," *Journal of Communication* 41, no. 1 (1992): 66–81.

45. Naomi Sakr, *Arab Television Today* (New York: I. B. Taurus, 2007), 2, 52; Kraidy and Khalil, *Arab Television Industries*, 17, 31.

46. Noha Mellor, *Modern Arab Journalism: Problems and Prospects* (Edinburgh: Edinburgh University Press, 2007), 50.

47. For the periodization of television into ages of scarcity, availability, and plenty see John Ellis, *Seeing Things: Television in the Age of Uncertainty* (London: I. B. Taurus, 2000).

48. Kraidy and Khalil, *Arab Television Industries*; for the expansion in Arab media choices and the emerging media industry also see Muhammad Ayish, "Television Broadcasting in the Arab World: Political Democratization and Cultural Revivalism," in *Arab Media Globalization and Emerging Media Industries*, ed. Noha Mellor, Muhammad Ayish, Nabil Dajani, and Khalil Rinnawi (Cambridge, MA: Polity, 2011); Muhammad Ayish, *Arab Television in the Age of Globalization: An Analysis of Emerging Political Economic, Cultural and Technological Patterns* (Hamburg: Deutsches Orient-Institut, 2003).

49. *Nahar*, March 5, 1992. United Nations estimates put the number of deaths at 120,000. United Nations Human Rights Council, "Implementation of General Assembly Resolution 60/251 of 15 March 2006 Entitled Human Rights Council," November 23, 2006, 18.

50. Popular histories of the war are Sandra Mackey's *Lebanon: A House Divided* (New York and London: W. W. Norton, 2006); and Fisk's *Pity the Nation*.

51. Before the war, Lebanon also had one radio station, later called Radio Lebanon. The outlet reflected the policies of its government sponsor because it survived on government support, rather than advertisements, after the French had handed it over in 1946. See Douglas Boyd, *Broadcasting in the Arab World: A Survey of the Electronic Media in the Middle East* (Ames: Iowa State Press, 1999), 69. In the early years of the war, over a hundred pirate rebel radio stations began operating, unchallenged by the weak government. According to Boyd, these clandestine stations were used by the disenfranchised to mobilize opposition or to survive. In addition, throughout the war, the Lebanese also turned for news to a number of international radio stations, such as the BBC, Radio Monte Carlo, and the Voice of America, as an expression of disapproval with the national broadcasting outlets. See Douglas Boyd, "Lebanese Broadcasting: Unofficial Electronic Media during a Prolonged Civil War," *Journal of Broadcasting & Electronic Media* 35, no. 3 (1991): 269–87, 269–70; Boulos, *Al-Televizion*, 1995; Marwan Kraidy, "Broadcasting Regulation and Civil Society in Postwar Lebanon," *Journal of Broadcasting & Electronic Media* 42, no. 3 (1998): 387–400, 391.

52. Interview with Sepouh Alvanthian, LBC director of programming, by author, Adma, 2004.

53. Marshall McLuhan, *Understanding Media: The Extensions of Man* (New York: McGraw-Hill, 1964), 9.

54. Gitelman, *Always Already New*, 6.

55. Ibid., 7.

56. James Zappen, *The Rebirth of Dialogue: Bakhtin, Socrates, and the Rhetorical Tradition* (Albany: State University of New York Press, 2004), 142.

57. Ussama Makdisi, "Reconstructing the Nation-State: The Modernity of Sectarianism in Lebanon," *Middle East Report* (July–September 1996): 23–26, 26.

58. John E. Joseph, *Language and Identity: National, Ethnic, Religious* (Basingstoke, UK: Palgrave, 2004).

59. Peter Ives, "Language and Collective Identity: Theorizing Complexity," in *Language and Identity Politics: A Cross-Atlantic Perspective*, ed. Christina Spati (New York: Berghahn Books, 2015), 17–37, 18.

60. Ives, "Language and Collective Identity," 19. Earlier linguistic theories, like those of Saussure and Chomsky, postulated the static and politically neutral nature of linguistic systems, which reflects popular speakers' views of language.

61. Alessandro Carlucci, *Gramsci and Languages: Unification, Diversity, Hegemony* (Leiden: Brill, 2013), 5.

62. Antonio Gramsci, *Selections from Cultural Writings*, eds. David Forgacs and Geoffrey Nowell-Smith (London: Lawrence and Wishart, 1985), 183–84.

63. Yasir Suleiman, *A War of Words: Language and Conflict in the Middle East* (Cambridge, MA: Cambridge University Press, 2004), 4. According to Sarah Thomason, "language serves as a powerful symbol for discontented groups." See *Language Contact: An Introduction* (Washington, DC: Georgetown University Press, 2001), 47.

64. Abdullah al-Ghathami, "Cultural Criticism: Theory and Method," in *Arab Cultural Studies: Mapping the Field*, ed. Tarik Sabry (London and New York: I. B. Taurus, 2011), 255–74.

65. Ghathami, "Cultural Criticism," 256, 269.

66. Ibid., 258.

67. Judith Irvine, "When Talk Isn't Cheap: Language and Political Economy," *American Ethnologist* 16 (1989): 248–67, 255.

68. Yasir Suleiman, *Arabic in the Fray: Language Ideology and Cultural Politics* (Edinburgh: Edinburgh University Press, 2013), 6.

69. Ibid., 7.

70. See Antonio Gramsci, *Selection from the Prison Notebooks*, ed. and trans. Q. Hoare and G. Nowell-Smith (London: Lawrence and Wishart, 1971), 323; Yasir Suleiman, "Arabic Folk Linguistics: Between Mother Tongue and Native Language," in *The Oxford Handbook of Arabic Linguistics*, ed. Jonathan Owens (Oxford: Oxford University Press, 2013), 264–80.

71. See Marc Lynch, *Voices of the New Arab Public: Iraq, Al-Jazeera, and Middle East Politics Today* (New York: Columbia University Press, 2006).

72. Abdelkabir al-Khatibi, *Al-Naqd al-Muzdawij* (Beirut: Dar al- ʿAwda, 1980).

73. See also Tarik Sabry, *Cultural Encounters in the Arab World: On Media, the Modern and the Everyday* (London and New York: I. B. Taurus, 2010), 182–83; Marwan Kraidy, "Globalizing Media and Communication Studies: Thoughts on the Translocal and the Modern," in *De-Westernizing Communication Research: Altering Questions and*

Changing Frameworks, ed. Georgette Wang (Abingdon; NY: Routledge, 2011), 50–76; Georgette Wang, "Beyond De-Westernizing Communication Research: An Introduction," in *De-Westernizing Communication Research: Altering Questions and Changing Frameworks*, ed. Georgette Wang (Abingdon; NY: Routledge, 2011), 1–17; Jayyusi, "Internationalizing Media Studies," 255.

74. Yasir Suleiman, *The Arabic Language and National Identity: A Study in Ideology* (Washington, DC: Georgetown University Press, 2003), 225.

75. Yasir Suleiman, *Arabic, Self and Identity* (New York: Oxford University Press, 2011), 29, 30. Suleiman criticizes political scholars for a "reluctance to take the study of nationalism in the Arab Middle East into the wider cultural arena of literary production, the arts, film, music, sports, tourism, festivals, school textbooks, architectural styles, naming practices, maps, stamps and other media of symbolic expression" as well as into the arena of language—"the most important of all systems of functional and symbolic expression" (Suleiman, *The Arabic Language and National Identity*, 2, 3). The closest discipline to study language and politics is sociolinguistics but so far it has been interested in Arabic's functional capacity rather than its symbolic connotations (ibid., 4). By contrast, Suleiman has shown that considering the political role of language in sociolinguistics provides a "thicker and deeper" analysis of the relation between language and society than registering how language varies. His study of Jordanian vernaculars is a case in point where he suggests that observed difference between male and female speech in Jordan is not rooted in attitudes toward gender but in attitudes toward vernaculars that are competing politically. After 1970 the Jordanian state started promoting a distinctly Jordanian pronunciation and removed Palestinian males from institutions of power; the latter accommodated their speech by shifting to the newly prestigious Jordanian variant (Suleiman, *A War of Words*, 127, 131–35). As this example shows, looking at language politics can help account for the historical complexity of the relationship between language and society, as well as the contextuality of language (Suleiman, *Arabic, Self and Identity*, 13).

76. Deborah Cameron, "Demythologizing Sociolinguistics: Why Language Does Not Reflect Society," in *Ideologies of Language*, ed. John Joseph and Talbot Taylor (London: Routledge, 1990), 79–93, 92.

77. Mikhail Bakhtin, *The Dialogic Imagination: Four Essays* (Austin: University of Texas Press, 1981). Bakhtin's theory has been particularly popular in literary and cultural studies. For instance, using a Bakhtinian approach, Hoda El Shakry explores how the heteroglossic Maghrebi novel requires multilingual reading practices and publics. "Heteroglossia and the Poetics of the Roman Maghrébin," *Contemporary French and Francophone Studies* 20, no. 1 (2017): 8–17.

78. Mikhail Bakhtin, *Speech Genres and Other Late Essays* (Austin: University of Texas Press, 1986), 91.

79. Simon Dentith, *Bakhtinian Thought: An Introductory Reader* (London; New York: Routledge, 1995), 71–73.

80. Ibid.

81. Sabry, *Cultural Encounters*, 47.

82. Ibid.

83. Ibid., 158.

84. Dentith, *Bakhtinian Thought*, 76.

85. Lieven de Cauter, "Towards a Phenomenology of Civil War: Hobbes Meets Benjamin in Beirut," *International Journal of Urban and Regional Research* 35, no. 2 (2011): 421–30, 425.

86. On one hand, there was "the mobility culture of a global elite traveling for choice, leisure and business; on the other, the differential mobilities of those various Others displaced by necessity rather than choice." Sara Fregonese, "Between a Refuge and a Battleground: Beirut's Discrepant Cosmopolitanisms," *Geographical Review* 102, no. 3 (2012): 316–36, 324.

87. Samira Aghacy found that modern Lebanese fiction narrated a process of modernization of Lebanese society without modernity. "Contemporary Lebanese Fiction: Modernization without Modernity," *International Journal of Middle East Studies* 38 (2006): 561–80.

88. For example, Elias Khoury's novels *Rihlat Gandhi al-Saghir* (Beirut: Dar al-Adab, 1989) and *Al-Jabal al-Saghir* (1977; reprint, Beirut: Dar al-Adab, 2003). See Aghacy, "Contemporary Lebanese Fiction," 564–65.

89. As Fregonese asserts, "coexistence and conflict, rather than constituting distinct elements of a contradiction, are parts of the same metasystem of sectarian governmentality that originated in Ottoman Lebanon's encounter with European colonial policies." Fregonese, "Between a Refuge and a Battleground," 332.

90. Samir Kassir, *Beirut* (Berkeley: University of California Press, 2010); Samir Khalaf and Philip Khoury, *Recovering Beirut: Urban Design and Post-War Reconstruction* (Leiden: Brill, 1993).

91. Suleiman, *A War of Words*, 93.

92. While Classical Arabic remains widely but exclusively used in the liturgical realm, the modified version is used in the official realm, the media, and modern literature.

93. Niloofar Haeri, *Sacred Language, Ordinary People: Dilemmas of Culture and Politics in Egypt* (New York: Palgrave Macmillan, 2003), xi.

94. Natalie Khazaal, "Re-evaluating Mohamed Choukri's Autobiography Al-Khubz al-Hafi: The Oppression of Morocco's Amazigh Population, the Sa'alik, and Backlash," *Middle Eastern Literatures*: incorporating *Edebiyat* 16, no. 2 (2013): 147–68.

95. Haeri, *Sacred Language*, 19.

96. See Niloofar Haeri, *The Sociolinguistic Market of Cairo: Gender, Class, and Education* (London; New York: Kegan Paul International, 1996).

97. Haeri, *Sacred Language*, 157.

98. Ibid., 149–51.

99. Ibid., 14. Saussure theorized modernity as the arbitrariness of the linguistic sign, although he has been challenged on that.

100. Moustapha Safouan, *Why Are the Arabs Not Free?: The Politics of Writing* (Boston: Wiley-Blackwell, 2007).

101. Acts of language communication are inherently acts of identity. Several processes underlie the construction of identity through language—identification, differentiation, and distanciation (Suleiman, *Arabic in the Fray*, 13). See also Suleiman, *Arabic Language and National Identity*.

102. Kais Firro, "Lebanese Nationalism versus Arabism: From Bulus Nujaym to Michel Chiha," *Middle Eastern Studies* 40, no. 5 (2004): 1–27.

103. Jacques Tabet, *La Syrie* (Paris: A. Lemerre, 1920), 151.

104. Some understood the Mardaites as a group from the Byzantine Empire that revolted against the Arab-Muslims; by contrast, others insisted that the Mardaites revolted against the Byzantine Empire. Firro, "Lebanese Nationalism," 13; Kamal Salibi, *House of Many Mansions, The History of Lebanon Reconsidered* (London: I. B. Tauris, 1985), 77–86.

105. Firro, "Lebanese Nationalism," 18.

106. Suleiman, *Arabic in the Fray*, 33.

107. Firro, "Lebanese Nationalism," 17.

108. Marwan Kraidy, *Reality Television and Arab Politics: Contention in Public Life* (Cambridge: Cambridge University Press, 2010).

109. Lila Abu-Lughod, *Dramas of Nationhood: The Politics of Television in Egypt* (Chicago: University of Chicago Press, 2004).

110. Armbrust, "Bourgeois Leisure."

111. Joan Scott, "Gender: A Useful Category of Historical Analysis," *American Historical Review* 91, no. 5 (1986): 1053–75, 1067–68.

112. Ibid., 1067.

113. Armbrust, "Bourgeois Leisure," 123.

1. History of Lebanese Television and the Television-Audience Relationship

1. The epigraph source is Marwan Najjar, email correspondence with author, 2013. The Boulos incident is recounted in Jean-Claude Boulos, *Al-Televizion: Tarikh wa Qisas* (Beirut: Sharikat al-Tab‘ wa-al-Nashr al-Lubnaniyya, 1995), 93.

2. Boulos (1934–2012) had an illustrious fifty-four-year career in television and advertising. He built the first television building in Lebanon in the late 1950s (his first and last engineering job), and in the early 2010s he got Iraq's television station al-Sumaria off the ground. In the meantime, he became the CEO of Télé Liban and the worldwide president of the International Advertising Association (IAA); he was named Officer of the

Arts and Humanities by the French government and Knight of the Order of the Cedar by the Lebanese president; he received multiple awards in advertising; he wrote several books; and he was even a rock 'n' roll singer in the 1960s.

3. Nabil Dajani, *Disoriented Media in a Fragmented Society: The Lebanese Experience* (Beirut: American University of Beirut, 1992), 91. In comparison, radio was established in Lebanon during the French protectorate in 1938 by the French as a reaction to Nazi propaganda, according to Dajani. The French aimed at preventing Lebanon from severing its loyalty to France (ibid., 67). Print periodicals, on the other hand, first appeared in Lebanon in the eighteenth century as a venue used by foreign Christian missionaries to attract and recruit new adherents; later print periodicals were popularized by Lebanese intellectuals who sought to reform the country and educate the masses (ibid., 21).

4. Boulos, *Al-Televizion*, 23–24.

5. Later one of the brothers, Fouad Boulos, became a member of the board of directors of CLT.

6. La Compagnie Libanaise de Television, SAL.

7. Boulos, *Al-Televizion*, 36.

8. Dajani, *Disoriented Media*, 93.

9. Nabil Dajani, *Lebanon: Studies in Broadcasting* (London: International Institute of Communications, 1979), 41.

10. The late Muhammad al-Qaisi (b. 1931) was a longtime artistic consultant at *Shabaka*'s publisher, Dar al-Sayyad. He was also an arts professor at the College of Arts, Lebanese University. Qaisi was known for his work in illustration, oil, and watercolor. He invented six new models of Arabic type and was the recipient of multiple medals and orders of honor, including the National Order of the Cedar—Lebanon's highest state order awarded by the president. Qaisi's work was shown in over fifty separate exhibitions, some sponsored by Lebanese dignitaries like first lady Mona Hrawi.

11. In 1974, between 75 and 87 percent of all homes had a television set, which put an end to earlier forms of communal viewership. Research Bureau Limited, "Middle East Media Survey," London, 1974.

12. Data from Lebanese Government, Ministry of Planning, "National Accounts for 1964–73."

13. I refer to the television programs discussed in this book by their original (Arabic) titles when I first introduce them and in most instances thereafter by the English translations of those titles so readers can track them more easily. According to a 1974 ABC survey, *Abu Melhem* was watched by 65.2 percent of all viewers, and topped other popular shows like the eponymous *Abu Salim* watched by 50 percent. ABC, "TV Audience Survey: Nov–Dec 1974," Beirut, 1975.

14. CLT also did not have many performers with television experience. Boulos, *Al-Televizion*, 46, 50.

15. "Sahrat al-Ahad ma' al-Mister Elie Baida," *al-Shabaka* 341, August 6, 1962, 42; "Sahrat al-Ahad," *al-Shabaka* 350, October 8, 1962, 42.

16. *Al-Shabaka* 400, September 23, 1963, 38.

17. Zaven Kouyoumdjian, *Lebanon on Screen: The Greatest Moments of Lebanese Television and Pop Culture* (Beirut: Hachette Antoine, 2017), 191–92.

18. George Ibrahim al-Khoury, "'Illat al 'Ilal fi al-Televizion," *al-Shabaka* 367, February 4, 1963, 8.

19. Egypt and Syria launched their television in 1960; Morocco in 1962; Sudan in 1963; Yemen in 1965; Greece, Israel, and Tunisia in 1966; Turkey and Jordan in 1968; and Kosovo and Oman in 1974.

20. Boulos, *Al-Televizion*, 119.

21. Ibid., 88.

22. "Abu al-Fahm . . . bila Fahm," *al-Shabaka* 344, August 27, 1962, 42.

23. George Ibrahim al-Khoury, "Baramij Sha'biyya? La, Innaha Mahzala," *al-Shabaka* 366, January 28, 1963, 8.

24. The French paper *Le Monde* used the occasion of CLT's launch to comment on the diminishing French influence in a postcolonial world. The exciting thing about a new Lebanese television service, it opined, was the loyalty that the Lebanese displayed for French expert supervision and technology (Boulos, *Al-Televizion*, 40–41). The article reflects some of the motives that drove the French to invest in Lebanese television, whose managing decisions were often brokered by the French and Lebanese heads of state. Given the financial situation of the Lebanese pioneers, though, loyalty was not the driving force. 'Izz al-Din and Arida had only six months to find one million Lebanese pounds (equivalent to USD$400,000 at the time) to establish the new television company before their license from the Lebanese government expired.

25. Ibid., 193.

26. Douglas Boyd, *Broadcasting in the Arab World: A Survey of the Electronic Media in the Middle East* (Ames: Iowa State Press, 1999), 72.

27. According to Boulos, the small size of the Lebanese advertising market didn't allow for two television stations to compete for audiences. However, as Kraidy has argued, some media during the war "achieved commercial solvency because of a strong advertising market." Marwan Kraidy, "State Control of Television News in 1990s Lebanon," *Journalism and Mass Communication Quarterly* 76, no. 3 (1999): 485–98, 487.

28. In the early 1960s, according to Boulos, CLT drained its capital and could not afford to get a second voice-recording camera, which it badly needed. Boulos, *Al-Televizion*, 57.

29. Ibid., 78.

30. Ibid., 118.

31. Lynn Spigel, *Make Room for TV: Television and the Family Ideal in Postwar America* (Chicago: University of Chicago Press, 1992), 138.

32. Ibid., 178.

33. https://www.youtube.com/watch?v=G9Jmz6Sou5I (see around min. 10).

34. "Akthiru min Najwa Qaz'un," *al-Shabaka* 325, April 23, 1962, 42.

35. George Ibrahim al-Khoury, "Layalin . . . wa Qanun al-Malahi," *al-Shabaka* 1857, October 7, 1991, 6–7.

36. "Akhbar al-Televizion," *al-Shabaka* 360, December 17, 1962, 43.

37. "Shawarib Najwa Qaz'un," *al-Shabaka* 354, November 5, 1962, 42.

38. Faruq al-Jamal, "Fi Nadhar Ashab al-Televizion," *al-Shabaka* 353, October 29, 1962, 10–11.

39. Al-Khoury, "Baramij Sha'biyya," 8.

40. Boulos, *Al-Televizion*, 69–70.

41. Ibid., 85.

42. "10 As'ila ma' Idha'i," *al-Shabaka* 372, March 11, 1963, 33.

43. "Al-Habs li-l-Rijal wa-l-Mar'a bi-Nus 'Aql," *al-Shabaka* 388, July 1, 1963, 42.

44. George Ibrahim al-Khoury, "Al-Lahja al-Lubnaniyya wa-l-'Uqda al-Muzmina," *al-Shabaka* 401, September 30, 1963, 6.

45. George Ibrahim al-Khoury, "Mushkilat al-Lahja al-Lubnaniyya: Al-Ara'," *al-Shabaka* 366, January 28, 1963, 9; "Al-Televizion Nuqtat Intilaq," *al-Shabaka* 402, October 7, 1963, 38.

46. Kouyoumdjian, *Lebanon on Screen*, 299.

47. Ibid., 179.

48. Al-Jamal, "Fi Nadhar Ashab al-Televizion," 10–11; Antoine Baroudy, "Al-Shabaka Tattahim al-Qanat 7 & 11 bi-Tashwih al-Nutq wa-l-Mantiq fi Lubnan," *al-Shabaka* 405, October 28, 1963, 12–15.

49. Boulos, *Al-Televizion*, 29.

50. Ibid., 95–96.

51. Ibid., 105.

52. Dajani, *Disoriented Media*, 95.

53. Ibid., 95–96.

54. Interview with Hassan Shaqqur by author, July 2017.

55. Boulos, *Al-Televizion*, 103.

56. Kouyoumdjian, *Lebanon on Screen*, 249.

57. Boulos, *Al-Televizion*, 97.

58. Kouyoumdjian, *Lebanon on Screen*, 94–102.

59. Dajani, *Disoriented Media*, 95.

60. Ibid., 96.

61. Ibid., 98.

62. Ibid., 100–101.

63. Ibid., 100.

64. Ibid., 101.

65. William Osterhaus, "TL 1979: Evaluation with Some Recommendations," October 1979.

66. Kouyoumdjian, *Lebanon on Screen*, 156.

67. Abd al-Ghani Tlis, "Min Haythu Nadri," *al-Shabaka* 1557, January 6, 1986, 58.

68. Abd al-Ghani Tlis, "Anta Mawjud Am La," *al-Shabaka* 1560, January 27, 1986, 56.

69. Abd al-Ghani Tlis, "Televizion al-Mashriq Yushriq Am La Yushriq?," *al-Shabaka* 1738, June 26, 1989, 44–45.

70. Abd al-Ghani Tlis, "Bayan al-Idara," *al-Shabaka* 1643, August 31, 1987, 60.

71. Abd al-Ghani Tlis, "Al-Idrab Aydan," *al-Shabaka* 1644, September 7, 1987, 64–65.

72. Abd al-Ghani Tlis, "Layla Karam wa-l-Ajr al-Ghali," *al-Shabaka* 1418, May 9, 1983, 70.

73. Antoine Baroudy, "Al-Yawm Tamthil wa-Ghadan 'Asir," *al-Shabaka* 1120, August 22, 1977, 53.

74. Abd al-Ghani Tlis, "Nasri Ha Huwa Sawtuhu Yakhtaniq," *al-Shabaka* 1727, April 10, 1989, 46.

75. Kouyoumdjian, *Lebanon on Screen*, 53–55.

76. Ibid.

77. Abd al-Ghani Tlis, "Nashat," *al-Shabaka* 1565, March 3, 1986, 54.

78. "Wujuh wa-Baramij fi-l-Mu'assasa al-Lubnaniyya li-l-Irsal," *al-Shabaka* 1563, February 17, 1986, 50–53.

79. Tlis, "Nashat," 54.

80. Abd al-Ghani Tlis, "'Ashi wa-l-Mu'assasa," *al-Shabaka* 1647, September 29, 1987, 60.

81. Tlis, "Nashat," 54.

82. Abd al-Ghani Tlis, "Ila Ayn," *al-Shabaka* 1578, June 2, 1986, 66.

83. Dajani, *Disoriented Media*, 105.

84. Tlis, "Televizion al-Mashriq," 44–45.

85. Dajani, *Disoriented Media*, 159, 161.

86. Abd al-Ghani Tlis, "Ni'mat al-Intishar wa-Televizion al-Khubz wa-l-Ma'," *al-Shabaka* 1321, June 29, 1981, 77.

87. Abd al-Ghani Tlis, "Studio 88," *al-Shabaka* 1649, October 12, 1987, 62.

88. 'Abdu al-Helu, "Al-Shatir Ziad . . . La Yahki," *al-Shabaka* 2091, April 1, 1996, 52–53.

89. Abd al-Ghani Tlis, "Gharib," *al-Shabaka* 1624, April 20, 1987, 62.

90. 'Abdu al-Helu, "Fi Lubnan 39 Mahatta Televizioniyya," al-*Shabaka* 1867, December 16, 1991, 16–17; Boyd, *Broadcasting in the Arab World*, 79.

91. Jean Shahin, "Fu'ad Na'im Mudir 'Am li-l-Televizion," *al-Shabaka* 1995, August 23, 1993, 14–16.

92. Abd al-Ghani Tlis, "Mumta'idun Mu'taridun," *al-Shabaka* 1876, February 17, 1992, 54–55.

93. Boulos, *Al-Televizion*, 130.

94. William Rugh, *Arab Mass Media: Newspapers, Radio, and Television in Arab Politics* (Westport, CT: Paeger, 2004), 202–4.

95. See Sarah El Richani, "The Lebanese Broadcasting System: A Battle between Political Parallelism, Commercialization, and De-facto Liberalism," in *National Broadcasting and State Policy in Arab Countries*, ed. Tourya Guaaybess (London: Palgrave Macmillan, 2013), 69–82; Marwan Kraidy, "Globalization avant la Lettre?: Cultural Hybridity and Media Power in Lebanon," in *Global Media Studies: Ethnographic Perspectives*, ed. Patrick Murphy and Marwan Kraidy (New York: Routledge, 2003): 276–95; Boyd, *Broadcasting in the Arab World*, 80.

96. El Richani, "The Lebanese Broadcasting System," 77.

97. Ibid., 75.

98. Ibid., 78.

99. Wassim Mroueh, "Local Television Stations Push for New Cable Fees," *The Daily Star* (Beirut), March 5, 2015.

100. Samya Kullab, "Tele-Liban Gets Glossy Hi-Tech Overhaul," *The Daily Star* (Beirut), January 31, 2014.

101. Abd al-Ghani Tlis, "Inqilab Abyad," *al-Shabaka* 1829, March 25, 1991, 49.

102. Ibid.

103. Ibid.

104. Abd al-Ghani Tlis, "Televizion Lubnan: Al-Bashar Awwalan Ya Majlis al-Idara," *al-Shabaka* 1927, February 8, 1993, 52–53.

105. 'Abdu al-Helu, "Al-Nihaya Allati Yaktubuha al-Nas," *al-Shabaka* 2085, February 19, 1996, 54.

106. Interview with Hassan Shaqqur by author, July 2017.

107. Ibid.

108. George Ibrahim al-Khoury, "Televizion Lubnan bi-l-Abyad wa-l-Aswad," *al-Shabaka* 2153, June 9, 1997, 6. According to former Télé Liban chair Fuad Naim, the government did not have a good understanding of the nature of the service provided by public broadcasting institutions like Télé Liban and therefore did not support the outlet. (Interview with Naim by Zahira Harb, Beirut, 2004.) See Zahira Harb, *Channels of Resistance in Lebanon: Liberation Propaganda, Hezbollah and the Media* (London: I. B. Taurus, 2011), 105.

109. Jean-Claude Boulos, *Al-Televizion: Rihla ila al-Jahim* (Beirut: Dar al-Nahar li-l-Nashr, 2007).

110. Kullab, "Tele-Liban Gets Glossy."

111. Interview with Hassan Shaqqur by author, July 2017.

112. Kullab, "Tele-Liban Gets Glossy."

113. Interview with Hassan Shaqqur by author, July 2017.

114. Ibid.

115. For an account of Pierre Daher's role at LBC, see Sarah El Richani, "Pierre Daher: Sheikh, Barron, and Moghul of LBC," in *Arab Media Moguls*, ed. Donatella Della Ratta, Naomi Sakr, and Jakob Skovgaard-Petersen (London and New York: I. B. Taurus, 2015), 49–62.

116. Carol Rizq, "Indictment Backs LF Lawsuit against LBC, Seeks Jail for Daher," *The Daily Star* (Beirut), October 15, 2010.

117. 'Al-Helu, "Al-Shatir Ziad," 52–53.

118. Boyd, *Broadcasting in the Arab World*, 81.

119. The phrase is an opening of traditional Arabic songs. It dates back thousands of years and is of unclear origins, perhaps Babylonian, old Egyptian, or Arabic.

120. Kraidy and Khalil, *Arab Television Industries*, 42.

2. Télé Liban: The Peace Bubble and the Crisis of Legitimacy

1. The epigraph is from Zaven Kouyoumdjian, *Lebanon on Screen: The Greatest Moments of Lebanese Television and Pop Culture* (Beirut: Hachette Antoine, 2017), 109.

2. Jean-Claude Boulos, *Al-Televizion: Tarikh wa Qisas* (Beirut: Sharikat al-Tab' wa-l-Nashr al-Lubnaniyya, 1995), 14.

3. Television and other media have been linked to galvanizing the fragile, war-prone situation. An exploration of the musical theater of the Rahbani brothers and Fayrouz, who were broadcast regularly from the mid-1950s to the outbreak of the war, has led Christopher Stone to convincingly argue their role in inflaming sensitivities that contributed to the civil war. According to him, their art produced a sectarian representation of Lebanon and Lebanese folklore that was conflated with Christian mountain nationalism and excluded the majority of Lebanese who were not Christian. Christopher Stone, "The Ba'albakk Festival and the Rahbanis: Folklore, Ancient History, Musical Theater, and Nationalism in Lebanon," *Arab Studies Journal* 11/12, nos. 2/1 (Fall 2003/Spring 2004): 10–39.

4. In addition, Lebanon enjoyed freedom of the press uncharacteristic of the Arab region. See Baha Abu-Laban, "Factors in Social Control of the Press in Lebanon," *Journalism and Mass Communication Quarterly* 43, no. 3 (1966): 510–18; William Rugh, *The Arab Press: News and Political Process in the Arab World* (Syracuse, NY: Syracuse University Press, 1987).

5. See Donald Browne, "Television and National Stabilization: The Lebanese Experience," *Journalism Quarterly* 52, no. 4 (1975): 692–98, 694; Marwan Kraidy, "Broadcasting Regulation and Civil Society in Postwar Lebanon," *Journal of Broadcasting & Electronic Media* 42, no. 3 (1998): 387–400.

6. See Kouyoumdjian, *Lebanon on Screen*, 103–7.

7. Ibid.

8. *Shabaka* reported that the news department had over a hundred people, but according to Hassan Shaqqur, that is an exaggeration. While around seventy people worked and supported the news department, the core staff was under twenty. Interview with Hassan Shaqqur by author, July 2017.

9. Nabil Dajani, *Disoriented Media in a Fragmented Society: The Lebanese Experience* (Beirut: American University of Beirut, 1992), 132.

10. Boulos, *Al-Televizion*, 183.

11. Adel Malek, *Harb al-Sanatayn wa-Ba'd* (Beirut: Dar Sa'ir al-Mashriq, 2016).

12. Boulos, *Al-Televizion*, 182.

13. Interview with Hassan Shaqqur by author, July 2017.

14. Bold text appears in the original.

15. Nabil Dajani, *Lebanon: Studies in Broadcasting* (London: International Institute of Communications, 1979), 8.

16. Marwan Hamade, "Le Liban, Ce Grand Absent," editorial, *L'Orient-Le Jour*, Beirut, October 20, 1974; Donald Browne, "Television and National Stabilization: The Lebanese Experience," *Journalism Quarterly* 52, no. 4 (1975): 692–98, 695.

17. Douglas Boyd, *Broadcasting in the Arab World: A Survey of the Electronic Media in the Middle East* (Ames: Iowa State Press, 1999), 74.

18. Interview with Hassan Shaqqur by author, Beirut, 2003.

19. Dajani, *Lebanon*, 56.

20. Boulos, *Al-Televizion*, 105.

21. Ibid.

22. Kouyoumdjian, *Lebanon on Screen*, 120.

23. This was a legitimate fear because there were already around a hundred pirate radio outlets. After seventeen dormant years, some of the rebel radio stations that had appeared during the 1958 civil conflict resumed transmission. The majority of these stations were sectarian, not commercial, and cared more about disseminating sectarian vitriol than serving the needs of the population. Radio initially cracked the bubble, but soon radio stations settled into a comfortable routine of partisan bubbles that did little to address public concerns and sensibilities, with the exception of The Voice of Lebanon that might merit additional exploration outside the scope of this book. The Voice of Lebanon began broadcasting on September 24, 1975, from the Christian neighborhood of Ashrafieh. Its effective organization, with numerous local and international correspondents, and its oppositional news coverage that challenged the government line propelled it to a reasonably respected international status and significant local audience. See Boyd, *Broadcasting in the Arab World*, 76–77.

24. The same strategy was used in July 1985 when news anchor Jacques Wakim was almost killed by a booby trap. Télé Liban's employees struck, withheld the evening newscast, and instead aired a text in standard Arabic as a notice of their anger.

25. Antoine Baroudy, "Fawda wa-Irtibak fi-l-Televizion," *Shabaka* 1030, October 20, 1975, 48.

26. Dajani, *Disoriented Media*, 97.

27. Baroudy, "Fawda wa-Irtibak," 48; Boulos, *Al-Televizion*, 106.

28. Ibid., 183.

29. Although international war is common, it is civil war that is the defining experience in our times. Between 1940 and 2000, 133 civil wars erupted; "civil wars" are defined as internal armed conflicts with 1,000 battle deaths per year minimum. See Monica Toft, "Getting Religion?: The Puzzling Case of Islam and Civil War," *International Security* 31, no. 4 (2007): 97–131. Since 1950 more than half of all nations have experienced civil conflict (twenty-five battle deaths per year minimum). See Christopher Blattman and Edward Miguel, "Civil War," *Journal of Economic Literature* 48, no. 1 (2010): 3–57.

30. See Stuart Allan and Barbie Zelizer, "Rules of Engagement: Journalism and War," in *Reporting War: Journalism in Wartime*, ed. Stuart Allan and Barbie Zelizer (New York: Routledge, 2004), 3–22. Most research on the wartime dilemmas of the media focuses on international war. A crucial way in which international war shapes the media is by confronting it with hard choices. One dilemma lies in the media's choice and ability to cover the war independently in the face of government efforts to muzzle media coverage. Since the US invasion of Grenada in 1983, media power and government management of media during war have been rising. See Trevor Thrall, *War in the Media Age* (Cresskill, NJ: Hampton Press, 2000.) Stig Hjarvard speaks of "mediatization," or the enormous role of the media, especially television, in cultural change. See Stig Hjarvard, *The Mediatization of Society and Culture* (London: Routledge, 2013). With this rising power, governments try to manage corporate media and muzzle its message. During war, the government may deliberately misinform the media, withhold information, or manipulate and oversee the media's reports by embedding journalists with the military. Nonetheless, individual journalists may circumvent these attempts for muzzling and propaganda. Howard Tumber and Jerry Palmer, *Media at War: The Iraq Crisis* (London: Sage, 2004.)

31. Thrall, *War in the Media Age.*

32. Fred Hallyday, "Manipulation and Limits: Media Coverage of the Gulf War, 1990–91," in *The Media of Conflict: War Reporting and Representations of Ethnic Violence*, ed. Tim Allen and Jean Seaton (London: Zed Books, 1999), 127–46, 129; David Morrison, *Television and the Gulf War* (New Barnet, UK: John Libbey, 1992).

33. Barbie Zelizer, "When War Is Reduced to a Photograph," in *Reporting War: Journalism in Wartime*, ed. Stuart Allan and Barbie Zelizer (New York: Routledge, 2004), 115–35.

34. Allan and Zelizer, "Rules of Engagement," 3–22.

35. Andrew Hoskins, "New Memory: Mediating History," *Historical Journal of Film, Radio and Television* 21, no. 4 (2001): 333–46; John Whiteclay Chambers II and David Culbert, *World War II, Film, and History* (New York: Oxford University Press, 1996);

Pierre Nora, "Between Memory and History: Les Lieux de Mémoire," *Representations* 26 (1989): 7–24.

36. Boulos, *Al-Televizion*, 183.

37. Ibid., 183–84.

38. Boulos, *Al-Televizion*, 184.

39. Dajani, *Lebanon*, 35.

40. Antoine Baroudy, "Raqm Qiyasi li-Idha'atina," *Shabaka* 1046–47, February 16, 1976, 55.

41. *Nahar*, April 10, 1977, 6.

42. Antoine Baroudy, "Sanam Ismuhu al-Bathth al-Mubashir," *Shabaka* 1017, July 21, 1975, 69.

43. Antoine Baroudy, "Mahabbat Jubran," *Shabaka* 1030, October 20, 1975, 48.

44. The diva's use of classical Arabic for the lyrics connected her art with a glorified, centuries-old tradition of Arabic *tarab* (musical entertainment). Written in an otherworldly language, Umm Kulthum's songs transported listeners into an imagined, wondrous foreign country. The clash between the intended state of emotional intoxication in Umm Kulthum's songs and the audience's sense of agony from the civil war likely gave radio transmissions a hallucinatory aura.

45. *Clear and Safe* was not the actual name of the program (which was *Nashrat al-Arsad al-Amniyya* [Security Bulletin]), but it became the name by which it was commonly known. Akhawi (1928–87) apparently used it spontaneously during a twenty-hour broadcast to describe the situation.

46. One assassination attempt was apparently by a man dressed as a priest; the other attempt was an abduction that the announcer intercepted by throwing himself out of the car.

47. Decades later, Akhawi's name remains the gold standard in addressing the concerns of people on the street. In 2005, for instance, the Memory for the Future movement resumed its earlier campaign, called "Understanding the War," accompanied by a prize for a short film on peace named after Akhawi and presented by his son Jad. Marianne Stigset, "Amid Folklore and Festivities, a Bid for National Reconciliation," *The Daily Star* (Beirut), April 9, 2005. Akhawi's understanding of how to communicate with the audience during conflict is considered unparalleled.

48. Boulos, *Al-Televizion*, 182.

49. Ibid.

50. The Hazmieh branch of Télé Liban was the former Télé Orient, while the Tallet al-Khayyat branch was the former CLT.

51. Boulos, *Al-Televizion*, 184.

52. Najjar recalls, "My family spent most of the shelter-seeking months there with our Muslim friends from Tripoli (the Akkari family, still very close to us), and I remember

having had nice times with the singer Abdul Karim el Shaar and with the star Ragheb Alame in Limassol (1983–84)." Email interview with Najjar by author, December 13, 2014.

53. Jean-Claude Khoury, "The Lebanese Radio and Television Stations Present: The Reluctant Partisans," *Monday Morning* (March 28, 1976), 41.

54. In February 1984, though, the news programs experienced a longer and more radical split when heavy fighting began between the Lebanese armed forces and the Shi'a militia Amal; the government resigned, and the US marines pulled out. Each station began broadcasting news in three languages. Boulos, *Al-Televizion*, 184–85.

55. Quoted in Kouyoumdjian, *Lebanon on Screen*, 117.

56. Quoted in ibid., 110.

57. Jean Said Makdisi, *Beirut Fragments: A War Memoir*, rev. ed. (New York: Persea Books, 1999), 36.

58. Dajani, *Disoriented Media*, 160–64.

59. See Amahl Bishara for "embodied journalism" in the Israeli-Palestinian conflict. Amahl Bishara, *Back Stories: US News Production and Palestinian Politics* (Stanford, CA: Stanford University Press, 2013), 161.

60. Dominic Boyer, *The Life Informatic: Newsmaking in the Digital Era* (Ithaca, NY: Cornell University Press, 2013), 11.

3. Audiences: Sarcasm, the New Hero of Television, and the Components of Modern Legitimacy

1. The epigraph is from Huda Barakat, *Hajar al-Dahak* [*The Stone of Laughter*] (Beirut: Riad al-Rayyis Books, 1990), 83.

2. For women's contribution to Lebanese war literature, see Miriam Cooke, *War's Other Voices: Women Writers on the Lebanese Civil War* (Cambridge: Cambridge University Press, 1987).

3. Jean Said Makdisi, *Beirut Fragments: A War Memoir*, rev. ed. (New York: Persea Books, 1999), 211. Also see Jean Said Makdisi, "Book Mark Living in Beirut: 'A Tightrope Over an Abyss of Panic' Memoir: A Palestinian Describes Her Efforts to Live a Normal Life in a City under Siege, and to Understand Passions That Would Erase It from the Map," *Los Angeles Times*, Home Edition (September 9, 1990), 2.

4. Marwan Kraidy, "Television and Civic Discourse in Postwar Lebanon," in *Civil Discourse and Digital Age Communications in the Middle East*, ed. Leo Gher and Hussein Amin (Stamford, CT: Ablex, 2000), 3–18, 8.

5. For a detailed description of similar wartime vocabulary, see Makdisi, *Beirut Fragments*, 49–65.

6. The house never lost its significance and after the war the city restored it as a museum, which opened in 2016.

7. A video clip of the series opening can be seen here: https://www.youtube.com/watch?v=VtAXJ8r72Cg.

8. The interview can be seen here: https://www.youtube.com/watch?v=Zl0nEGxurr4.

9. "Relative Calm" exposes the raging disillusionment with media language, but it hardly gives justice to Ziad's resistance to the peace bubble through his plays, songs, and radio skits, which abound in Lebanese colloquialisms, puns, witticisms, and twists of the vernacular. His work also exposed and parodied the peace bubble that his famous parents, Fayrouz and Aasi Rahbani, helped to maintain by creating an idealized Lebanon. The regularity with which he is quoted is probably the best sign of just how effectively Ziad had made his fellow citizens a part of the public debate of critical political and social issues. For a detailed discussion of Ziad's work, see H. al-Dahir, "Yukmil al-Masira al-Rahbaniyya al-Ibdaʿiyya baʿda Ghiyab Mansour," *al-Anwar,* March 26, 1995; Christopher Stone, "Ziyad Rahbani's 'Novelization' of Lebanese Musical Theater or the Paradox of Parody," *Middle Eastern Literatures* 8, no. 2 (July 2005): 151–70; Elise Salem, *Constructing Lebanon: A Century of Literary Narratives* (Gainesville: University Press of Florida, 2003); R. ʻAnini, "Ru'yat al-Hayat wa-l-Fann fi Masrah Ziyad Rahbani," *Al-Tariq* 48.6–49.1 (1989–90): 147–96.

10. Mamun Fandy, "Information Technology, Trust and Social Change in the Arab World," *Middle East Journal* 54, no. 3 (2000): 378–94.

11. Ibid., 383.

12. The show featured for decades on the Lebanese channel Future Television (est. 1993). It was launched after the end of the war; however, its title is perhaps an eerily unconscious throwback to the danger that had been lurking in wartime open spaces. Zahi Wehbi, interview by author, Beirut, August 2013.

13. In 1982, literary critic Roger Allen predicted that Arabic novels would be "written for the ear" after writers started engaging explicitly with the Arabic oral literary tradition. The Lebanese Civil War might have proved him right. It is widely known that oral accounts depend on multiple iterations and are characterized by discrepancies and distortions. However, instead of taking issue with oral accounts, wartime writers began mistrusting writing's claim to be the medium of the unchanging word.

14. Elias Khoury, interview by Elise Salem, July 1995 (in Salem, *Constructing Lebanon,* 107). Much in step with his fellow writers and the times, Elias Khoury frequently disparaged the written word in favor of the spoken because he believed that, without an intervention from the spoken tongue, a writer could not tell stories. As Sami Sweidan has observed, in Khoury's novel *al-Wujuh al-Bayda'* (*White Faces*) (Beirut: Dar Ibn Rushd, 1981), the author's language is taken over by spoken narration. Sami Sweidan, *Abhath fi al-Nass al-Riwa'i al-ʻArabi* (Beirut: Mu'assasat al-Abhath al-ʻArabiyya, 1986), 241.

15. Interview by author, August 2013, Beirut.

16. Many writers like Hanan al-Shaykh, Huda Barakat, and Rachid al-Daif ditched traditional lyrical styles; Daif's language was stripped to the bare essentials, while Shaykh's

writing imitated "uneducated" styles. Mona Takieddine Amyuni, "Style and Politics in the Poems and Novels of Rashid al-Da'if," *International Journal of Middle East Studies* 28, no. 2 (May 1996): 177–92, 177; interview with Rachid al-Daif by Amyuni, January 31, 1998. This unidealized, unromantic, and at times uneducated-sounding language embraced the impudence, courage, and crudeness of the street. The war generation rebelled against the romantic themes of earlier poetry and fiction, which had glorified war and revolution. For example, Zahi Wehbi observes that the Arabic poem, the *qasida*, came down from its romantic tower and incorporated the language of the *shabab* (the street toughs and the young war generation) and the vocabulary from people's daily experience of the war (e.g., death, bullet, etc.). Zahi Wehbi, interview by author, August 2013, Beirut.

17. The increased interplay of spoken and formal registers became a new trend. A tribute to the oral appeared in different forms, even in titles. For example, *Hikayat Zahra (The Story of Zahra)* (Beirut: Dar al-Adab, [1980] 2004) by Hanan al-Shaykh bears the name of its genre, *hikaya*, or oral narrative, in the title. Another example comes from Elias Khoury's novel *Rihlat Gandhi al-Saghir* (*The Journey of Little Gandhi*) (Beirut: Dar al-Adab, 1989), where Gandhi's death scene is repeated in several different chapters, but every time the story varies from earlier versions mimicking oral narratives. *'Ammiyya* privileged intimate revelations and everyday experience. Many writers immersed themselves in describing the daily routines of physical and emotional survival during the conflict. Famously, Huda Barakat's novels abound in descriptions of daily chores, house cleaning, and other domestic routines. In his 1989 novel *Taqaniyat al-Bu's* (*Techniques of Anguish*), Rachid al-Daif portrays a school teacher out of work who busies himself with the daily routines of supplying water, ensuring electricity, preparing food, and so forth during the tough years of wartime deficiencies. Even films that leaned toward sanitized versions of the civil war, such as Ziad Doueiri's 1998 *West Beirut*, depicted the daily struggles for food, medication, and survival (e.g., the scene at the bakery that depicted a violent struggle over bread).

18. For more on the role of coffee shops as sites of public conversation, see Zahi Wehbi, *Qahwa Sada: Fi Ahwal al-Maqha al-Bayruti* [*Black Coffee: On the Plight of the Beiruti Coffeeshop*] (Beirut: Al-Dar al-'Arabiyya li-l-'Ulum Nashirun, 2010).

19. Yasir Suleiman, *The Arabic Language and National Identity: A Study in Ideology* (Washington, DC: Georgetown University Press, 2003), 215.

20. Salem, *Constructing Lebanon*, 173.

21. See Joseph Zeidan, *Arab Women Novelists: The Formative Years and Beyond* (Albany: SUNY University Press, 1995).

22. Etel Adnan, *Al-Sitt Marie-Rose* (Beirut: al-Mu'assasa al-'Arabiyya li-l-Dirasat wa-l-Nashr, 1978); Huda Barakat, *Hajar al-Dahak*; Rachid al-Daif, *Unsi Yalhu Ma' Ritta: Kitab al-Balighin* (Beirut: Al-Mu'assasa al-Jami'iyya li-l-Dirasat wa-l-Nashr wa-l-Tawzi', 1983); Mahmoud Darwish, *Dhakira li-l-Nisyan: Sirat Yawm, al-Zaman—Ab, al-Makan—Bayrut* (Ramallah: Wizarat al-Thaqafa & Dar al-Nashir, [1986] 1997); Elias Khoury,

Al-Jabal al-Saghir (Beirut: Dar al-Adab, [1977] 2003); Elias Khoury, *Rihlat Ghandi al-Saghir*; Jean Said Makdisi, *Beirut Fragments*; Hanan al-Shaykh, *Hikayat Zahra*.

23. Makdisi, *Beirut Fragments*, 41–42, emphasis added.

24. Darwish, *Dhakira li-l-Nisyan*, 30.

25. Ibid., 30–31.

26. Barakat, *Hajar al-Dahak*, 80–81.

27. Ibid., 83.

28. Ibid., 80.

29. See Michael Warner, "Publics and Counterpublics," *Public Culture* 14, no. 1 (2002): 49–90, 61.

30. Al-Daif, *Unsi Yalhu Ma' Ritta*. Daif is one of the best-known wartime and post-war Lebanese writers and a professor of Arabic literature in Beirut. His works have been translated into Dutch, English, French, German, Greek, Italian, Polish, Portuguese, and Spanish.

31. Al-Daif, *Unsi Yalhu Ma' Ritta*, 9.

32. Ibid., 15–19.

33. Of course, there were always exceptions like Akhawi, for instance.

34. Emphasis added. Darwish, *Dhakira li-l-Nisyan*, 32.

35. Ron Krabill, *Starring Mandela and Cosby: Media and the End(s) of Apartheid* (Chicago: University of Chicago Press, 2010).

36. Agnes Ku, "Revisiting the Notion of 'Public' in Habermas's Theory—Toward a Theory of Politics of Public Credibility," *Sociological Theory* 18, no. 2 (2000): 216–40, 229.

37. The magazine maintains a website under the name Achabakamagazine.com.

38. Nabil Dajani, *Disoriented Media in a Fragmented Society: The Lebanese Experience* (Beirut: American University of Beirut, 1992), 156.

39. Saad Mkhalalati was also briefly a contributor to the column.

40. Abd al-Ghani Tlis, "Al-Sha'b al-Lubnani bayna Qadha'if al-Midfa'iyya wa Qadha'if . . . al-Televizion," *al-Shabaka* 1317, June 1, 1981, 32–33.

41. Majdi Fahmi, "Sinemat Saqatat fi Harb Lubnan," *al-Shabaka* 1046–47, February 16, 1976, 16–19.

42. Tlis, "Al-Sha'b al-Lubnani bayna Qadha'if," 32–33.

43. George Ibrahim al-Khoury, "Al-Televizion Ya'tadhir," *al-Shabaka*, December 5, 1977, 5; Abd al-Ghani Tlis, "Al-Hatif al-Mushta'il," *al-Shabaka* 1481, July 23, 1984, 62.

44. Abd al-Ghani Tlis, "Al-Sana al-'Ashira Ya . . . Televizion," *al-Shabaka* 1468, April 23, 1984, 62.

45. Abd al-Ghani Tlis, "Al-Da'uq fi Tasrih," *al-Shabaka* 1473, May 28, 1984, 62.

46. Saad Mkhalalati, "Kalimat Naqd La Budda Minha: Hawla Televizion Lubnan," *al-Shabaka* 1205, April 9, 1979, 62.

47. Abd al-Ghani Tlis, "Fikra li-l-Televizion," *al-Shabaka* 1406, February 14, 1983, 70.

48. Abd al-Ghani Tlis, "Istifta' 'ala al-Hatif," *al-Shabaka* 1420, May 23, 1983, 66.

49. Abd al-Ghani Tlis, "Risala Majhula," *al-Shabaka* 1658, December 14, 1987, 70.

50. Abd al-Ghani Tlis, "Ila Sharl Rizq: Madha Fa'ala Televizion Lubnan," *al-Shabaka* 1295, December 29, 1980, 43.

51. Dajani, *Disoriented Media*, 156.

52. Abd al-Ghani Tlis, "Muhawala, Law Annaha Tanjah," *al-Shabaka* 1190, December 25, 1978, 60.

53. Abd al-Ghani Tlis, "Wara' al-Akhbar," *al-Shabaka* 1364, April 27, 1982, 70.

54. Abd al-Ghani Tlis, "Yakfi," *al-Shabaka* 1582, June 30, 1986, 64.

55. "Layla Huna wa-Layla Hunak," *al-Shabaka* 1526, June 3, 1985, 60.

56. Ibid.

57. Antoine Baroudy, "Al-Suwar al-Mutaharrika," *al-Shabaka* 1123, September 12, 1977, 53.

58. Abd al-Ghani Tlis, "Al-Adab al-Sha'bi," *al-Shabaka* 1392, November 8, 1982, 76.

59. Abd al-Ghani Tlis, "La Ya Marwan!," *al-Shabaka* 1404, January 31, 1983, 68.

60. Ibid.

61. Abd al-Ghani Tlis, "Thartharat al-Adab al-Sha'bi," *al-Shabaka* 1408, February 28, 1983, 70.

62. Abd al-Ghani Tlis, "Bi-l-Idhn minkum," *al-Shabaka* 1412, March 28, 1983, 72.

63. Abd al-Ghani Tlis, "Tahiya," *al-Shabaka* 1313, May 4, 1981, 42.

64. Tlis, "Bi-l-Idhn minkum," 72.

65. Saad Mkhalalati, "Takshira ila," *al-Shabaka* 1225, August 27, 1979, 65.

66. Abd al-Ghani Tlis, "Al-Sabq," *al-Shabaka* 1642, August 24, 1987, 56.

67. George Ibrahim al-Khoury, "Al-Televizion al-Shaykh . . . Kayfa Yarji' ila Sibahu," *al-Shabaka* 1587, August 4, 1986, 6–7.

68. Abd al-Ghani Tlis, "Sha'b Muntasir wa-Televizion Mahzum," *al-Shabaka* 1463, March 19, 1984, 64.

69. Abd al-Ghani Tlis, "Ayyuha al-Televizion, Ayn al-Thaqafa," *al-Shabaka* 1365, May 3, 1982, 66.

70. Antoine Baroudy, "Al-Televizion wa-l-Karasi," *al-Shabaka* 1108, May 30, 1977, 53.

71. Abd al-Ghani Tlis, "Ni'mat al-Intishar wa-Televizion al-Khubz wa-l-Ma,'" *al-Shabaka* 1321, June 29, 1981, 77.

72. Abd al-Ghani Tlis, "Al-Wujuh al-Televizioniyya al-Dahika Tazuruna Layliyyan wa-La Tudjir," *al-Shabaka* 1284, October 13, 1980, 38–40.

73. Ibid.

74. Antoine Baroudy, "Risala wa-Sura," *al-Shabaka* 1136, December 12, 1977, 52.

75. Abd al-Ghani Tlis, "Pier Ghanim: Al-Mudhi' al-Sha'ir," *al-Shabaka* 1504, December 31, 1984, 65.

76. Antoine Baroudy, "Al-Mudhi' al-Aqrab ila al-Qalb?," *al-Shabaka* 1188, December 11, 1978, 56.

77. Antoine Baroudy, "Yukhatibuna min Hunak," *al-Shabaka* 1176, September 18, 1978, 55.

78. Abd al-Ghani Tlis, "Ismuhu Maurice," *al-Shabaka* 1639, August 3, 1987, 50.

79. Tlis, "Al-Wujuh Al-Televizioniyya al-Dahika," 38–40.

80. Abd al-Ghani Tlis, "Mismar," al-Shabaka 1295, December 29, 1980, 44.

81. Tarif Shams al-Din, "Mudhi'at al-Televizion: Sa'idat am Ba'isat?," *al-Shabaka* 1298, January 19, 1981, 40–43.

82. Sarukh, "Ila Charles Rizq," *al-Shabaka* 1215, June 18, 1979, 44.

83. George Ibrahim al-Khoury, "Al-Akhbar," *al-Shabaka* 1034, November 17, 1975, 5.

84. Shams al-Din, "Mudhi'at al-Televizion," 40–43.

85. Antoine Baroudy, "Charlotte al-Mudhi'a," *al-Shabaka* 1125, September 26, 1977, 53.

86. Abd al-Ghani Tlis, "Qarsa," *al-Shabaka* 1314, May 11, 1981, 43.

87. Abd al-Ghani Tlis, "Qarsa am Tahiya," *al-Shabaka* 1306, March 16, 1981, 43.

88. Abd al-Ghani Tlis, "Aydan: Thiyab li-l-Mudhi'in," *al-Shabaka* 1322, July 6, 1981, 73.

89. Antoine Baroudy, "Fi al-Sadis 'Ashar min Kull Shahar," *al-Shabaka* 1126, October 3, 1977, 52.

90. George Jordaq, "Ma' Aswat al-Mudhi'at 1," *al-Shabaka* 1126, October 3, 1977, 32–33.

91. George Jordaq, "Ma' Aswat al-Mudhi'at 2," *al-Shabaka* 1127, October 10, 1977, 32–33.

92. George Jordaq, "Ma' Aswat al-Mudhi'at 5" *al-Shabaka* 1130, October 31, 1977, 32–33.

93. George Ibrahim al-Khoury, "Madrasat al-Mudhi'in," *al-Shabaka* 1431, August 8, 1983, 3.

94. Al-Khoury, "Al-Akhbar," 5.

95. Tlis, "Al-Wujuh Al-Televizioniyya al-Dahika," 38–40.

96. Sonya Farah, "Ni'mat 'Azuri: Dhuruf Lubnan Saraqat Ibtisamataha," *al-Shabaka* 1532, July 15, 1985, 22–23.

97. Abd al-Ghani Tlis, "Tahiya," *al-Shabaka* 1322, July 6, 1981, 73.

98. Tlis, "Qarsa," 43.

99. Abd al-Ghani Tlis, "Qif Ya Fu'ad!," *al-Shabaka* 1423, June 13, 1983, 70.

100. Antoine Baroudy, "Al-Mudhi' al-'Asabi Camille Menassa," *al-Shabaka* 1184, November 13, 1978, 60.

101. Sonya Farah, "Al-Mudhi'a al-Falakiyya Maggie Farah: Innahu 'Am al-Hasm fi Lubnan," *al-Shabaka* 1354, February 15, 1982, 24–25.

102. Baroudy, "Charlotte al-Mudhi'a," 53.

103. Abd al-Ghani Tlis, "Mahmud Yasin . . . bi-l-Lubnani," *al-Shabaka* 1316, May 25, 1981, 39.

104. Antoine Baroudy, "Al-Tante 'Imm Melhem,'" *al-Shabaka* 1032, November 3, 1975, 48.

105. Antoine Baroudy, "Jean Khoury min Haythu La Yadri," *al-Shabaka* 1121, August 29, 1977, 52.

106. Ibid., 52.

107. George Jordaq, "Ma' Aswat al-Mudhi'at 5," *al-Shabaka* 1130, October 31, 1977, 32–33.

108. Sarukh, "Ila Su'ad al-'Ashi," *al-Shabaka* 1177, September 25, 1978, 36.

109. Younis, "Jalla Man La Yukhti'," *al-Shabaka* 1418, May 9, 1983, 70.

110. Younis, "Jawab al-Khitab," *al-Shabaka* 1444, November 7, 1983, 72.

111. Abd al-Ghani Tlis, "Al-'Amid Kan'an Mudir 'Am Televizion Lubnan: Abwabuna Maftuha Amama Jami' al-Imkanat," *al-Shabaka* 1427, July 11, 1983, 70.

112. Antoine Baroudy, "Al-Khutta 'al-Hasima,'" *al-Shabaka* 1016, July 14, 1975, 70.

113. Antoine Baroudy, "Qunbula Lughawiyya Jadida li-Jean-Claude," *al-Shabaka* 1017, July 21, 1975, 70.

114. Tlis, "Qif Ya Fu'ad!," 70.

115. Abd al-Ghani Tlis, "Ayyuha al-Mudhi', Hal Ta'rif Man Anta?," *al-Shabaka* 1253, March 10, 1980, 94.

116. Abd al-Ghani Tlis, "Taksir al-Qawa'id al-Lughawiyya!," *al-Shabaka* 1417, May 2, 1983, 66.

117. Dajani, *Disoriented Media*, 133.

118. Ibid., 132.

119. Ismat al-Ayyubi, "'Al-Waw' wa-'l-Nun' Zinat al-Akhbar wa-Hakadha Yabqa al-Rus Ghadibun," *al-Nahar*, December 1, 1977, 7.

120. M. B., "Shasha Saghira mithla Musalsal 'Poor Man,'" *al-Nahar*, December 7, 1977.

121. Shafiq Naime, "Al-Dawla Tamna' Masrahiyyat 'Shi Mitl al-Kizeb' bi-Maf'ul Raja'i!," *al-Shabaka* 1384, September 13, 1982, 16–17.

122. Ibid.

123. "Sahafat Lubnan Tabda' al-Yawm Tatbiq al-Raqaba al-Dhatiyya," *al-Safir*, April 17, 1975, 3.

124. Antoine Baroudy, "Muraqaba Jadida li-l-Baramij al-Qadima," *al-Shabaka* 1048, February 23, 1976, 48.

125. Ibid.

126. Abd al-Ghani Tlis, "'Sada al-Sinin' Yatawaqqaf wa-'Alamat al-Istifham Takbur," *al-Shabaka* 1252, March 3, 1980, 88.

127. George Jordaq, "Ta'diban li-l-Qawm al-Salihin wa-'Iqaban lahum," *al-Shabaka* 1430, August 1, 1983, 60–61.

128. Ibid.

129. Jean Shahin, "Sharif al-Akhawi Dakhala al-Tarikh min Bab al-Mihna," *al-Shabaka* 1033, November 10, 1975, 19–21.

130. Sonya Farah, "Al-Mudhi'a al-Falakiyya," 24–25.

131. Abd al-Ghani Tlis, "Al-Haqiqa fi-l-Maghara," *al-Shabaka* 1477, June 25, 1984, 68.

132. Antoine Baroudy, "Ghayr Salika 'wi-Tfaddalu 'Abadu,'" *al-Shabaka* 1030, October 20, 1975, 48.

133. Tlis, "Al-Sha'b al-Lubnani bayna Qadha'if," 32–33.

134. Fandy, "Information Technology," 394.

135. Néstor García Canclini, *Consumers and Citizens: Globalization and Multicultural Conflict* (Minneapolis and London: University of Minnesota Press, 2001), 23.

136. Sune Haugbolle, *War and Memory in Lebanon* (New York: Cambridge University Press, 2010).

137. For several months in 1976 Radio Lebanon also broadcast Jean Chamoun and Ziad Rahbani's popular program *We're Still O.K.* The program discussed the war and politics in a series of sarcastic sketches and later became popular in pirated tapes.

138. Asef Bayat, *Life as Politics: How Ordinary People Change the Middle East* (Stanford, CA: Stanford University Press, 2010, 2013), 12, 93.

139. Charles Tripp, *The Power and the People: Paths of Resistance in the Middle East* (Cambridge: Cambridge University Press, 2013), 393.

140. Dominic Boyer, *The Life Informatic: Newsmaking in the Digital Era* (Ithaca, NY: Cornell University Press, 2013), 11.

141. Lilie Chouliaraki, "Digital Witnessing in War Journalism: The Case of Post Arab Spring Conflicts," *Popular Communication* 13, no. 2 (2015): 105–19.

142. For witnessing in protection of civilians, see Chouliaraki, "Digital Witnessing"; Stuart Allan, *Citizen Witnessing: Revisioning Journalism in Times of Crisis* (Cambridge, UK and Malden, MA: Polity, 2013).

143. See Anja Wallenberg and Jason Pack, "Rebels with a Pen: Observations on the Newly Emerging Media Landscape in Libya," *Journal of North African Studies* 18, no. 2 (2013): 191–210.

144. See Luke Goode, "Social News, Citizen Journalism, and Democracy," *New Media and Society* 11, no. 8 (2009): 1287–1305.

145. Paul Spiegel and Peter Salama, "War and Mortality in Kosovo, 1998–99: An Epidemiological Testimony," *The Lancet* 355, no. 9222 (2000): 2204–9.

146. Peter Dahlgren, *Media and Political Engagement: Citizens, Communication, and Democracy* (New York: Cambridge University Press, 2009), 57–79.

4. LBC: An Illegitimate Militia Seeks Legitimacy in Participating Audiences and Accommodating Media

1. The epigraph is from Rémi Favret, "Deadly Harvest: Lebanon Has the Perfect Cash Crop to Finance Its Perpetual State of War," *The Globe and Mail* (Toronto), November 22, 1986, D5.

Marie-Joelle Zahar, "Is All the News Bad News for Peace? Economic Agendas in the Lebanese Civil War," *International Journal* 56, no. 1 (2000/2001): 115–28, 125–26.

2. Jonathan Marshall, *The Lebanese Connection: Corruption, Civil War and the International Drug Traffic* (Stanford, CA: Stanford University Press, 2012), 96–97.

3. Zahar, "Is All the News Bad News," 126.

4. Vito got his nickname because his charges with crime tended to be dismissed; i.e., they did not stick. Marshall, *The Lebanese Connection*, 92.

5. Collin Knox, "The Lebanese Connection: Bekaa Valley Drugs Fuel Endless Conflict," *Soldier of Fortune* (May 1988): 54–69, 54.

6. Favret, "Deadly Harvest," D5.

7. Today, the magazine has a website by subscription, www.almassira.com.

8. The relationships between *Masira* and its readership and between LF and its constituency were homologous.

9. Pierre Gemayel led the Phalangists from 1936 to his death from a heart attack in 1984. The Phalange organization started as a paramilitary youth group but turned into a political party in the late 1950s and 1960s. Its separatist ideology espoused Lebanon's independence as a unique Phoenician-heritage nation (home to its Christian population), rather than as part of a pan-Arab one. Following its transformation to a party, the Phalange focused on diplomacy and negotiation.

10. Zahar, "Is All the News Bad News," 118–19. According to Zahar, militia is "a generic label that includes all non-state actors who resort to violence in order to achieve their objectives" ("Protégés, Clients, Cannon Fodder: Civilians in the Calculus of Militias," *International Peacekeeping* 7, no. 4 (2000): 107–28, 108).

11. Zahar, "Is All the News Bad News," 121–22.

12. R. T. Naylor, "The Insurgent Economy: Black Market Operations of Guerrilla Organizations," *Crime, Law and Social Change* 20, no. 1 (1993): 13–51, 32.

13. Zahar, "Is All the News Bad News," 121–22.

14. Drug production and trafficking in Lebanon were instrumental in prolonging the civil war, even though they were not the reason for its outbreak. A substantial body of literature studies the connection between economic agendas such as black-market activities (from "off the books" to crime) and civil wars. The literature describes two motivations for continued violence during conflicts—greed and grievances. Those scholars (like World Bank economist Paul Collier), who argue that economic interests (greed) play a

decisive role in starting violent conflict, disfavor other, more common explanations for conflict such as ethnic and religious divisions, inequality, authoritarianism, and so on. The theoretical and empirical soundness of the greed explanation has been criticized broadly. Thus, most scholars argue that economic agendas are instead major factors in the continuance of violence during civil conflict (after the conflict has started for other reasons) as such agendas pose obstacles to peace. Combatants may want violence to continue because they profit from extracting resources and protecting them with military means, but they also may need violence as a means to push for changing the system.

15. As Elizabeth Picard has observed, the division of the country into many enclaves controlled by different militias did not impede the production and smuggling of drugs; on the contrary, it increased the profit from it. See "Trafficking, Rents, and Diaspora in the Lebanese War," in *Rethinking the Economics of War: The Intersection of Need, Creed, and Greed*, eds. Cynthia Arnson and William Zartman (Washington, DC: Woodrow Wilson Center Press, 2005), 27–67, 33.

16. Marshall, *The Lebanese Connection*, 11.

17. *Los Angeles Times*, October 17, 1981, 33.

18. Drug cultivation and trafficking were part of the Lebanese informal economy long before the war. Once the war started, the government collapsed and could no longer enforce drug laws. As the subsistence of a portion of the population was threatened due to the conflict, drugs became a lucrative trade. Moreover, international pressure could no longer keep the drug economy from growing, while foreign drug agencies avoided going to Lebanon for fear of being abducted (Marshall, *The Lebanese Connection*, 11). Favret, who visited the Lebanese Beqaa Valley in 1986, remarked that the drug trade was "the industry that pays for all the guns, the ammunition and the men in this bitter and bloody war" and that, according to the DEA, drug profits accounted for half of the entire Lebanese economy. He claimed that the single crop of marijuana was "enough for the Lebanese war to be self-perpetuating" (Favret, "Deadly Harvest," D5).

19. The Lebanese Diaspora in North America and Europe was often the link connecting producers and traffickers to consumers. Joseph Geha's 2012 novel *Lebanese Blonde* portrays the life of a Lebanese immigrant family in Toledo, Ohio's suburb "Little Syria." The family openly runs a funeral home while secretly smuggling hashish and makes plans to stash enough money aside to go back to Lebanon and live like pashas. The novel's title comes from a potent strain of hashish named after Lebanese immigrant women who dye their hair blonde to fit in with American cultural norms of the 1970s. The novel is not just an expression of nostalgia for the lost life of an American city with a thriving immigrant community but also a testimony to the significance of the drug trade during the Lebanese civil war. Joseph Geha, *Lebanese Blonde* (Ann Arbor: University of Michigan Press, 2012).

20. Favret, "Deadly Harvest," D5.

21. Marshall, *The Lebanese Connection*, 92.

22. Jürgen Endres, "Economic Ambitions in War: Lebanese Militias as Entrepreneurs," Working Papers Series. Kbh: Copenhagen Peace Research Institute, 2000, 5.

23. Marshall, *The Lebanese Connection*, 84.

24. Barbara Newman, *The Covenant: Love and Death in Beirut* (London: Bloomsbury, 1991), 130–31.

25. Zahar, "Is All the News Bad News," 118.

26. Ibid., 118–19, 124.

27. Ibid., 124. According to Zahar, the black-market activities demanded that LF develop this extensive infrastructure, not the other way around.

28. Economic agendas during war constitute a major reason to continue fighting; they oppose peace-seeking civilian agendas. Combatants do not feel a tremendous amount of pressure from their populations to work toward peace and to behave differently as long as their illegal economy is booming. Nonetheless, as Zahar has argued, black-market gains can become a liability in three ways: the government can retaliate and cease assets; the inflow of revenues can trigger in-fighting over their control; the illegal origin of their strength can become a liability domestically and internationally (negative consequences). Ibid., 119.

29. Marshall, *The Lebanese Connection*, 97. In 1984, the DEA and the ATF (the US Bureau of Alcohol, Tobacco, Firearms, and Explosives) started an investigation into the "guns-for-drugs traffic" between Lebanon and Detroit—the city with one of the largest Lebanese Diasporas in the United States—where a special Middle East investigation unit was created. Ibid., 95.

30. As *Le Monde* reported later, a tribunal in Marseilles convicted Geagea sympathizers of trafficking heroin and hashish for LF (May 19, 1990). Aoun's television scooped daily footage of drugs seizures from LF barracks, while he blasted, "We want to build a sound republic, not a heroin republic that the militiamen intend to establish." He alleged that his attack on LF came as an attempt to satisfy the US government's policies toward curbing drug trafficking. Sahar Baasiri, "Aoun Says Rival Militia Involved in Drug Trafficking," *UPI* (February 13, 1990).

31. Marshall, *The Lebanese Connection*, 110.

32. When Elias Hrawi—Aoun's rival for the presidency—proposed a farmers' plan that substituted cannabis with legal cash crops, Syria and Washington discussed financial and technical assistance. Ibid., 110.

33. *Le Monde*, April 5, 1989.

34. After the end of the civil war in 1990, LF became a political party but was soon outlawed, and in 1994 Geagea was imprisoned for eleven years on charges of bombing a church and contracting political assassinations, which he vehemently disputes. He was released in 2005 after Parliament granted him amnesty as a result of the anti-Syrian Cedar Revolution (that followed the assassination of Lebanon's Prime Minister Rafiq

Hariri on Valentine's Day). Shortly after, he enlisted LF into the ranks of the March 14 forces—an alliance of Lebanon's anti-Syrian parties.

35. Zahar, "Is All the News Bad News," 125.

36. Ibid.

37. Ibid., 122, 124.

38. Ibid., 126.

39. Ibid., 122.

40. Jean-Claude Boulos, *Al-Televizion: Tarikh wa Qisas* (Beirut: Sharikat al-Tab' wa-al-Nashr al-Lubnaniyya, 1995), 139. According to Nassim al-Khoury, Bachir had laid plans for LBC as early as 1980. Nassim al-Khoury, *Al-I'lam al-'Arabi wa-Inhiyar al-Sulta al-Lughawiyya* (Beirut: Markaz Dirasat al-Wahda al-'Arabiyya, 2005), 259. See also the interview with an LBC employee by Silva Abu Hamad and Nadine Shebli, *Sana'*, Beirut, Lebanese University (May 1993), 47.

41. Zahar, "Is All the News Bad News," 120.

42. Néstor García Canclini, *Consumers and Citizens: Globalization and Multicultural Conflict* (Minneapolis and London: University of Minnesota Press, 2001), 5, 24.

43. Ibid., 28, 29. Consumption, according to Canclini, is not an irrational compulsive expenditure but rather a thoughtful process in which the citizen behaves politically (ibid., 37).

44. As Canclini writes, spaces allowed for the public interest have contracted, and in the 1980s, many states surrendered partial control to private companies. Popular movements and liberation movements hybridized with the market and mass culture (ibid., 47).

45. Ibid., 22, 23, 25.

46. Ibid., 27.

47. *Masira*'s publication history is based on interviews with Amjad Iskandar, 'Imad Moussa, C. N., and others by author, August 2013.

48. This illustration is also a poster. See Zeina Maasri, *Off the Wall: Political Posters of the Lebanese Civil War* (New York: I. B. Taurus, 2008).

49. One of the perks that *Masira* didn't lose as an LF affiliate was being able to headquarter in a rent-free building that the militia owned. In the early 1990s, the journal also had its own printing house, property of LF. But when the militia-turned-party was banned in 1994 and the state appropriated its printing house, *Masira* returned to the older method of hiring out the loyal printer LF had used for decades. Until the makeover, the "internal bulletin" version of *Masira* did not need an official license because it was not sold on the market. When the journal applied for a license, Lebanese publications law did not permit publishing political periodicals under new names. Therefore, new magazines were forced to publish under names of out-of-print but still licensed publications. *Masira* settled on a franchise from *Najwa*. A new publication displayed, even highlighted, the name of the old periodical; hence, *Masira*'s cover read *Masira-Najwa*.

50. Today, things have slowed down considerably and the number of employees is slashed radically. Instead, *Masira* hires freelancers, keeping only five to six regular employees whose salaries can be supported by its budget.

51. As of this writing, ads for *Masira* are broadcast by Radio Free Lebanon instead of LBC, due to bitterness over the ownership lawsuit between the television's management and LF.

52. C. N. has asked that his identity be kept private.

53. According to Iskandar, no names were necessary because everyone at *Masira* was working for the cause. This anonymity made "Charbel" somewhat of a mystery (*ghumud*)—if someone alleged that he or she was working for the journal, no one could verify or disprove it.

54. There is lack of agreement on the appropriateness of the term "graphic novel" and its difference from the term "comic strip."

55. Allen Douglas and Fedwa Malti-Douglas, *Arab Comic Strips* (Bloomington: Indiana University Press, 1994), 3.

56. Ibid., 2.

57. Ibid., 224.

58. Ibid., 6, 224, 1.

59. It is considered the first real American graphic novel.

60. The strip uses formal generic features such as the size and shape of frames to depart from the linear narrative sequence and introduce parallel levels of historical generalization (ibid., 34).

61. Ibid., 47, 50, 52.

62. Jeremy Dauber, "Comic Books, Tragic Stories: Will Eisner's American Jewish History," *Association for Jewish Studies Review* 30, no. 2 (2006): 277–304, 278–79.

63. Douglas and Malti-Douglas, *Arab Comic Strips*, 222, 223, 226.

64. Iskandar, interview by author, Beirut, 2013.

65. Brian Peters, "Qu(e)ering Comic Book Culture and Representations of Sexuality in Wonder Woman," *CLCWeb: Comparative Literature and Culture* 5, no. 3 (2003): 52–60, 53.

66. Common explanations of the war also include an international component labeling it as "the war of others"; i.e., forces and interests outside Lebanon.

67. Ussama Makdisi, "Reconstructing the Nation-State: The Modernity of Sectarianism in Lebanon," *Middle East Report 200, Minorities in the Middle East: Power and the Politics of Difference* (July–September 1996): 23–26.

68. As Makdisi argues, before the nineteenth century, when the modern phenomenon of sectarianism was forged, Lebanese communities were religiously mixed and politics depended on a hierarchical system of notable families (*a'yan*) and common folk (*ahali*). Prompted by demographic and economic changes during the nineteenth century and the interaction between Western powers and the local population, elites

developed a new type of religion-based politics, and sectarianism as a community-organizing principle took off. But its meaning and application were far from clear until World War I. Peasants, elites, and clergy contested what a "true" Maronite meant, for example. While elites peddled the idea of a Maronite sect (*ta'ifa*) to maintain their position against the threat of rival elites and commoners, commoners employed it for social liberation (for example, when Maronite peasants rose against Maronite landlords in 1858). The struggle testified that the commoners were breaking into an unrepresentative social order. See ibid., 24–25.

69. Ibid., 25. See also Kamal Salibi, *Crossroads to Civil War: Lebanon 1958–1976* (New York: Caravan Books, 1976).

70. Of course, some readers could interpret *qabaday* as it is sometimes used to praise masculine behavior (especially strength, bravery, and success); nonetheless, many readers would also interpret it less kindly.

71. Michael Johnson, *All Honorable Men: The Social Origins of War in Lebanon* (New York: I. B. Taurus, 2002), 48.

72. Ibid., 49.

73. Ibid., 51.

74. Ibid.

75. Salibi, *Crossroads to Civil War,* 142. Qulaylat led over a thousand predominantly lower-class urban Sunni militia members of the Independent Nassarite Movement "Murabitun" headquartered in his native Beirut neighborhood Mahallat Abu Shakir. Before that, Qulaylat had been swinging from pledging allegiance to radical anti-Sadat elements to becoming a client of Libya's Muammar Gaddafi.

76. Having no name also erases Frem from the historical memory of future generations.

77. Nemer Frayha, "Religious Conflict and the Role of Social Studies for Citizenship in the Lebanese Schools between 1920 and 1983" (PhD diss., Stanford University, 1985), 341–42. Indeed, some of the communal events (such as Bachir's election to the presidency in 1982, his assassination twenty-one days later, as well as subsequent commemorations of these events) are clearly meaningless without the leader.

78. One can also make the point that Charbel is a representation of a collective—that of the rank-and-file LF member. However, in and of himself Charbel is not a site for constructing the collective identity of LF but a single example of it.

79. Dauber, "Comic Books, Tragic Stories," 282–87. This tension is addressed by scholars with regards to American Jewish autobiography and biography; see the two special issues of the journal *Prooftexts* 18, nos. 2–3 (July–September 1998) dedicated to American Jewish autobiography.

80. Iskandar, interview by author, January 23, 2015.

81. These were issues 29, 39, and 43.

82. Ahmad Beydoun, "Restoring Lebanese Culture," in *State and Society in Lebanon*, ed. Leila Fawaz (London: Center for Lebanese Studies and Tufts University, 1991), 63–74, 67.

83. "Breaking the Chain of Hate: Visit to the UK of Lebanese Former Militiamen, April 19–25" (brochure), *Initiatives of Change* (London: Agenda for Reconciliation, 2002), 6.

84. Frayha, "Religious Conflict," 341.

85. Nakhle Wehbe and Adnan el-Amine, *Systeme d'Enseignement at Division Sociale au Liban* (Paris: Le Sycomore, 1980). In the absence of an authoritative source on the war, students turn to their families, sects, or political parties whose perspectives are framed by the cult of dead leaders, amnesiac or mythologized war narratives. For instance, Maronite sources claim that the establishment of Greater Lebanon was a Lebanese cause and those who were killed for it in the fight against the Ottomans were heroes, while Muslim sources claim that Greater Lebanon was a "scrambled French fabrication detached from the Arab hinterland" and those killed were traitors. See Kamal Abouchedid, Ramzi Nasser, and Jeremy Van Blommestein, "The Limitations of Inter-Group Learning in Confessional School Systems: The Case of Lebanon," *Arab Studies Quarterly* 24, no. 4 (2002): 61–82, 72. See also Anja Peleikis, "The Making and Unmaking of Memories: The Case of a Multi-Confessional Village in Lebanon," in *Memory and Violence in the Middle East and North Africa*, ed. Ussama Makdisi and Paul Silverstein (Bloomington: Indiana University Press, 2006), 133–50; Sune Haugbolle, "Memory as Representation and Memory as Idiom," in *Breaking the Cycle: Civil Wars in Lebanon*, ed. Youssef Choueiri (Center for Lebanese Studies, Oxford; London: and Stacey International, 2007), 121; Rima Maktabi, "Lebanon's Missing History: Why School Books Ignore the Past," CNN (June 8, 2012).

86. Second installment, April 13, 1984.

87. The graphic novel avoids mentioning LF's defeats or cherry-picks parts that can be recast as victories. For example, during the Mountain War (September 1983–February 1984), LF sought expansion in areas with rural Christian populations (mainly in the Chouf). The result was confrontations with the local Druze community followed by LF's defeat and the displacement of Christians from Chouf and Aley. The novel, however, rewrites these battles as LF's vows to fight to the death, followed by the militia distributing food and supplies to the local population and helping them to rebuild their destroyed homes.

88. A vague comment that "one day, the hostile military pressure on one of the fronts increased" precedes the adventure/spy story but is unconvincing in portraying LF's actions as retaliation.

89. Douglas and Malti-Douglas, *Arab Comic Strips*, 224–25. However, there is a trend in the new millennium to produce some animation in the vernacular; for example

the US animated sitcom *The Simpsons* (Fox Broadcasting Company) was dubbed in the Egyptian vernacular instead of *Fusha*.

90. It also stems from the fact that in the twentieth century comics came from secular intellectual elites who tend to valorize *Fusha*.

91. As the accepted language of writing, *Fusha* was not strictly considered alienating in the rest of the journal, which discussed issues like politics, history, and military strategy rather than everyday conversations among regular people.

92. Whereas other Lebanese comics magazines still circulated throughout the region, reaching as far as Morocco despite the civil war, *Masira* was different. At first, it had limited member distribution, then limited national distribution. This was one among several reasons why using *Fusha* in the novel as the medium of communication was not crucial.

93. Zaven Kouyoumdjian, *Lebanon on Screen: The Greatest Moments of Lebanese Television and Pop Culture* (Beirut: Hachette Antoine, 2017), 160–61.

94. Nassim al-Khoury even divides the history of television in Lebanon into "before LBC" and "after LBC" (*Al-I'lam al-'Arabi*, 258).

95. It was impossible to view wartime news bulletins from Télé Liban and compare them to those of LBC in order to provide quotes in support. During the development of *Pretty Liar*, Télé Liban denied nonemployees access to its archives, large chunks of which are known to be lost or destroyed. In addition, it regards its archive as special property that should be well protected from outsiders rather than as a national treasure available for research, which would increase its value and that of the station.

96. Kouyoumdjian, *Lebanon on Screen*, 161.

97. Abd al-Ghani Tlis, "Televizion al-Mashriq Yushriq Am La Yushriq?," al-*Shabaka* 1738, June 26, 1989, 44–45.

98. Abd al-Ghani Tlis, "Akhbar al-Mu'assasa," al-*Shabaka* 1617, March 2, 1987, 60.

99. Kouyoumdjian, *Lebanon on Screen*, 159.

100. Ibid., 162.

101. Ibid., 163.

102. Ibid.

103. Ibid.

104. "Wujuh wa-Baramij fi-l-Mu'assasa al-Lubnaniyya li-l-Irsal," al-*Shabaka* 1563, February 17, 1986, 50–53, 52.

105. Kouyoumdjian, *Lebanon on Screen*, 159.

106. Nassim al-Khoury observes that the use of index cards as mnemonic devices by LBC's on-site reporters was quickly copied on other stations. *Al-I'lam al-'Arabi*, 262.

107. Tlis, "Akhbar al-Mu'assasa," 60.

108. Boulos, *Al-Televizion*, 141.

109. Nassim al-Khoury, *Al-I'lam al-'Arabi*, 261.

110. Mahmoud al-Batal, "Identity and Language Tension in Lebanon: The Arabic of Local News at LBCI," in *Language Contact and Language Conflict in Arabic: Variations on a Sociolinguistic Theme*, ed. Aleya Rouchdy (London: Routledge Curzon, 2002), 91–115, 113.

111. See an interview with LBC's news director George Ghanim by Cynthia 'Atalla, LBC, March 12, 1999.

112. Nassim al-Khoury, *Al-I'lam al-'Arabi*, 261.

5. Télé Liban in Defense of *Fusha*

1. Abd al-Ghani Tlis, "Risalat Qari' ila al-Televizion," *al-Shabaka* 1369, May 31, 1982, 66. The epigraph is from *Mister Mandur*, Episode 6, 1985, Télé Liban.

2. Abd al-Ghani Tlis, "'Al-'Ammiyya Tatrah al-Sawt?,'" *al-Shabaka* 1344, December 7, 1981, 76.

3. Abd al-Ghani Tlis, "'Al-Shabaka' Taftah Malaff al-Kitaba al-Televizioniyya: Jorj Ibrahim al-Khuri: Ana ma' al-Jamal wa-l-Ibda' wa-l-Fann," *al-Shabaka* 1293, December 15, 1980, 40.

4. Abd al-Ghani Tlis, "'Al-Shabaka' Taftah Malaff al-Kitaba al-Televizioniyya: Niqash 'ala al-Waraq al-Hurr," *al-Shabaka* 1303, February 23, 1981, 38.

5. Abd al-Ghani Tlis, "'Al-Shabaka' Taftah Malaff al-Kitaba al-Televizioniyya: Wajih Radwan: Al-Kitaba Asbahat li-l-Tafihin wa-l-Sathiyyn," *al-Shabaka* 1300, February 2, 1981, 42.

6. Tlis, "Al-'Ammiyya Tatruh al-Sawt?" 76.

7. Abd al-Ghani Tlis, "Antwan wa-Barnamij al-Watan," *al-Shabaka* 1440, October 10, 1983, 73.

8. Tlis, "Al-'Ammiyya Tatrah al-Sawt?," 76.

9. Work on *My Aunt's Home* began in 1986, but it first aired in 1988. *Miss Teacher* and *Mister Professor* can be watched in its entirety on YouTube (https://www.youtube.com/watch?v=V5zhOYYynVc). *What a Fortunate Home*, Season 1 can also be seen on YouTube (https://www.youtube.com/playlist?list=PLE85A645C874890E8), and it has a dedicated Facebook page (https://www.facebook.com/niyyelelbeit/). To my knowledge, none of the other shows have been made available on YouTube except for a few short clips.

10. Zaven Kouyoumdjian, *Lebanon on Screen: The Greatest Moments of Lebanese Television and Pop Culture* (Beirut: Hachette Antoine, 2017), 420.

11. The show was produced by London Weekend Television, directed by Stuart Allen, and written by Vince Powell.

12. The format might have been inspired by the American sitcom *Welcome Back, Kotter* (1975–79, aired by ABC) that was based on a social studies remedial class.

13. "1.5 Miliun Dular li-Mahu al-Ummiyya fi Lubnan," *Al-Sharq al-Awsat*, H. H. Saudi Research and Marketing, September 14, 2000. http://www.aawsat.com/details.asp?section=30&article=74127&issueno=7961.

14. Gabriella Gonzalez et al., *Facing Human Capital Challenges of the 21st Century: Education and Labor Market Initiatives in Lebanon, Oman, Qatar, and the United Arab Emirates* (RAND Corporation, 2008), 216–17, based on United Nations Development Programme, *Arab Human Development Report: Creating Opportunities for Future Generations* (New York: UNDP, Regional Bureau for Arab States, 2002). "[I]nvestments in education have produced what is a highly literate population in comparison with the populations of other countries in the Middle East, and Lebanon's illiteracy rate has continued to decline despite the Civil War" (Gonzalez et al., *Facing Human Capital*, 216).

15. Toufic Gaspard, *A Political Economy of Lebanon, 1948–2002: The Limits of Laissez-Faire*, Social, Economic and Political Studies of the Middle East Series (Leiden: Brill, 2004), 77.

16. Zeena Zakharia, "Language and Vulnerability: How Educational Policies Exacerbate Inequalities in Higher Education," *Middle East Institute Viewpoints: Higher Education and the Middle East*, Washington DC, 2010. http://www.mei.edu., 42; Zeena Zakharia, "Positioning Arabic in Schools: Language Policy, National Identity, and Development in Contemporary Lebanon," in *Critical Approaches to Comparative Education: Vertical Case Studies from Africa, Europe, the Middle East, and the Americas, ed.* Frances Vavrus and Leslie Bartlett (New York: Palgrave Macmillan, 2009), 215–31.

17. Even in 2009, state involvement in bridging the gender gap in literacy is lacking, according to Anita Nassar, Assistant Director of the Institute for Women's Studies in the Arab World (IWSAW) at Lebanese American University. Patrick Galey, "Lebanon Illiteracy Report Shows Alarming Urban-Rural Divide," *The Daily Star* (Beirut), July 4, 2009, http://www.dailystar.com.lb/News/Local-News/Jul/04/Lebanon-illiteracy-report-shows-alarming-urban-rural-divide.ashx#ixzz2ZR4vRVtq. According to a UNDP report, in 2006 rural regions like the Beqaa and Nabatieh had three times higher illiteracy rates (16.82 and 16.74 percent respectively) than urban centers like Beirut (6.06 percent). United Nations Development Programme, *Lebanon National Human Development Report: Toward a Citizen's State* (New York: UNDP, Regional Bureau for Arab States, 2009), 53.

18. They were similar to centers that appeared in the southern US states in the 1980s with the same goal. For example, one US endeavor called Project Read began in the state of Georgia in 1988 as a response to a television program on illiteracy that ABC and public television had broadcast earlier. See Strat Douthat, "Southern Cities Aim to Wipe Out Adult Illiteracy," *Los Angeles Times*, November 6, 1988, http://articles.latimes.com/1988-11-06/news/mn-268_1_adult-illiteracy.

19. I was guided by Kouyoumdjian's selection of important fictional series in *Lebanon on Screen*.

20. Douglas Boyd, *Broadcasting in the Arab World: A Survey of the Electronic Media in the Middle East* (Ames: Iowa State Press, 1999), 78.

21. Nabil Dajani, *Disoriented Media in a Fragmented Society: The Lebanese Experience* (Beirut: American University of Beirut, 1992), 139. Only 20 percent of all entertainment programs on Télé Liban were local, the rest were foreign, and just over half were subtitled. Eighty-two percent of workers watched them and 81 percent found them important. Lebanese elites typically watched foreign programs, yet 36 percent also followed local series and 34 percent found them important.

22. "Layla Karam: Fi Beirut Ibnat Madina wa-fi al-Janub Takhbiz 'ala al-Saj," *al-Shabaka* 1426, July 4, 1983, 21–23.

23. Suad Joseph, *Encyclopedia of Women and Islamic Cultures*, vol. 2, *Family, Law, and Politics* (Leiden: Brill, 2005), 1025. Organizations such as the Movement Social, AFEL (Association du Foyer de l'Enfant Libanais), The Good Shepherd Association, Association Dar al-Amal, and Foundation Terre des Hommes actively developed specialized programs for "literacy, vocational training, and the reintegration of children in the formal educational system," although without an independent body of studies, assessing their credibility and utility has been impossible (CAS and UNICEF, *State of the Children in Lebanon 2000* [Beirut: CAS, 2002], 38).

24. In a lecture at Texas A&M University, Najjar argued that the goal of education, including the one that Mandur espouses, is to bring about a "desirable behavior change" and that television is an important path to such change. ("Television Drama," lecture at Texas A&M University, November 25, 2013.)

25. Abd al-Ghani Tlis, "Tawaddahat Ma'alim 'Sami': Marwan Najjar Yaktub, al-Atfal Yumaththilun," *al-Shabaka* 1190, December 25, 1978, 61.

26. Najjar was also approached to do a show on the history of Arab Andalusia in a way that would transform boring education into an entertaining learning experience.

27. Abd al-Ghani Tlis, "Al-Mushaghib Marwan," *al-Shabaka* 1404, January 31, 1983, 68.

28. Abd al-Ghani Tlis, "Law La," *al-Shabaka* 1407, February 21, 1983, 64.

29. Abd al-Ghani Tlis, "Marwan Yusalih wa-Yukhasim," *al-Shabaka* 1549, November 11, 1985, 56.

30. Abd al-Ghani Tlis, "Mawqif al-Haqq," *al-Shabaka* 1600, November 3, 1986, 62. *Shabaka* speculated that he may have been unhappy with the performance of his script.

31. Jean Shahin, ""Ariseyn Midri min Weyn' Dahak Yatafajjar Farhan," *al-Shabaka* 1615, February 16, 1987, 22–24.

32. Interview with Najjar by author, August 2013.

33. It is doubtful that the episode alone triggered such response, given the decade-long hard work by a number of children's NGOs to initiate a law against child labor in Lebanon.

34. Interview with Najjar by author, December 2015.

35. Interview with Joseph Abu Nassar by author, August 2013.

36. Ibid.

37. Gibran imagined Lebanon as a place that belongs to the peasants, shepherds, young boys and girls, parents, and poets. He saw it in the beauty and strength of its rocks, valleys, and mountains; the purity of its water; and the fragrance of its air. For him it was a flock of birds fluttering in the early morning as shepherds led their sheep into the meadow and in the evening as farmers returned from their fields and vineyards.

38. See Yasir Suleiman, *The Arabic Language and National Identity: A Study in Ideology* (Washington, DC: Georgetown University Press, 2003), 227.

39. *Mister Mandur*, Episode 6, 1985, Télé Liban.

40. In the mid-1990s, this researcher began teaching English at the Maqaṣid school in the Beirut neighborhood of Mar Ilyas. The school is part of a religion-based network of Sunni schools that has branches all over Lebanon. (School networks are groups of religious or secular schools that share common interests and are joined under a local, national, or regional umbrella organization that usually keeps the network's policies closely in line with its orientation.) I was assigned ninth grade English, the equivalent of a low intermediate level. On my first day, a student in the back lit up a cigarette and began puffing while his friends cast him merry glances and an occasional verbal encouragement, "*Ya, salaam!*" To add insult to injury, another student asked me out to a movie. The rest were distracted—chatting or daydreaming—and certainly not paying attention to me. Despite my plea for help after class, the school administration only suggested that I start playing "bad cop."

41. *Mister Mandur*, Episode 1, 1985, Télé Liban.

42. Lebanese educators regarded their task as facilitating the flow of information from textbook to student. Accordingly, teachers were trained to lecture or have students memorize material and recite it for exams. See Nemer Frayha, "Religious Conflict and the Role of Social Studies for Citizenship in the Lebanese Schools between 1920 and 1983," PhD diss., Stanford University, 1985, 161–62.

43. United Nations Development Programme, *A Profile of Sustainable Human Development in Lebanon* (New York: UNDP, 1997), chapter 3 F, Education and Sustainable Human Development, 6. http://www.undp.org.lb/programme/governance/advocacy/nhdr/nhdr97/chpt3f.pdf.

44. Frayha, "Religious Conflict," 163–66. During the Mandate (1923–46) there were two training schools for public teachers; one was a two-year program established in 1924 and later named *Dar al-Mu'allimin* (Teachers' College) (Hassan Qubaysi, "Al-Dawla wa-l-Ta'lim al-Rasmi fi Lubnan," in *Al-Dawla wa-l-Ta'lim fi Lubnan*, ed. Munir Bashshur [Beirut: Al-Hay'a al-Lubnaniyya li-l-'Ulum al-Tarbawiyya, 1999], 105–83, 129; Frayha, "Religious Conflict," 160). Teachers' school graduates were assigned at the time to city schools, while applicants for teaching positions who had a primary studies certificate but no teacher training were assigned to rural schools (ibid.). Private schools had many

foreign teachers trained under more rigorous conditions abroad. Until the late 1970s, primary teachers were expected to have at least a Brevet; afterward they were required to have Bac Part II, while high school teachers needed a B.A. in the field they taught.

45. UNESCO, *L'Université Libanaise, La Faculté de Pédadogie, Centre de Recherches et de Développement Pedagogiques CRDP* (Beirut: UNESCO, 1980), 22.

46. Frayha, "Religious Conflict," 162.

47. S. Michel, "Muhtawa al-Manahij," *Al-Majalla al-Tarbawiya* 2 (1982): 7.

48. Frayha, "Religious Conflict," 143. Frayha also describes a private school administrator who coerced three teachers to relinquish 20 percent of their salary, yet made them sign a monthly government schedule stating that they were paid the full amounts.

49. Although this report was published in 2002, similar conditions and hence conclusions applied for the earlier wartime period as well. CAS and UNICEF, *State of the Children*, 31–32; Educational Center for Research and Development, *Learning/Difficulties for Students of the Second Cycle of Basic Education: A Sample of the Sixth Basic Class* [in Arabic] (Beirut: ECRD Press, 2001).

50. "Hind Abi al-Lama' wa-Ibrahim Mir'ashli Yaftahan Madrasa fi al-Televizion," *al-Shabaka* 1490, September 24, 1984, 30–31.

51. George Jordaq, "Khiffa wa-Tahshish," *al-Shabaka* 1502, December 17, 1984, 38–39.

52. Diana Hindi, "Al-Ustadh Ibrahim Yuwazzi' al-Shahadat 'ala Talamidhihi," *al-Shabaka* 1509, February 4, 1985, 16–18.

53. *Miss Teacher and Mister Professor*, Episode 1, 1984, Télé Liban.

54. A good example of the trickle-down linguistic nationalism is the scene where Fadlu's son Sami explains complicated grammatical categories to his father. Fadlu objects to the "lesson" by interrupting his son with the phrase *hallaktani sharhan* (you made me sick of [listening to] this explanation). Yet, he also feels obligated to raise his language register to *Fusha*. That is why he uses the accusative form of "explanation" *sharhan* and pronounces distinctly the third "a" in *hallaktani* (see Note Table). But in his attempt at *Fusha* Fadlu uses the wrong register of "you made me sick": the spoken form II instead of the formal form IV. Sami proceeds to educate his dad on language and trickles down Mandur's linguistic nationalism (*Mister Mandur*, Episode 2, 1985, Télé Liban).

Comparison of Linguistic Registers

Fadlu's Language	*Fusha*	*Lebanese*
hallaktani sharhan	*ahlaktani sharhan*	*hallaktni shareh*
form II	form IV	form II
3rd "a"	3rd "a"	—
accusative noun ending	accusative noun ending	—

55. *Mister Mandur,* Episode 1, 1985, Télé Liban.

56. Ibid.

57. *Mister Mandur,* Episode 1, 1985, Télé Liban. Added italics. The full song is:

No matter how much we tire and wander around
Or how much our mothers plead with us
We'll only learn Arabic
As per the method of Master Mandur.

The Arabic language is very beautiful
Provided the teacher would be smiling.

If on occasion my tongue slips
Over a tiny unguarded mistake
He will turn this world upside down
Demanding correct speech.

No one's as smart and wise as him
Always alert to capture mistakes
Breaking rulers for broken rules
Facing those who wouldn't understand.

Language is thought's stallion
Thought is the knight
The former never stumbles
The latter never faints.

We think he wants to correct a word
A short vowel, a little "o," a short "a"
A blunder that has lost its way
He ends up correcting the whole family.

He forgives wrongdoing
And tolerates childishness
But he wants to fix this world
And teach the planet how to spin
Mr. Mandur, Mandur, Mandur.

58. Abd al-Ghani Tlis, "'Al-Shabaka' Taftah Malaff al-Kitaba al-Televizioniyya: Marwan Najjar: Nahnu Afdal min al-'Ulama' fi Biladina," *al-Shabaka* 1296, January 5, 1981, 38–39.

59. *Professor No*, 1986, Hana'a Media Productions.

60. Ibid.

61. Jean Qassis, "'Al-Ustadh Mandur' Atlaq Shuhratahu," *al-Dalil*, March 12, 1999, 2.

62. He attributes being typecast as a comedy actor to his small stature that "can not carry a dramatic role." George Diab, interview by author, Beirut, August 2004. He also developed a rapport with Najjar who had cast him in the earlier theater play *Mouse Game* (1980). As their professional relationship blossomed in the next twenty-five years, they did many plays and television films together, so Diab worked with few other writers.

63. Qassis, "'Al-Ustadh Mandur," 2.

64. As the language of writing and formal oration, *Fusha* signals a formal, dignified atmosphere and has been called the "language of solemnity." On the other hand, it is considered a hard, "grammatical" language that can sound pompous. In contrast, *'ammiyya*, the language of conversation, is considered a "language of intimacy." Assem Nasr has shown how important *'ammiyya* is for conveying a feeling of closeness and a connection with the audience. Assem Nasr, "Bridge over Troubled Waters: A Content Analysis of Television Advertisements in Lebanon," *GMJ: Mediterranean Edition* 9, no. 1 (2014): 1–12, 6. In Lebanese television advertisements, where language is vital for communicating a product's identity, *'ammiyya* expresses intimate local culture, he argues, because it mirrors the viewers' linguistic identity and their anxieties and hopes. Nonetheless, being in command only of *'ammiyya* is often a marker of illiteracy, an attitude that illustrates the complicated language loyalties of Arab speakers. It prompts negative value judgments about a speaker's colder relationships to nationalist formalism, revered traditions, and high culture.

65. As an expert in phonetics, Professor Henry Higgins, the lead character in *My Fair Lady*, is ashamed that the English, as he sees it, cannot learn to speak their language properly. The poor classes' enunciation and accent contradicts Higgins's image of the English as more civilized and cultured than others, such as Arabs, who according to him learn Arabic "with the speed of summer lightning," (*My Fair Lady*, 1964, Warner Bros., dir. George Cukor, screenplay by Alan Jay Lerner). The failure to accumulate linguistic capital on *My Fair Lady* is cured by the power of idealization. Miss Eliza Doolittle is "a prisoner of the gutter," marked by her Cockney accent (ibid.). Despite her phonetic somersaults or enlisting the help of preposterous scientific equipment that Higgins owns, the miracle of proper English eludes her until Higgins tells her, "Just think of what you're dealing with. The majesty and grandeur of the English language is the greatest possession we have. The noblest thoughts that ever floated through the hearts of men are contained in its extraordinary imaginative and musical mixture of sounds. And that is what you set yourself out to conquer, Eliza. And conquer it you will. Now try again!" (ibid.). Inspired by this idealized image, Eliza succeeds and her words ring out in the clearest standard English: "The rain in Spain stays mainly in the plain." (ibid.). What Eliza learns

is the skill of idealization. In a matter of seconds, she grasps that creating an idealized reality is the cure for her "disease," no matter how absurd this might seem (after all, English also allows obscenities, lies, or death threats, for instance).

66. Ien Ang, *Living Room Wars: Rethinking Media Audiences for a Postmodern World* (London: Routledge, 1996), 146.

67. In comparison, 83 percent believed it was appropriate as the language of print. Nassim al-Khoury, *Al-I'lam al-'Arabi wa-Inhiyar al-Sulta al-Lughawiyya* (Beirut: Markaz Dirasat al-Wahda al-'Arabiyya, 2005), 315.

6. LBC and Language Pessoptimism

1. The epigraph is from "Why Can't the English?" (from *My Fair Lady*). Lyrics by Alan Jay Lerner. Music by Frederick Loewe. Copyright © 1956 (Renewed) Alan Jay Lerner and Frederick Loewe. Publication and Allied Rights Assigned to Chappell & Co. All Rights Reserved. Used by Permission of Alfred Music.

2. In Lebanese Arabic, the proverb is expressed as "*Akbar minnak l-boom, afham minnak l-bseyne.*"

3. In Lebanese Arabic, *Akbar minnak byom, afham minnak bsine.*

4. The show had two offshoot theater plays—*Awbat Khalti* (*My Aunt's Gang*, 1992) and *Niyyalak Ba'dak Saber* (*Saber and Company* [lit., "You're So Lucky to Still Be Patient/Saber"], 2001).

5. Inaya Jaber, "'Niyyal al-Bayt' 'ala LBC: Al-Jasad Afsah wa-l-Madmun Arhab," *al-Safir*, January 12, 1998; Jana Nasralla, "'Niyyal al-Bayt' 'ala Shashat LBC: 'Afawiya Sakhira wa-la Tandhir aw Mubashara," *al-Nahar*, June 28, 1999; Maher al-Shawwa, "Niyyal al-Bayt 'Ad ba'da 'Am 'ala Inqita'ih," *al-Dalil*, 2001, 2.

6. The sequel also named Kamal's wife Jina to resemble the name of Salame's wife Lina.

7. Abd al-Ghani Tlis, "Ahbabna 'Bayt Khalti,'" *al-Shabaka 1693*, August 15, 1988, 60–61; Antoine Sarkis, "'Beyt Khalti' Yatajaddad wa-'Madinat al-Alwan' Taftah Abwabha," *al-Nahar al-'Arabi wa-l-Duali*, 1989, 6; Jaber, "'Niyyal al-Bayt'"; Nasralla, "'Niyyal al-Bayt' 'ala Shashat LBC."

8. Samir Kamel, "Niyyal al-Bayt 'ala Shashat LBC: Kumidiya Nadhifa fi Lughatiha wa-Madmuniha," *al-Nahar*, July 2, 1998; Nasralla, "'Niyyal al-Bayt' 'ala Shashat LBC."

9. Tlis, "Ahbabna 'Bayt Khalti,'" 60–61; Hanadi al-Diri, "Al-Mu'aththirat al-Khassa li-l-Marra al-'Ula fi Musalsal Televizioni Mahalli," *al-Nahar*, July 12, 1999; Sarkis, "'Beyt Khalti.'"

10. Kamel, "Niyyal al-Bayt 'ala Shashat LBC"; Nasralla, "'Niyyal al-Bayt' 'ala Shashat LBC."

11. George Hayek, "Karl Salame: Ibn 'al-Awba' al-Mudallal," *al-Nahar* (Akhbar wa-Ara'), January 15, 1999.

12. Ibid.

13. Nibal Zughaib, "Camille Salame wa-'Niyyal al-Bayt' Thalithuhuma Kumidiya al-Mawaqif!," *al-Afkar* ("Musalsal tahta al-Daw'"), January 25, 1999, 52–53.

14. Interviews with Camille Salame, George al-Asmar, Gabriel Yamine, and Toni Mhanna by author, 2003–2013.

15. As George al-Asmar (Dara) shared, the price of each commercial slot was very steep. Interview by author, Beirut 2013.

16. Nasralla, "'Niyyal al-Bayt' 'ala Shashat LBC."

17. Ibid.; Al-Diri, "Al-Mu'aththirat al-Khassa."

18. Tlis, "Ahbabna 'Bayt Khalti'"; Shawwa, "Niyyal al-Bayt."

19. Jean Qassis, "'Niyyal al-Bayt . . . ' fi Thalathin Halqa Shakhsiyat 'Bayt Khalti' Tudahhikuna Mujaddidan," *al-Dalil* ("Television"), October 2, 1998, 2.

20. Jaber, "Niyyal al-Bayt."

21. Kamel, "Niyyal al-Bayt 'ala Shashat LBC."

22. Zughaib, "Camille Salame."

23. Hayek, "Karl Salame"; Zughaib, "Camille Salame."

24. Qassis, "'Niyyal al-Bayt," 2.

25. Tlis, "Ahbabna 'Bayt Khalti,'" 60–61.

26. Shawwa, "Niyyal al-Bayt."

27. Jaber, "'Niyyal al-Bayt'."

28. Nasralla, "'Niyyal al-Bayt' 'ala Shashat LBC."

29. Tlis, "Ahbabna 'Bayt Khalti,'" 60–61.

30. Shawwa, "Niyyal al-Bayt."

31. Nasralla, "'Niyyal al-Bayt' 'ala Shashat LBC."

32. Salame's writing was seen as the series' best "qualification" (Jaber, "'Niyyal al-Bayt'"), which boasted respectable language and eschewed "ugliness" (Nasralla, "'Niyyal al-Bayt' 'ala Shashat LBC"), so that the whole family, including kids, could watch every episode (Zughaib, "Camille Salame").

33. Nasralla, "'Niyyal al-Bayt' 'ala Shashat LBC."

34. Tlis, "Ahbabna 'Bayt Khalti,'" 60–61.

35. Nasralla, "'Niyyal al-Bayt' 'ala Shashat LBC."

36. Zughaib, "Camille Salame."

37. Elise Salem, *Constructing Lebanon: A Century of Literary Narratives* (Gainesville: University Press of Florida, 2003), 163.

38. Huda Barakat, *Hajar al-Dahak* (Beirut: Riad al-Rayyis Books, 1990), 244.

39. Later, he is hired as a full-time Arabic teacher at a school.

40. *Khadim* is Arabic for servant and waiter.

41. In one exception, Dara calls him "Master."

42. Kamal Salibi, *House of Many Mansions, The History of Lebanon Reconsidered* (London: I. B. Tauris, 1988).

43. *My Aunt's Home*, Season 2, Episode 1, 1989, LBC.

44. Ibid.

45. In Arabic, *Bet sitti hajar 'adim, udtein w-dar w-matbakh w-il-hammem barraat el-bet b-il-ha'le*. Ibid.

46. Salem, *Constructing Lebanon*, 50.

47. Quoted in ibid., 44.

48. Robin Ostle, "Modern Poetry," in *Encyclopedia of Arabic Literature*, ed. Julie Scott Meisami and Paul Starkey, vol. 2 (New York: Routledge, 1998), 606–9, 608. Although the prominence of this romantic and neoclassical school is long over, it is still popular in the Gulf.

49. In Arabic, *Haydek el-bet ahla, bi-nnahawi*. *My Aunt's Home*, Season 2, Episode 1, 1989, LBC.

50. Mikhail Bakhtin, "From the Prehistory of Novelistic Discourse," in *The Dialogic Imagination: Four Essays*, ed. Michael Holquist (Austin and London: University of Texas Press, 1981), 41–83, 45.

51. Salem, *Constructing Lebanon*, 242.

52. Hassan Abdallah, "Thaqafat Tams al-Haqa'iq," *al-Adab*, Special winter issue *Istifta' al-Adab al-Kabir: al-Muthaqqafun wa-l-Hazima* (1983): 45; Yumna al-Eid, *Al-Kitaba: Tahawwul fi al-Tahawwul: Muqaraba li-l-Kitaba al-Adabiyya fi Zaman al-Harb al-Lubnaniyya* (Beirut: Dar al-Adab, 1993), 135.

53. Barakat, *Hajar al-Dahak*, 243.

54. The story of the camel is continued in the next episode. *Niyyal al-Bayt*, Season 2, Episodes 3 and 4, 2000–2001, LBC.

55. In Arabic, *Ya jamal, ya Bub'a—ya sabir 'a-l-sahari; safart yom al-urb'a—terikni la-hari*. Ibid.

7. War, Modernity, and the Crisis of Patriarchy

1. The epigraph is from Abdullah al-Ghathami, "Cultural Criticism: Theory and Method," in *Arab Cultural Studies: Mapping the Field*, ed Tarik Sabry (London; New York: I. B. Taurus, 2012), n.p. © 2012 Abdullah al-Ghathami. Reproduced with permission of The Licensor through PLSclear.

2. "Kayfa Saqat al-Doktor Jacque Kundakjian fi-l-'Mutafawwiqun,'" *al-Shabaka* 1259, April 21, 1980, 24–25. My emphasis.

3. Ibid.

4. Personal interview with Najjar by email. My emphasis.

5. Zaven Kouyoumdjian, *Lebanon on Screen: The Greatest Moments of Lebanese Television and Pop Culture* (Beirut: Hachette Antoine, 2017), 271.

6. Elizabeth Thompson, *Colonial Citizens: Republican Rights, Paternal Privilege, and Gender in French Syria and Lebanon* (New York: Columbia University Press, 2000).

7. Ibid., 6.

8. Suad Joseph, "Connectivity and Patriarchy among Urban-Class Arab Families in Lebanon," *Ethos* 21, no. 4 (1993): 452–84.

9. Suad Joseph, "The Public/Private: The Imagined Boundary in the Imagined Nation/State/Community: The Lebanese Case," *Feminist Review* 57 (1997): 73–92, 85, 86.

10. Suad Joseph, "Conceiving Family Relationships in Postwar Lebanon," *Journal of Comparative Family Studies* 35, no. 2 (2004): 275–93, 275.

11. Samir Makdisi, *Lessons from Lebanon: The Economics of War and Development* (London: I. B. Taurus, 2004), 44.

12. Fawwaz Traboulsi, *A History of Modern Lebanon* (London: Pluto Press, 2008), 205–19.

13. Michael Johnson, *All Honorable Men: The Social Origins of War in Lebanon* (New York: I. B. Taurus, 2002).

14. Ibid.

15. For a discussion of militarized masculinity, see Sune Haugbolle, "The (Little) Militia Man: Memory and Militarized Masculinity in Lebanon," *Journal of Middle East Women's Studies* 8, no. 2 (2012): 115–39.

16. Joseph, "Conceiving Family Relationships," 275.

17. Ibid., 271–72.

18. Makdisi, *Lessons from Lebanon*, 43.

19. Ibid., 45.

20. Ibid., 6, 35.

21. Ibid., 47.

22. Ibid., 47–48. Manufacturing had grown at first, but later experienced a drop.

23. Ibid., 49.

24. Ibid., 74.

25. Zeina Zaatari, "The Culture of Motherhood: An Avenue for Women's Civil Participation in South Lebanon," *Journal of Middle East Women's Studies* 2, no. 1 (2006): 33–64; Suad Joseph, "Problematizing Gender and Relational Rights: Experiences from Lebanon," *Social Politics: International Studies in Gender, State, and Society* 1, no. 3 (1994): 271–85.

26. Interestingly, Lebanese war novels, according to Samira Aghacy, depict domestic space as a refuge where men find comfort and relief from the war but where they also feel marginalized and anxious about losing their male identity and turning into women. Samira Aghacy, "Domestic Spaces in Lebanese War Fiction: Entrapment or Liberation," in *Crisis and Memory: The Representation of Space in Modern Levantine Narrative*, ed. Ken Seigneurie and Samira Aghacy (Wiesbaden: Dr. Ludwig Reichert Verlag, 2003), 83–99.

27. This is also typical of anticolonial contexts like Mandate Palestine.

28. Deniz Kandiyoti, "Bargaining with Patriarchy," *Gender and Society* 2, no. 3 (1988): 274–90, 282.

29. Female participation in the labor force increased from 17.5 percent of all women in 1970–75 to 27.8 percent in 1990. Lamia Rustum Shehadeh, ed., *Women and War in Lebanon* (Gainesville: University Press of Florida, 1999), 54, 55, 59. Women whose income is necessary for a household's survival are often treated more equally to men.

30. Maha Charani, *Three Voices, One Heart: A War Story of Three Generations of Middle-Class Lebanese Muslim Women* (Saarbrücken: VDM Verlag Dr. Muller 2008), 30.

31. The civil war caused a "conscious and more systematic exclusion of women from numerous industrial tasks" in favor of unskilled domestic and foreign males. Malek Abisaab, *Militant Women of a Fragile Nation* (Syracuse, NY: Syracuse University Press, 2010), 122.

32. Ibid., 117, 122.

33. Ibid., 126.

34. Ibid., 29. Although women contributed significantly to the Lebanese economy, class also played a role in marginalizing or empowering them differently. Middle- and upper-class women, for example, engaged in labor activism in order to fight their seclusion, as negative attitudes toward female labor were primarily stemming from their circles. By contrast, negative attitudes were less significant for lower-class women who were more concerned with income and accepted less desirable unskilled jobs to survive. Ibid., 55.

35. Chiara Saraceno, "The Italian Family: Paradoxes of Privacy," in *History of Private Life V: Riddles of Identity in Modern Times*, ed. Philippe Ariès et al. (Cambridge, MA: Harvard University Press, 1991), 451–502. See also Shehadeh, *Women and War in Lebanon*, 50–52.

36. Charani, *Three Voices*, 95. Another woman shares: "During the war, all we worried about was how to finish washing the dishes and the clothes before the water and the electricity were cut off for the day. That was my worry" (109–10).

37. Zaatari, "The Culture of Motherhood," 43.

38. Charani, *Three Voices*, 4.

39. Ibid., 118.

40. For instance, the number of female lawyers quadrupled from 5.8 to 24.3 percent between 1980 and 1993, while the number of female engineers and architects increased thirty-four times from 0.2 to 6.78 percent. Shehadeh, *Women and War in Lebanon*, 56.

41. Ibid., 66.

42. Ibid., 53.

43. See Miriam Cooke, *War's Other Voices: Women Writers on the Lebanese Civil War* (Cambridge: Cambridge University Press, 1987).

44. Joseph Zeidan, *Arab Women Novelists: The Formative Years and Beyond* (Albany: SUNY Press, 1995), 233.

45. Interview by Charani, *Three Voices*, 109–10.

46. Ibid., 130–31.

47. Abisaab, *Militant Women*, 116.

48. Naila Nauphal, *Post-War Lebanon: Women and Other War-affected Groups* (Beirut: Dar al-Shawra, 1997).

49. Charani, *Three Voices*, 91–92.

50. Bouthaina Shaaban, "The Hidden History of Arab Feminism," *Ms. Magazine* (May/June, 1993), 76–77.

51. Shehadeh, *Women and War in Lebanon*, 149.

52. Hala Maksoud, "The Case of Lebanon," in *Arab Women between Defiance and Restraint*, ed. S. Sabbagh (New York: Olive Branch Press, 1996), 89–94; Hanifa al-Khatib, *Tarikh Tatawwur al-Haraka al-Nisa'iyya fi Lubnan wa Irtibatuha bi-l-'Alam al-'Arabi: 1800–1975* (Beirut: Dar al-Hadatha li-l-Tiba'a wa-l-Nashr, 1984).

53. Roger Moukarzel's 1978 photograph can be viewed at http://i2.cdn.turner.com/cnnnext/dam/assets/120425093008-roger-moukarzel-war-lebanon-horizontal-large-gallery.jpg.

54. Jocelyn Khweiri, "From Gunpowder to Incense," in *Women and War in Lebanon*, ed. Lamia Rustum Shehadeh (Gainesville: University Press of Florida, 1999), 209–26, 225. After 1985, the downtown Beirut unit of the Nizamiyyat, which had fought in the most dangerous area during the war, abandoned military action and formed a pacifist movement calling for education (Shehadeh, *Women and War in Lebanon*, 157). The documentary *Lebanon's Women Warriors* aired on al-Jazeera on April 21, 2010.

55. Charani, *Three Voices*, 49.

56. Samantha Wehbi, "Lebanese Women Disability Rights Activists: War-Time Experiences," *Women's Studies International Forum* 33, no. 5 (2010): 455–63, 460.

57. Haugbolle, "The (Little) Militia Man," 130; "Rihla fi Nufus Milishiyin Sabiqin," al-*Nahar*, February 12–13, 1998.

58. Fadia Nassif and Tar Kovacs, *Les Rumerurs dans la Guerre du Liban: Les mots de la Violence* (Paris: CNRS Édition, 1998), 272–323.

59. Walter Armbrust, "Bourgeois Leisure and Egyptian Media Fantasies," in *New Media in the Muslim World: The Emerging Public Sphere*, ed. Dale Eickelman and Jon Anderson (Bloomington: Indiana University Press, 2003), 102–28, 102.

60. See Salim Tamari, "Bourgeois Nostalgia and the Abandoned City," *Comparative Studies of South Asia, Africa, and the Middle East* 23, nos. 1/2 (2003): 173–80.

61. See Najib Hourani, "The Militiaman Icon—Cinema, Memory, and the Lebanese Civil Wars," *CR: The New Centennial Review* 8, no. 2 (2008): 287–307, 303.

62. Of course, focusing on boys is understandable also given that Mandur was blackmailed for alleged sexual harassment of a female student.

63. Pierre Bourdieu, *Masculine Domination* (Stanford, CA: Stanford University Press, 2001), 21.

64. Abu Melhem was played by Adib Haddad. Later, Karam's role was given to Salwa Haddad, Adib's own wife.

65. "Al-Habs li-l-Rijal wa-l-Mar'a bi-Nus 'Aql," *al-Shabaka* 388, July 1, 1963, 42.

66. Abd al-Ghani Tlis, "Layla Karam Burkan Yanfajir!," *al-Shabaka* 1379, August 8, 1982, 14–15.

67. See Carol Adams, *The Sexual Politics of Meat: A Feminist-Vegetarian Critical Theory, Anniversary edition* (1990; reprint, London: Bloomsbury Academic, 2015); and Carol Adams, *The Pornography of Meat*, reprint ed. (2004; reprint, New York: Lantern Books, 2015).

68. Ghathami, "Cultural Criticism," 267.

69. Clare Chambers, *Sex, Culture, and Justice: The Limits of Choice* (University Park, PA: Penn State University Press, 2008), 68.

Conclusion: The Case for the Study of Lebanese Broadcast Television

1. The epigraph is from Vivian Haddad, "'Al-Dunya Hayk' Ya'khudh fi Rihla li-Midhaq al-Sab'inat bi-Qalib Hadith," *al-Sharq al-Awsat*, March 26, 2017.

2. A YouTube video created by the campaign provides a wealth of information: https://www.youtube.com/watch?v=KEEeWUI_Z38.

3. Arabic is typically written without short vowels as readers understand the unvoweled words from context—in English, cat, cot, and cut would be written "ct" and listeners would understand the meaning if, for example, they were told to "sleep on a ct." Arabic learners are sometimes encouraged to add short vowels to words to help them learn the language.

4. See Lara Deeb and Mona Harb, *Leisurely Islam: Negotiating Geography and Morality in Shi'ite South Beirut* (Princeton, NJ: Princeton University Press, 2013).

5. Cafes and restaurants have been popular in Lebanon since urbanization at the beginning of the twentieth century. Popular working-class cafes frequented by males to play cards and backgammon were all over residential neighborhoods, squares, and alleys (Chawqi Douaihy, *Maqahi Bayrut al-Sha'biyya: 1950–1990* [Beirut: Dar al-Nahar, 2005]). Cafes also helped migrants to find jobs and receive mail from their families and political leaders to connect to their base. Mixing of the genders in eating-out establishments became popular around the 1940s in downtown Beirut when restaurant culture became widespread (Christa Salamandra, *A New Old Damascus: Authenticity and Distinction in Urban Syria* [Bloomington: Indiana University Press, 2004]). With commercialization, new desires for modern urban lifestyles, and the advent of television in the late 1950s and early 1960s, a more affluent clientele was attracted to the new sidewalk cafes in cosmopolitan areas like Hamra. A number of cafes there became gathering spots for intellectuals, political activists, and people in the arts. By contrast, working men visited the older-style cafes and working-class women paid social visits to relatives' and neighbors' homes (Aseel

Sawalha, *Reconstructing Beirut: Memory and Space in a Postwar Arab City* [Austin: University of Texas Press, 2010], 92).

6. Whereas before the war the number of coffee shops was around 120, at the beginning of the twenty-first century there were fewer than 50 (Douaihy, *Maqahi Bayrut*).

7. Hamra and a few gentrified residential neighborhoods like Gemmayzeh became popular destinations for eating out and night life.

8. The four styles are often used in the same establishment to decorate separate rooms.

9. Deeb and Harb, *Leisurely Islam*, 125.

10. Only fewer than a quarter of the cafes in the religiously conservative Dahieh neighborhood also offer a prayer room, according to Deeb and Harb, *Leisurely Islam*, 119.

11. Deeb and Harb, *Leisurely Islam*, 25.

12. Ibid., 126.

13. Haddad, "'Al-Dunya Hayk.'"

14. Gladys Saade, "Lebanese Television Archives," *The Electronic Library* 22, no. 2 (2004): 139–43, 139.

15. Ibid., 140.

16. Ibid., 141–42.

Bibliography

Primary Television Shows Analyzed

Bayt Khalti (*My Aunt's Home*), 1986/1988–90, LBC

Al-Mu'allima wa-l-Ustadh (*Miss Teacher and Mister Professor*), 1984, Télé Liban

Niyyal al-Bayt (*What a Fortunate Home*), 1998–2001, LBC

Al-Ustadh Mamnu' (*Professor No*), 1986, Hana'a Media Productions

Al-Ustadh Mandur (*Mister Mandur*), 1985, Télé Liban

Primary Literary Sources Analyzed

Adnan, Etel, *Al-Sitt Marie-Rose* (*Sitt Marie-Rose*), 1978

Barakat, Huda, *Hajar al-Dahak* (*The Stone of Laughter*), 1990

Al-Daif, Rachid, *Unsi Yalhu ma' Ritta: Kitab al-Balighin* (*Unsi Plays with Ritta: A Book for Adults*), 1983

Darwish, Mahmoud, *Dhakira li-l-Nisyan: Sirat Yawm, al-Zaman—Ab, al-Makan—Bayrut* (*Memory for Forgetfulness, August, Beirut, 1982*), 1986

"Hikayat Batal Ismu Charbel" (*The Story of a Hero Called Charbel*), 1984

Khoury, Elias, *al-Jabal al-Saghir* (*Little Mountain*), 1977

Khoury, Elias, *Rihlat Gandhi al-Saghir* (*The Journey of Little Gandhi*), 1989

Makdisi, Jean Said, *Beirut Fragments, 1990*

Al-Shaykh, Hanan, *Hikayat Zahra* (*The Story of Zahra*), 1980

Primary Print Publications Analyzed

Al-Masira (Beirut, 1983–)

Al-Nahar (Beirut, 1933–)

Al-Safir (Beirut, 1974–2016)

Al-Shabaka (Beirut, 1956–)

Interviews

Abu Nassar, Joseph, journalist, *Nahar,* and actor, West Beirut
Ahmad, audience member
Alvanthian, Sepouh, director of programming, LBC
Al-Asmar, George, actor, *My Aunt's Home* and *What a Fortunate Home*
C. N., illustrator, "The Story of a Hero Called Charbel," *Masira*
Diab, George, actor, *Mister Mandur*
Feghali, Jean, journalist and cofounder, *Masira*
Fuad, audience member
Georgette, audience member
Imad, audience member
Iskandar, Amjad, editor-in-chief and executive director, *Masira*
Khabbaz, George, actor, *Talibin al-Qurb* (*The Matchseekers*); *al-Profesor* (*The Professor*)
Khalil, Charbel, creator, *Bas Mat Watan* (When a Nation Died/Smiles of a Nation); general manager, Comedy's Production s.a.r.l.
Maaluf, Elie, television producer, *Talamidh Akhir Zaman* (*Latter-Day Students*)
Maya, audience member
Mhanna, Tony, actor, *My Aunt's Home* and *What a Fortunate Home*
Moussa, Imad, journalist, LBC, and cofounder, *Masira*
Najjar, Marwan, television writer, *Mister Mandur*
Sabah, audience member
Salame, Camille, television writer, *My Aunt's Home* and *What a Fortunate Home*
Shaqqur, Hassan, director of programming, Télé Liban
Tlis, Abd al-Ghani, columnist, *al-Shabaka*; host of *Masa al-Nur* (*Good Evening*), Télé Liban
Vassia, audience member
Wehbi, Zahi, host of *Khallik bi-l-Bayt*, Future TV
Yammine, Gabriel, actor, *My Aunt's Home* and *What a Fortunate Home*

Selected Bibliography

"121 Terrestrial TV Stations Broadcast in 18 Arab Countries." January 9, 2013. http://www.broadcastprome.com/news/121-terrestrial-tv-stations-broadcast-in-18-arab-countries/#.WQVWn1eFitA.

"1.5 Miliun Dular li-Mahu al-Ummiyya fi Lubnan." *Al-Sharq al-Awsat.* H. H. Saudi Research and Marketing. September 14, 2000. http://www.aawsat.com/details.asp?section=30&article=74127&issueno=7961.

ABC. "TV Audience Survey: Nov–Dec 1974." Beirut, 1975.

Abdallah, Hassan. "Thaqafat Tams al-Haqa'iq." *Al-Adab* special winter issue *Istifta' al-Adab al-Kabir: Al-Muthaqqafun wa-l-Hazima* (1983).

Abisaab, Malek. *Militant Women of a Fragile Nation.* Syracuse, NY: Syracuse University Press, 2010.

Abouchedid, Kamal, Ramzi Nasser, and Jeremy Van Blommestein. "The Limitations of Inter-Group Learning in Confessional School Systems: The Case of Lebanon." *Arab Studies Quarterly* 24, no. 4 (2002): 61–82.

Abu Nassar, Joseph. Interview by author. In person. Beirut, August 2013.

Abu-Laban, Baha. "Factors in Social Control of the Press in Lebanon." *Journalism and Mass Communication Quarterly* 43, no. 3 (1966): 510–18.

Adams, Carol. *The Sexual Politics of Meat: A Feminist-Vegetarian Critical Theory.* Anniversary edition. London: Bloomsbury Academic, [1990] 2015.

———. *The Pornography of Meat.* Reprint edition. New York: Lantern Books, [2004] 2015.

Adnan, Etel. *Al-Sitt Marie-Rose.* Beirut: al-Mu'assasa al-'Arabiyya li-l-Dirasat wa-l-Nashr, 1978.

Aghacy, Samira. "Domestic Spaces in Lebanese War Fiction: Entrapment or Liberation." In *Crisis and Memory: The Representation of Space in Modern Levantine Narrative,* edited by Ken Seigneurie and Samira Aghacy. Wiesbaden: Dr. Ludwig Reichert Verlag, 2003, 83–99.

———. "Contemporary Lebanese Fiction: Modernization without Modernity." *International Journal of Middle East Studies* 38, no. 4 (2006): 561–80.

Akar, Bassel. "The Space between Civic Education and Active Citizenship in Lebanon." In *Rethinking Education for Social Cohesion,* edited by Maha Shuayb. Basingstoke: Palgrave Macmillan, 2012, 154–70.

Allan, Stuart. *Citizen Witnessing: Revisioning Journalism in Times of Crisis.* Cambridge, UK and Malden, MA: Polity, 2013.

Allan, Stuart, and Barbie Zelizer. "Rules of Engagement: Journalism and War." In *Reporting War: Journalism in Wartime,* edited by Stuart Allan and Barbie Zelizer. New York: Routledge, 2004, 3–22.

Allen, Thomas, F. Clifton Berry Jr., and Norman Polmar. *CNN: War in the Gulf: From the Invasion of Kuwait to the Day of Victory and Beyond.* Kansas City: Andrews McMeel, 1991.

Allen, Tim, and Jean Seaton, eds. *The Media of Conflict: War Reporting and Representations of Ethnic Violence*. London and New York: Zed Books, 1999.

Alvanthian, Sepouh. Interview by author. In person. Beirut, 2004.

Amyuni, Mona Takieddine. "Style and Politics in the Poems and Novels of Rashid al-Da'if." *International Journal of Middle East Studies* 28, no. 2 (May 1996): 177–92.

Ang, Ien. *Living Room Wars: Rethinking Media Audiences for a Postmodern World*. London: Routledge, 1996.

Anini, R. "Ru'yat al-Hayat wa-l-Fann fi Masrah Ziyad Rahbani." *Al-Tariq* 48.6–49.1 (1989–1990): 147–62, 175–96.

Arab Media Outlook 2011–2015: Forecasts and Analysis of Traditional and Digital Media in the Arab World. 4th ed. In *Dubai Press Club* (N.p.: 2012).

Al-Asmar, George. Interview by author. In person. Beirut, 2003.

———. Interview by author. In person. Beirut, 2013.

Armbrust, Walter. "Bourgeois Leisure and Egyptian Media Fantasies." In *New Media in the Muslim World: The Emerging Public Sphere*, edited by Dale Eickelman and Jon Anderson. Bloomington: Indiana University Press, 2003, 102–28.

Ayish, Muhammad. "Arab World Television in Transition: Current Trends and Future Prospects." *Orient* 41, no. 3 (2000): 415–34.

———. "Political Communication on Arab World Television: Evolving Patterns." *Political Communication* 19, no. 2 (2002): 137–54.

———. *Arab Television in the Age of Globalization: An Analysis of Emerging Political Economic, Cultural and Technological Patterns*. Hamburg: Deutsches Orient-Institut, 2003.

———. "Arab State Broadcasting Systems in Transition: The Promise of the Public Service Broadcasting Model." *Middle East Journal of Culture and Communication* 3 (2010): 9–25.

———. "Television Broadcasting in the Arab World: Political Democratization and Cultural Revivalism." In *Arab Media: Globalization and Emerging Media Industries*, edited by Noha Mellor et al. Cambridge and Malden, MA: Polity Press, 2011.

Baasiri, Sahar. "Aoun Says Rival Militia Involved in Drug Trafficking." *UPI*, February 13, 1990.

Bakhtin, Mikhail. *The Dialogic Imagination: Four Essays*. Edited by Michael Holquist. Austin and London: University of Texas Press, 1981.

———. *Speech Genres and Other Late Essays*. Austin: University of Texas Press, 1986.

Bala Tul Sire. Future TV. March 27, 2016. https://www.youtube.com/watch?v=2AxOWNB3qw8.

Barakat, Huda. *Hajar al-Dahak*. London: Riad al-Rayyes Books, 1990.

Al-Batal, Mahmoud. "Identity and Language Tension in Lebanon: The Arabic of Local News at LBCI." In *Language Contact and Language Conflict in Arabic: Variations on a Sociolinguistic Theme*, edited by Aleya Rouchdy. London: Routledge Curzon, 2002, 91–115.

Bayat, Asef. *Life as Politics: How Ordinary People Change the Middle East*. Stanford, CA: Stanford University Press, 2013.

Beydoun, Ahmad. "Restoring Lebanese Culture." In *State and Society in Lebanon*, edited by Leila Fawaz. London: Center for Lebanese Studies and Tufts University, 1991, 63–74.

Bishara, Amahl. *Back Stories: US News Production and Palestinian Politics*. Stanford, CA: Stanford University Press, 2013.

Blattman, Christopher, and Edward Miguel. "Civil War." *Journal of Economic Literature* 48, no. 1 (2010): 3–57.

Boulos, Jean-Claude. *Al-Televizion: Tarikh wa Qisas*. Beirut: Sharikat al-Tab' wa-l-Nashr al-Lubnaniyya, 1995.

———. *Al-Televizion: Rihla ila al-Jahim*. Beirut: Dar al-Nahar li-l-Nashr, 2007.

Bourdieu, Pierre. *Masculine Domination*. Stanford, CA: Stanford University Press, 2001.

Boyd, Douglas. "Lebanese Broadcasting: Unofficial Electronic Media during a Prolonged Civil War." *Journal of Broadcasting & Electronic Media* 35, no. 3 (1991): 269–87.

———. *Broadcasting in the Arab World: A Survey of the Electronic Media in the Middle East*. Ames: Iowa State Press, 1999.

Boyer, Dominic. *The Life Informatic: Newsmaking in the Digital Era*. Ithaca, NY: Cornell University Press, 2013.

Browne, Donald. "Television and National Stabilization: The Lebanese Experience." *Journalism Quarterly* 52, no. 4 (1975): 692–98.

Cameron, Deborah. "Demythologizing Sociolinguistics: Why Language Does Not Reflect Society." In *Ideologies of Language*, edited by John Joseph and Talbot Taylor. London: Routledge, 1990, 79–93.

Canclini, Nestor Garcia. *Consumers and Citizens: Globalization and Multicultural Conflict*. Minneapolis and London: University of Minnesota Press, 2001.

Carlucci, Alessandro. *Gramsci and Languages: Unification, Diversity, Hegemony.* Leiden: Brill, 2013.

CAS and UNICEF. *State of the Children in Lebanon 2000.* Beirut: Central Administration of Statistics, 2002.

Chambers, Clare. *Sex, Culture, and Justice: The Limits of Choice.* University Park, PA: Penn State University Press, 2008.

Chambers, John Whiteclay, II, and David Culbert. *World War II: Film, and History.* New York: Oxford University Press, 1996.

Charani, Maha. *Three Voices, One Heart: A War Story of Three Generations of Middle-Class Lebanese Muslim Women.* Saarbrücken: VDM Verlag Dr. Muller, 2008.

Chouliaraki, Lilie. "Digital Witnessing in War Journalism: The Case of Post Arab Spring Conflicts." *Popular Communication* 13, no. 2 (2015): 105–19.

Cooke, Miriam. *War's Other Voices: Women Writers on the Lebanese Civil War.* Cambridge: Cambridge University Press, 1987.

"Court Throws Out World Cup Lawsuit against Tele Liban." *The Daily Star* (Beirut), July 5, 2014.

Al-Dahir, H. "Yukmil al-Masira al-Rahbaniyya al-Ibda'iyya ba'da Ghiyab Mansour." *Al-Anwar,* March 26, 1995.

Dahlgren, Peter. *Media and Political Engagement: Citizens, Communication, and Democracy.* New York: Cambridge University Press, 2009.

Al-Daif, Rachid. *Unsi Yalhu Ma' Ritta: Kitab al-Balighin.* Beirut: Al-Mu'assasa al-Jami'iyya li-l-Dirasat wa-l-Nashr wa-l-Tawzi', 1983.

———. *Taqaniyat al-Bu's.* Beirut: Riad al-Rayyis li-l-Kutub wa-l-Nashr, [1989] 2001.

Dajani, Nabil. *Lebanon: Studies in Broadcasting.* London: International Institute of Communications, 1979.

———. *Disoriented Media in a Fragmented Society: The Lebanese Experience.* Beirut: American University of Beirut, 1992.

Darwish, Mahmoud. *Dhakira li-l-Nisyan: Sirat Yawm, al-Zaman—Ab, al-Makan—Bayrut.* Ramallah: Wizarat al-Thaqafa & Dar al-Nashir, [1986] 1997.

Dauber, Jeremy. "Comic Books, Tragic Stories: Will Eisner's American Jewish History." *Association for Jewish Studies Review* 30, no. 2 (2006): 277–304.

Davis, Thomas. *40 Km into Lebanon: Israel's 1982 Invasion.* Darby, PA: Diane Publishing, 1995.

De Cauter, Lieven. "Towards a Phenomenology of Civil War: Hobbes Meets Benjamin in Beirut." *International Journal of Urban and Regional Research* 35, no. 2 (2011): 421–30.

Deeb, Lara, and Mona Harb. *Leisurely Islam: Negotiating Geography and Morality in Shi'ite South Beirut*. Princeton, NJ: Princeton University Press, 2013.

Dentith, Simon. *Bakhtinian Thought: An Introductory Reader*. London; New York: Routledge, 1995.

Diab, George. Interview by author. In person. Beirut, August 2003.

Al-Diri, Hanadi. "Al-Mu'aththirat al-Khassa li-l-Marra al-'Ula fi Musalsal Televizioni Mahalli." *Nahar*, July 12, 1999.

Douaihy, Chawqi. *Maqahi Bayrut al-Sha'biyya: 1950–1990*. Beirut: Dar al-Nahar, 2005.

Douglas, Allen, and Fedwa Malti-Douglas. *Arab Comic Strips*. Bloomington: Indiana University Press, 1994.

Douthat, Strat. "Southern Cities Aim to Wipe Out Adult Illiteracy." *Los Angeles Times*, November 6, 1988. http://articles.latimes.com/1988-11-06/news/mn-268_1_adult-illiteracy.

Educational Center for Research and Development. *Learning/Difficulties for Students of the Second Cycle of Basic Education: A Sample of the Sixth Basic Class* [in Arabic]. Beirut: ECRD Press, 2001.

Eickelman, Dale, and Jon Anderson, eds. *New Media in the Muslim World: The Emerging Public Sphere*. 2nd ed. Bloomington: Indiana University Press, 2003.

Al-Eid, Yumna. *Al-Kitaba: Tahawwul fi al-Tahawwul: Muqaraba li-l-Kitaba al-Adabiyya fi Zaman al-Harb al-Lubnaniyya*. Beirut: Dar al-Adab, 1993.

Ellis, John. *Seeing Things: Television in the Age of Uncertainty*. London: I. B. Taurus, 2000.

Endres, Jürgen. "Economic Ambitions in War: Lebanese Militias as Entrepreneurs." Working Papers Series. N.p.: Copenhagen Peace Research Institute, 2000.

Fandy, Mamun. "Information Technology, Trust and Social Change in the Arab World." *Middle East Journal* 54, no. 3 (2000): 378–94.

Favret, Rémi. "Deadly Harvest: Lebanon Has the Perfect Cash Crop to Finance Its Perpetual State of War." *The Globe and Mail* (Toronto), November 22, 1986, D5.

Firro, Kais. "Lebanese Nationalism versus Arabism: From Bulus Nujaym to Michel Chiha." *Middle Eastern Studies* 40, no. 5 (2004): 1–27.

Fisk, Robert. *Pity the Nation: The Abduction of Lebanon*. New York: Thunder's Mouth Press/Nation Books, 2001.

Frayha, Nemer. "Religious Conflict and the Role of Social Studies for Citizenship in the Lebanese Schools between 1920 and 1983." PhD diss., Stanford University, 1985.

Freedman, Des, and Daya Kishan Thussu, eds. *Media and Terrorism: Global Perspectives*. Thousand Oaks, CA: Sage, 2012.

Fregonese, Sara. "Between a Refuge and a Battleground: Beirut's Discrepant Cosmopolitanisms." *Geographical Review* 102, no. 3 (2012): 316–36.

Galey, Patrick. "Lebanon Illiteracy Report Shows Alarming Urban-Rural Divide." *The Daily Star* (Beirut), July 4, 2009, http://www.dailystar.com.lb/News/Local-News/Jul/04/Lebanon-illiteracy-report-shows-alarming-urban-rural-divide.ashx#ixzz2ZR4vRVtq.

Gaspard, Toufic. *A Political Economy of Lebanon, 1948–2002: The Limits of Laissez-Faire*. Social, Economic and Political Studies of the Middle East Series. Leiden: Brill, 2004.

Geha, Joseph. *Lebanese Blonde*. Ann Arbor: University of Michigan Press, 2012.

Ghanim, George. Interview by Samantha 'Atalla. LBC, March 13, 1999.

Al-Ghathami, Abdullah. "Cultural Criticism: Theory and Method." In *Arab Cultural Studies: Mapping the Field*, edited by Tarik Sabry. London and New York: I. B. Taurus, 2011, 255–74.

Gitelman, Lisa. *Always Already New: Media, History, and the Data of Culture*. Cambridge and London: MIT Press, 2006.

Gonzalez, Gabriella, et al. *Facing Human Capital Challenges of the 21st Century Education and Labor Market Initiatives in Lebanon, Oman, Qatar, and the United Arab Emirates*. Santa Monica, CA: RAND Corporation, 2008.

Goode, Luke. "Social News, Citizen Journalism, and Democracy." *New Media and Society* 11, no. 8 (2009): 1287–1305.

Gramsci, Antonio. *Selections from Cultural Writings*. Edited by David Forgacs and Geoffrey Nowell-Smith. London: Lawrence and Wishart, 1985.

———. *Selections from the Prison Notebooks of Antonio Gramsci*. Edited by Quintin Hoare and Geoffrey Nowell Smith. 11th ed. New York: International Publishers; London: Lawrence and Wishart, [1971] 1992.

Haddad, Vivian. "'Al-Dunya Hayk' Ya'khudh fi Rihla li-Midhaq al-Sab'inat bi-Qalib Hadith." *al-Sharq al-Awsat*, March 26, 2017.

Haeri, Niloofar. *The Sociolinguistic Market of Cairo: Gender, Class, and Education*. London; New York: Kegan Paul International, 1996.

———. *Sacred Language, Ordinary People: Dilemmas of Culture and Politics in Egypt*. New York: Palgrave Macmillan, 2003.

Hamade, Marwan. "Le Liban, Ce Grand Absent." Editorial. *L'Orient-Le Jour,* Beirut, October 20, 1974.

Hallyday, Fred. "Manipulation and Limits: Media Coverage of the Gulf War, 1990–91." In *The Media of Conflict: War Reporting and Representations of Ethnic Violence,* edited by Tim Allen and Jean Seaton. London: Zed Books, 1999.

Harb, Zahira. *Channels of Resistance in Lebanon: Liberation Propaganda, Hezbollah and the Media.* London: I. B. Taurus, 2011.

Haugbolle, Sune. "Memory as Representation and Memory as Idiom." In *Breaking the Cycle: Civil Wars in Lebanon,* edited by Youssef Choueiri. Center for Lebanese Studies. Oxford; London: Stacey International, 2007.

———. *War and Memory in Lebanon.* Cambridge: Cambridge University Press, 2010.

———. "The (Little) Militia Man: Memory and Militarized Masculinity in Lebanon." *Journal of Middle East Women's Studies* 8, no. 1 (2012): 115–39.

Hayek, George. "Karl Salame: Ibn 'al-Awba' al-Mudallal." *Al-Nahar* (Akhbar wa-Ara'), January 15, 1999.

Hjarvard, Stig. *The Mediatization of Society and Culture.* New York: Routledge, 2013.

Hoskins, Andrew. "New Memory: Mediating History." *Historical Journal of Film, Radio and Television* 21, no. 4 (2001): 333–46.

Hourani, Najib. "The Militiaman Icon—Cinema, Memory, and the Lebanese Civil Wars." *CR: The New Centennial Review* 8, no. 2 (2008): 287–307.

Initiatives of Change. "Breaking the Chain of Hate: Visit to the U.K. of Lebanese Former Militiamen, April 19–25." Brochure. London: Agenda for Reconciliation, 2002.

Irvine, Judith. "When Talk Isn't Cheap: Language and Political Economy." *American Ethnologist* 16, no. 2 (1989): 248–67.

Iskandar, Amjad. Interview by author. In person. Beirut, August 2013.

———. Interview by author. Email. January 2015.

Ives, Peter. "Language and Collective Identity: Theorizing Complexity." In *Language and Identity Politics: A Cross-Atlantic Perspective,* edited by Christina Spati. New York: Berghahn Books, 2015, 17–37.

Jaber, 'Inaya. "'Niyyal al-Bayt' 'ala LBC: Al-Jasad Afsah wa-l-Madmun Arhab." *Al-Safir* 8173, December 12, 1998, 19.

Jayyusi, Lena. "Internationalizing Media Studies: A View from the Arab World." *Global Media and Communication* 3, no. 3 (2007): 251–55.

Johnson, Michael. *All Honorable Men: The Social Origins of War in Lebanon*. New York: I. B. Taurus, 2002.

Joseph, John E. *Language and Identity: National, Ethnic, Religious*. Basingstoke, UK: Palgrave, 2004.

Joseph, Suad. "Connectivity and Patriarchy among Urban-Class Arab Families in Lebanon." *Ethos* 21, no. 4 (1993): 452–84.

———. "Problematizing Gender and Relational Rights: Experiences from Lebanon." *Social Politics: International Studies in Gender, State, and Society* 1, no. 3 (1994): 271–85.

———. "The Public/Private: The Imagined Boundary in the Imagined Nation/State/Community: The Lebanese Case." *Feminist Review* 57 (1997): 73–92.

———. "Conceiving Family Relationships in Postwar Lebanon." *Journal of Comparative Family Studies* 35, no. 2 (2004): 275–93.

———. *Encyclopedia of Women and Islamic Cultures*. Vol. 2, *Family, Law, and Politics*. Leiden: Brill, 2005.

Kamel, Samir. "Niyyal al-Bayt 'ala Shashat LBC: Kumidiya Nadhifa fi Lughatiha wa-Madmuniha." *Al-Nahar* (Television), July 12, 1998.

Kandiyoti, Deniz. "Bargaining with Patriarchy." *Gender and Society* 2, no. 3 (1988): 274–90.

Kassir, Samir. *Beirut*. Berkeley: University of California Press, 2010.

Khalaf, Samir, and Philip Khoury, *Recovering Beirut: Urban Design and Post-War Reconstruction*. Leiden: Brill, 1993.

Khalil, Charbel. Interview by author. In person. Beirut, 2004.

Al-Khatib, Hanifa. *Tarikh Tatawwur al-Haraka al-Nisa'iyya fi Lubnan wa–Irtibatuha bi-l-'Alam al-'Arabi: 1800-1975*. Beirut: Dar al-Hadatha, 1984.

Al-Khatibi, Abdelkabir. *Al-Naqd al-Muzdawij*. Beirut: Dar al-'Awda, 1980.

Khazaal, Natalie. "Re-evaluating Mohamed Choukri's Autobiography Al-Khubz al-Hafi: The Oppression of Morocco's Amazigh Population, the Sa'alik, and Backlash." *Middle Eastern Literatures*: incorporating *Edebiyat* 16, no. 2 (2013): 147–68.

Khazen, Jihad. "Freedom of the Press in the Arab World: Censorship and State Control in the Arab World," *Press/Politics* 4, no. 3 (1999): 87–92.

Khiabany, Gholam. "Iranian Media: The Paradox of Modernity." *Social Semiotics* 17, no. 4 (2007): 479–501.

Khoury, Elias. Al-*Jabal al-Saghir*. Beirut: Dar al-Adab, [1977] 2003.

———. *Al-Wujuh al-Bayda'*. Beirut: Dar Ibn Rushd, 1981.

———. *Rihlat Gandhi al-Saghir*. Beirut: Dar al-Adab, 1989.

Khoury, Jean-Claude. "The Lebanese Radio and Television Stations Present: The Reluctant Partisans." *Monday Morning*, March 28, 1976, 41.

Al-Khoury, Nassim. *Al-I'lam al-'Arabi wa-Inhiyar al-Sulutat al-Lughawiyya*. Beirut: Markaz Dirasat al-Wahda al-'Arabiyya, 2005.

Khweiri, Jocelyn. "From Gunpowder to Incense." In *Women and War in Lebanon*, edited by Lamia Rustum Shehadeh. Gainesville: University Press of Florida, 1999, 209–26.

Knox, Collin. "The Lebanese Connection: Bekaa Valley Drugs Fuel Endless Conflict." *Soldier of Fortune* (May 1988): 54–69.

Kouyoumdjian, Zaven. *As'ad Allah Masa'kum: Mi'at Lahdha Sana't al-Televizion fi Lubnan*. Beirut: Hachette Antoine, 2015.

———. *Lebanon on Screen: The Greatest Moments of Lebanese Television and Pop Culture*. Beirut: Hachette Antoine, 2017.

Krabill, Ron. *Starring Mandela and Cosby: Media and the End(s) of Apartheid*. Chicago: University of Chicago Press, 2010.

Kraidy, Marwan. "Broadcasting Regulation and Civil Society in Postwar Lebanon." *Journal of Broadcasting & Electronic Media* 42, no. 3 (1998): 387–400.

———. "State Control of Television News in 1990s Lebanon." *Journalism and Mass Communication Quarterly* 76, no. 3 (1999): 485–98.

———. "Television and Civic Discourse in Postwar Lebanon." In *Civil Discourse and Digital Age Communications in the Middle East*, edited by Leo Gher and Hussein Amin. Stamford, CT: Ablex, 2000, 3–18.

———. "Globalization avant la Lettre?: Cultural Hybridity and Media Power in Lebanon." In *Global Media Studies: Ethnographic Perspectives*, edited by Patrick Murphy and Marwan Kraidy. New York: Routledge, 2003, 276–95.

———. *Reality Television and Arab Politics: Contention in Public Life*. Cambridge: Cambridge University Press, 2010.

———. "Globalizing Media and Communication Studies: Thoughts on the Translocal and the Modern." In *De-Westernizing Communication Research: Altering Questions and Changing Frameworks*, edited by Georgette Wang. Abingdon; New York: Routledge, 2011, 50–76.

———. *The Naked Blogger of Cairo: Creative Insurgency in the Arab World*. Cambridge, MA: Harvard University Press, 2016.

Kraidy, Marwan, and Joe Khalil. *Arab Television Industries*. London: Palgrave Macmillan, 2009.

Ku, Agnes. "Revisiting the Notion of 'Public' in Habermas's Theory—Toward a Theory of Politics of Public Credibility." *Sociological Theory* 18, no. 2 (2000): 216–40.

Kullab, Samya. "Tele-Liban Gets Glossy Hi-Tech Overhaul." *The Daily Star* (Beirut), January 31, 2014.

Laipson, Ellen, and Clyde Mark. "Conflict in Lebanon: From the Missile Crisis of April 1981 through the Israeli Invasion, August 1982." Washington, DC: Congressional Research Service, Library of Congress, 1983.

Lambek, Michael. *Knowledge and Practice in Mayotte: Local Discourse of Islam, Sorcery, and Spirit Possession.* Toronto: University of Toronto Press, 1993.

Lughod, Lila Abu. *Dramas of Nationhood: The Politics of Television in Egypt.* Chicago: University of Chicago Press, 2005.

Lynch, Marc. *Voices of the New Arab Public: Iraq, Al-Jazeera, and Middle East Politics Today.* New York: Columbia University Press, 2006.

Maasri, Zeina. *Off the Wall: Political Posters of the Lebanese Civil War.* New York: I. B. Taurus, 2008.

Mackey, Sandra. *Lebanon: A House Divided.* New York and London: W. W. Norton, 2006.

Makdisi, Jean Said. "Book Mark Living in Beirut: 'A Tightrope Over an Abyss of Panic' Memoir: A Palestinian Describes Her Efforts to Live a Normal Life in a City under Siege, and to Understand Passions That Would Erase It from the Map." *Los Angeles Times*, Home Edition, September 9, 1990, 2.

———. *Beirut Fragments: A War Memoir.* Rev. ed. New York: Persea Books, 1999.

Makdisi, Samir. *Lessons from Lebanon: The Economics of War and Development.* London: I. B. Taurus, 2004.

Makdisi, Ussama. "Reconstructing the Nation-State: The Modernity of Sectarianism in Lebanon." *Middle East Report 200: Minorities in the Middle East: Power and the Politics of Difference* (July–September 1996): 23–26.

Maksoud, Hala. "The Case of Lebanon." In *Arab Women between Defiance and Restraint*, edited by Suha Sabbagh. New York: Olive Branch Press, 1996.

Maktabi, Rima. "Lebanon's Missing History: Why School Books Ignore the Past." CNN. Updated June 8, 2012. http://www.cnn.com/2012/06/08/world/meast/lebanon-civil-war-history/index.html.

Malek, Adel. *Harb al-Sanatayn wa-Ba'd.* Beirut: Dar Sa'ir al-Mashriq, 2016.

Marshall, Jonathan. *The Lebanese Connection: Corruption, Civil War and the International Drug Traffic.* Stanford, CA: Stanford University, 2012.

McLuhan, Marshall. *Understanding Media: The Extensions of Man*. Columbus, OH: McGraw-Hill, 1964.

Mellor, Noha. *Modern Arab Journalism: Problems and Prospects*. Edinburgh: Edinburgh University Press, 2007.

———. "Arab Journalists as Cultural Intermediaries." *Press/Politics* 13, no. 4 (2008): 465–83.

———. "Media: An Overview of Recent Trends." In *Arab Media: Globalization and Emerging Media Industries*. Edited by Noha Mellor et al. Cambridge, MA: Polity, 2011, 12–28.

Mhanna, Toni. Interview by author. In person. Beirut, 2013.

Michel, S. "Muhtawa al-Manahij." *Al-Majalla al-Tarbawiyya* 2 (1982): n.p.

Miller, Flagg. *The Moral Resonance of Arab Media: Audiocassette Poetry and Culture in Yemen*. Cambridge, MA, and London: Harvard University Press, 2007.

Miller, Tim, Val Jervis, and Tim Hogg. "Terrestrial Broadcasting and Spectrum Use in the Arab States: A Report for the GSMA." London: Plum Consulting, 2015.

Morrison, David. *Television and the Gulf War*. London: John Libbey, 1992.

Mroueh, Wassim. "Local Television Stations Push for New Cable Fees." *The Daily Star* (Beirut), March 5, 2015.

Najjar, Marwan. Interview by author. In person. Beirut, 2003.

———. Interview by author. In person. Beirut, 2013.

———. "Television Drama." Lecture at Texas A&M University, November 25, 2013.

———. Interview by author. Email. November 2014.

———. Interview by author. Email. December 2014.

———. Interview by author. Email. December 2015.

———. Interview by author. Email. December 2016.

———. Interview by author. Email. August 2017.

Nasr, Assem. "Bridge over Troubled Waters: A Content Analysis of Television Advertisements in Lebanon." *GMJ: Mediterranean Edition* 9, no. 1 (2014): 1–12.

Nasralla, Jana. "'Niyyal al-Bayt' 'ala Shashat LBC: 'Afawiyya Sakhira wa-la Tandhir aw Mubashara." *Al-Nahar*, June 28, 1999.

Nassif, Fadia, and Tar Kovacs. *Les Rumerurs dans la Guerre du Liban: Les mots de la Violence*. Paris: CNRS Édition, 1998.

Nauphal, Naila. *Post-War Lebanon: Women and Other War-affected Groups*. Geneva: International Labor Organization, 1997.

Naylor, R. T. "The Insurgent Economy: Black Market Operations of Guerrilla Organizations." *Crime, Law and Social Change* 20, no. 1 (1993): 13–51.

Newman, Barbara. *The Covenant: Love and Death in Beirut.* London: Bloomsbury, 1991.

Nora, Pierre. "Between Memory and History: Les Lieux de Mémoire." *Representations* no. 26, Special Issue: Memory and Counter-Memory (Spring 1989): 7–24.

Osterhaus, William. "TL 1979: Evaluation with Some Recommendations." October 1979.

Ostle, Robin. "Modern Poetry." In *Encyclopedia of Arabic Literature,* vol. 2, edited by Julie Scott Meisami and Paul Starkey. New York: Routledge, 1998, 606–9.

PARC press release. June 5, 2009.

Peleikis, Anja. "The Making and Unmaking of Memories: The Case of a Multi-Confessional Village in Lebanon." In *Memory and Violence in the Middle East and North Africa,* edited by Ussama Makdisi and Paul Silverstein. Bloomington: Indiana University Press, 2006, 133–50.

Peters, Brian. "Qu(e)ering Comic Book Culture and Representations of Sexuality in Wonder Woman." *CLCWeb: Comparative Literature and Culture* 5, no. 3 (2003): 52–60.

Picard, Elizabeth. "Trafficking, Rents, and Diaspora in the Lebanese War." In *Rethinking the Economics of War: The Intersection of Need, Creed, and Greed,* edited by Cynthia Arnson and William Zartman. Washington, DC: Woodrow Wilson Center Press, 2005, 27–67.

Pintak, Lawrence. "Border Guards of the 'Imagined' *Watan*: Arab Journalists and the New Arab Consciousness." *Middle East Journal* 63, no. 2 (2009): 191–212.

Pintak, Lawrence, and Jeremy Ginges. "The Mission of Arab Journalism: Creating Change in a Time of Turmoil." *Press/Politics* 13, no. 3 (2008): 193–227.

Qabbani, Nizar. *Jumhuriyyat Jununistan: Lubnan Sabiqan.* Beirut: Manshurat Nizar Qabbani, 1988.

Qassis, Jean. "'Niyyal al-Bayt . . . ' fi Thalathin Halqa Shakhsiyyat 'Bayt Khalti' Tudahhikuna Mujaddadan." *Al-Dalil* ("Television"), October 2, 1998, 2.

———. "'Al-Ustadh Mandur' Atlaq Shuhratahu." *Al-Dalil,* March 12, 1999, 2.

Qubaysi, Hassan. "Al-Dawla wa-l-Ta'lim al-Rasmi fi Lubnan." In *Al-Dawla wa-l-Ta'lim fi Lubnan,* edited by Munir Bashshur. Beirut: Al-Hay'a al-Lubnaniyya li-l-'Ulum al-Tarbawiyya, 1999, 105–83.

Research Bureau Limited. "Middle East Media Survey." London: n.p., 1974.

El Richani, Sarah. "The Lebanese Broadcasting System: A Battle between Political Parallelism, Commercialization, and De-facto Liberalism." In *National Broadcasting and State Policy in Arab Countries*, edited by Tourya Guaaybess. London: Palgrave Macmillan, 2013, 69–82.

———. "Pierre Daher: Sheikh, Barron, and Moghul of LBC." In *Arab Media Moguls*, edited by Donatella Della Ratta, Naomi Sakr, and Jakob Skovgaard-Petersen. London and New York: I. B. Taurus, 2015, 49–62.

"Rihla fi Nufus Milishiyyin Sabiqin." *Al-Nahar*, February 12–13, 1998.

Rizk, Carol. "Indictment Backs LF Lawsuit against LBC, Seeks Jail for Daher." *The Daily Star* (Beirut), October 15, 2010.

Rugh, William. *The Arab Press: News and Political Process in the Arab World*. Syracuse, NY: Syracuse University Press, 1987.

———. *Arab Mass Media: Newspapers, Radio, and Television in Arab Politics*. Westport, CT: Praeger, 2004.

Saade, Gladys. "Lebanese Television Archives." *The Electronic Library* 22, no. 2 (2004): 139–43.

Sabry, Tarik. *Cultural Encounters in the Arab World: On Media, the Modern and the Everyday*. London and New York: I. B. Taurus, 2010.

Safouan, Moustapha. *Why Are The Arabs Not Free?: The Politics of Writing*. Boston: Wiley-Blackwell, 2007.

Sakr, Naomi. "Freedom of Expression, Accountability and Development in the Arab Region." *Journal of Human Development* 4, no. 1 (2003): 29–46.

———. *Arab Television Today*. New York: I. B. Taurus, 2007.

Salamandra, Christa. *A New Old Damascus: Authenticity and Distinction in Urban Syria*. Bloomington: Indiana University Press, 2004.

Salame, Camille. Interview by author. In person. Beirut, 2003.

———. Interview by author. In person. Beirut, 2013.

———. Interview by author. Email. December 2015.

———. Interview by author. Email. March 2016.

Salem, Elise. *Constructing Lebanon: A Century of Literary Narratives*. Gainesville: University Press of Florida, 2003.

Salibi, Kamal. *Crossroads to Civil War: Lebanon 1958-1976*. New York: Caravan Books, 1976.

———. *House of Many Mansions: The History of Lebanon Reconsidered*. London: I. B. Tauris, 1988.

Saraceno, Chiara. "The Italian Family: Paradoxes of Privacy." In *History of Private Life V: Riddles of Identity in Modern Times*, edited by Philippe Ariès et al. Cambridge, MA: Harvard University Press, 1991, 451–502.

Sarkis, Antoine. "'Bayt Khalti' Yatajaddad wa-'Madinat al-Alwan' Taftah Abwabaha." *Al-Nahar al-'Arabi wa-l-Duali* (1989): 6.

Sawalha, Aseel. *Reconstructing Beirut: Memory and Space in a Postwar Arab City*. Austin: University of Texas Press, 2010.

Scott, Joan. "Gender: A Useful Category of Historical Analysis." *American Historical Review* 91, no. 5 (1986): 1053–75.

Shaaban, Bouthaina. "The Hidden History of Arab Feminism." *Ms. Magazine*, May/June, 1993.

Al-Shabaka. Beirut, 1962–1997.

El Shakry, Hoda. "Heteroglossia and the Poetics of the Roman Maghrébin." *Contemporary French and Francophone Studies* 20, no. 1 (2017): 8–17.

Shaqqur, Hassan. Interview by author. In person. Beirut, 2003.

———. Interview by author. Phone. July 2017.

Al-Shawwa, Maher. "Niyyal al-Bayt 'Ad ba'da 'Am 'ala Inqita'ih." *Al-Dalil* ("Television") (2001), 2.

Al-Shaykh, Hanan. *Hikayat Zahra*. Beirut: Dar al-Adab, [1980] 2004.

Shehadeh, Lamia Rustum, ed. *Women and War in Lebanon*. Gainesville: University Press of Florida, 1999.

Spiegel, Paul, and Peter Salama. "War and Mortality in Kosovo, 1998–99: An Epidemiological Testimony." *The Lancet* 355, no. 9222 (2000): 2204–9.

Spigel, Lynn. *Make Room for TV: Television and the Family Ideal in Postwar America*. Chicago: University of Chicago Press, 1992.

Sreberny, Annabelle. "The Analytic Challenges in Studying the Middle East and Its Evolving Media Environment." *Middle East Journal of Culture and Communication* 1 (2008): 8–23.

Stigset, Marianne. "Amid Folklore and Festivities, a Bid for National Reconciliation." *The Daily Star* (Beirut), April 9, 2005.

Stone, Christopher. "The Ba'albakk Festival and the Rahbanis: Folklore, Ancient History, Musical Theater and Nationalism in Lebanon." *Arab Studies Journal* 11–12, nos. 2–1 (2003–2004): 10–39.

———. "Ziyad Rahbani's 'Novelization' of Lebanese Musical Theater or the Paradox of Parody." *Middle Eastern Literatures* 8, no. 2 (July 2005): 151–70.

Suleiman, Yasir. *The Arabic Language and National Identity: A Study in Ideology*. Washington, DC: Georgetown University Press, 2003.

———. *A War of Words: Language and Conflict in the Middle East*. Cambridge: Cambridge University Press, 2004.

———. *Arabic, Self and Identity: A Study in Conflict and Displacement*. New York: Oxford University Press, 2011.

———. "Arabic Folk Linguistics: Between Mother Tongue and Native Language." In *The Oxford Handbook of Arabic Linguistics*, edited by Jonathan Owens. Oxford: Oxford University Press, 2013, 264–80.

———. *Arabic in the Fray: Language Ideology and Cultural Politics*. Edinburgh: Edinburgh University Press, 2013.

———, ed. *Language and Identity in the Middle East and North Africa*. London: Curzon Press, 1996.

Sweidan, Sami. *Abhath fi al-Nass al-Riwa'i al-'Arabi*. Beirut: Mu'assasat al-Abhath al-'Arabiyya, 1986.

Tabet, Jacques. *La Syrie*. Paris: A. Lemerre, 1920.

Tamari, Salim. "Bourgeois Nostalgia and the Abandoned City." *Comparative Studies of South Asia, Africa, and the Middle East* 23, nos. 1/2 (2003): 173–80.

Tawil-Souri, Helga. "Arab Television in Academic Scholarship," *Sociology Compass* 2, no. 5 (2008): 1400–1415.

"Televizion Lubnan Yunaffidh Wa'dahu: Al-Mubarayat Mubasharatan li-Jami' al-Nas." *Al-Akhbar*. http://www.al-akhbar.com/node/208650.

"Terrestrial TV 'Stays Static in Arab World.'" *Trade Arabic Business News Information*, Amman, June 7, 2009.

"The 1982 Israeli Invasion of Lebanon: The Casualties." *Race and Class* 24, no. 4 (April 1983): 340–43.

Thomason, Sarah. *Language Contact: An Introduction*. Washington, DC: Georgetown University Press, 2001.

Thompson, Elizabeth. *Colonial Citizens: Republican Rights, Paternal Privilege, and Gender in French Syria and Lebanon*. New York: Columbia University Press, 2000.

Thrall, Trevor. *War in the Media Age*. Cresskill, NJ: Hampton Press, 2000.

Tlis, Abd al-Ghani. "We Loved 'My Aunt's Home.'" *Al-Shabaka*, January 1989, 60–61.

Toft, Monica. "Getting Religion? The Puzzling Case of Islam and Civil War." *International Security* 31, no. 4 (2007): 97–131.

Traboulsi, Fawwaz. *A History of Modern Lebanon*. London: Pluto Press, 2008.

Tripp, Charles. *The Power and the People: Paths of Resistance in the Middle East*. Cambridge: Cambridge University Press, 2013.

Tumber, Howard, and Jerry Palmer. *Media at War: The Iraq Crisis.* London: Sage, 2004.

UNESCO. *L'Université Libanaise, La Faculté de Pédadogie, Centre de Recherches et de Développement Pedagogiques CRDP.* Beirut: UNESCO, 1980.

United Nations Development Programme. *A Profile of Sustainable Human Development in Lebanon.* Beirut: UNDP, 1997. Chapter 3 F. Education and Sustainable Human Development, 6. http://www.undp.org.lb/programme/governance/advocacy/nhdr/nhdr97/chpt3f.pdf.

———. *Arab Human Development Report: Creating Opportunities for Future Generations.* New York: UNDP, Regional Bureau for Arab States, 2002.

———. *Lebanon National Human Development Report: Toward a Citizen's State.* Beirut: UNDP, Regional Bureau for Arab States, 2009.

Wallenberg, Anja, and Jason Pack. "Rebels with a Pen: Observations on the Newly Emerging Media Landscape in Libya." *Journal of North African Studies* 18, no. 2 (2013): 191–210.

United Nations Human Rights Council. "Implementation of General Assembly Resolution 60/251 of 15 March 2006 Entitled Human Rights Council." November 23, 2006.

Wang, Georgette. "Beyond De-Westernizing Communication Research: An Introduction." In *De-Westernizing Communication Research: Altering Questions and Changing Frameworks,* edited by Georgette Wang. Abingdon; New York: Routledge, 2011, 1–17.

Warner, Michael. "Publics and Counterpublics." *Public Culture* 14, no. 1 (2002): 49–90.

Wehbe, Nakhle, and Adnan el-Amine. *Système d'Enseignement et Division Sociale au Liban.* Paris: Le Sycomore, 1980.

Wehbi, Samantha. "Lebanese Women Disability Rights Activists: War-time Experiences." *Women's Studies International Forum* 33, no. 5 (2010): 455–63.

Wehbi, Zahi. *Qahwa Sada: Fi Ahwal al-Maqha al-Bayruti.* Beirut: Al-Dar al-'Arabiyya li-l-'Ulum Nashirun, 2010.

———. Interview by author. In person. Beirut, August 2013.

Yamine, Gabriel. Interview by author. In person. Beirut, 2003.

Zaatari, Zeina. "The Culture of Motherhood: An Avenue for Women's Civil Participation in South Lebanon." *Journal of Middle East Women's Studies* 2, no. 1 (2006): 33–64.

Zahar, Marie-Joelle. "Protégés, Clients, Cannon Fodder: Civilians in the Calculus of Militias." *International Peacekeeping* 7, no. 4 (2000): 107–28.

———. "Is All the News Bad News for Peace? Economic Agendas in the Lebanese Civil War." *International Journal* 56, no. 1 (2000/2001): 115–28.

Zakharia, Zeena. "Positioning Arabic in Schools: Language Policy, National Identity, and Development in Contemporary Lebanon." In *Critical Approaches to Comparative Education: Vertical Case Studies from Africa, Europe, the Middle East, and the Americas*, edited by Frances Vavrus and Leslie Bartlett. New York: Palgrave Macmillan, 2009, 215–31.

———. "Language and Vulnerability: How Educational Policies Exacerbate Inequalities in Higher Education." *Middle East Institute Viewpoints: Higher Education and the Middle East. Washington, DC*, 2010. http://www.mei.edu.

Zappen, James. *The Rebirth of Dialogue: Bakhtin, Socrates, and the Rhetorical Tradition*. Albany: State University of New York Press, 2004.

Zayani, Mohamed. "Arab Media Studies: Between the Legacy of a Thin Discipline and the Promise of New Cultural Pathways." In *Arab Cultural Studies: Mapping the Field*, edited by Tarik Sabry. London and New York: I. B. Taurus, 2011, 55–78.

Zboray, Ronald, and Mary Zboray. *Encyclopedia of War and American Society*. Edited by Peter Karsten. Thousand Oaks, CA: Sage, 2006.

Zeidan, Joseph. *Arab Women Novelists: The Formative Years and Beyond*. Albany: SUNY Press, 1995.

Zelizer, Barbie. "CNN, the Gulf War, and Journalistic Practice." *Journal of Communication* 42, no. 1 (1992): 66–81.

———. "When War Is Reduced to a Photograph." In *Reporting War: Journalism in Wartime*, edited by Stuart Allan and Barbie Zelizer. New York: Routledge, 2004, 115–35.

Zughaib, Nibal. "Camille Salame wa-'Niyyal al-Bayt' Thalithuhuma Kumidiya al-Mawaqif!" *Al-Afkar* ("Musalsal tahta al-Daw'"), January 25, 1999, 52–53.

Index

Natalie Khazaal is an assistant professor of International Studies and Arab Culture at Texas A&M University. She has published on the role of Arab media in representations of minorities as well as on other cultural studies topics related to Arabic language and literature. She is coauthor of the first and second editions of *Ultimate Arabic* (Living Language/Random House, 2006, 2009).